THE CANTERBURY TALES

Unwin Critical Library
GENERAL EDITOR: CLAUDE RAWSON

The Canterbury Tales

DEREK PEARSALL

London and New York

First published in 1985
by George Allen & Unwin (Publishers) Ltd

Reprinted 1993, 1994
by Routledge
11 New Fetter Lane, London EC4P 4EE

Simultaneously published in the USA and Canada
by Routledge
29 West 35th Street, New York, NY 10001

Printed and bound in Great Britain by
Biddles Ltd, Guildford and King's Lynn

British Library Cataloguing in Publication Data

Pearsall, Derek Albert.
    The Canterbury tales.
1. Chaucer, Geoffrey. Canterbury tales
I. Title
821'.1   PR1874

Library of Congress Cataloging in Publication Data

Pearsall, Derek
    The Canterbury tales.
Bibliography: p.
Includes index.
1. Chaucer, Geoffrey, d. 1400. Canterbury tales.
I. Title   II. Series
PR1874.P43   1985   821'1   85–6104

ISBN 0–415–09444–5

CONTENTS

INTRODUCTION

Chaucer's poems are the only literary works of the English Middle Ages which have a continuous history of publication, and amongst Chaucer's poems the *Canterbury Tales* have always commanded the widest readership and the most enthusiastic appreciation. They remain part of the permanent literary and sub-literary culture of English-speaking people, and the individual tales have a further importance as the only pieces of medieval English writing of which a majority of educated readers will have had first-hand experience.

The segmentation of the *Canterbury Tales* for purposes of reading and study is a circumstance that needs to be taken into account: the experience of reading the whole work through from beginning to end is, I take it, a rare one. Though books on the *Canterbury Tales* tend, perhaps by their nature, to demonstrations of the unity and structural coherence of the *Tales*, it seems proper to recognise the circumstances in which the work is habitually read, for they may accord with its nature. There are, in fact, a number of reasons why it seems appropriate and opportune to stress the value of an approach which treats the *Canterbury Tales* as a series of poems rather than as a poem. One reason lies in the experience of reading the large number of studies of the *Tales* that have been made and of finding the critic's determination to theorise the work into some kind of unity distracting him from the important things that lie before him in the individual tales, pushing him away from the centre towards the periphery. Good critics will often stray from the common truth of their response to individual tales in evolving theories of unity, often as a defence against bad critics, who have nothing *but* theories.

A second reason for stressing the diversity of the *Tales*, and the essential independence and uniqueness of individual tales, has to do with the practical realities of a critical approach to a text which is unfinished. The facts of the matter are not in dispute: Chaucer, when he died, was nowhere near completing what he had planned for the *Tales*; the best surviving manuscripts show evidence of continuing revision; the order of the *Tales*, as deduced by the editors of those manuscripts, is not Chaucer's. What we read, therefore, is a sequence of fragments, some very substantial, some consisting of only one tale, put together by an intelligent compiler from what survived of Chaucer's unfinished work on the *Tales*. There are at least nine breaks in that sequence. It is possible, of course, to overstate the importance of this kind of evidence, and to end up by claiming that interpretation of the work as a whole is impossible or even improper. This is obviously not true, since there is much evidence of design in the poem, and of Chaucer's determination to exploit as fully as he could the potentialities of that design. The dramatic framework of the pilgrimage often creates sequences or juxtapositions of tales in which the meaning of the individual tales is suggestively enriched; some tales, though not many, grow directly out of the roadside drama and the character of the pilgrims who tell them. The pilgrimage itself is present, decisively at the beginning and end of the work, more obscurely elsewhere, as a figure of a comprehensive and totally purposive interpretation of the life that seems here so spontaneously lived. Structural and thematic echoes and anticipations constantly provoke new and unexpected insights.

It is here, though, in speaking of the design of the work, that one comes upon the third reason for asserting the primacy of the individual tales, for the design of the work is nothing more than a means of granting to individual tales the greatest possible degree of autonomy. The scheme of the *Tales* has a quality of drama and naturalism that has become so familiar that there is a temptation to forget how extraordinarily original and innovative it was, and how exceptional it has remained. It creates a powerful orbit within which the tales move, and sometimes adds a significant dimension to their meaning: it is difficult to imagine a tale, once allocated to the *Canterbury Tales*, escaping back into anonymity. However, the scheme, by its very nature, does not lend itself to any significant interpretative evaluation: the direct conclusions to which it would lead are either banal (life is a pilgrimage) or trivial and untrue (this is what life is like). In fact, when one compares Chaucer's design for the *Canterbury Tales* with other medieval designs for collections of tales, it seems that he has deliberately set out to create a form which will defy systematic interpretation, and which will preserve the maximum of provisionality and openness. There are times indeed when the work seems so fully released from its author, and from his authoritative intentions and voice, that it begins to take on an independent existence of its own. At such times, one might recognise the truth of the perception that sees the role of the author as a 'guest' within his own text (so Barthes, cited in Spearing, 1983, pp. 198–9).

The tales gain much from the dramatic impetus as well as the suggestive openness of the context in which they are placed. But the chief freedoms are those that are won for the activity of Chaucer's narrative art within the individual tales themselves. In taking over the different genres of narrative that were traditionally current in the Middle Ages, he is able, through the fiction of the tale-telling, to exploit, challenge and often defy the expectations that they carry of the relationship between fiction and reality. Instead of contenting his readers with replications of kinds of literary experience that they are used to, he constantly creates questions and disturbances, so that readers are jolted into re-examining their customary assumptions. Romance is counterpointed against the ridiculous, comedy has an edge of pathos or even tragedy, satire is metamorphosed into humour. The relationship between author, narrator and reader, being in a state of constant flux, is the subject of a quest in almost every tale, and the nature of Chaucer's experimentation is such that some tales will return progressively more complex answers on successive readings, each reading being suggestive of new ideas. The sense of being involved in a creative process of discovery is very strong, and Chaucer is constantly investigating those complexities in the relation of author to reader and of author to fiction and fictional character, and in the nature of the agreement between author and reader on the judgment of moral questions, that preoccupy modern theoreticians of narrative technique. One such is Wolfgang Iser, who speaks in these terms of later prose fiction in his book *The Implied Reader*:

> What was presented in the novel led to a specific effect: namely, to involve the reader in the world of the novel and so help him to understand it – and ultimately his own world – more clearly ... The reader discovers ... a new reality through a fiction which, at least in part, is different from the world he himself is used to; and he discovers the deficiencies inherent in prevalent norms and in his own restricted behaviour. (1974, pp. xi, xiii)

The characteristic experience of the reader at the end of the best of the tales is not that of satisfaction at the elucidation of a design but that of excitement at a precarious feat completed, in which one's imaginative energies and powers of discrimination have been fully stretched and examined, and many unexpected vistas opened up. Chaucer is exceptional in the extent to which he will allow his handling of stories to create problems, to ask questions, and to suggest ambiguities that are not easily resolved. Many of these problems, questions and ambiguities are the product of Chaucer's new way with old stories, and with stories in familiar genres: his characteristic technique is to immerse the stories that he draws from traditional and literary sources in a richer kind of understanding, so that they take on meanings different from and sometimes quite contrary to those which were recognised when they served their original simple moralising and idealising functions. 'The effect thus created', as Diekstra (1981, p. 216) says, 'is that of a clash between two modes of apprehending reality, which in Chaucer's hands, gives rise to a third and richer view, though often ironical and unresolved.' Elizabeth Salter, who is notable for the fullness and sensitivity with which she has responded to the challenges presented by Chaucer to the reader, has this to say, with an apt passing comment on the preoccupations of critics:

> Chaucer criticism still deals in the skilful administering of *placebos* to readers whose own sensibilities must register that Chaucer is characterized among English poets for the extent to which he will allow his ranging materials to pose questions, dictate problematic situations, suggest richly ambiguous characters and scenarios – not all of which can or will be dealt with in the logical formal structure of the total work. (1983, p. 121)

The encouragement that Chaucer gives to new kinds of imaginative and intellectual activity, the shock to habituated perceptions, is something that he is helped achieve through the freedom granted to individual tales, and the constant shifting of points of view. The awareness that he stimulates, of ourselves and of the way in which we manipulate our experience of reality, is central to his concerns as a poet, and the character of individual tales and the organisation of the tales as a whole are constant in their determination not to press for or permit a systematic kind of moral or ideological interpretation that will obscure or gloss over the complex realities of reading, evaluation and self-evaluation. Beyond this education of perception, to recognise and respond to which is the proper object of reading and criticism, the general moral purpose of the *Tales* is clear: it is always to give the advantage to a humane and generous understanding, and, perhaps as no small part of this, to dissolve disapproval in laughter, to tease us out of ill temper.

CHAPTER 1

Date and Manuscripts

The attribution of the *Canterbury Tales* to Geoffrey Chaucer has never been questioned: the list of the poet's works in the Prologue to *The Legend of Good Women*, the attribution of the *Legend* to 'Chaucer' in the Introduction to the Man of Law's Tale, and the further list of the poet's works in the 'retracciouns' at the end of the Parson's Tale, which includes the *Legend* and 'the tales of Caunterbury',[1] all concur in establishing the place of the *Canterbury Tales* in the Chaucer canon. It may be noted that the title given by Chaucer to the work – and given too in the rubrics to the earliest and best manuscripts of the *Tales*, the Hengwrt and Ellesmere manuscripts (see Appendix A) – is different from the title now generally accepted, and is evidently more authentic, as Pratt (1975) argues. However, the modern title soon became well established, perhaps under the influence of John Lydgate, who always refers to the 'Canterbury talys', presumably because it makes an easier rhyme.

Though the Chaucer canon, and the place within it of the *Canterbury Tales*, is secure, the dating of the works within the canon is a more speculative matter, and the chronology of Chaucer's writings is a spider's web of hypothesis. The absence of any mention of the *Tales*, as such, in the list of Chaucer's works in the Prologue to the *Legend of Good Women* suggests they were not then written, or known to the prospective audience of the *Legend*, or in a state to be mentioned. The *Legend* certainly follows close on *Troilus and Criseyde*, since it purports to be Chaucer's act of penitence for the trespass he committed against the name of women in describing Criseyde's infidelity. Chaucer was at work on the early part of *Troilus* after 1382, as may be deduced from his complimentary reference to Queen Anne, who married Richard II in that year (i. 171–2), and it was certainly finished and in circulation well before 1388, when Thomas Usk, who refers to the *Troilus* in his *Testament of Love* (Skeat, 1897, p. 123), was executed. If *Troilus* was finished in 1386, then the *Legend* may be allocated to 1386–7. The *Canterbury Tales* would then occupy the remaining years of Chaucer's life.

What is being spoken of here, of course, is a date for the inception of the scheme of the *Canterbury Tales*, a date when the idea of the pilgrimage as a framework for a series of stories came into Chaucer's head and pushed everything else out. The order of composition of individual tales and links is a matter for further and still more fragile hypothesis, since there are, again, no manuscripts dating from within the presumed period of composition (1387–1400), and no very helpful topical allusions. Everything must be deduced from the evidence of internal relationship, and from the ambiguous evidence of stratification and revision provided by the manuscripts. It is by no means a necessary assumption that Chaucer began by writing the General Prologue, nor that the General Prologue as it stands in the manuscripts was what Chaucer originally wrote. Likewise, the Parson's Tale is not specially likely to have been written last, though the Retractions may be an addition made near the end of Chaucer's life. The use made of material from the Parson's Tale in others of the *Canterbury Tales* suggests that it was written early.

There are, however, in this chaos of speculation, a few certainties and a few reasonable deductions. Among the certainties is the fact that the Knight's Tale and the Second Nun's Tale, whether or not in their surviving form, were written before the *Tales* were thought of or begun. They are mentioned in the list of Chaucer's works in the Prologue to the *Legend*, which as we have seen is to be dated 1386–7:

> He made the book that hight the Hous of Fame,
> And eke the Deeth of Blaunche the Duchesse,
> And the Parlement of Foules, as I gesse,
> And al the love of Palamon and Arcite
> Of Thebes, thogh the storye ys knowen lyte;
> And many an ympne for your halydayes,
> That highten balades, roundels, virelayes;
> And for to speke of other holynesse,
> He hath in prose translated Boece,
> [And Of the Wreched Engendrynge of Mankynde,
> As man may in pope Innocent yfynde;]
> And maad the lyf also of Seynt Cecile.[2]

It is impossible to know how far Chaucer revised the stories of 'Palamon and Arcite' and 'Seynt Cecile' for inclusion in the *Canterbury Tales*, or at what stage he did so. Whether Chaucer would go on referring to the stories of 'Palamon and Arcite' and 'Seynt Cecile' in the revised Prologue to the *Legend* (made after 1394) after he had converted them into

Canterbury tales is a matter of opinion. There is no inherent objection to a late date for the integration of the two poems into the *Tales*. Chaucer evidently added some lines near the beginning of the Knight's Tale (I.889–92) to adapt it to the story-telling contest, and the whole of the apology for omitted matter (I.872–92) may have been introduced as more appropriate to the new context: it comes in rather abruptly, and line 871 runs on to 893 very naturally. Beyond this there are no signs of any attempt to adapt the poem to the pilgrimage-frame, apart from the very last line ('And God save al this faire compaignye', I.3108), while the survival of a line wholly inappropriate to supposed 'live' narration,

> But of that storie list me nat to write (I.1201),

might be taken to suggest that any revision undertaken was rather perfunctory. So too with the Second Nun's Tale, the text of which retains several references to written composition, including this very explicit one:

> Yet preye I yow that reden that I write (VIII.78).

On the other hand, such lapses of dramatic congruity do occur in other links and tales (V.1549, VII.964), and they perhaps indicate no more than that Chaucer was rather careless about minor matters of dramatic consistency. It should be recognised that such slips are of a kind quite different from the conventional lapse into literariness in the frame-narrative, whereby the poet, purporting to 'tell' his story to a listening audience (e.g. General Prologue, I.35, 720, 858), reminds us that he is actually writing a book for us to read:

> And therfore, whoso list it nat yheere,
> Turne over the leef and chese another tale (I.3176–7).

Such allusions violate no conventional propriety of literary address. The references in the Knight's Tale and Second Nun's Tale, however, jar within the context of the very fiction Chaucer has spent some effort fabricating, and, though they do not stand alone, they may be taken as further indications that Chaucer did little or nothing to revise the tales for inclusion in the *Tales*. The reference of the narrator of the Second Nun's Tale to himself/herself as an 'unworthy sone of Eve' (VIII.62) is a similar indication, though an attempt has been made to argue that a 'son of Eve' could be a nun (Gardner, 1947).

From a practical point of view, it can be seen that the scheme of the *Tales* gave Chaucer, amongst many significant creative opportunities, the chance to gather a number of fugitive pieces, for which there was no immediate literary 'occasion' and which might otherwise be dispersed and given little attention (as has happened to *Anelida and Arcite*), and allot them reasonably appropriate places in the larger and more secure literary environment of the *Canterbury Tales*. There may be and most probably are more in this category than the two of which we have external evidence, though the tendency of scholars to relegate tales they find uncongenial to the pre-*Canterbury Tales* era, as 'early work', has made speculation of this kind a little suspect. Two of the religious tales in rhyme royal stanzas (Clerk's, Man of Law's) and the one in eight-line stanzas (Monk's) have been favoured candidates for this kind of treatment, a further assumption being that stanzaic form is also a mark of early composition. The model for these suppositions was the Second Nun's Tale, though the Prioress's Tale, also in rhyme royal, was always exempted from the category, being clearly designed for the Prioress. The force of these arguments for an early date was felt so strongly that the Knight's Tale itself, known to be pre-*Canterbury Tales*, was long assumed to have been, in its original form, in rhyme royal (see Robinson, 1957, p. 669). There is no evidence for this whatsoever, nor for an early date for the Clerk's or Man of Law's Tales. Indeed the latter, which borrows extensively, both in Prologue and Tale, from the *De Miseria Condicionis Humane (De Contemptu Mundi)* of Pope Innocent III, can plausibly be assigned to the period when Chaucer was working on his own translation of the *De Miseria* (Lewis, 1978, pp. 5–31). This must have been sometime between the composition of the original (F) version of the Prologue to the *Legend of Good Women* and the composition of the revised version (G) which Chaucer undertook when his direct reference to Queen Anne (F 496–7) became, with her death in 1394, painfully inappropriate. As we have seen, Chaucer introduces a mention of his (now lost) translation into prose, 'Of the Wreched Engendrynge of Mankynde', in G 414 which is not in F, and there is no reason to suppose that he would not have listed this in F if he had, then, written it. The Man of Law's Tale can only be dated early, therefore, if it is supposed that Chaucer larded an early work with citations from a Latin treatise that later took his fancy. As for the rhyme royal stanza, it cannot be concluded that its presence indicates an early date: Chaucer uses it quite consistently in the *Canterbury Tales* for purposes of stylistic decorum, that is, as a form of 'high style' suitable for religious narratives with a strong emotional content. With the Monk's Tale, there is more temptation to succumb to considerations of taste, and suggest an early date. How could Chaucer, one might think, interest himself in such a jejune notion of tragedy *after* he had written the Knight's Tale and *Troilus?* On the other hand, the Monk's Tale is one of the few which contain an allusion securely datable from external evidence. It is an allusion to the fall from power and subsequent death of Barnabo Visconti (VIII.2405), who died 19 December 1385. Against this, it is commonly argued that the Bernabo stanza, along with the other 'modern instances' (Pedro of Castile, Peter of Cyprus, and Ugolino of Pisa, VII.2375–457), is a late addition to a poem composed at an earlier date. An early dating for the two prose tales, the *Tale of Melibee* and the Parson's Tale, might be argued on other grounds: that the use made of material from the two works elsewhere in the *Tales* suggests that they were written early in the *Canterbury Tales* period, if not before.

Beyond these indications of early or relatively early date, there is little to go on, though there has been a good deal of speculation based on more or less likely accounts of the development of the plan of the *Canterbury Tales*. The evidence that the Shipman's Tale was originally designed for a woman, in the narrator's opening remarks about husbands and their responsibilities towards their wives, seems clear:

> The sely housbonde, algate he moot paye,
> He moot us clothe, and he moot us arraye,
> Al for his owene worshipe richely,
> In which array we daunce jolily.
> And if that he noght may, par aventure,
> Or ellis list no swich dispence endure,
> But thynketh it is wasted and ylost,
> Thanne moot another payen for oure cost,
> Or lene us gold, and that is perilous. (VII.12–19)

To argue that the Shipman is here mimicking the kind of thing that wives might say, himself speaking 'in a piping falsetto' (Chapman, 1956, p. 5), and that the text therefore bears no signs of stratification, seems a little desperate. The lines are more naturally taken as evidence of the continuous, evolving and unfinished nature of Chaucer's work on the *Tales*, and of how little inclination or opportunity he had for systematic revision.

If, then, the lines were originally designed for a woman, it must have been the Wife of Bath, and the reallocation of the Tale to the Shipman indicates that Chaucer later developed a larger role for the Wife of Bath. The larger role is certainly there, in her Prologue and Tale, and the impact of the Wife of Bath on the maturing development of the *Tales* as a whole is clearly evident in the references to her and her ideas elsewhere: in the Merchant's Tale, where she is alluded to by name in the discourse of a character within the story (IV.1685–7); at the end of the Clerk's Tale, where she is named (IV.1170) in the concluding stanzas (IV.1163–76), which, with the ironical Envoy (1177–212), are evidently a later replacement for the original single concluding stanza;[3] and in the Franklin's Tale, where the references to *soveraynetee* in marriage (V.751) and to the joy of marriage (V.804–6) – the latter, in their turn, echoing the mordantly ironic lines in the Merchant's Tale (IV.1337–41) – must awaken some reminiscence of the Wife's manifesto concerning women's *maistrye* in marriage and her pronouncements on the 'wo that is in mariage' (III.3).

We are dealing, it will be seen, with the sequence of tales that has come to be known as the 'Marriage-group', and although there will have to be several reservations about the integrity and dramatic purpose of this group, which it might be preferable in any case to call 'the Wife of Bath group', there can be no reasonable doubt that the development of the Wife of Bath was an important creative influence in the mature stages of the writing of the *Canterbury Tales*.[4] There is, indeed, external evidence of the impact of the Wife on Chaucer and his circle of readers and listeners in the brilliant little *Envoy to Bukton* (dated 1396 in Robinson, 1957, p. 864), where Chaucer, offering mock-serious warnings against marriage to his friend, concludes:

> The Wyf of Bathe I pray yow that ye rede
> Of this matere that we have on honde.
> God graunte yow your lyf frely to lede
> In fredam; for ful hard is to be bonde (29–32).

These remarks indicate that the Wife of Bath had become something of a talking point in London literary circles in the 1390s, and there is good evidence that Chaucer responded to this interest by adding some lines to the Wife of Bath's Prologue which tended to make her even more outrageous and provocative.[5]

There are other signs of stratification in the text which are capable of interpretation in relation to the date of individual parts of the *Canterbury Tales*. The cancellation of the Nun's Priest's Epilogue (VII.3447-62), for instance, and the re-use of some of its material in the Host's words to the Monk (e.g. VII.1945), suggest that the development and integration of Fragment VII was undertaken during the mature phase of composition of the *Tales*. But this is no more than would be expected, and in any case has more to do with the evolution of the plan of the *Tales*, to be discussed later, than with the dating of individual tales.

One other indicator of date is perhaps worth mentioning, namely the evidence of date to be derived from Chaucer's use of particular sources. Something has already been said of the date of his work on a translation of the *De Miseria Condicionis Humane*, and the clues about the dating of the Man of Law's Tale that this may give. It might be argued further (Lewis, 1978, p. 31) that the influence of the *De Miseria* on the Pardoner's Tale, since it is broader, less specific, more fully 'digested', indicates a later date for that Tale, as does the absence there of the Latin glosses, which in the Man of Law's Tale seem to be drawn directly from the Latin text which Chaucer was at that time working with. Further, the presence in the Pardoner's Tale of glosses from St Jerome's *Epistola adversus Jovinianum* would suggest that the Tale was being written at about the same time as the Wife of Bath's Prologue and the Franklin's Tale, which also make extensive use of Jerome's treatise. The fact that a lengthy summary of 'Jerome agayns Jovynyan' is introduced into the revised version of the Prologue to the *Legend of Good Women* (G.281), which as we have seen is to be dated after 1394, gives us perhaps a date in the mid-1390s for Chaucer's work on these tales.

It is very rarely that absolute datings, even of this tentative kind, can be arrived at. It sometimes seems that Chaucer is almost deliberately niggardly with datable topical allusion, as if he wishes to locate his poetry in some more permanent region of consciousness than the merely historical. The various other kinds of evidence that scholars have used to provide absolute datings are either useless or highly implausible. An example of useless evidence is the deduction that the Nun's Priest's Tale must have been written after 1381 since it contains a reference to the Peasants' Revolt (VII.3394). As an example of implausible dating one might cite the attempts at astronomical dating of poems where Chaucer attaches a day to a date,[6] which depend entirely on the assumption that Chaucer, when he did such a thing, looked up the current year's calendar. Such an assumption is quite unnecessary. Finally, as examples of a procedure for dating which it would be over-charitable to call implausible, there are the various attempts to provide 'occasions' for individual tales or to see in them covert allegories of topical events.[7]

THE MANUSCRIPTS OF THE CANTERBURY TALES: TEXT

The physical evidence of the existence of the *Canterbury Tales* is in some 82 manuscripts (see Appendix A), ranging in date from very early to very late in the fifteenth century. To this number of witnesses should be added the first printed edition, that of William Caxton in 1478, which, since it was based on a manuscript now lost, is a printed text with the status of a manuscript. Later printed editions, up to the time of the modern scholarly editions based on known manuscripts, derive largely or wholly from Caxton and have no such status. The number of surviving manuscripts is very large for a vernacular work, and in fact only *The Prick of Conscience* survives in more copies,[8] a comparison much to the disadvantage of the *Canterbury Tales* in terms of their actual popularity since *The Prick of Conscience* had all the advantages for preservation of a dogmatic religious subject-matter. The 82 manuscripts include 14 perfect or near-perfect copies of the whole received text of the *Tales*, forty-one which are complete except for accidental loss of a few leaves or a tale or two, seven very fragmentary copies which may be presumed to represent once-complete manuscripts, and twenty which contain a tale or tales or a passage deliberately excerpted from the larger work for inclusion in an anthology or miscellany. It is hard to know how many manuscripts once existed, and are represented by those that survive, but the work was, we can be sure, popular and widely known from the time that it began to be circulated.

The manuscripts of the *Canterbury Tales* are interesting from many points of view, but their principal value for readers of Chaucer is as witnesses to what Chaucer wrote. In theory, every manuscript, however late and however debauched the general character of the text it presents, may contain readings that go back to the author's copy. In theory, even a sixteenth- or seventeenth-century printed text may have the benefit of authentic readings picked up from casual consultation of a good manuscript now lost. Fortunately, these theories do not work out in practice, and the number of manuscripts that has to be employed in the construction of a good text is in fact remarkably small. The reason for this appears to be that the manuscripts that provided the ancestors for the largest surviving groups of manuscripts were from the start, by chance, rather poor, whether from the effects of scribal carelessness or of editorial care in the 'improvement' of the text. Routine workshop production of copies of the *Tales* in the fifteenth century tends therefore to be of rapidly diminishing interest for the establishment of the text. The exhaustive work of Manly and Rickert on the manuscripts of the *Canterbury Tales* may be open to objection on a number of counts,[9] but it demonstrates clearly that nearly all the important questions relating to the text of the *Canterbury Tales* turn in the end upon a small group of manuscripts surviving from the first quarter of the century,[10] with the addition of two eccentric manuscripts from the second quarter. Of these latter, one, British Library Additional 35286, is a manuscript of good independent descent but itself very careless and unreliable, while the other, Cambridge University Library Gg.4.27, seems to have been the product of an attempt to make a collection of Chaucer's poems (it includes *Troilus*, the *Legend*, the *Parliament* and several of the minor poems, as well as the *Canterbury Tales*) by someone who had access to some good early exemplars. It introduces many variants of its own and is eccentrically spelt, but it has some value as a check against the best early manuscripts.

Of the 'first generation' manuscripts, three (British Library Additional 10340, the Merthyr fragment, and Longleat 29) are mere fragments. Of the remaining eight manuscripts in this early group, five are of importance because they are the earliest representatives of the four family groups identified by Manly and Rickert, though not themselves the ancestors of those groups. Group *a* is represented by Cambridge University Library Dd.4.24, group *b* by the Helmingham manuscript (the early portion, that is, of this composite manuscript), group *c* by Corpus Christi College, Oxford, 198 and British Library Lansdowne 851, and group *d* by the Petworth manuscript. To these groups, with all their ramifications and cross-affiliations, belong the majority of the manuscripts of the *Canterbury Tales*, and these five manuscripts, therefore, are of importance in establishing the character of that large number of manuscripts. However, the textual quality of these groups is, as has been said, poor, with the exception of group *a*, which has a special claim on our interest and will be discussed further. The others are of little or no importance for the establishment of the original text. One of the remaining manuscripts, British Library Harley 7334, has had an interesting history: probably a copy from the same hand as Corpus 198, it is a beautifully written and carefully edited text of the *Tales*, and was sufficiently attractive to early editors to persuade Thomas Tyrwhitt (1775) to use it occasionally in his eclectic text of the *Canterbury Tales*, and Thomas Wright to make it the copy for his edition of the *Tales* in 1847. A kind of glamour hung about it even after W. W. Skeat (1894) had decided to use the less readily accessible Ellesmere manuscript as the basis for the *Tales* in his great edition of Chaucer, and it was only with regret that its claims to represent, if not the original text, at least an early draft or an authorial revision of that text, were finally buried (Tatlock, 1909; Robinson, 1957, p. xxxviii). The manuscript provides a lesson in the dangers of mistaking skilful and intelligent editorial improvement for the poet's own work.

We are left with two manuscripts, the Ellesmere and the Hengwrt. The Ellesmere is the most famous manuscript of the *Canterbury Tales*: carefully written and put together, beautifully produced, with handsome miniatures of the pilgrims set in the margin at the head of their tales, it contains an excellent text, and has held sway in editions of the *Tales* for nearly a century. To the extent that Robinson's edition is modelled upon Skeat's, the Ellesmere text *is* the *Canterbury Tales*, since Robinson's is the edition most extensively used for citation in critical books and articles. Yet it is clear, when comparison is made with the Hengwrt manuscript, that the Ellesmere manuscript itself is quite extensively edited. This editing was carried out in a highly intelligent and responsible manner, and was designed to 'improve' grammar and syntax, to clear up apparent irregularities and inconsistencies, to eliminate what were thought to be infelicities, and to regularise Chaucer's metre according to a ten-syllable pattern. It is impossible, without extensive citation, to show the large effects of these comparatively minor changes, but one or two examples may help to suggest the meticulous care that has been taken with such matters.[11]

1   *Hg* Wel sikerer was his crowyng in his logge
       Than is a clokke or any abbey orlogge (VII.2853–4)
     El Than is a clokke or an abbey orlogge.

The change of *any* to *an* makes the syntax more systematic (*an* now parallels *a*), eliminates the need for elision in *any ͜ abbey*, and brings the line to a soporific decasyllable.

2   *Hg* Comth of the grete superfluitee (VII.2927)
     El Cometh of greet superfluytee

The Ellesmere reviser has a pedantic dislike for the syncopated third person singular, which he removes at every opportunity. Here it causes him some metrical problems, which he solves at the cost of an unidiomatic omission of the definite article, which in turn means that he cannot use the singular weak adjective with -*e*.[12] The resultant line is quite flat, and lacks the bounce of Hengwrt.

3 *Hg* Which causeth folk to dreden in hir dremes
     Of arwes, and of fyr with rede lemes,
     Of rede bestes, that they wol hem byte (VII.2929–31)
   El Of grete bestes, that they wol hem byte

In his care to avoid the repetition of *rede*, which (like a modern publisher's copy-editor) he regards as *per se* a stylistic infelicity, the Ellesmere reviser actually removes the very point of Pertelote's discourse, which is to stress that people with an excess of red choler will dream of red things (like foxes).

4 *Hg* As wel of joye as tribulaciouns (VII.2980)
   El As wel of joye as of tribulaciouns

Here again is demonstrated the pedantic care for syntactical neatness. Compare these lines from General Prologue 49:

> *Hg* As wel in cristendom as hethenesse
> *El* As wel in cristendom as in hethenesse

It is not surprising, in a way, that modern editors have been so impressed with Ellesmere, when the preoccupations of the Ellesmere reviser with neatness and regularity and consistency so much resemble their own. Yet clearly Ellesmere presents a text, not of what Chaucer wrote, but of what his editorial executors thought he should have written, or would have written if he had known as well as they did what he wished to write.

There can be no question of the intrinsic superiority of Hengwrt as a witness to what Chaucer wrote. This superiority is displayed not only in its more accurate representation of a flexible, idiomatic and successful metrical practice, and in its freedom from editorialisation, but also in numerous readings of a substantive and significant nature. To take an example: as one of the possible interpretations of divine predestination in its relation to human freewill, the Nun's Priest offers the following:

Hg Or ellis if fre choys be graunted me
   To do that same thyng or do it noght,
   Though God forwoot it er that I was wroght (VII.3246–8)
El Though God forwoot it er that it was wroght

The reading of Hengwrt, striking, unexpected and audacious as it is, is preferable on every count: it strengthens the assertion of God's fore-knowledge – active not only before the doing of the deed but before the birth of the doer – in a dramatic manner; and *wroght* is more appropriate to the creation of a man than the doing of a deed. The Hengwrt reading is accepted in the modern editions of Donaldson (1958) and Pratt (1974), and Robinson (1957) planned to accept it in his second edition, as is clear from the Table of Altered Readings at page 885. Unfortunately, some-thing went wrong, and both *it* and *I* were omitted in the second edition, with who knows what consequences for the interpretation of the passage by untextual readers. Manly and Rickert (1940) comment favourably on the Hengwrt reading in their notes, but accept Ellesmere in their text, one of the unfortunate consequences of their decision to use Skeat's edition, with its inbuilt Ellesmere inclination, as their base-text for collation. Nevertheless, in those places where their text does move away from Skeat, it moves consistently towards Hengwrt.

Hengwrt is thus, from every point of view, the best manuscript of the *Canterbury Tales* – an early and uneditorialised manuscript of incontest-ably high quality, with excellent spelling, paragraphing and punctu-ation, a mirror in which we may believe, without illusion, that we see Chaucer clearly. However, it is only recently, in Blake (1980) and the Variorum Chaucer (e.g. Pearsall, 1983), that it has been used as the copy-text for editions of the *Canterbury Tales*, and the explanation of this odd state of affairs must be sought in the incomplete and disordered appearance it makes beside Ellesmere. From the point of view of Ellesmere, it lacks certain portions of the text, whether by mechanical defect (the latter half of the Parson's Tale) or by omission (the Canon's Yeoman's Prologue and Tale); it lacks certain of the links and the added lines of both the Wife of Bath's Prologue and the Nun's Priest's Prologue (VII.2771–90); it uses some of the other links, with the names of the pilgrims changed, to arrange the tales in a totally different, and to all appearances worse, order. It was evidently put together in a great hurry, and the changes of ink, the spaces left for matter known to exist but not immediately available, the fudging of the lay-out to hide errors in such calculations, all indicate that the copyist was dealing with exemplars that were arriving on his desk in fragmentary form and unpredictable sequence.[13] The hustle and bustle of the writing-shop, as Chaucer's literary executors, having presumably scoured the poet's study for the *Canterbury Tales* papers, now tried to bring out as a matter of urgency the first copy of the whole text of the long-awaited masterpiece, could hardly be more vividly conveyed.

As to the relationship between Hengwrt and Ellesmere, there have been wide differences of opinion, ranging from the dismissal of all that is not in Hengwrt as spurious (e.g. Blake, 1979, 1980, 1981a) to the acceptance of Ellesmere as the superior manuscript, representing authorial revision and deriving from superior copies that came to light after the publication of Hengwrt (e.g. Robinson, 1957, p. 888). The former view is logically tenable and in some ways easier to defend, demanding fewer hypotheses, but it is repugnant to lovers of Chaucer's poetry, who would accept an infinitude of ingenious hypotheses rather than lose the Canon's Yeoman. The latter view is superficially appealing, but cannot be accepted in its entirety, because of the inferior status of Ellesmere in general as a witness to what Chaucer wrote. There are many intermediate hypotheses which might, without any proof being possible, explain how the best text of the *Canterbury Tales* comes to have un-Chaucerian elements, and how a later, inferior text might incorporate genuine material. It is not difficult to believe that the haste with which Hengwrt was put together led to some hurried decisions in the disposition of what was available, and some editorial manipulation of linking material, and that meanwhile some items were missed altogether. When Ellesmere was made, a few years later, copied by the same scribe,[14] perhaps under the instructions of the same editor or editors, there was more time for a leisured scrutiny of the papers, and a more reasoned ordering of them, and a chance too to incorporate extra material that had subsequently come to light, whether from Chaucer's own shelves and cupboards or from friends close to him who had been favoured with portions of the *Tales* prior to publication.[15] The Ellesmere editor, with all the text before him, in an order that he approved, was now able to embark on the careful editing of his copy which we have already described, and to prepare the whole work for de luxe presentation. The contentiousness of the debate between Hengwrt and Ellesemere, as it concerns the quality of their texts, is, it will be seen, more apparent than real, and arises principally from a tyrannical interpretation of the editorial function, and the imperative need of editors and readers for unequivocal assertions concerning the author's text. For the fact is that the *Canterbury Tales* are unfinished, and surviving manuscripts may record various stages in the development of the work in progress. There is not one of these manuscripts that constitutes an 'act of publication' on the author's part, where he commits himself publicly to the delivery of his text to his readers. Thus the Ellesmere manuscript may have the authority of witnessing to certain later stages in Chaucer's work on the *Tales*, and likewise the manuscripts of the *a* group, and especially its earliest representative, Cambridge University Library Dd.4.24, may have readings that can be regarded as cancelled 'first shots'. The Cambridge manuscript and its fellows have many good readings that may be placed in this category (e.g. Pearsall, 1983, pp. 99–100), and of course they, and they alone, have the Nun's Priest's Epilogue, which is evidently genuine though equally evidently superseded in the developing plan of the *Tales*.

THE MANUSCRIPTS OF THE CANTERBURY TALES: ORDER OF TALES

It will be seen that questions of textual authority inevitably merge into questions concerning the order of the *Canterbury Tales*, and concerning the extent to which the surviving manuscripts offer evidence of Chaucer's developing plan and final intentions for the *Tales* as a whole. Some remarks have already been made, in the discussion of the dating of the tales, concerning stages in the evolution of the plan of the *Tales*, but what needs to be stressed here is the fragmentary nature of the evidence and the unfinished state of the work. The *Tales* come down to us in a series of unlinked fragments, and there is no manuscript evidence that Chaucer arranged these fragments in any final order. It used to be believed that the order of the tales in different manuscripts derived from various arrangements tried successively by Chaucer himself, but this belief has been shown to be untenable, and Manly and Rickert conclude thus:

> The evidence of the MSS seems to show clearly that Chaucer was not responsible for any of the extant arrangements. (1940, vol. 2, p. 475)

This is the position from which any discussion of the subject must start. It is not, on the face of it, a happy position, and it is not surprising that editors and readers of the poem have been reluctant to accept it. Fifteenth-century editors and scribes were prolific in the invention of spurious links to join together the unlinked fragments (Robbins and Cutler, 1965, p. 462), and in modern times there has been a wealth of interpretative speculation concerning the arrangement that Chaucer had in mind.[16] Much of this speculation we shall see to be quite unfounded, but it will be as well first to map out the known parts of the terrain.

The integrity and position of Fragment I (General Prologue, Knight's Tale, Miller's Tale, Reeve's Tale, unfinished Cook's Tale) is undisputed. As a sequence, it is, judging from the highly developed sense of dramatic form, mature or late work, and the plan for the story-telling contest (I.761–821), with four tales to be told by each pilgrim, two on the way to Canterbury and two on the way back, may well be a late development (Owen, 1977). The four-tale plan is never referred to elsewhere in the *Tales*: on the contrary, the Franklin is told that everyone must keep his promise to tell 'a tale or two' (V.698), and the Host says to the Parson,

For every man, save thou, hath toold his tale (X.25)[17]

It has also been argued (e.g. Hammond, 1908, p. 254; Nevo, 1963) that the group of six pilgrims introduced as a group at the end of the General Prologue (I.542–4) is a late addition, designed to accommodate further tales that Chaucer had written or wished to write. That the plan of the *Tales* was still evolving, and the General Prologue still under revision, even at this late stage, is suggested by the evidence of lines 163–4:

Another NONNE with hire hadde she,
That was hir chapeleyne, and preestes thre.

The absurdity of having three priests attendant upon the two nuns, the fact that a single Nun's Priest is addressed by the Host and asked for a tale (VII.2809), and the disruption to Chaucer's numbering of the company of 'nyne and twenty' pilgrims (I.24) if more than one Nun's Priest is admitted, all suggest that Chaucer left line 164 unfinished at 'chapeleyne', to await the addition of the portraits of the Nun and Nun's Priest, and that the line was completed by an early scribe.[18]

The integrity and position of Fragment X (Parson's Prologue and Tale) is likewise undisputed. The end of the work is clearly alluded to in the Parson's Prologue:

Now lakketh us no tales mo than oon (X.16)

and all the manuscripts that have the Fragment have it at the end of the *Tales*, though a few lack the Retraction. The *Tales* thus have a fixed beginning and end.

Within these limits, the integrity if not the position of certain fragments is assured. Fragment VII (Shipman's Tale, Prioress's Tale, Chaucer's tales of *Thopas* and *Melibee*, Monk's Tale, Nun's Priest's Tale) is another example of mature work on the development of blocks of tales with strong dramatic continuity. The removal of the Nun's Priest's Endlink, as we have seen, was the prelude to the further development of the Host's remarks to the Monk, and the expanded form of the Nun's Priest's Prologue (that is, including VII.2771–90) was introduced at a still later stage to provide the opportunity for the richly comic exchange between the Knight and the Host over the merits of the Monk's Tale. This was one of the revisions, indubitably authentic, missed by Hengwrt. Another fragment which has well-attested integrity is Fragment III (Wife of Bath's Prologue and Tale, Friar's Tale, Summoner's Tale), which again has a close-knit dramatic continuity, even to the extent of anticipating the Friar-Summoner quarrel before the Wife has finished speaking (III.829–56), and allowing the Pardoner to interrupt her in mid-career (III.163–87). With the Summoner and the Friar, likewise, each interrupts the other when he is well embarked on his tale (III.1332,1761). These are unique innovations in the dramatic structure of the *Tales* and, with the further evidence of unusually extensive revision within the body of the Wife's Prologue, as described above, point to a very late if not the latest stage in Chaucer's work on the *Tales*. Another well-integrated fragment is Fragment VI (Physician's Tale, Pardoner's Tale), which shows, in the Physician-Pardoner Link and in the 'epilogue' to the Pardoner's Tale, the same attention to the dramatic development of the Host's role as Fragment VII. The evidence for an earlier version of the Link, preserved in British Library Harley 7334, is poor, though it is accepted by Manly and Rickert (1940, vol. 2, p. 325) and by Severs (1954). Finally, there are two fragments each containing a single tale and its prologue, Fragment II (Man of Law) and Fragment IX (Manciple), which regularly appear thus.

The integrity of all the above fragments is attested by all manuscripts except obviously unreliable ones, and, more important, by both Hengwrt and Ellesmere. There is similar agreement on a limited number of sequences: IX–X, with very few anomalies;[19] VI–VII, with rather more anomalies, but still with the agreement of Hengwrt and Ellesmere; and I–II, with a smaller number of anomalies, but without the agreement of Hengwrt.[20] Beyond this, though there is a wide measure of agreement between Ellesmere and other good manuscripts on the integrity of Fragments IV, V and VIII and on the ordering of the ten fragments, there is no support from Hengwrt, and we move therefore from the order of the *Tales* certainly attributable to Chaucer to the order which may be the work of his early fifteenth-century editors.

At this point, it will be convenient to set out the relationship between Hengwrt and Ellesmere, which is the crux of the matter, in the form of a chart. In this chart, the Monk's Tale, Nun's Priest's Tale (end of Fragment VII) and Manciple's Tale (Fragment IX) in Hengwrt, which all authorities agree have been accidentally displaced in the manuscript by mis-arrangement of quires (Ruggiers, 1979, p. xxiii) from their proper position following the first part of Fragment VII, have been treated as if they were in their proper position.

Hengwrt	*Ellesmere*
I	I
III	II
II	III
Squire's Tale (without Prologue)	IV (Clerk, Merchant)
Squire-Franklin Link as 'Merchant's Prologue'	V (Squire, Franklin)
Merchant's Tale	VI
Merchant's Epilogue – Squire's Prologue (without break) as 'Host's Words to Franklin'	VII
Franklin's Prologue and Tale	VIII (Second Nun, Canon's Yeoman)
Second Nun's Tale	
Clerk's Prologue, Tale and Epilogue	IX
VI	
VII	X
IX	
X	

It is possible to argue, as we have seen (Blake, 1979, 1980, 1981a), that there was nothing to be had of Chaucer's but what the scribe of Hengwrt had, and that therefore those links that appear in Hengwrt in the 'wrong' places were actually composed *ad hoc* to fill gaps in the exemplars and were later more judiciously appropriated in Ellesmere, and that the portions of text that do not appear at all in Hengwrt (the 'real' Merchant's Prologue, and the Canon's Yeoman's Prologue and Tale) are likewise spurious. These arguments, as I have said, are repugnant, and it is inherently unlikely that there was a hack in the workshop who could write so perfectly in Chaucer's idiom that he has bamboozled everyone. A further objection is that lines that appear in the 'Host's Words to the Franklin' in Hengwrt actually appear in metrically superior form in their 'correct' places in the Squire's Prologue in Ellesmere (see Manly and Rickert, 1940, vol. 2, p. 476; Benson, 1981, pp. 105–6):

> *Hg* Sire Frankeleyn, com neer, if it youre wille be
> And sey us a tale, for certes ye
> Konnen theron as muche as any man.
> *El* Squier, com neer, if it youre wille be,
> And sey somwhat of love; for certes ye
> Konnen theron as muche as any man. (V.1–3).

The simplest and most likely explanation of the variation is that the Ellesmere lines are authentic and were mutilated in the attempt to fit them to a different purpose in Hengwrt. The scribe of Hengwrt, or editor, if there was one, seems to have been in a position where he was juggling with a number of separate exemplars, containing the various fragments of the *Tales* as they had been worked up by Chaucer. Not all of these fragments arrived together, and some of them were still in disarray (IV,V) or partly missing (VIII), with projected links still on separate sheets of paper. He did the best he could with what he had, working on the principle that there should be some kind of pilgrimage interlude, whether prologue, epilogue or genuine link, between tales (Blake, 1979, p. 8). Where he could find nothing of the right sort, he pressed into service what he could find. The editor of Ellesmere, with more leisure, with Hengwrt or something like it to work with,[21] and with added material more recently come to light, was able to rearrange the tales in the disordered fragments (IV,V) in the manner which was presumed to be intended by Chaucer, and to attach the Canon's Yeoman's Prologue and Tale to the Second Nun's Tale (which is clearly the position intended for it: see VIII.554) to form Fragment VIII. He did his work with care and intelligence – the same qualities that inspired his editorial work on the text, though in this case with happier consequences – and clearly intended that Chaucer's great poem should have the dignified and ordered treatment that was associated with learned works in Latin.

Emphasis was placed on the ordered structure and unity of the work through the carefully organised lay-out and the introduction of the pilgrim-portraits at the head of the tales, while the Latin glosses that were already scattered through manuscripts such as Hengwrt, and which may be presumed to derive in part from Chaucer, were expanded and added to so as to give the whole work the prestige of the *compilatio* from learned *auctoritates*.[22]

The order of the fragments was still a headache, and the Ellesmere editor was in the same position as the modern editor, of having to piece out from the surviving evidence what he deduced to have been Chaucer's intentions. Fragments I and IX–X presented no problem, and Fragments VI–VII seem to have been well settled together. It was clear to him that the newly united Fragment IV, with its explicit references to the Wife of Bath, should be placed as near as possible after Fragment III, and that Fragment V, with its somewhat less explicit references to her views on *soveraynetee*, might well be placed immediately afterwards. The Canon's Yeoman's Tale has a prominent reference to 'Boghtoun under Blee' in its opening lines (VIII.556), and the Ellesmere editor, knowing that this village was close to Canterbury, may have decided that this was a good enough reason to put Fragment VIII as near as possible to the end of the sequence. All that was left to do was to arrange II, III–V and VI–VII in some sort of order between I and VIII–X, and, without much else to guide him, he settled on the order we now have.

It is doubtful whether it can be improved upon as a hypothesis concerning what Chaucer would have done with the fragments if he had been given a few hours and told to put his papers in order. Even if Chaucer could be asked to come back and do this, the order so arrived at would not represent his 'intentions', since those intentions are unrealised in the unfinished work as he left it and as we have it. All orderings of the *Tales* are therefore provisional and merely pragmatic. However, modern editors and scholars have been unable to rest content with this state of affairs, and a number of theories have been put forward, in an attempt to establish a more definite order for the *Tales*.

One assumption that much excited Henry Bradshaw and F. J. Furnivall when they were working on the manuscripts of the *Tales* in 1868 (see Furnivall, 1868, pp. 9–43) was that Chaucer had an itinerary worked out for the pilgrimage, with tales allotted to morning, afternoon and evening of a three-and-a-half day one-way journey from London to Canterbury.[23] This assumption, not unreasonable for the working practice of a nineteenth-century novelist, was what guided their speculations concerning the 'correct' order of the *Canterbury Tales*. What they had to work with was a series of references to places and times of day on the journey between London and Canterbury, some of them rather general (I.822, II.5–6, 13–14, III.2294, VI.321–2, X.5, 12), some of them quite specific, to 'the wateryng of Seint Thomas' (I.825–6), Deptford and Greenwich (I.3906–7), Sittingbourne (III.847), Rochester (VII.1926), Boughton-under-Blee (VIII.556), and 'Bobbe-up-and-down' (IX.2). It did not escape the notice of Bradshaw that all the geographical places mentioned are in the order in which they come on the road to Canterbury, except for Rochester, which should come before Sittingbourne. He therefore proposed what has come to be called the 'Bradshaw shift', whereby Fragment VII is moved to follow Fragment II, and, with the aid of the cancelled Man of Law's Epilogue, integrated with it to form, in the new nomenclature, Fragment B. Supporting arguments for the shift were drawn from the need for tales to pad out parts of the theoretical itinerary, which inspired also the shift of Fragment VI, a 'floating' or geographically unattached fragment, to follow new Fragment B, thus forming Fragment C. The arguments based on the itinerary time-table have now been largely abandoned, since it is recognised, and will be argued further in Chapter 2 below, that Chaucer sought no such naturalistic consistency, but the 'Bradshaw shift' has won many supporters.[24] It has indeed common sense on its side, since, though one might have reservations about Chaucer's interest in the time it took to tell a tale or the stopping places on the journey, it would not be reasonable to suppose that he would deliberately or carelessly put the places on the way to Canterbury in the wrong order. However, the manuscripts give no support whatsoever to the Bradshaw shift;[25] on the contrary, they make it clear that the Man of Law's Epilogue cannot be used to link Fragments II and VII. Though it was intended by Chaucer at one point as a link, he did not make up his mind what was to follow, and after toying with various possibilities he abandoned it. A further explanation of its history would assume that it was originally intended to follow the *Tale of Melibee*, which was itself originally ascribed to the Man of Law (whence his reference in the Introduction to his Tale, 'I speke in prose', II.96), and to be followed by a tale told by the Summoner.[26]

When Melibeus was transferred to Chaucer himself and the Summoner involved in the quarrel with the Friar, this endlink ceased to have any proper function and became a mere vestigial organ, a sort of literary vermiform appendix. (Manly and Rickert, 1940, vol. 2, pp. 189–90)

It does not appear in any of the best manuscripts, and is not available for the use to which it has been put. The discrepancy in the geography is something to which Chaucer would no doubt eventually have given his attention, but, in the unfinished state in which his text survives, it must remain a discrepancy.

Attempts have been made to advance further arguments in favour of the Bradshaw shift, particularly on the grounds that the presence of Fragment VII before Fragment III allows for some development of the 'marriage-debate' to prepare for the rather abrupt announcement by the Wife of Bath:

> Experience, though noon auctoritee
> Were in this world, is right ynogh for me
> To speke of wo that is in mariage (III.1–3)

In particular, it is argued by Germaine Dempster (1953; also Keiser, 1977–8) that the development of Fragment VII, and the larger role given to the Host, are part of this preparation, especially the Host's comments on his shrewish wife after the telling of *Melibee* (VII.1889–1923). However, the role of the 'marriage-debate' has been much exaggerated by scholars, who are inclined to see every reference to the relationships between men and women (and few tales are free from such references) as an episode in the debate, and thereby weaken and dissipate the cross-connections that do exist within what I have called 'the Wife of Bath group'. The Wife of Bath's opening remarks, further-more, follow on only weakly from the Nun's Priest's Tale, and the manuscripts offer no support for a linkage of Fragments VII and III. The attempt by Pratt (1951, pp. 1162–3) to argue that the Nun's Priest's Epilogue is actually the opening of the Nun's Priest–Wife of Bath Link, fractured and half-lost, is ingenious, but it goes clean against the manuscript evidence, which shows that the Nun's Priest's Epilogue, another 'vermiform appendix', was cancelled by Chaucer; it survives only in the manuscripts of the *a* group, which preserve some of his early drafts. Manuscript evidence is not unassailable, but it must be respected, and the dangers of neglecting it are well illustrated in the misuse of Pratt's argument by Gibbons (1954), who argued that the second part of the putative Nun's Priest–Wife of Bath Link is not lost, but present in six lines that appear in four manuscripts. The manuscripts have no authority, and the lines are certainly spurious, as Brosnahan (1961) demonstrates conclusively.

There is not much else that has been said that is worth pausing over, though Pratt's argument (1951, p. 1158) that Fragment VI should not come before Fragment III, on the grounds that the Pardoner's interruption of the Wife of Bath would be dramatically inappropriate if it followed the grotesque business of the Pardoner's 'epilogue', is very sound. But since the Ellesmere editor put it later anyway, it cannot be said that much ground has been gained.

There is no doubt that the Ellesmere manuscript has the best order of the *Tales*. The editor did his work well, and he arrived at the most satisfactory solution of an impossible problem. It has to be recognised that any modern editor must likewise acquiesce in the pragmatic realities of his role. Even if he accepts, as he must, that the Ellesmere order is not Chaucer's order, that indeed there *is* no Chaucerian order, he must still print the *Tales* in some order. Since the Ellesmere order is the best available, and the one that Chaucer might have settled for if he had been given the chance (or wished) to make a decision on the matter, this is the one that the modern editor must accept, as Robinson (1957, p. 889), in his own admirable comments on the matter, makes clear.

There discussion might end, it would seem. The consequences, however, need to be considered, for the presentation of Chaucer's unordered fragments as 'the Book of the Tales of Canterbury' gives a spurious authority to a purely pragmatic editorial decision. It is a widely accepted belief, enforced by the nature of 'the book', that the *Canterbury Tales* as they are presented in modern editions are the *Tales* as Chaucer intended them to be, and it is not uncommon to find the unfinished state of the work, and its existence as a series of fragments, treated as a mere hiccough in the author's communication of his text to his readers. So powerful is the influence of 'the book', so imperative the need of readers for complete, unified and unequivocal texts, that the concrete and perceivable realities of the existence of the *Tales* are denied, and any number of myths of unity promoted. 'The work', we are told, 'is unfinished but complete' (Howard, 1976, p. 1), whatever that may mean, and meanwhile the evidence of stratification is equally commonly neglected, passages from different stages in the work's development being conflated, without remark, for the purposes of interpretation (e.g. Lumiansky, 1955, pp. 109–12). The facts speak otherwise, and it is an editor's responsibility not to encourage this kind of behaviour. If, for instance, it were true that the Man of Law's Epilogue was originally designed to make a link to the Shipman's Tale when it was still assigned to the Wife of Bath, this would be no justification for emending it to make a link to the present Wife of Bath's Prologue. This is what Donaldson does in his edition of *Chaucer's Poetry* (1958), and, though he acknowledges (1958, pp. 190, 1074; 1970b, pp. 202–3) that to do so is a matter of mere editorial convenience and supposes nothing of Chaucer's intentions, the very fact of doing so imparts authority to 'the text' thus reconstituted, and may mislead others who are less conscious of the reservations that are necessary concerning the text.

The witness of the manuscripts is that the *Canterbury Tales* are unfinished, and that Chaucer left the work as a partly assembled kit with no directions. This is how, ideally, it should be presented, partly as a bound book (with first and last fragments fixed) and partly as a set of fragments in folders, with the incomplete information as to their nature and placement fully displayed. This would not make studies of the structure and design of the *Tales* impossible or illicit as Blake (1981b, p. 58) seems to suggest; it would merely ensure that such studies were conducted within a proper context of understanding.

CHAPTER 2

Plan and Order

The *Canterbury Tales* were begun by Chaucer, as we have seen, about 1387, after he had completed *Troilus and Criseyde* and after he had begun and presumably abandoned the *Legend of Good Women*. It is thus the work of his latest years, though it shows no signs of age or fading power, and indeed is remarkable for its vigour and freedom and its extraordinary innovative and experimental character. It may have been that Chaucer gained this freedom from his security in the achievement of his *magnum opus*, *Troilus and Criseyde*, for there can be no doubt that the literary care lavished on that poem is of a kind quite different from what we find in the *Canterbury Tales*, and is designed to make it worthy of comparison with the work of the great poets of the past:

> Go, litel bok, go, litel myn tragedye,
> Ther God thi makere yet, er that he dye,
> So sende myght to make in som comedye!
> But litel book, no makyng thow n'envie,
> But subgit be to alle poesye;
> And kis the steppes, where as thow seest pace
> Virgile, Ovide, Omer, Lucan, and Stace. (V.1786–92)

The conscious regard for posterity, and for the accurate transmission and true understanding of the text (V.1793–8), the self-conscious solemnity of the opening invocation and closing prayer of the poem, the elaborate structure and highly-wrought style, all claim a confident place for Chaucer in the pantheon of poets, and are quite exceptional in the English poetry of the Middle Ages. The *Canterbury Tales* are bound to suffer in comparison with *Troilus* because of their unfinished state, but their very incompleteness and open-endedness are part of the challenge they offer to our powers of perception and understanding. They do not show Chaucer relaxing amid the familiar furniture of his mind, but rather a spirit of innovation and experiment in which he can explore imaginative territories of the existence of which there is little hint in *Troilus*.

First, though, there was *The Legend of Good Women*, the occasion of which springs directly from *Troilus and Criseyde*. Chaucer explains in the Prologue to the *Legend* how he was commanded by the God of Love to tell tales of good women wronged by men, as a penance for having spoken ill of women in the person of Criseyde. Chaucer promises nineteen tales, but actually delivers only nine and a half, and it is clear that, though he may have begun the work with the best of intentions, he soon tired of the subject. The handling of the tales grows increasingly casual, and the conventional patter of *abbreviatio* ('Now is it tyme I make an ende sone ... And shortly lest this tale be to long ...', 2341, 2675) becomes intrusive. Chaucer may have undertaken the *Legend* because he was keen to try his hand at short narrative poems within a fictional frame, but if he did so he soon found that he had chosen the wrong kinds of narrative and the wrong frame. The monotony of the externally imposed theme meant that he was imprisoned in certain kinds of story and certain ways of telling a story, and, though the Prologue is a masterpiece in its own right and the legends have interest as experiments in short narrative, there is no question why he abandoned the enterprise. It was probably a valuable lesson for him.

Everything that Chaucer had not got in the *Legend* he sought for himself in the *Canterbury Tales*. The framework that he devises for his collection of stories here is so natural, so spontaneous and so convincing that it hardly seems to be a matter of artistic choice. Chaucer seems quite simply to be telling us 'how it was'. But this of course is the character of the best artistic choices of this kind, and we should not allow the experience of familiarity to dull our recognition of the extraordinary originality of his scheme.

The fictional framework is simple: the poet portrays himself meeting a group of pilgrims at the Tabard Inn at Southwark, where they are gathered together to make their pilgrimage to the shrine of St Thomas à Becket at Canterbury. The Host of the Tabard proposes that they enliven the journey by telling tales on the way, and make a competition of it, the winner,

> 'That is to seyn, that telleth in this caas
> Tales of best sentence and moost solaas,' (I.797–8)

to be treated to 'a soper at oure aller cost' on their return to Southwark. They are each to tell two tales on the way there and two more on the way back, and the Host is to make the rules and be the judge. The tale-telling competition is mentioned from time to time through the framing narrative of the *Tales* (eg., I.3117–19, 3127, II.33–42, 1167, IV.10–11, 22–5, V.696–8, VII.1927, 2803–4, IX.12, X.15–21), though sometimes it seems to be quite forgotten, as for instance in the preoccupation of the Reeve, Friar and Summoner with 'quiting' other pilgrims rather than 'quiting' their tales (I.3119, 3127, 3864, 3916, 4324, III.1292; cf. I.4362). The four-tale contest is never mentioned again, and pilgrims are usually told that they have to tell a tale, with the implication and on one occasion the explicit statement (X.25) that only one tale is required. On one occasion the promise is said to be 'a tale or two' (V.698), while the Friar and the Summoner, entirely out of a superfluity of spleen and with no reference to the tale-telling contest, offer 'a tale or two' and 'tales two or thre' respectively (III.842, 846). The Monk likewise, put out by the Host's raillery and determined to stand on his dignity, offers 'a tale, or two, or three' or possibly of 'tragedies . . . an hundred' (VII.1968–71), but there is no hint that he does so for any other reason than to make the Host's head ache at the prospect. The precise terms of the tale-telling contest seem, therefore, to be something that Chaucer worked out at a later stage and incorporated in the General Prologue, without making the necessary adjustments elsewhere. This is a more likely explanation than that he gradually and silently abandoned the plan as first announced, or – though it may seem superfluous to mention such a supposition – that the Host did so. The strength of the argument advanced here is in the clear evidence of stratification in the surviving texts of the *Tales*, the many unadjusted discrepancies, and the certainty that Chaucer did not intend the *Tales* to be read through as a continuous and integrated sequence as they now stand in printed editions.[1]

The four-tale scheme is an extremely ambitious one, and Chaucer came nowhere near completing it. There are twenty-four tales in all, including one from each of twenty-one of the twenty-nine pilgrims,[2] and two from Chaucer. One tale, the Cook's, is fragmentary, and three tales (Squire's, *Thopas*, Monk's) are 'dramatically' unfinished, that is, interrupted. One tale, the Canon's Yeoman's, comes from a new character who breaks into the pilgrimage. Thus, seven pilgrims do not tell tales at all, namely, the Yeoman, the Plowman, and the five Guildsmen. For the latter, they are described so perfunctorily in the General Prologue that it is difficult to know why Chaucer included them at all, unless he intended them as what Coghill (1949, p. 154) calls 'blank cheques', like the Nun's Priest. As for the Yeoman and the Plowman, the suspicion hovers that Chaucer included them for form's sake, so as to be able to make some claim that he had not neglected the common herd of men, but that he had no intention of telling tales suitable to numbskulls and virtuous peasants.

With so much of a one-tale scheme completed, and with all the 'interesting' pilgrims having had their say, it would seem that it would have been remarkably easy for Chaucer to cut his coat according to his cloth, and, by explicitly reducing or not expanding the scale of the contest, removing the superfluous pilgrims, tidying up discrepancies and writing in a few links, to hand the work down more or less 'complete'. That he did not do so may be due to death, loss of interest, or a reluctance to acquiesce in the compromising and curtailment of a grand artistic vision, even when prospects for completion were remote. The four-tale scheme may even have been a wryly defiant protest against such acquiescence. Whatever the case, the unrevised and fragmentary state of the *Canterbury Tales* has not inhibited those who have rushed to complete Chaucer's schemes for him. Fifteenth-century editors were soon at work with additional links and tales, and modern editors and scholars, more scrupulous about interference with the text, have busied themselves in the fitting together of the fragments in plausible sequences. Much has already been said in Chapter One of these rearrangements, and of the premises from which they derive. The illusion of reality that Chaucer creates in the frame narrative is so compelling that there is a constant temptation to take the illusion for reality, to assume that the *Tales* are incompletely naturalistic merely because they are incomplete, and to embark on thoroughgoing naturalistic interpretations of the fictional frame. An itinerary and a time-table are worked out, and the tales squeezed in here and there according to suppositions of a real journey. Workers at this task assume that they are doing what Chaucer would naturally have done himself if he had not died in the midst of his foul papers; but they are, as Jordan (1967) says, 'smoothing the road to Canterbury for a journey Chaucer's pilgrims never made' (p. 117). A nineteenth-century novelist would normally assume a fundamental obligation to make sure that his characters did nothing in space and time that they could not, literally, have done, but Chaucer had no such ambitions, and it would have been the merest folly for him to have chosen the pilgrimage frame, with all its attendant absurdities – how could the pilgrims all have heard the speaker, strung out two by two on a narrow, ill-kempt, pot-holed, muddy road? how could such a group have possibly met up and maintained fellowship on the road? what were many of them doing there anyway? and how do so many of them come to be graced with perfect mastery of the pentameter couplet? – if he had.

On the contrary, the 'carelessness' of consistency which has so exasperated Chaucer's critics and so spurred them to efforts on his behalf may be the absence of a kind of care which would have prepared the *Tales* for an inappropriate kind of attention. Chaucer valued the illusion created by the pilgrimage framework, and fostered it where he valued it; but he did not value it overmuch. The vagueness and inconsistency of spatial and other naturalistic reference inhibits precisely the kind of naturalistic interpretation which would ultimately collapse the illusion completely. Though Howard (1976) speaks well of the 'spectral, removed quality' of the pilgrimage (p. 164), and suggests that this 'placelessness' has 'a kind of iconographic meaning' in relation to the pilgrimage (of man's life) through the wilderness (of the world), it does not seem to be a matter of design on Chaucer's part: he did not leave the *Tales* deliberately in a state of disorder because he consciously recognised the limitations of naturalism and wished to thwart its pernicious influence. It is rather that his habits of mind, his artistic motives, his methods of work – and above all, his concern for the intrinsic significance of the individual tales – made certain kinds of organisation, the lack of which seems to us inexplicable, seem to him unimportant. We might listen to a great art-historian, speaking of a similarly ambiguous commitment to naturalism in the Boucicaut Master:

> Historians of art, attentive to triumphs of naturalism, should nevertheless recognize that he was a great artist even when he was not consistently 'advanced'. (Meiss, 1968, p. 70)

Recognising that the 'naturalistic surge of his style' is what first strikes us, and content to accept Panofsky's brilliant account of the artist's innovations in such things as aerial perspective, Meiss prefers to concentrate on

> the limitations of this naturalism – to some extent a deliberate limitation by the painter . . . engendered in part by his sense of the peculiarities of painting in books . . . and of an appropriate relation of a miniature and a folio. (pp. 12, 70)

Chaucer, one might suggest, is just as aware of the peculiarities of poems that pretend to be imitations of human life, and of the relation of the tale to the frame. If any countenance, finally, needed to be offered to Chaucer's practice, it might be found in the activities of his successors.

Lydgate allows the continuing pilgrimage journey to penetrate the telling of his 'Canterbury tale' of *The Siege of Thebes*, making several references to the passage of time in the course of the tale and to the progress of the journey; while the author of *The Tale of Beryn*, another 'Canterbury tale', attributed to the merchant in the solitary manuscript in which it survives, has a description of the arrival of the pilgrims at Canterbury and their lively adventures there, and an account of their activities as a group more extended than anything to be found in Chaucer.[3] The effect, though highly amusing, is trivialising – the dissipation of the overmastering reality of illusion in the pursuit of the vain illusion of reality.

Yet determination to curb eccentricity should not tempt us to underestimate the importance of the frame-narrative in the *Canterbury Tales*. Chaucer spent some considerable pains on the elaboration of this frame-narrative, and he clearly saw in it many advantages and opportunities. Some of these are obvious practical advantages: if, as seems apparent, Chaucer's inclination was now, after the completion of the great Boccaccian poems, 'Palamon and Arcite' and *Troilus and Criseyde*, to the writing of shorter verse narratives, the framework of the *Canterbury Tales* gave him plausible occasions for almost any tale he might wish to tell. In particular, it gave him the excuse, indeed a veritable obligation, to follow his 'cherles' into the realms of low life, and to indulge his taste for fabliaux. There are four of these, as strictly defined (tales of trickery and sexual intrigue with a bourgeois setting), namely, the Miller's, Reeve's, Merchant's and Shipman's Tales, and two further tales, the Friar's and the Summoner's, which are more broadly anecdotal. Without exception, they are amongst Chaucer's most striking and characteristic achievements, and there is no need to say that for him the indulgence of a taste was in actual fact an imaginatively strenuous engagement with new and unexpected materials. However, to others, and perhaps in a way to himself, he needed to explain how he came to be writing poems which were so inappropriate to the great poet he had now become, 'the noble philosophical poete in Englissh' as Thomas Usk called him, in his *Testament of Love* (ed. Skeat, 1897, p. 123). The role of the poet in the Middle Ages, in his relationship to his acknowledged public audience, laid many constraints upon the individual imagination. Chaucer had evaded these constraints in the past by adopting the role of the poet-dreamer, whose recognised responsibility is to report the contents of his dream, but who is not placed in a position of responsibility or authority in relation to those contents; or by adopting the role of the reporter of existing stories (*Troilus and Criseyde*), for which again he takes no responsibility. In these ways, Chaucer removes from himself the burden of authority which lay upon the poet and which would tend to direct him, if he did not adopt one of these disguises, into authoritative and dogmatic discourse concerning the Christian religion. There was no other authority from which the poet could claim to speak, and certainly no poet could claim to speak directly from the authority of experience, as would a Wordsworth or a Shelley. This is not to say that he did not in reality speak from experience, of course; only that the conventions of public poetry (and all poetry was public) did not allow that claim to be made. Even poets who wished to speak about nothing but the Christian religion, like Dante and Langland, would write under the cover of allegory and vision, for to claim that their own life and experience were of significance would be an act of usurpation of a divine prerogative. There could be no writing of 'My Life and Thoughts' or of *The Prelude* in the Middle Ages: as Stevens (1973) says, 'To claim an experience, event or feeling as meaningful *because it happened to me* would have struck a medieval audience as foolish and presumptuous' (p. 213).

In the *Canterbury Tales*, therefore, Chaucer advances himself as the reporter of events in which he participated but in which his own role is peripheral and primarily that of observer. David (1976) puts the matter quite bluntly: 'Through the invention of the frame story, Chaucer is able to escape his moral obligations as a poet' (p. 75). He assumes no overt responsibility for invention, and the extraordinary freedom that he thereby achieves is nowhere more piquantly demonstrated than in the Wife of Bath's claim to speak from that very position which was denied to the poet:

> Experience, though noon auctoritee
> Were in this world, is right ynogh for me
> To speke of wo that is in mariage. (III.1–3)

With the 'cherles', likewise, Chaucer can ease himself out of the position of acknowledged responsibility in claiming that he is acting merely as an accurate reporter of historical events:

> But first I pray yow, of youre curteisye,
> That ye n'arette it nat my vileynye,
> Thogh that I pleynly speke in this mateere,
> To telle yow hir wordes and hir cheere,
> Ne thogh I speke hir wordes proprely.
> For this ye knowen al so wel as I,

Whoso shal telle a tale after a man,
He moot reherce as ny as evere he kan
Everich a word, if it be in his charge,
Al speke he never so rudeliche and large,
Or ellis he moot telle his tale untrewe,
Or feyne thyng, or fynde wordes newe. (I.725–36)

Of course, what he is saying is not 'true', since everyone is perfectly well aware that what he is excusing himself for is what he has chosen to do. But to recognise this, and to laugh merely, and dismiss the passage as tongue-in-cheek, would be to miss an inner truth in the ludicrous subterfuge. As Elizabeth Salter says, speaking of this passage and the one quoted below, 'These should not be taken as humorous disclaimers of art but, on the contrary, as serious passages, laying claim to art of a particular nature – the art of the dramatist which "involves a kind of abdication"'.[4] As often, in his comments upon the operation of his art, Chaucer is expressing, under a guise of assumed innocence, a perception of a difficult and maybe even for him partly obscured reality. 'Truth to life' is not something to be laughed off, even if the terms in which he speaks of it here (chiefly, the possibility that he may have to use bad language or rude words)[5] themselves provoke laughter. In making us laugh at the discrepancy between what he claims he must do and what he actually does, Chaucer alerts us to the complexity of the 'truth' to which the poet must be faithful, and reminds us that it exists, in part at least, as something in the mind of the poet.

When he returns to this subject, in the introduction to the Miller's Tale, Chaucer speaks in similar terms:

And therfore every gentil wight I preye,
For Goddes love, demeth nat that I seye
Of yvel entente, but for I moot reherce
Hir tales alle, be they bettre or werse,
Or elles falsen som of my mateere.
And therfore, whoso list it nat yheere,
Turne over the leef and chese another tale;
For he shal fynde ynowe, grete and smale,
Of storial thyng that toucheth gentillesse,
And eek moralitee and hoolynesse.
Blameth nat me if that ye chese amys.
The Millere is a cherl, ye knowe wel this;
So was the Reve eek and othere mo,
And harlotrie they tolden bothe two. (I.3171–84)

To 'falsen' one's 'mateere' has here the ostensible sense of not reporting word for word what the Miller said (which Chaucer had presumably taken down in shorthand), but it is impossible to miss the layer of resonance of such language. Chaucer's use of 'mateere' recalls Jean de Meun's 'ce requeroit la matire', as cited in the last footnote, but also the famous distinction made by Chrétien de Troyes, in the prologue to the *Lancelot* (line 25) between *matiere* (given narrative material) and *san* (sense or significance imparted to the material in the poet's treatment, in this case the treatment specified by his patroness). This distinction has often been discussed, as by Vinaver (1971), Luttrell (1974) and Robertson (1951b): Luttrell (pp. 47–8) associates Chrétien's distinction with that made by Alain de Lille, in the *Anticlaudianus*, between *materia historialis* and *materia mistica*, but this association is misleading if it forces Chrétien into the allegorists' camp, which is where he finds himself in Robertson's forceful essay. Chrétien seems rather to be referring to the activity of mind of the creative artist, not the intentions of the allegorist. Chaucer, in speaking of *mateere*, is doing the same, though with the significant difference that he speaks of the 'matter' of experience rather than the 'matter' of given stories. His apparent disingenuousness thus conceals a more ambitious claim, the ulterior acknowledgement that is made being that of the poet's responsibility to be true to the matter of reality, of life as he perceives and experiences it. The acknowledgement of this responsibility does not involve a rejection of books and *auctoritee* in favour of *experience*, and should not be regarded as an opportunity to see Chaucer's poetic career in over-simplified terms as a progress from the one to the other.[6] Rather, in all his poetry, including the *Canterbury Tales*, experience and *auctoritee* are the two poles between which his poetic creativity flows. To bind himself to the one, as a 'realist', would be to relinquish the freedom he has won from subservience to the other. Chaucer's language here tends to dissolve these traditional categories, in just the same way that his exhortation not to make 'ernest' of 'game' is a playful way of indicating, not that the tales of 'harlotrie' are trivial and unmemorable, but that the activity of the poet has a legitimate sphere of operation in which edification is not sought for nor to be expected.[7]

These arguments have taken us a long way from the pragmatic considerations which attach to Chaucer's choice of the pilgrimage frame, but it has perhaps become clear that the provision of 'occasions' for a great variety of narrative poems was no small advantage to have won. On a more purely practical level, one might add that the scheme gave him convenient slots not only for poems he might write in the future but also for some poems that he had already written, such as the 'Palamon and Arcite' and the 'lyf of Seynt Cecile', which he mentions in the Prologue to the *Legend of Good Women*, and which had perhaps been gathering dust in his study for some years. The fugitive nature of such pieces in an age of manuscript is something to be stressed. Most of the shorter poems of the Middle Ages float in the sea of anonymity, detached from whatever moorings they might once have had in time and place and in the work of particular writers. For the medieval poet who was conscious of the scattering and loss and 'un-authorised' copying to which his writings might be subject, one solution, though of course it would not have manifested itself as a solution to this problem, was to write single long integrated poems, like Jean de Meun or Dante or Langland. Another solution was to assemble originally independent pieces in the protected stockade of an authorised collection, as Machaut did (Chichmaref, 1909, pp. lxxii–viii), and to hope that the author and his canon and a sense of the coherence of his canon would be preserved in this way. This idea may have appealed to Chaucer, but he was clearly much more influenced by a third and favourite method of giving integrity and unity to independent or diverse materials, namely, the device of the frame.

There are many types of tale-collection in the Middle Ages, though two broad categories may be isolated. One type depended for its integrity on the existence outside the tales of an abstract organising principle. This type may be called 'inorganic'. Its most obvious representatives are the collections of stories which are united in being common witnesses to the supreme truth, beyond narrative reality, of Christian truth, such as the *Legenda Aurea* and other collections of saints' legends and related material, or the *Gesta Romanorum*. Sometimes such tales will be arranged according to an additional external organising principle, as when legendaries are arranged according to the order of the Church's year, or a collection like the *Alphabetum Narrationum* (ed. Banks, 1894–5) in alphabetical order of title. The other type may be called 'organic', and here the collection of tales is presented, with varying degrees of dramatic plausibility, as springing from a narrative situation which acts as a frame for the whole work. So Scheherazade, in the *Thousand and One Nights*, tells a tale a night to save her neck; the daughters of Minyas, in Ovid's *Metamorphoses* (IV.31–388), absent themselves from the festival of Bacchus and tell tales, while they spin, to beguile the passing hours; the seven tutors of the son of the Emperor Diocletian tell each a tale a day, in *The Seven Sages of Rome* (ed. Brunner, 1933), to gain reprieve for the son from his father's threat of execution; Fiammetta, in Boccaccio's

Filocolo (IV.19–70), presides over a gathering where questions of love are presented in the form of stories. There are also some variations on these types, and mixtures. Chaucer's *Legend of Good Women* is clearly a secular version, or perversion, of the first type, the supreme truth to which the legends witness being the truth of women: the work is called 'the Seintes Legende of Cupide' in the introduction to the Man of Law's Tale (II.61). Gower's *Confessio Amantis* has a genuine narrative frame, the stories which it largely consists of being told by Genius, the priest of Venus, as part of his catechetical instruction concerning love to the penitent Lover. However, the instruction is given in seven books (i.e., excluding Prologue and Book VII) according to the division of the seven deadly sins, so that the poem partakes also of an externally imposed principle of ordering. Boccaccio's *De Casibus Virorum Illustrium* has a frame-narrative in which the poet at his desk is visited by figures or groups of figures from the past, whose fateful stories he tells (sometimes they tell their own). Lydgate's *Fall of Princes*, drawn from Boccaccio through a French intermediary, pays only intermittent attention to this frame, whose power and significance Lydgate hardly seems to understand, so that the poem is unified only by the inorganic scheme of a monotonous and unexclusive Fate.

It will be seen that there is some variety and richness in the types of organisation devised for collections of tales, and a clear indication as to the usefulness and desirability of such collections. However, there is little here that provides any sort of parallel with the *Canterbury Tales*. What all these collections lack, and what the *Tales* so manifestly have, is firstly, a sense of the organic autonomy of the frame narrative, its capacity to develop and expand, even in unexpected directions, according to the laws of its own fictional existence; and secondly, where there is more than one narrator, any attempt to differentiate the tales according to the character or status or other discernible attributes of the tellers. There is one collection that might seem to offer something of the first, a collection indeed which uses the narrative frame of the journey, the *Novelle* of Giovanni Sercambi (ed. Sinicropi, 1972), written in 1374, and there has been some speculation about Chaucer's possible knowledge of the work (e.g., Pratt and Young, 1941). But if he did know it, he would have got little more than the bare suggestion of the pilgrimage from it. In the *Novelle*, the author is represented as himself telling all the stories to a large company of travellers as they wander about Italy to escape the plague (it is a peregrination, not a pilgrimage); the pilgrims remain an undifferentiated mass, and few of them are distinguished or characterised, apart from Aluisi, the *preposto*, who acts as leader of the group, a little like the Host; the tales themselves all have Latin titles affixed at the head (*De Sapientia, De Simplicitate*, etc.) as if they were preachers' *exempla*. A few similarities with the *Tales* may be observed, but they are only such as might readily arise from the coincidence of subject.

With one Italian work, however, the *Tales* have a definite kinship, and a description of this work, the *Decameron* of Boccaccio, will help to demonstrate some of the special qualities of the *Tales*.[8] Boccaccio, after a Preface in which he says he writes principally for the delectation of ladies, begins with a powerful description of Florence ravaged by plague in 1348. Seven young ladies and three young men meet by chance and decide to go out to a country villa to escape the plague, and to seek some relaxation in amusing pastimes from the horrors around them. When they arrive, it is decided that one shall be chosen for each day to rule their pleasures for that day, and the first, Pampinea, decrees that they shall tell tales. The tale-telling will take place after the time of siesta, to fill the space before dinner and the evening's dancing and singing. All ten are to tell tales on each day, and each day will be dedicated to a particular theme (tales of adventures reaching a happy end, tales of things gained or regained that were much desired, tales of love ending unhappily, and so on), though there is no set theme for the first day, since there has been no time to think up suitable tales, and Emilia, on the ninth day, gives everyone a free choice. Dioneo, who from the start is given the character of the most licentiously spoken of the group,[9] is granted exemption from the rule of the theme of the day, and he always speaks last on a subject, usually highly improper, of his own choice. They stick rigidly to this scheme, with its minor variations, throughout the ten days, which are actually part of a stay of fourteen days because of their decision not to have any tales on Friday or Saturday, for a mixture of religious and practical reasons (women have to wash their hair on Saturdays). However, Boccaccio does introduce a few diversions: there is a change of venue on Day 3, the first Sunday, when they move to a different villa; on Day 6, the beginning of the tale-telling is interrupted by a quarrel among the servants about the virginity of a woman on her wedding-night – at which the ladies laugh so heartily that you could have pulled their teeth out; and at the end of Day 6, because the tale-telling finishes early (tales of witty retorts), they make a visit to the beautiful 'Valle delle Donne', where next day they spend the whole day and have the tale-telling near the lake where they earlier swam.

It will be seen that Boccaccio gives minute and scrupulous attention to the literal plausibility of his frame-narrative or 'cornice', and at every point we know where the characters are and what day and what time of day it is. The frame-narrative develops with complete naturalness and spontaneity, and is related firmly to surrounding realities (the plague-ridden city, the villas, landscapes, servants, meals, other entertainments). Attention is drawn to the fact that tales take more or less time to tell (e.g., Aldington, 1930, pp. 177, 335), and there is frequent retrospective reference to previous tales, even to tales of previous days (e.g., Aldington, 1930, pp. 196, 316, 386). In fact, Boccaccio does carefully all the things that Chaucer is so careless of. At the same time, he does little or nothing to develop the frame-narrative in unexpected or dramatic ways, and it takes on, quite early, a rigidity which Boccaccio shows little inclination to disturb. The links between tales and between days are mostly brief, repetitive and uninventive. Likewise, there is little attempt to develop any association between teller and tale, apart from the case of Dioneo. The men are given the more improper tales, and Filostrato's choice of subject for his day (tales of love ending unhappily, Day 4) reflects his character in so far as his name is his character. Apart from this, there is nothing, and Boccaccio, in choosing for the frame-narrative an undifferentiated group of characters of the same age and background, clearly sought nothing.

There are further parallels and contrasts with Chaucer to be seen in Boccaccio's own comments on his work. He explains in his opening narrative that he will not reveal the real name of his characters, so that they will not have to blush at the recital of what they said and listened to. Nor should they be obliged to blush, for it was an occasion when the horrors of plague gave some excuse for the relaxation of the usual inhibitions and restrictions of polite society. Dioneo throughout acts as a spokesman in defence of licence (e.g. pp. 31, 302, 335), and Boccaccio himself makes a brief entrance at the beginning of Day 4, to offer his defence against those detractors who say that he serves women ill in writing of them so. In his conclusion he recurs to these matters more fully. He replies to objections that the tales have not been suitable for modest ladies to hear or tell, by saying that he had to relate them as they were told, or else alter them completely ('Altramenti raccontar'); that the occasion was not a serious one, and somewhat freed from restraint by circumstance; that any ill interpretation is due to those who wish to take it so, who might pervert the scriptures if they wished. He asserts that he had to write down what he heard,[10] since he was only the scribe and not the inventor. Anyone who wants can read the tales they like and leave those they dislike – 'Turne over the leef and chese another tale,' as Chaucer put it, in the Miller's Prologue (I.3177) – and for this reason he gives a summary of the story at the head of each tale.

What Boccaccio does here with such brazen confidence is of course what we saw Chaucer doing rather more tentatively. Boccaccio knew exactly what he was doing: he knew that he could shake off censure by insisting that the tales are diversions to amuse women and therefore beneath the serious notice of scholars and fellow-poets, and he also knew that he could rely on a wide readership among the merchant and upper middle class families of northern Italy, amongst whom most manuscripts are to be found (Branca, 1976b, pp. 198–201). He had also fortified himself against any rebuke for his triviality by demonstrating his full powers in the magnificent prose pieces that frame the work: the sombre 'overture' with its description, based on the *Historia Langobardi* of Paulus Diaconus, of the plague in Florence; and the last tale, told, significantly enough, by Dioneo, of Gualtieri and Griselda. Boccaccio must have been delighted to receive these comments from Petrarch, his poetic guide and mentor, in a letter written in 1371:

> My hasty perusal afforded me much pleasure. If the humour is a little too free at times, this may be excused in view of the age at which you wrote, the style and language which you employ, and the frivolity of the subjects, and of the persons who are likely to read such tales ... Along with much that was light and amusing, I discovered some serious and edifying things as well ... (Musa and Bondanella, 1977, p. 185)

Petrarch singles out for special praise the overture and the tale of Griselda, and his letter includes his own famous translation of that tale into Latin, which in its turn provided Chaucer's direct source for his Clerk's Tale.

It is hard to believe that the *Decameron* did not provide a germ of growth or even a direct source of inspiration for the *Canterbury Tales*. Chaucer had already done English versions of Boccaccio's earlier poems, the *Teseida* and the *Filostrato*, in his 'Palamon and Arcite' and *Troilus and Criseyde*. Here now was the model for a work of 'extraliterary' inspiration, drawing on the life of the contemporary community, on popular tales, on well-known scatological anecdotes: after the world of high classical tragedy, the world of 'the human comedy', as Kittredge (1915,

p. 154) long ago called the *Tales*, and as Francesco de Sanctis, the great nineteenth-century literary historian, before him called the *Decameron* – 'la commedia umana' (1870–1, vol. 1, p. 329). Six of Chaucer's tales have analogues or possible sources in the *Decameron*, the Miller's (Day 3, Tale 4), Reeve's (9.6), Clerk's (10.10), Merchant's (7.9), Franklin's (10.5) and Shipman's (8.1) Tales, and in addition his Man of Law's Tale may be seen as a palinode to Boccaccio's lubricious tale of Alatiel (Day 2, Tale 7). Like Boccaccio, he buttressed his collection with massive demonstrations of traditional literary power (the Knight's Tale) and religious orthodoxy (the Parson's Tale), and like Boccaccio too he combined the serious and the irreverent, the exemplary and the anecdotal, and a representation of European life with a wide-ranging critique of society. Chaucer, in England, had no rich and numerous upper middle-class audience such as Boccaccio could rely on, but he was used to creating his own audience and the taste by which he would be appreciated. He wrote in verse: in England literary prose was primarily used for devotional writing.

The differences, though, between the *Decameron* and the *Tales* in their use of the frame-narrative, and quite apart from the differences between the framed tales of the two works in terms of the quality of imaginative engagement, remain of fundamental importance. Chaucer's carelessness with the naturalistic details of the frame-narrative has been mentioned, and may be a sign of a greater wisdom. But above all, there is the extension of the social range of the tale-tellers, the attempt to match tale and teller, and the inimitable explosive drama of the frame-narrative. This narrative seems to develop naturally and organically, and is as far as it could be from a mere excuse for stringing stories together. The social range of the cast, whether or not it was ever likely that such a group would in real life come together, makes the potential drama even more intriguing and unpredictable, as many modern film-makers have observed, in their stories of heterogeneous social groups suspended from normal life in special and prolonged proximity, as in lifeboats, train-journeys and air-disasters.

From the beginning, almost, nature rules. When the Knight's tale is over, the Host calls upon the Monk, possibly the next in rank if we unchivalrously pass over the Prioress, and it seems that we are to descend soberly down the social ladder. But at this point the Miller erupts onto the well-ordered scene, already drunk, scarcely able to stay on his horse, shouting 'in Pilates voys', and demanding to tell a tale. The Host helplessly acquiesces, and the Miller announces his tale of a carpenter and his wife, but immediately the Reeve, who we later learn is 'of carpenteris craft' (I.3861), starts up and demands that he stop his 'lewed dronken harlotrye' and tell no tale to the slander of man or woman. The next tale is thus already, so to speak, 'set up'. At the end of the Reeve's Tale there is no predictable 'tidying-up' of the quarrel with the Miller, but instead the Cook breaks in, overcome with ecstasy at the witty conclusion of the 'argument of herbergage'.

Fragment VII is another sequence in which the sense of evolving drama, of the natural but unexpected, is strong. The Host here plays a major dramatic role, whether inviting the Prioress to tell a tale with exquisitely overdone politeness and a regular cascade of subjunctives (VII.447–51), or using Chaucer, and later the Monk, as the target for some easy and patronising raillery, or giving a virtuoso account of the difference between his wife Goodelief and the wise and patient (allegorical) wife of Melibee (VII.1889–1923).

Examples could be further multiplied of the irresistible sense of dramatic momentum in the *Canterbury Tales* links: the smouldering hatred of the Friar and Summoner bursting forth in smooth viciousness and foul-mouthed obscenity (III); the sweet blandness of the Franklin's 'interruption' of the Squire, congratulating him on a tale well-told before he has finished telling it (V); the sudden bursting into the pilgrimage group of the Canon and his Yeoman (VIII); the vivid exchange between drunken Cook and fastidious Manciple, ending with what the Host laughingly salutes as the triumph of Bacchus (IX). The sense of dramatic evolution, of a naturally unfolding organism, is so strong that it tempts us to a thoroughgoing 'dramatic' reading of the *Tales*, in which the meaning of the work is most fully bodied forth in the frame-narrative and its implications. The limitations of such a view, in some sense limitations that Chaucer built into his poem, have already been discussed in relation to naturalistic interpretations of the frame-narrative, but the argument needs now to be extended.

It is possible, for instance, to think of the idea of the tale-telling contest as an important kind of unity provided by the frame-narrative and to agree with writers such as Gaylord (1967), Scheps (1975–6) and Olson (1982, pp. 156–63) that the comments made on the tales, by the Host and others, constitute a framework of critical understanding. The difficulty with this view is that all the comments made are either predictable and perfunctory (e.g., I.3109–13, 3855–8) or else ludicrously inapposite. The Host, in particular, always misses the point of what he has heard, and is a living example of how not to understand stories. His way of applying the story of the allegorical wife Prudence to his real wife Goodelief is a case in point. But this is so obvious that there is no way in which it could be said to inform our understanding of the tale of *Melibee*. The reader who needs the Host's comic literalism is in no position to relish it. All the matter of 'sentence' and 'solaas', too, is contrived so as to be read back into the frame: it offers nothing to the interpretation of the tales, for an approach to the interpretation that contented itself with the assertion that tales should be one or the other, or even a judicious mixture of the two, would sink to the level of the Host's own version of literary reality. There are some remarks about stories made by Chaucer himself, of course, which bear a different kind of interpretation, but these, as we have seen, merely masquerade as part of the frame-narrative and are actually *sotto voce* comments, in his characteristic style, on the practice of his art. The same may be said of the comments of Chaucer the pilgrim in the introduction to his tale of *Melibee*, where he says, in effect, that though the truth may be one there are many different ways of telling it. This is an observation of a different order of significance from any made by the characters of the pilgrimage, even the Knight in his interruption of the Monk's Tale.

These readings of the frame-narrative may seem to devalue what earlier I commended so enthusiastically. They contribute to the unfolding drama of the links, but place that drama on a lower level of meaning-fulness than the tales. This, I think, is fair. The thought of England seems always to produce a homely effect on Chaucer, and an impression of muddy lanes, cramped houses, large wooden objects, and wooden-headed people, contrived upon by a few sly tricksters. England, as the world of low realism, is part of the decorum of styles. As such, it has a place in contributing to the total effect in individual tales; but in the frame this effect is, as a whole, unrealised. The links are a series of opportunities seized rather than elements in a grand design. For the truly epic real-isation of this England, we must go to Shakespeare's vision of Eastcheap, the inn near Gadshill, the road to Sutton Coldfield, rural Gloucestershire.

There is, however, a more emphatic case that has been made for the 'dramatic' significance of the frame-narrative in the *Canterbury Tales*, and this has to do with the adaptation of tale to teller, and in particular the claim that the tales are primarily to be read as a display of the teller's character or as motivated by the dramatic needs of the frame-narrative. This view, first and most persuasively presented by Kittredge, has had a profound influence on the reading of the *Canterbury Tales*, and it is worth seeing what Kittredge originally said:

The Canterbury Pilgrimage is . . . a Human Comedy, and the Knight and the Miller and the Pardoner and the Wife of Bath and the rest are the *dramatis personae* . . . The Pilgrims do not exist for the sake of the stories, but *vice versa*. Structurally regarded, the stories are merely long speeches expressing, directly or indirectly, the characters of the several persons. They are more or less comparable, in this regard, to the soliloquies of Hamlet or Iago or Macbeth. But they are not mere monologues, for each is addressed to all the other personages, and evokes reply and comment, being thus in a real sense, a part of the conversation. (1915, pp. 154–5)

The attractiveness of this scheme is obvious: it is comprehensive, and offers a total interpretation of the *Tales*; it creates coherence where there is the appearance of fragmentation; it compares Chaucer favourably with Shakespeare; and it is easy to grasp, develop and amplify, since there are no constraints on the imagined activities of 'characters' of whom we know little or nothing. It is not surprising, therefore, that the 'dramatic principle' had been popular with explicators of the *Canterbury Tales*, perhaps most notoriously so in Lumiansky (1955), and has seemed generally to enhance understanding.

However, the understanding that is enhanced is the kind of understanding that we find easiest to offer, and not that which, in admitting the strenuous and exhilarating engagement with the 'differentness' of Chaucer's poetry, draws us to appreciate those things that were not previously perceivable or acceptable to us. The 'dramatic principle' is a way of making Chaucer respond to familiar twentieth-century preoccupations with 'character' and with psychological realism and complexity in the portrayal of individual literary characters. Take for instance the Clerk's Tale, and the way in which Kittredge appropriates it to his 'dramatic' reading of the *Canterbury Tales*:

We should not forget that the Clerk's Tale, like the Wife's long sermon, is addressed to the Canterbury Pilgrims, not us, though we are privileged to overhear. We must not only listen, but look. In our mind's eye, we must see the Pilgrims, and watch their demeanor. Naturally, they are interested, and equally of course, they understand what the Clerk is doing. He is replying to the Wife of Bath, – confuting her heresies, and at the same time vindicating his own order from her abusive raillery. (1915, p. 194).

The modern reader, quite out of sympathy with the allegorical mode and religious matter of the tale, sees here a welcome avenue of escape both from the tedium of the tale and from the embarrassment of believing that Chaucer was content with such tedium. New life is breathed into a dreary old poem. The real result, however, is the surrender of the poem to modern susceptibilities, and the jettisoning of a superb piece of narrative poetry, which brings together in fascinating juxtaposition potentially contradictory techniques of exemplary and mimetic writing, for a moment of character-drama. This is not to say that that character-drama is not present in the Clerk's 'epilogue' and Envoy (III.1163–1212). Here, in a passage which shows clear signs of having been added in revision, Chaucer returns to the frame-narrative and the unfolding drama which he there so much relishes. To allow that drama to penetrate back into the *Tale*, however, and to realign retrospectively its meanings, is to mistake accident for substance.

The point can be made more emphatically in a consideration of the tale of *Melibee* and the Monk's tale. Both are 'framed' as jokes at the Host's expense, the first as Chaucer's revenge for having been 'letted' of his tale of *Thopas*, and the second as the product of the Monk's determination to put down the Host for his impudence. The joke is there to be enjoyed, and the Host's limitations of understanding and frustrations are amusingly portrayed. But it would be trivial to take this drama back into the two tales, to say that *Melibee* is *really* an interminably dull and dreary moralistic allegory or that the Monk's Tale is *really* boring. Incompetence and 'boringness' have their place in literature, but they must of course be displayed in a manner that fills us with delight at the spectacle, as in the tale of *Thopas* itself or in Jane Austen's portrayal of Miss Bates. It would be absurd to suppose otherwise, and again it will be seen that the frame-narrative operates as a frame and not as an ironically informative clue to the 'real' meaning of a tale. The depredations that have been wrought on the *Canterbury Tales* by practitioners of the latter mode of interpretation are too numerous to be retailed here at length, though a few may be mentioned: the Knight's Tale reveals its teller as a mercenary soldier of the worst kind as well as an incompetent narrator, and is 'a hymn to tyranny' in the mouth of a cold-blooded professional killer (Jones, 1980); the Prioress's Tale is chiefly remarkable as an exposure of the hypocrisy of its teller and of her blind and bigoted anti-semitism (Schoeck, 1956); the Man of Law's Tale reveals its teller as an incompetent and pretentious time-server who understands nothing of the religious values he purports to celebrate (Delasanta, 1970–1); the

Second Nun's Tale is an example of the arrogance of militant Christianity (Engelhardt, 1975, pp. 294–6). In each case a tale which is not to modern taste is appropriated to some fashionable modern ideology by the employment of the 'dramatic principle' as a means of ironisation.[11] Chaucer writes badly so as to characterise the inadequacy of his pilgrim-narrators and thus refute what they say. By this means Chaucer can be·recruited to worthy causes, and all need of effort at true understanding is removed.[12]

There are, of course – to return from these solipsistic fantasies to the experience of reading the *Tales* – some tales in which the presence of the teller is more than usually strong. A distinct category, for instance, and in the present study a distinct chapter, is created for those tales which are preceded by extended quasi-autobiographical monologues, namely, the Wife of Bath's, Pardoner's and Canon's Yeoman's Tale. Naturally, these prologues prompt a more than usual interest in character display. It should be recognised, however, that the relation of tale to teller in at least the first two cases remains at the level of external congruence, and that the element of unstructured and unconscious self-revelation – the quality so prized in Browning's dramatic monologues – is limited to what has already been signalled in the more explicit context of the prologue. So the Wife of Bath's Tale is an *exemplum* of her manifesto concerning wifely sovereignty, and the Pardoner's Tale, more simply, an example of his preaching practice. The Canon's Yeoman's Tale is in some ways more suggestive, because of the curious relationship that exists between the autobiographical and fictional parts of his 'tale'. The former is laced with fiction and illusion, the latter inextricably entangled with personal experience, and Chaucer seems to suggest, in a remarkably subtle but incompletely achieved manner, the fluid relationship between the world of experience and the world of fiction.

Elsewhere, Chaucer is content with a general appropriateness of tale to teller, whereby the Knight tells a lofty romance of love and chivalry, the Squire a romance of a lighter and more sentimental kind, the Prioress and her Nun religious legends, while the Parson delivers a weighty discourse which is not a tale at all. The needs of the frame-narrative are observed with varying degrees of care and dramatic elaboration, but once a tale has properly got under way it is rare for there to be any reminder of the person or the character of the person who is telling it. At the end of the tale we return to the world of the pilgrimage with that ready and delighted acceptance of multiple fictional illusion which is instinctive to all readers except those brought up exclusively on certain kinds of novel.

Sometimes a dimension is added to our enjoyment of a tale by the manner in which it is drawn out of the drama of the frame-narrative. The tales deriving from quarrels or presumed quarrels (Reeve's, Friar's, Summoner's) exist in our reading within a consciousness of the motives of the teller which gives piquancy to the choice of subject, but of course there is no way in which the *manner* of the telling – the style, language, treatment of subject – reveals the character of the teller. All are told with equally consummate artistry. As Muscatine says,

> When Chaucer mediated carefully between teller and tale, he sought not an idiomatic but a tonal and attitudinal relationship. No medieval poet would have sacrificed all the rich technical means at his disposal merely to make a story sound as if such and such a character were actually telling it. (1957, p. 172)

The sense of an added dimension, though, is not to be devalued, for Chaucer is clearly aware of the extra dramatic effect to be derived at times from appropriateness of attribution. The fact that the Miller and the Reeve, the Friar and the Summoner tell tales about people like themselves, or like each other,[13] gives the tales a dramatic edge which is lacking in Boccaccio's similarly coarse and improper tales.

There are some exceptions to these general rules. Some tales, for instance, have been allocated to pilgrims with little or no care for appropriateness or congruence: nothing in what is heard of the Man of Law or Physician in the General Prologue prepares us for the tales that they tell (to call this dramatically realistic *because* unexpected is hardly sensible), and the Merchant's Tale is appropriated to the Merchant only through a late-added prologue (Manly and Rickert, 1940, Vol. 2, p. 266), which introduces new information about him quite unrelated to his merchant-ness. The Shipman's Tale is not in any way appropriate to the Shipman (perhaps a better-navigated version of the tale of Constance would have suited him), except in so far as he may be presumed to be a coarse fellow. The Nun's Priest's Tale is surely misread if it is read as mockery of or satire directed by its teller, or as spoken by any voice but the maturest and wittiest voice of the poet himself: the wheeling on of the unknown Nun's Priest is a comical device.

There are one or two tales, on the other hand, where it seems to me that the dramatic 'colouring' is quite strong and has a part in the interpretation of the tale as tale: the Franklin's Tale and, more enigmatically, the Manciple's Tale come to mind. Opinion as to the presence of such colouring must remain properly flexible – as long as a curb is placed on the misuse of the dramatic principle for the purposes of 'ironical' refutation and ideological reconstitution – for Chaucer did provide a dramatic framework for the *Tales* and evidently enjoyed exploiting some of the dramatic possibilities that he thereby created. Principally, though, what he sought in the frame-narrative of the *Canterbury Tales* was variety, flexibility, independence and *indirection* in the mode of narrative discourse.[14] To suppose that the *Tales* are always or never dramatically conceived would be to restore Chaucer to the straitjacket he struggled so hard to escape. In his earlier poems, Chaucer had always been concerned to create a narrator through whom the narrative could be communicated without Chaucer himself being committed to a fixed point of view. The narrators of the dream-poems and of *Troilus* are developed because of Chaucer's need for freedom from a premature and restrictive commitment to fixed attitudes or interpretations. The *Canterbury Tales* provide the perfect vehicle for this indirection. Whoever is telling a tale, we can be assured it is not Chaucer; and when it purports to be Chaucer, it is not really Chaucer; and when it really is Chaucer, he pretends that it is someone else. This is not artistic or moral evasiveness, or the throwing off of responsibilities that a poet should properly bear, but rather the taking on of the larger responsibility for comprehending many points of view and recognising the multifacetedness of experience. It is a sense of the relativity of perception and judgement, but it is not moral relativism.

With this said, it may seem that a fundamental element in the frame-narrative, and an important source of unity for the *Tales*, is being neglected – the pilgrimage. There is no question that the pilgrimage is a potent image for the journey of man through life,[15]

> This world nys but a thurghfare ful of wo,
> And we been pilgrymes, passynge to and fro (I.2847–8)

and for the spiritual journey of man from the world of creatural experience (the city, London, the Tabard Inn) to the world of true spiritual understanding (the heavenly city, Canterbury, the shrine of St Thomas). Chaucer begins his poem with some delicate play on the spiritual significance and secular reality of pilgrimages, which clearly, whilst describing the latter, alerts us to the former. The coming of Spring, we are told, fills all nature with renewed life and makes the birds sing all night with joy of love. But also,

Thanne longen folk to goon on pilgrimages ... (I.12)

The association between the promptings of nature and the desire to go on
pilgrimage both sacralises nature and also desacralises pilgrimage. It
leaves us with the sense that the pilgrim may be answering two different
kinds of call, as Hoffman (1954) says, and the progress of the General
Prologue persuades us that for nearly all of them it is the wrong one. Only
the Knight is spoken of as going on pilgrimage with any sense of purpose
(I.77–8). Soon the pilgrimage is forgotten: the pilgrims seems to be on a
kind of holiday, with the Host as their tour-leader. The object of the
journey is briefly alluded to by the Host (I.769–70) but the main
preoccupation is with making the journey as pleasant as possible. Maybe
this is like life. Subsequently there is no mention of the pilgrimage to
Canterbury, or of the reasons for undertaking it, only references to the
journey or the places on the way, or unrelated and unpointed references
to pilgrimages within the tales (e.g. III.557, VII.2986). Then, as they
approach the end of their journey, comes the Host's request that the
Parson, as a man fit to 'knytte up wel a greet mateere' (X.28), should tell
the last tale, and the Parson's majestic response:

> I wol yow telle a myrie tale in prose
> To knytte up al this feeste, and make an ende.
> And Ihesu, for his grace, wit me sende
> To shewe yow the wey, in this viage,
> Of thilke parfit glorious pilgrymage
> That highte Jerusalem celestial. (X.46–51)

The Parson asks for and receives the assent of the whole body of pilgrims
to his proposal, and the Host, acting formally as their spokesman –

> Oure Hoost hadde the wordes for us alle (X.67)

– figuratively hands over the conduct of the pilgrimage to the Parson, as
the pilgrims form themselves into a solemn congregation.

The allegorical nature of the pilgrimage is authoritatively stated by the
Parson, and it is a not unreasonable view that sees the Parson's Tale as
equally authoritative in relation to the *Tales* as a whole, a schematic moral
commentary on all that has gone before, and an explicit statement of the
truth that lies behind the many appearances and versions of truth that we
have seen. It is the 'best' of the tales, and in thus looking back to the

original announcement of the theme of pilgrimage in the General Prologue, and in thus viewing the journey of the pilgrims and the journey of man's life as figures of the way of Penitence (X.81), the Parson's Tale points to the essential religious truths which constitute the unity of the *Canterbury Tales*. Such an interpretation has weight, especially in so far as it respects the monumental character of the Parson's Tale – for there is no serious credence to be given to the idea that the Parson's Tale reflects the Parson's character, and that as such it is located as one of a number of possible versions of truth. However, the interpretation is of value only in relation to the conclusion of the frame-narrative, where Chaucer is observing a decorum of closure which Boccaccio likewise recognised in the *Decameron*:

> For, as it seemed, it was for to doone,
> To enden in som vertuous sentence. (X.62–3)

The Parson's Tale is not a different kind of tale which by its difference acts as a critique of the tale-telling that has gone before: it is not a tale at all, and belongs to a different order of discourse. Its reference is not to the world of reality as that reality is perceived in stories, but to reality itself, and its aim is not knowledge and understanding but action. This aim is achieved in the Retraction.

The argument concerning the underlying religious unity of the *Canterbury Tales* which is derived from the conclusion of the frame-narrative and the Parson's Tale is radically defective in practice because it demands that the nature of the tales as tales be denied and that they be reconstituted as ideological discourse by retrospective realignment.[16] The unity that is thereby achieved is not an artistic or purposed unity but simply the known unity of all the matter of creation, including literary discourse, as witness to God's truth. Chaucer acknowledges this truth when he spoke as a man, and a man of religion, in his Retraction:

> For oure book seith, 'Al that is writen is writen for oure doctrine', and that is myn entente. (X.1083)

But, as a poet, he uses this very dictum, at the end of the Nun's Priest's Tale (VII.3438–43), as a playful warning against ideological appropriation. In his writing of the *Tales*, Chaucer had to hand a number of traditional types of narrative – romance, fable, fabliau, saint's legend – which had in common that they all depended for their *sense* on some

external and received body of values. Narrative is conceived of and
justified as the illustration or demonstration of some truth already
known, from sources more reputable than fiction, to be true. Stories for
Chaucer, however, are more important than this. They do not merely
reinforce what can be said clearly in other ways and in other words; they
may operate at a profound level of consciousness, both inviting participation and at the same time transforming that act of participation into a
recognition of the illusion that prompts it. They are models, in their
enigmatic mode of existence, for the reality which we perceive and judge,
and return the reader to himself with a heightened consciousness of that
reality, and of the acts of perception and judgement, of self-perception
and self-judgement, which order it. Chaucer's endeavour is to release
narrative from external pressure, and to allow it a self-validating,
non-exemplary significance of its own which grows out of its intrinsic
nature as an imitation of human life. [17] Not all the tales attempt to do all of
this, and not all that do succeed, but this is the controlling pattern of his
creative activity, and the bending of the materials of narrative to this will
is the fascination of watching him at work.

The openness and flexibility of the *Canterbury Tales* frame gave
Chaucer, as we have seen, every opportunity to explore these new ideas
of narrative, and if it is right to identify freedom as what he sought, then
concepts of unity or of the function of the frame-narrative that limit that
freedom are mistaken. Much of the pressure to unify the *Tales* comes, of
course, from the practice of writing books about them, which in their
turn need their own principles of organisation. Those who have rejected
the unifying schemes derived from the frame-narrative, such as the
Human Comedy and the Pilgrima e of Life, have resorted to a number of
expedients. One method has been to give the frame and links some
preliminary notice, and then to dismiss them as only a partial realisation
of Chaucer's intentions, and to concentrate on the tales as tales, grouped
according to traditional concepts of genre. [18] Though such studies may
properly claim to represent the nature of the work in what they do, and to
be relevant to Chaucer's artistic purposes, they are principally ways of
re-ordering and classifying the parts of the work as an aid to thought and
study. A rather stricter rationale is observed by Kean (1972), whose
arrangement of the tales in her discussion is designed to demonstrate the
importance of certain 'major themes' (Fortune and free will; marriage in
relation to Nature, and to order and disorder; the nobleness of man) in
individual tales and in the development of the series as whole (p. 110).
She sees this not as a means of eliciting an 'organising principle' (p. 74),

but as a way of giving some account of ideas which preoccupied Chaucer and which are 'part of a philosophically consistent way of looking at the world' (p. 110).

Somewhat more ambitious is the kind of approach that accepts the frame-narrative and the sequence of tales more or less as they have settled by inertia in the received text, and which finds in the continuities and abrupt discontinuities of the sequence a type of 'Gothic' structure.[19] The juxtaposition of real and unreal worlds, the co-ordination of naturalistic illusion with forceful denial of illusion, finds a ready analogy in the complex programmes of illustration of Beatus pages in fourteenth-century English psalters. Such comparisons are encouraged by the resemblances thought to exist between the assocation of tale and frame and the association of main picture and marginal illustration. Many other types of Gothic art have been brought in, such as rose-windows and cathedrals, to support the argument that the apparent disunity and fragmentation and inorganic assembly of the *Canterbury Tales* is actually a form of Gothic unity. In so far as such interpretations of the structure of the *Tales* act as a warning against unhistorical naturalistic and dramatic readings such as we have described, they serve a valuable purpose, though the practice of making analogies between literature and the visual arts is for the most part too fanciful and impressionistic to be more than suggestive. There is in fact much to be said for accepting the stimulus of analogy and then forgetting it, recognising that the shifts of perspective between tale and frame are ways of juxtaposing different points of view and of exploring the various ways in which 'the world of the tales (art) and the world of the links (experience)' amend each other.[20] This view has the great merit above others of acknowledging and responding to realities of immediate association that exist between tales and links without coercing these into a theory of unity that perforce must leap over many hermeneutic barriers.

Another approach discerns the unity of the *Canterbury Tales* in a multitude of echoes and anticipations of words, phrases and motifs. This is certainly a form of local structuring that is used by Chaucer to great effect, and we shall see notable examples of tale-bonding in such pairs of tales as the Knight's and the Miller's Tales and the Monk's and Nun's Priest's Tales. The 'Wife of Bath group', too, has a scatter of allusions that seem to create a loosely unified sequence. The systematic development of this approach, however, must be viewed sceptically:

> *The Canterbury Tales* as a poem, even in its unfinished state, is a
> knitting of a number of threads in complex patterns, a design which
> may be called thematic interlace. . . . The labyrinthine inter-
> connections of threads defy full elucidation, so complex are the
> contrasts, juxtapositions, parallels, and tensions. The imagination and
> perception of the reader are free to move in all directions to make
> connections and find significance with few specific directions, or none,
> from Chaucer. (Leyerle, 1976, pp. 108–9, 121)

The four 'themes' that Leyerle selects for treatment are sexuality, food
and drink, gold, and death. These seem sufficiently comprehensive: I
suppose 'life' might be another. Howard's idea of the 'structure' of the
Canterbury Tales, in *The Idea of the Canterbury Tales*, is essentially similar
to Leyerle's, though worked out in terms of the 'concatenated binary
principle' (1976, p. 225), that is, one tale is linked to the next tale. His
idea of the attraction of his scheme is much the same: 'One can hardly
ever *stop* showing how everything leads to everything else' (p. 226). The
use of 'analogy as an organizing principle' (p. 71) in Allen and Moritz
(1981) is a more sophisticated version of such associationism, in which
the fourfold classification of the stories of Ovid's *Metamorphoses* made by
medieval commentators is used as the basis for a fourfold division of the
Canterbury Tales into tales natural, magical, moral and spiritual (p. 24).
This game of free associations is an activity not of the critically alert mind
striving to participate with Chaucer in his imaginative engagement with
his matter, but of the mind idling among its reminiscences of the *Tales*.
Essentially, it distracts attention from the individual feats of imagination
which constitute the individual tales.

The conclusion must be that the tales as tales stand first in any reading
or critical scrutiny of the *Canterbury Tales*. The frame-narrative has
vitality and significance and an irresistible sense of actuality, and occasionally the tales gain a dimension of meaning from their place in that
frame, but there are very few tales whose strength is essentially dependent on the frame or whose meaning is defective without it. It might have
been different if Chaucer had completed the work, but I doubt it, for the
techniques of accommodation of tale to frame that he wished to exploit
are fully displayed. A study of the *Tales* must therefore respect what
there is of completed sequence without straining to impose upon the
work theories of order and unity which distort the nature of what we
have. A good model might seem to be Alfred David's *The Strumpet Muse*
(1976), which contains (pp. 52–240) perhaps the best full-length study of

the *Tales*, in which David passes the tales in review, giving to each its full imaginative independence and his own undistracted attention. However, the conflict between the moralist and the artist, which is a recurrent theme, as David sees it, in Chaucer's poetry, becomes for the critic, in the end, a controlling image for the understanding of the whole nature and development of the work:

> In writing the *Canterbury Tales*, Chaucer came to master the art of illusion but at the same time to regard with growing skepticism its potential for expressing moral truths. The relationship between teller and tale often comments poignantly on the inadequacies of poetry, and each teller shows some new face of the poet's Strumpet Muse. (1976, pp. 6–7)

This is a rich and stimulating view of the *Tales*, but, organised and systematised into a unifying theory, according to a fixed ordering of the *Tales*, it becomes something of a straitjacket.

A compromise seemed therefore to be called for, and I originally intended that the present study should be organised according to such a principle of compromise. Fragments I and VII were to be treated in separate chapters as integrated groups, and Fragments III–IV–V likewise treated in a single chapter, as constituting a more loosely integrated sequence. The remaining fragments were to be thrown together in a chapter of left-overs, though concluding of course with Fragment X. Attempts to write about the *Tales* in this way led, I found, in practice, to constant distraction, especially that provoked by the tendency to give excessive prominence to less important matters. Meanwhile, the importance of the *Tales* as tales was neglected, and their affiliations with tales of a similar kind, with the genres from which they draw their primary contextual significance as narratives, were obscured. I therefore fell back on the organisation by genres which had proved useful in the past (see note 18 above). It needs a little sleight-of-hand to associate the tales which grow out of monologues with the 'portraits' of the General Prologue, but the three broad major genres, of romances, comic tales and religious tales, fall together very naturally. The Parson's Tale can still come last.

CHAPTER 3

Some Portraits

Whatever state the *Canterbury Tales* were in when Chaucer left them unfinished, the General Prologue was evidently intended to stand first. It may itself have been written early, when the scheme of the *Tales* was first devised, about 1387; or written as a first draft, and subsequently added to as new ideas suggested themselves to Chaucer (the six pilgrims added as a group at line 542, as well as the plans for the four-tale contest, have been suggested by Hammond, 1908, p. 254, Nevo, 1963, and Owen, 1977, as likely to have been introduced in revision); or written late. Occasional lack of 'fit' between pilgrim and tale would appear to support the case for early composition of the General Prologue. The Merchant's Tale provides an example. The Merchant is described in the General Prologue exclusively in terms of his profession. When the tale of January and May was allocated to him, a brief prologue was written, assigning him a new role as a disillusioned husband, but the new role is not specially appropriate to him as a merchant. A similar argument might be advanced in respect of the 'new' Monk who emerges in the Link preceding the Monk's Tale.

It must be admitted, though, that any arguments of this kind, entered into with a view to establishing the order and date of composition of portions of the *Tales*, can easily get stuck in a familiar revolving-door of speculation. It could readily be argued, for instance, and perhaps more plausibly, that it is no part of Chaucer's intention in the General Prologue to reveal all: he keeps for the most part reasonably in touch with the illusion that he is telling us what might be discerned by an observer or elicited by an interlocutor; he does not induct us, as an omniscient author, into all the mysteries of human nature; and he leaves some things to emerge in the course of the pilgrimage. To develop portraits so as to make them accord with subsequent revelations would disturb this illusion. Some exception to these generalisations about the General Prologue portraits might be made in relation to the last six pilgrims, or at least to five of them – the Reeve, Miller, Summoner, Pardoner and Manciple – since Chaucer's addition of himself to the group is merely mischievous. Here the 'fit' of pilgrim to tale is consistently close and well-worked out, and in the case of the Reeve and Pardoner exceptionally close, and it may well be that the group was added late, when Chaucer had developed more fully his ideas about the strategy of the *Tales*. The group follows immediately after the description of the Plowman, who would originally have made a natural close, both as the lowest in social class and as the ideal representative of the third of the three traditional estates of society (the Knight and the Parson being the other two).

Whatever the order of composition, the position of the General Prologue in relation to the rest of the *Tales* makes it appropriate that the discussion of the *Tales* should begin with it, just as it will be appropriate for discussion to end with the Parson's Tale. The General Prologue is dedicated, apart from its brief introduction and the closing paragraphs that initiate the tale-telling contest, to portraiture, and it is further appropriate therefore that it should be associated, in this chapter, with those three prologues and tales that are likewise dedicated to portraiture. The Wife of Bath, Pardoner and Canon's Yeoman are set distinctly aside from the other pilgrims, as commonly recognised (e.g. Ruggiers, 1967, p. 123), in that all three are given extended autobiographical monologues which lead directly into their tales. The perception of relationship between character of teller and tale, which elsewhere is a suggestion, a temptation, a provocative juxtaposition or a delusion, is here an obligation, for there is no way in which these three tales can be read except as extensions of the portraits begun in explicit self-revelation. To discuss the Wife of Bath's Tale, for instance, in relation to the genre of 'romance' to which it theoretically belongs would miss the dramatic dimension which gives the tale its essential, not merely an added significance, and would entail constant explanation of its differentness. An added advantage of the present arrangement is that it identifies in a decisive way those tales in which the 'dramatic principle' can be demonstrated to be of fundamental interpretative significance, and forces a recognition of the difference between these tales and the others, and of the very limited sphere of operation of the dramatic principle in the latter.

THE GENERAL PROLOGUE

The opening sentence of the General Prologue is a wonderful assertion of poetic control, almost a declaration, in itself, of the coming-of-age of English poetry:

> Whan that Aprill with his shoures soote
> The droghte of March hath perced to the roote,
> And bathed every veyne in swich licour
> Of which vertu engendred is the flour;
> Whan Zephirus eek with his sweete breeth
> Inspired hath in every holt and heeth
> The tendre croppes, and the yonge sonne
> Hath in the Ram his halve cours yronne,
> And smale foweles maken melodye,
> That slepen al the nyght with open ye
> (So priketh hem nature in hir corages);
> Thanne longen folk to goon on pilgrimages,
> And palmeres for to seken straunge strondes,
> To ferne halwes, kowthe in sondry londes;
> And specially from every shires ende
> Of Engelond to Caunterbury they wende,
> The hooly blisful martir for to seke,
> That hem hath holpen whan that they were seeke. (1–18)

Unlike the opening sentence of *Paradise Lost*, which is similarly confident and self-conscious as a demonstration of the poet's mastery of his craft, the technical skill here is in the harmonising of an unobtrusively 'natural' syntax and metre into a long flowing verse paragraph which has something of the character of inspired conversation. Chaucer does not make an imperative claim on our attention, as does Milton, but rather eases himself into our confidence as the 18-line sentence smoothly unfolds, with barely a concession to syntactical inversion or other kinds of artificial poeticism. The opening of Milton's poem is like the launching of a great ship down the slipway; the opening of Chaucer's is like the imperceptible edging away from shore, so that we hardly realise at what point we have given ourselves over to the new medium. The construction of the sentence is firm yet unemphatic, carefully contrived yet basically simple: 'Whan . . . and . . . Whan . . . and . . . and . . . Thanne . . . and . . . and . . .' It is a sentence whose music seems to have rung in the ears even of the unmusical Lydgate, though his attempt to imitate it, in the opening lines of the Prologue to his *Siege of Thebes*, ends in disaster.

At the end of the sentence, we have come a long way, from the springtime renewal of nature to the renewal of health, through the intercession of St Thomas a Becket, for those who have been 'seeke', in body or spirit. The turning-point in this progression is line 12, where it is said that spring is the time when people think of going on pilgrimage.

This, though it is a playful turning aside of one conventional expectation of the poetic spring-opening ('In the spring a young man's fancy...'), is not itself a paradox, since spring is the time of spiritual as well as natural regeneration, the time when the 'drought' of Lent comes to an end as well as the 'droghte' of March:

> The pilgrimage is set down in the calendar of seasons as well as in the calendar of piety; nature impels and supernatural draws. 'Go, go, go', says the bird; 'Come', says the saint. (Hoffman, 1954, p. 31)

The absence of discrimination between the secular and spiritual impulse, the easy continuity between the one and the other, do not seem designed to provoke ironical unease, but to hint rather at some optimistically conceived unity of the world of natural reality and the world of the spirit. It is springtime, and like the springtime of the world, where no shadow falls over the sunny prospect, and 'where the mirror of Nature could not but reflect the divine order'.[1] Chaucer has chosen, too, to emphasise a scientific and philosophical perception of spring, not a human and social one, and in doing so he allows attention to dwell undistracted on the goodness of Nature, its reliable and beneficent tendency. He draws less on the conventional spring-openings of romance and lyric, or on the realities of an English spring-time – though there is nothing inherently unEnglish about April showers – than on the accounts given of the seasons in scientific treatises and encyclopaedias (see Tuve, 1937), where spring has its place in the immutably mutating cycle of growth, decay and regeneration. The language he uses is technical – 'licour', 'vertu', 'engendred', 'inspired' – and suggests the operation of a benevolent higher authority. Even the song of the birds is detached from its usual association with the pleasures and pains of human love – an association that is soon to be made explicit in the description of the Squire (97–8) – and attributed simply to the impulsion of Nature.

Chaucer celebrates here what is to be celebrated, nature and supernature in harmony, and sets his great poem, at its beginning, under the canopy of a wise and amiable governance. This is no ill reflection of his own spirit, though there will be much to disturb and question easy complacency in the course of the poem, and the ending will perforce, in its contemplation of the last things, take a different turn. There are many who wish to visit the strenuous moralism of the Parson's Tale upon the opening of the General Prologue, and find something suspicious in any occasion given to thoughts of pilgrimage by an improvement in the weather. They might find their ancestor in Henryson, who in his *Fables* gave his own account of the cycle of the seasons as 'Concorddand till owr opurtunitie' (ed. Fox, 1981, line 1676) in their reminder of mortality. Spring, the time of pleasure, warmth and growth, is when we should prepare for the coming winter, as the fable of 'The Preaching of the Swallow' demonstrates. Likewise, at the beginning of the *Testament of Cresseid*, Henryson gives a description of spring which might seem to be designed as a moral corrective to, and not merely a Scottish version of, Chaucer's holiday-mood description of more or less the same time of year. Here, Henryson seems to say, is the harsh reality of springtime, and of life.

Quha wait gif all that Chauceir wrait was trew? (ed., Fox, 1981, l. 64)

he asks, something more than rhetorically.

Holiday and holy-day remain for Chaucer, though, still in some sort of approximate harmony, and his ensuing account of his meeting with the other pilgrims at the Tabard Inn at Southwark is unassailably good-natured. The 'ful devout corage' (22) which inspires his own pilgrimage to Canterbury is implicitly visited upon the 'nyne and twenty' (24) that he falls in with (see note 18 to Chapter One); the inn is rated very comfortable; all seem desirous of 'felaweshipe' (32). There seems no reason to take all this as the rosy-spectacled ramblings of an incurable innocent. On the contrary, the sense of goodwill that is communicated is a deeply important first impression in our reading of the *Tales*.

What follows is something that Chaucer's literary friends would have had cause to dissuade him from, if he ever discussed his intentions with them. He proposes nothing less than a complete gallery of portraits of all his new-found fellow-pilgrims:

> But nathelees, whil I have tyme and space,
> Er that I ferther in this tale pace,
> Me thynketh it acordaunt to resoun
> To telle yow al the condicioun
> Of ech of hem, so as it semed me,
> And whiche they weren, and of what degree,
> And eek in what array that they were inne. (35–41)

It seems like a recipe for certain disaster, for repetitive schematisation and yawning monotony, something that a deranged *rhétoriqueur* might have dreamed up. In the event it turns out, against all the odds and perhaps in some way – given Chaucer's taste for experimentation – because of them, to be one of Chaucer's most characteristic successes, and an apt epitome, in its attitudes to art, authority and the matter of experience, for what follows, as well as a prologue to it.

The principle is variety, if the certainty of not knowing what to expect next can be called a principle, and it operates in the ordering of the portraits, in the ordering of the detail within the portraits, in the choice of detail, and in the expression of point of view. In all these aspects of treatment, no single method of presentation is allowed to become established strongly enough to create an expectation that it will be maintained. Here, to begin, is the list of portraits, with the number of lines allotted to each:

Knight	36
Squire	22
Yeoman	17
Prioress	45
Monk	43
Friar	62
Merchant	15
Clerk	24
Lawyer	22
Franklin	30
5 Guildsmen	18
Cook	9
Shipman	23
Doctor	24
Wife of Bath	32
Parson	52
Plowman	13
Miller	22
Manciple	20
Reeve	36
Summoner	46
Pardoner	46

The ordering of the portraits is broadly one of descending social class,[2] passing from the landed gentry through the professional classes and the lower mercantile and trading groups to the Plowman. Appended to this, however, is a rogues' gallery of miscellaneous predators (Nevo, 1963), associated only in the skill with which they batten upon the society that has just been described. This group ends with the Summoner and Pardoner, the last representatives of the second estate, of the clergy, whose members have been quite untraditionally sprinkled among the secular portraits. The general impression of hierarchy and the traditional ordering of the estates is further disturbed by the counterpointing against it of other kinds of grouping, suggestive of the multiplicity of ways in which man as a social being can be viewed. The Parson and the Plowman are linked by brotherhood, of both blood and spirit; the Knight, Squire and Yeoman by kinship and service; the five Guildsmen and their Cook by service alone; the Prioress, Monk and Friar by religious profession; the Man of Law and Franklin by common interest; the Summoner and the Pardoner by something probably unspeakable. Between and within these groupings there is further play of certain juxtapositions, well described by Hoffman (1954) and Owen (1977, pp. 48–86), some of them apparently almost happy chances: the progressive movement from inward virtue to outward show in the Knight–Squire–Yeoman sequence, and from doubtful devoutness to undoubted undevoutness in the Prioress–Monk–Friar sequence; the sandwiching of the spare and austere Clerk between those two windbags, the Merchant and the Lawyer; the bizarre conjunction of Wife of Bath and Parson. The total effect is one of inexhaustible richness and profusion, both in the world of characters that is portrayed and in the enthusiasm and appetite for the observing and recording of that world. The density of texture, the sheer amount of detail, is such that to annotate the Prologue adequately would be to write a complete description, and a very subtle and penetrating critique, of late fourteenth-century society, or at least those parts of it within the band that excludes the aristocracy and the poor peasantry (the Reeve and the Plowman are peasants of the better-off kind, more like *kulaks*).

Within the portraits, Chaucer demonstrates what he has learnt from the top-to-toe descriptive technique of rhetorical tradition,[3] namely, to avoid it altogether. His ordering of detail is quite unsystematic, and comment on different aspects of physical appearance, behaviour, array, opinion, attitude, inward moral life and professional occupation is presented in the order in which it seems to have occurred to the memory of the observer. A portrait may begin with a general impression of the character –

A Frere ther was, a wantowne and a merye (208)

A Sergeant of the Lawe, war and wys (309)

– or equally with some physical detail that seems to have caught the attention of the observer in a quite random way, like the 'forked berd' of the Merchant (270) or the daisy-white beard of the Franklin (332). Likewise, a portrait may end with some remark that sounds like an encapsulation of the character –

And gladly wolde he lerne and gladly teche. (308)

Was nowher swich a worthy vavasour. (360)

– or it may end with a quite arbitrarily remembered detail:

His palfrey was as broun as is a berye (207)

A bokeleer hadde he maad hym of a cake. (668)

Within the portraits, there is no discernible pattern in the ordering of detail, neither within the individual portrait nor from portrait to portrait. Chaucer achieves a special effect, in fact, from the juxtaposition of unrelated detail, a suggestion of incongruity which enhances the illusion of random recall and also creates in us a natural desire to look for the missing link that will rationalise the discontinuity. The description of the Cook ends thus:

> But greet harm was it, as it thoughte me,
> That on his shyne a mormal hadde he.
> For blankmanger, that made he with the beste. (385–7)

The punctuation is important here, and modern punctuation is perhaps over-scrupulous in removing the temptation to read *For*, hoveringly, as conjunction, 'because', rather than preposition, 'as for'. The implied suggestion of the causative relationship – that the quality of his 'blank-manger' is somewhat compromised by the suppurating sore on his shin – is too delightfully disgusting to be ignored altogether, but it is we that are responsible for it, not Chaucer. The same pleasure is to be derived from the bland laying side by side of these two statements about the Wife of Bath:

She was a worthy womman al hir lyve:
Housbondes at chirche dore she hadde fyve. (459-60)

The rhyme is specially effective here in uniting two observations which
are in themselves discrete, and making us wonder whether there is any
proportionate relationship between the Wife's degree of worthiness and
the number of her husbands. Chaucer merely observes.

The portraits are very varied, too, in the kind and amount of detail that
is selected for presentation. There are the full-scale portraits, in which a
number of approaches, physical, behavioural and occupational, are
developed: Prioress, Monk, Friar, Wife of Bath, Reeve, Summoner,
Pardoner. These are the great achievements of the Prologue. At the other
end of the scale the idealised portraits of the Parson and Plowman are
distinguished from all the others by the almost total absence of detail of
appearance or array. The only thing about the Plowman we have from
observation is that he rode in a tabard upon a mare; the Parson's only
contact with physically observable reality is the 'staf' that he carries when
he visits his parish on foot, and of course that is no part of present
observation, since he goes to pilgrimage on horseback.

The fiction of the General Prologue is that Chaucer has just met all
these people and is describing what he has seen and heard of them. This
fiction may owe something, as Cunningham (1952) observes, to the
tradition of dream-poetry, which allowed a medieval poet to talk with
some degree of seriousness about what he had seen and 'experienced', a
kind of subject-matter that would conventionally be regarded as of the
utmost triviality (Stevens, 1973, p. 123). The fiction is of the greatest
importance to Chaucer, since it relieves him of the obligation to sys-
tematise his presentation of the pilgrims according to some single
unifying moral principle. Moral observations, of course, are made in
passing from time to time, and there is explicit approval of the Parson
and equally explicit disapproval of the Summoner (659). They mostly
have the character, though, of impromptu comments, and they do not
contribute to the establishment of any explicitly stated moral *schema*
according to which all the pilgrims are to be judged.

The fiction of observation and report is the one established at the
beginning of the Prologue – it will be a description of the pilgrims 'so as it
semed me' (39) – and it is reinforced from time to time with reminders of
the personal voice of the narrator ('I gesse . . . I trowe . . . I undertake
. . .'). He declares the limitations of his knowledge when speaking of the
Merchant:

> But, sooth to seyn, I noot how men hym calle. (284)

The effect of such a remark is not only to give the immediacy of first-hand report, but also to 'authenticate', as Bloomfield (1964) puts it, the reality of the Merchant, since if his name is not known to the narrator it must be available to be known somewhere, and where else but in the world of reality? At times, Chaucer speaks as if he has just been having a conversation with the pilgrim he is describing, which he rushes to set down on paper, with all the enthusiasm of a cub-reporter.

> Now is nat that of God a ful fair grace
> That swich a lewed mannes wit shal pace
> The wisdom of an heep of lerned men? (573–5)

he asks, catching up the Manciple's own glee and self-satisfaction at the way he can put it over on his supposed superiors. His enthusiasm for the Monk's cause, so benignly defended by Beichner (1954), and for the new ideas that he just heard from him concerning the monastic rule is such that he takes up cudgels on his behalf, and in so doing proves a very embarrassing advocate:

> And I seyde his opinion was good.
> What sholde he studie and make hymselven wood,
> Upon a book in cloystre alwey to poure,
> Or swynken with his handes, and laboure,
> As Austyn bit? How shal the world be servd?
> Lat Austyn have his swynk to hym reserved! (183–8)

However, Chaucer is quite content to allow the fiction of reportage to operate in this suggestive way, and to reap the benefits that accrue; he knows the powers and limitations of illusion, and he takes no pains to maintain it consistently. We are not to imagine, for instance, that the Yeoman has actually appeared on pilgrimage clad from head to foot in his hunting gear, with bow and sheaf of peacock-arrows at the ready. Nor are we to imagine that the Prioress has brought her dogs with her for the other inmates of the Tabard to kick about, or that the narrator has just glimpsed her in the taproom sorrowing over a mouse caught in a trap. As always, in traditional narrative and dramatic writing, we recognise intuitively the proper sphere of operation of, and the proper pleasure to be taken in illusion, and do not irritably ask the author to keep his tongue in his cheek so that we know where it is.

The constant shifting of point of view in the General Prologue so perceptively described by Muscatine (1966, p. 96), the movement in and out of the fiction of reportage, the absence of the morally normative system of evaluation that would be expected in what is presumed to be a satirical account of society, have produced some dilemmas for interpretative commentary. The reaction has been to look for the clues to the hidden system through which Chaucer enforces a moral and satiric critique of society. One method has been to stress, as David (1976, pp. 58–62) does, the generalised function of the portraits of the Knight, Parson and Plowman as idealised versions of the proper functioning of the three estates, and as yardsticks against which all the other pilgrims are to be measured. The most influential approach, however, has been that of Donaldson (1954; 1958, pp. 873–901), who, with some passing glances at the development of the 'fallible first-person singular' in the novel, sees the whole Prologue as placed in the mouth of a naive and gullible 'Chaucer the Pilgrim'. It is not so much Chaucer with his tongue in this cheek as a consistently conceived *persona*, 'acutely unaware of the significance of what he sees, no matter how sharply he sees it', and in general 'the victim of the poet's pervasive – not merely sporadic – irony' (1954, p. 3).

Donaldson's presentation of his argument is persuasive and witty, and is valuably supplemented by Woolf (1959). There are certainly many points in the Prologue when one is tempted to identify the elusiveness of the author with the presence of a guileless pilgrim-narrator or 'cub-reporter'. At times, indeed, it seems a better way of explaining what is going on than any other, as when the narrator rushes in to support the Monk –

And I seyde his opinion was good (183)

– and in his good-natured enthusiasm and desire to be helpful demolishes the Monk's case by speaking respectfully of 'the world' and disrespectfully of St Augustine. At other times, the identification of the role of the pilgrim-narrator is no more than a way of dramatising the operation of what is usually called irony. When the Monk is spoken of, for instance, as

A manly man, to been an abbot able (167)

there are no readers who will not recognise that 'manliness' is rather an inappropriate qualification for fitness to be an abbot. The agreement of author and reader on this point is presumably understood to be taken for granted, and the invention of a narrator-figure who really believes that manly men make the best abbots merely literalises the surface meaning. Criticism of a society in which abbots frequently are characterised more by manly than spiritual virtues is available to both forms of reading as a further ironical sideswipe. Similarly with the description of the Friar's discrimination in the company he keeps:

> He knew the tavernes wel in every toun
> And everich hostiler and tappestere
> Bet than a lazar or a beggestere;
> For unto swich a worthy man as he
> Acorded nat, as by his facultee,
> To have with sike lazars aqueyntaunce.
> It is nat honest, it may nat avaunce,
> For to deelen with no swich poraille,
> But al with riche and selleres of vitaille. (240–8)

The ironic signal, which indicates to the reader that he is to enter into a conspiracy against the apparent meaning of the text, is in the contrast between what the Friar does and what everyone knows his order was expected to do, and especially in the innocent-seeming collocation of honesty with profitability (246). Again, the presence of an intervening narrator-figure who is genuinely ignorant of what friars should be, and who genuinely believes that the failure to pursue financial advantage is an unseemly form of conduct, serves chiefly to strengthen the ironic signal.

It is the implication of consistency, however, that constitutes the weakness of the argument for the existence of a Chaucerian pilgrim-*persona*. If he is always present, and if everything he says is subject to the poet's 'pervasive irony', then the very complexity that was sought through variation in point of view becomes imperilled. If everything is ironical, nothing is interesting, since the reader has been deprived of those conspiratorial pleasures, those satisfactions of knowing that he has joined an elite fraternity of knowingness (see Booth, 1974, p. 37), and instead has simply to decode praise as blame and vice versa. The concept of *persona*, which Donaldson invented as a means of enhancing an observed ironic effect, becomes a means to refute the text, to validate misreading and to justify ideological appropriation. A line in the description of the Prioress,

> Ful semely after hir mete she raughte (136)

occurs in a generally piquant context, since all readers would find some
oddity in the prominence given to the Prioress's table manners, even if
they hesitated to state categorically that to show true devoutness it is
necessary to eat like a pig. However, the dictionaries have another
meaning for *raughte*, past tense of *reche*, apart from the obvious meaning
'reached, stretched out her hand', and it has got around amongst scholars
(e.g., Copland, 1970) and students that *raughte* means 'belched'. 'The
persona of Chaucer', we are told, 'is the victim of the poet's pervasive
irony' (Garbáty, 1969–70, p. 18). In other words, the attempt of that
star-struck simpleton, 'Chaucer the pilgrim', to portray the Prioress as a
delicate and gracious lady collapses in this picture of her belching *ad
libitum*, albeit in 'semely' fashion. It is fortunate that the facts are at hand
to demonstrate that the supposed irony is an imposition on the text: the
word *reche*, modern English 'reach', as explained in the *Oxford English
Dictionary*, means 'to spit, to make an effort to clear the throat, to spit or
bring up (blood or phlegm), to make an effort to vomit, to retch', and not
'belch'. Anyone who does not know the difference between these two
activities is in no position to talk about sophisticated things like irony.

Recently, the description of the Knight has been turned on its head by
the reading into it of the systematic kind of irony that Donaldson's
concept of *persona* makes possible. Chaucer's apparent admiration for
the Knight, says Jones (1980), is ironic, and he is really portraying a
cold-blooded professional mercenary of the kind that was making itself
notorious in the late fourteenth-century. The battles that he fought were
squalid engagements, fought for profit rather than religion, and he never
fought for king and country. From line 61 of the Prologue,

> At mortal batailles hadde he been fiftene,

it is clear that the Knight 'has killed at least fifteen men . . . The Knight,
it appears, is a very efficient and merciless killer' (1980, p. 77). The score
is raised to eighteen at Tramyssene:

> And foughten for oure feith at Tramyssene
> In lystes thries, and ay slayn his foo. (62–3)

'This bloody record of killings', says Jones, reveals the Knight's 'homi-
cidal character' (pp. 84–5). 'He nevere yet no vileynye ne sayde',
Chaucer tells us in line 70, but chivalry, Jones retorts sternly, is not just a
matter of avoiding bad language. It is sometimes rather difficult to know

what Chaucer could have said in praise of the Knight that could not have been demonstrated to be ironical on the application of such principles. One fears for the Parson. Jones's theory has been dismantled by historical scholars such as Keen (1983) and Lester (1982), but the reader who has a care for validity in interpretation would want to point out too how conveniently the development of the concept of *persona*, and the systematic ironisation it makes possible, meet the need for ideological appropriation. There are certain opinions that all decent people must share, and they include the abhorrence of violence and killing; to be admired, Chaucer must share these opinions too; irony is the means of ensuring that he does.

The concept of *persona*, of the pilgrim-narrator, has not been without its critics,[4] and quite early in its career Bronson (1960, pp. 27–8) tried to restore some sense of the reality of the performer, and his varied repertoire, and to catch more of the hovering and flickering quality of Chaucer's irony and self-mockery. Other writers, more recently, have tried to chip away at the monolith of the *persona*, and David (1976) makes a reasonable case for a modified and more flexible concept of the performer's art of self-impersonation:

A point that has not been sufficiently stressed is that such a 'persona' does not impose the restrictions of dramatic consistency that we would expect from a character in a novel or a play. The author or lecturer who is impersonating himself may at any moment step out of his dramatic part to wink at his audience or address it seriously. (p. 218)

The restoration of the narrator to the conventions of oral performance or reading aloud needs no elaborate suppositions concerning the nature of Chaucer's audience, since those conventions persisted long after the time when such practices ceased to be customary (see Chapter 7).

The systematic undercutting of meaning, which *persona*-based irony made possible, provided the opportunity for the equally systematic moral or ideological reconstruction of the Prologue which many critics wanted. The restoration of flexibility and variety to narrative tone and tone of voice involves a recognition of the existence of moral contrarieties, which is not so different from what Donaldson wished to advocate, and even of a degree of moral indeterminacy and relativism. It might seem tempting at this point to haul out and refurbish the old picture of the kindly observer of humanity, who sees all, forgives all and condemns none. The truth of this picture to the irresistible impression of generosity and goodwill that is communicated by the Prologue is accepted by Baldwin:

> Uniformly with Chaucer there are affection, good will, and objectivity visited upon his characters, so that they get the chance to be what, independently, they *have* to be, given the working out of those characteristics with which they have been endowed ... We have with Chaucer ... the release of the character without meddling or compulsion. (1955, pp. 26–7)

There is, however, too much moral judgement implicitly asked of us in the General Prologue to allow such a statement to stand unchallenged, and there are some questions still to be answered.

Two things are notable in the General Prologue. One is that all the characters are described in terms of their profession or occupation, and often exclusively in those terms. Their very identity is vested in their occupation, which provides the only name by which they are known, with the exception of the Prioress and the Friar (whose names are never again mentioned in the *Tales*). The reason for the specialisation of the portraits, in their concentration upon occupational characteristics, is found by Jill Mann (1973) in Chaucer's debt to estates satire. She takes this to be of more fundamental importance to the evolution of the Prologue portraits than other possible sources, such as the examples of rhetorical description of persons that Chaucer found in writers like Benoit de Saint-Maure and Joseph of Exeter (and which he used in *Troilus and Criseyde*, V.799–840), or the collections of exemplary traits that he found in treatises on the vices and virtues or on medical and physiognomical characteristics, or that he drew from general iconographic tradition.[5] She shows further how estates satire, in which society is criticised in general through the isolation of the faults appropriate to its various estates and occupations, not only provided a model for a sequence of portraits but also the materials for some of the most important of the portraits, such as those of the Monk and the Friar.

The other notable feature of the General Prologue is the approbation extended to virtually every pilgrim in respect of his performance of his profession or trade, an approbation often expressed in superlative terms:

> He was a verray, parfit gentil knyght (72)

> He was the beste beggere in his hous (252)

So greet a purchasour was nowher noon (318)

In al this world ne was ther noon hym lik,
To speke of phisik and of surgerye (412–13)

Ne was ther swich another pardoner. (693)

The approbation is quite proper and well-supported as far as the bare fact
of performance goes, but takes no account of the moral quality of the
activities engaged in. So the Doctor is 'a verray, parfit praktisour' (422),
just as the Knight is 'a verray, parfit gentil knyght'; the Monk, on the
strength of his fine boots and horse, is 'a fair prelaat' (204); and the
Pardoner, for all his chicanery, is 'in chirche a noble ecclesiaste' (708).
What seems to have happened is that Chaucer has taken over the kind of
detail customarily employed to satirise the representatives of the estates
and demonstrate their folly and wickedness, and has removed the
elements of explicit moral condemnation. Each pilgrim seems to float
free on a raft of his own values, or, to put it another way, is described in
the terms he might have wished to see himself described in if he were
applying for a job. The standards applied are social and professional, not
moral. The morality is left for someone else to think about, and Chaucer
does not seem to wish to make it particularly easy for the moralist to get to
work. This, for instance, is how a genuine moralist describes the musical
accomplishments of friars:

> Thei studien on the holy day aboute experymentes or wiche craft or
> veyn songis and knackynge and harpynge, gyternynge and daunsynge
> and othere veyn triflis to geten the stynkyng love of damyselis. (Mann,
> 1973, p. 45)

Here, by contrast, is Chaucer's Friar:

> And certeinly he hadde a murye note:
> Wel koude he synge and pleyen on a rote . . .
> And in his harpyng, whan that he hadde songe,
> His eyen twynkled in his heed aryght,
> As doon the sterres in the frosty nyght. (235–6, 266–8)

The context, it is true, implies that the Friar employs his musical abilities
to impress people, especially women, but the actual description of his
music-making is free from any suggestion of sordid and lascivious intent,

and it is left to the reader, if he wishes, to supply it. The preceding account of the Friar's skill and obligingness as a confessor may seem more openly satirical. 'Yet', as Speirs says, 'the quietude of the amused contemplation, undistorted by exasperation with human delinquency or by exertion of the will to abuse or chastise, is such that even here "satire" seems not to be the right word' (1951, pp. 110–11). 'Comedy' seems a more appropriate term, as Morgan (1981) says, and may likewise better suit the last lines of the description of the Doctor, which are similarly bland:

> For gold in phisik is a cordial,
> Therefore he lovede gold in special. (443–4)

The ironic implication, that the Doctor's love of gold has other motives than its value in medication, is so far from being driven home that it is the reader again who is placed in the position of asserting the moral commentary. It is in cases like this that the concept of a naive *persona* has been employed, and perhaps not entirely legitimately, to make the irony decisive.

The portrait of the Prioress is probably the subtlest and most sustained example of the withdrawal of the author from all the normally entrenched positions of the moral commentator. The mention of her 'gretteste ooth', for instance, is given an unexpected prominence: it is strange, we may feel, that such attention should be given to her restraint in the practice of something that she should not have been doing anyway. But the 'should not' is made to come from the reader, and from the expectations of a prioress's behaviour that he has derived from what he must now think to be irrelevant or prejudiced sources. In any case the offence, if it be offence, is so mild, and so swiftly mitigated, that the satiric barb barely penetrates its presumed target, and all the efforts of scholars (e.g., Steadman, 1959) have produced nothing on 'Seinte Loy' to make swearing by him anything worse than faintly whimsical. The agreement between author and reader on the moral criteria for the criticism of behaviour, which must be presupposed in the establishment of the existence of disparaging irony, is thus not clearly set forth. Since the kind of behaviour which might be deemed to be improper in respect of the strictest interpretation of the rule of life appropriate to the pilgrim is not in itself offensive, the reader must feel that his urge to disapprove is unduly harsh.

There are many other details in the description of the Prioress that have provoked a raising of the eyebrows, but where the fuller effect is to oblige the reader to identify himself as a harsh and unjust moralist or at best as embarrassingly unsubtle. The references to the Prioress's singing, for instance, have been said to imply a specially affected and self-conscious mannerism: it seems to be true, however, that a nasal intonation was normal, and of course it would need a peculiar kind of moralist to complain that she pays too much attention to her singing. The comment on the Prioress's French has perhaps a touch of slyness in it, in the hint of patrician condescension to those who know only the 'provincial' Anglo-Norman now spoken among the genteel classes. It would of course be more of a moral criticism of the Prioress if she had worked hard to cultivate Parisian French, as a way of keeping up with the *haute monde*; the satire here, being social in its norms, draws attention to its own irrelevance in relation to any considered moral criticism of the Prioress, and tempts the reader who has been growing indignant at the Prioress's worldliness into agreeing that she is not worldly enough.

The description of the Prioress's table-manners has been alluded to already. If people are to eat at table, it may be thought, it is better to have good manners than bad ones, or none at all. There is a literary joke, of course, embedded in the description, since the detail is taken from the account given in the *Roman de la Rose* (13378–402) of the advice tendered by La Vieille to a young woman about how she should comport herself at table if she wants to make herself attractive to men. The joke, which Chaucer's readers may be presumed to have enjoyed, is in the incongruity of literary collocation, and not in any satire directed against the Prioress, for she can hardly be severely criticised for behaving in a civilised way when she is so touchingly deprived of the practical benefits of civility. The moralist, again, finds himself disarmed, and if he lights upon the suggestions of effortfulness at the end of the description as signs of labour and affectation (137–41) he will find himself in the same unholy alliance as before with the social satirist.

The remainder of the description of the Prioress would provide material for commentary on similar lines, especially the final provocative mention of her motto, 'Amor vincit omnia', but perhaps enough has been said to demonstrate the audacity of Chaucer's proceeding here. What he does is persistently to obstruct the conventional impetus to an ultimately unequivocal moral judgement, even to remove the possibility of such judgement. Moral judgement is shown constantly to be conditioned by emotional, historical and subjective factors, so that we are led 'to discover in ourselves the coexistence of different methods of judging people' (Mann, 1973, p. 197). A number of choices are offered to the reader, not in order to leave him in a state of indecision, but so as to make clear to him that the choice is his. When Lowes spoke, in his famous phrase, of 'the engagingly imperfect submergence of the feminine in the ecclesiastical' (1919, p. 41) he did not mean that the delight was to be itself submerged and obliterated in the final judgement of imperfection. The two remain continually present to the reader; the author is not going to simplify the world for him, or feed his delusions of moral certitude, by deciding on his behalf.

Even portraits that are less subtle and richly wrought than that of the Prioress, and evidently less equivocal, have a similar quality of reservation and qualification. The viciousness of rogues like the Summoner and the Pardoner is described in the same phlegmatic manner as their physical ugliness and repulsiveness, not so much to stress, in the medieval way, the iconographic connection between the physical and the moral, as to suggest that both have the objective status of observed attributes. Immorality almost becomes a trait of character, and not an offence against a generally accredited moral system. The Parson, to take a case at the opposite extreme of conventional moral valuation, is portrayed in so remote and admiring and almost unreal a way that he begins to take on the character of a framed picture of rural virtue:

> Wyd was his parisshe, and houses fer asonder,
> But he ne lefte nat, for reyn ne thonder,
> In siknesse nor in meschief to visite
> The ferreste in his parisshe, muche and lite,
> Upon his feet, and in his hand a staf (491–5)

The Parson's excellence, it seems to be suggested, is excellence in his chosen profession, and in the exemplification of values that pertain to that profession. How interesting, and how admirable, that there are people who choose to behave in this way! But there is no insistence on the relevance of such ideals of behaviour to those who are not parsons.

Attention to the manner of treatment, to the ordering, internal organisation and manipulation of point of view in the portraits, is better able to elucidate what is happening in the General Prologue, and above all what is innovative, than the discussion of the relation of the portraits to reality. Such discussion has tended to preoccupy commentators, and, when it has gone beyond the necessary and properly historical documentation of referential denotation and, where possible, connotation, it has led to some rather sterile arguments concerning the extent to which Chaucer drew on his observation of real historical persons, and similarly unproductive debates concerning the relationship between the 'typical' and the 'individual'.[6] The former has no chance of contributing much to our understanding of what we read, since even when we can identify a Harry Bailly, innkeeper, or a Roger of Ware, Cook, and even if we had a complete dossier on them from an unimpeachably authoritative source, the associations and comparisons that can and might be made are of merely curious interest. As for the latter, there is so little basis for deciding what is typical and what individual, and so little agreement on what the terms mean, if they mean anything at all, that nothing more than casual and gossipy impressions can usually be conveyed. One would return, therefore, to Mann's conclusion:

> The centre of interest in the *Prologue* is not in any depiction of human character, in actuality for its own sake; it is in our relationship with the actual, the way in which we perceive it and the attitudes we adopt to it. (1973, p. 200)

This is an accurate description of the experience of reading the Prologue, and of the way we are continually made to draw back and examine the mode of operation in us of judgement and discrimination. This is in itself a positive activity, and not an invitation to moral relativism, where it takes all sorts to make a world, or to a deconstruction of moral perception, where judgement lies merely in the eye of the observer. Something more might be added, though, in recognition of the power of educating and enriching perception, as well as clarifying its nature, that Chaucer has. Coghill says:

> He is one of those rare poets who can strongly affect, not only our passions and intelligence, but our wills too: he creates generosities in them. (1956, p. 60).

THE WIFE OF BATH'S PROLOGUE AND TALE

The Wife of Bath's Prologue, and to some extent the Wife of Bath herself, have been constructed by Chaucer out of the commonplaces of Latin clerical teaching and satire, on marriage and women, and their vernacular derivatives. These one-sided marriage-debates and misogynistic diatribes must have seemed one of the more sterile legacies of his traditional reading, but, as often, Chaucer has converted the detritus of clerical culture into a new and vigorous life. It must have pleased him to include, as one of the essential elements of the Wife's narrative of her five husbands, an account of the 'book of wikked wyves' (III.685) from which her fifth husband, Jankyn, used to read provocative extracts, since what Chaucer describes is an anti-feminist anthology of just the kind he himself might have known (Pratt, 1962):

> He cleped it Valerie and Theofraste,
> At which book he lough alwey ful faste.
> And eek ther was somtyme a clerk at Rome,
> A cardinal, that highte Seint Jerome,
> That made a book agayn Jovinian ... (671–7)

It is the *Epistola Valerii ad Rufinum de non Ducenda Uxore*, the *Liber Aureolus de Nuptiis* of Theophrastus, and the *Epistola adversus Jovinianum* of St Jerome that provide Chaucer with much of the material for his account of the 'book', and Jerome also contributes much of the argumentation and many of the biblical texts for the Wife's opening defence of marriage. According to his usual custom, Chaucer does not mention the French works which he placed under even heavier contribution, namely the satirical *Lamentations de Matheolus*, which he uses extensively (see Thundy, 1979), particularly in the Wife's report of the abuse that she used to tell her three old husbands they would heap on her and her sex, or would have done if they had dared (235–378); and the *Roman de la Rose*. In Jean de Meun's portion of the last-named work there is a long account (8437–9330) of the rebuke of a jealous husband to his wife, which contains much of the abuse of women that the Wife attributes to her husbands, and also a character called La Vieille, who may have provided the original inspiration for the Wife of Bath. She is an ageing prostitute who gives advice to the young beginner in the profession on how to make herself attractive to men, to use her sexual powers to get their money from them, to seduce, cajole and intimidate them into submission. She speaks, she says, from experience; gives way to momentary regret for her past youth, and then scorns her regret; declares that no woman should give her sexual favours without cash in hand; repudiates all restraint on freedom of appetite; and laments the one time she gave away her heart, to a disdainful Casanova who mastered her sexually and led her a dog's life.[7] The parallels between La Vieille and the Wife of Bath are, it will be seen, quite close.

At the same time, everything is different, and it is worth examining some of the ways in which Chaucer has humanised, domesticated and anglicised the rampant shrew and raging nymphomaniac of the European satirical imagination. The intentions of these writers, the long line of whom stretches back through late classical antiquity to Juvenal and forward to Chaucer's contemporary, Deschamps, are transparently didactic and satirical. Even with Jean de Meun, who makes the most extensive use of an off-centred dramatic technique, the fierce animus against women comes stridently through the carefully orchestrated babble of discordant voices. He never allows us to forget, either, that the young woman (or rather the young man, Bel Acueill, who, according to the requirements of personification allegory, represents the obliging part of her nature) who is being instructed in the art of prostitution is none other than the idol of the Lover's dreams. So much, Jean de Meun seems to say, as La Vieille advises Bel Acueill on the crafty manipulation of multiple night-visitors (14197–262), for *fine amour*. La Vieille declares that the purpose of her training is to enable women to use their sexual powers and women's wiles to gain financial supremacy, to suck men dry and destroy them (13581–4). Some part of this sexual aggressiveness remains in the Wife of Bath, as for instance when she describes the manner in which she tormented the near-impotence of her three old husbands:

> As help me God, I laughe whan I thynke
> How pitously a-nyght I made hem swynke! (201–2)

There are, however, important differences.

For one thing, the whole of her campaign is conducted within marriage, and the language of commerce that she uses (e.g., 214, 268, 314, 414–17, 447) has to do, not with prostitution, but with her own interpretation of the marriage 'debt'. Further, the nature of her first three marriages, to rich old men, is such as to suggest that she is not so much preying upon men as using those powers that she has in order to win herself a measure of independence in a world that is unfair to her sex. The husbands appear to be the victims, but it needs no great effort of the imagination, and no great wrenching of the facts of historical record on the role of women in the Middle Ages (as distinct from the role assigned to them by clerical authority), to recognise a certain rough legitimacy in the way the Wife has turned the economic tables on her would-be exploiters, and to recognise too a degree of bourgeois shrewdness and

healthy common sense, excellently brought out by Carruthers (1979), in
her contempt for the 'books of deportment' which purported to show
how wives should be governed. She has no implacable hatred of
mankind, bears no vindictive ill-will towards her three old husbands,
and, when she has secured her position financially, she is not averse to
recognising the pleasure they get out of her counter-accusations:

> Of wenches wolde I beren hem on honde,
> Whan that for syk unnethes myghte they stonde.
> Yet tikled I his herte, for that he
> Wende that I hadde of hym so greet chiertee! (393–6)

There is a touch of affection in the way she stage-manages their submission so as to make them believe they have got what they want:

> What eyleth yow to grucche thus and grone?
> Is it for ye wolde have my queynte allone?
> Wy, taak it al! lo, have it every deel!
> Peter! I shrewe yow, but ye love it weel. (443–6)

Even her troublesome fourth husband she remembers with a certain
generosity (489–90) and she wishes him well (500–2).

Chaucer, in fact, having taken over into his portrait of the Wife many
of the traits of the traditional virago, has done much to subdue the
element of the grotesque, or at least to complicate our response to the
Wife so that we see in her something more than a monster of appetite and
unreason. The number of her husbands is excessive, though perhaps
more an occasion for mirth than horrified rebuke, and not in itself, we
should remember, directly contrary to Christian teaching, as St Augustine reluctantly admitted (see Cook, 1978–9, p. 53). What is important is
the Wife's own concern that she is not immune from criticism:

> Housbondes at chirche dore I have had fyve, –
> If I so ofte myghte have ywedded bee . . . (6–7)

She is conscious of the proprieties that she may have transgressed ('I hate
hym that my vices telleth me', she says at another point, line 662), and
very concerned to defend herself from the accusation of having behaved
in an immoral or un-Christian way. The concern is as significant as the
joyful illogicality of the defence. She has, in fact, many of the instincts of

a conformist *petite bourgeoise*, and her determination to pursue her predatory career within the traditional bounds of marriage is a quite touching confirmation of the values that her predecessors shamelessly repudiated.[8] She takes her revenge on her adulterous fourth husband by engaging in affairs to make him jealous, but she assures us with the greatest earnestness that she never herself stooped to adultery (481–8). Whether she is lying or not – an unanswerable question anyway – makes no difference, since it is the concern, and the moral consciousness that prompts it, that distinguishes the Wife from the iconographic figures of female lust and domination on which she is modelled. Her suggested horoscope for herself derives from the same desire to pre-empt the accusation of immorality, by explaining that she is as she is because of forces beyond her control:

> Myn ascendent was Taur, and Mars therinne.
> Allas! allas! that evere love was synne!
> I folwed ay myn inclinacioun
> By vertu of my constellacioun;
> That made me I koude noght withdrawe
> My chambre of Venus from a good felawe. (613–18)

The horoscope is accurate enough in relation to her disposition, as Curry (1926, pp. 91–107) and Wood (1970, pp. 172–80) agree, but her claim that her disposition leaves her no choice would have been regarded as disingenuous at best, and is intended by Chaucer to be seen to be inadequate. However, the need to make it, and the consciousness of a world of moral value in which mysterious entities like 'love' and 'synne' are sensed to have their being, and she herself perhaps not, are what lift the Wife of Bath out of the common run of trulls and termagants.

There is a puzzle, of course, and an apparent contradiction, in the last couplet quoted above, which seems to suggest a regular career of adultery, something that the Wife has elsewhere strenuously denied. It may have arisen mechanically, through the manner in which Chaucer brought different kinds of material together in assembling the Wife's Prologue, but few would be prepared to leave the matter in such an unsatisfactory state. The iconographers will claim that inconsistencies of this kind – and there are not a few of them in the Wife of Bath's Prologue – are in the very nature of inorganic art, which presents 'characters' in terms of bundles of attributes, each one of them significant of some moral quality or failing. Touches of verisimilitude may be added to give vitality, but these are a mere sauce to the exegetical meal, and consistency is not, on principle, sought. Thus Robertson:

> Alisoun of Bath is not a 'character' in the modern sense at all, but an elaborate iconographic figure designed to show the manifold implications of an attitude ... She is a literary personification of rampant 'femininity' or carnality. (1962, pp. 330, 321)

As an explanation of La Vieille, or of almost any of the Wife of Bath's literary predecessors, this would do very well indeed. As we read La Vieille's discourse, we are conscious at every point that it is to be seen *through*, and there is not much doubt about what is to be seen through it. She is a demonstration that women out of order are out of reason, and that freedom breeds unbridled lust and desire to dominate. The Wife of Bath's monologue is not so transparent: it demands to be looked *into*, puzzles and intrigues the observer, offers opportunities for contrary responses, creates, though itself a monologue, the effect of a dialogue, within the speaker and also within the reader.

At the same time, Robertson's strictures on interpretation of the Wife of Bath as 'a "character" in the modern sense' are worth heeding, especially if 'the modern sense' be taken to include amateur psychologising of a vaguely Freudian drift. It is very easy to explain all inconsistencies of the kind noted above, indeed to eliminate all possibility of inconsistency, if the Prologue is seen as the product of the fantasising imagination evading the mind's own areas of inner conflict (as by Parker, 1969–70). With Chaucer's text converted to a stream of unconscious suggestion, there is no reason to hesitate in opening one's *Guide to Psychosexual Disorders*, and diagnosing the Wife as a neurotic pervert who probably murdered her fourth husband (Rowland, 1972, 1972–3), or as a 'sociopath' who preys upon society because she cannot make personal relationships and thinks feeling gets in the way of success (Sands, 1977–8), or as 'that familiar figure, the bossy woman who likes to be mastered in the bedroom' (Burton, 1978–9, p. 47). Molly Bloom lurks on the fringes of consciousness, as does Martha in *Who's Afraid of Virginia Woolf?* Archetypal resemblances there may be in men's observation and consciousness of certain kinds of women, but this is where the writer's problems begin, not where he grounds his achievement. It is notable, furthermore, that all such psychologically interpretative exercises treat the character as a 'case' and the author as analyst: the reader replicates the analysis and understand the diagnosis. The process is little removed, except in its initial premises, from that of iconographic exegesis, and since the premises are less plausible, the exegesis is inferior.

However, the notion of 'character', even 'in the modern sense', is not best identified in terms of this loose kind of psychological fantasising. The preoccupation of nineteenth-century novelists with 'character' for instance, is not a special form of deviancy and literary sentimentality, as Robertson would imply, but a willingness to become involved, and to involve the reader, in those problems of judgement and understanding which are equally the concern of Chaucer. A comparison is to hand in the 'dramatic monologues' of Browning. Poems such as *My Last Duchess*, *Bishop Blougram's Apology*, *Fra Lippo Lippi* and *Andrea del Sarto* could claim to be among the most fully-developed and single-minded manifestations of character-consciousness: they insist on 'the facts from within' (Langbaum, 1957, p. 78), and the form provides, like the Wife of Bath's Prologue, a more or less independent structure, without formal narrative context and without explicit authorial intervention, for the display of character. What we get is not the uninhibited flow of consciousness, but the careful articulation of a many-sided debate on crucial matters of experience in religion, morality and aesthetics, in which the speaker's character acts as a nexus of conflict. Through the speaker's discourse, and the judgements he makes, and the judgements we make on him, Browning draws out, in an apparently objective and spontaneous manner, the complexity of such matters. Within the form, there is ample opportunity for the creation of the illusion of immediacy, through impromptu asides, self-conscious self-commentary, cryptic but undeciphered allusion, and various other kinds of parenthetic by-play. Browning can, at his best, as in *My Last Duchess*, achieve an effect of totally unforced revelation: the speaker, with his single-mindedness, his aesthetic ruthlessness, his impeccable manners, compels our admiration, our participation in his view of things, so that moral judgement, when it enters in after being so long suspended, produces mingled outrage and fascination. The straining against each other of the two kinds of response is the means to a particularised, intense kind of understanding. As Blougram says:

> Our interest's on the dangerous edge of things.
> The honest thief, the tender murderer,
> The superstitious atheist, demirep
> That loves and saves her soul in new French books –

> We watch while these in equilibrium keep
> The giddy line midway: one step aside
> They're classed and done with. (395–401)

It is this 'dangerous edge of things' that Chaucer explores in the Wife of Bath. Everything, even the expression of points of view directly opposed to her own, is absorbed into the mould of her consciousness and reproduced according to her characteristic style of expression, so that we are never unaware of her. Yet at the same time we are never unaware of the influence of that consciousness in shaping what we hear, and of the conflicting demands that are made on us to understand and to judge. It is character 'in performance' that we observe, and involve ourselves in according to the dramatic requirements of such perform-ance, not a surgery of the unconscious. To press too hard for psycho-logically consistent explanations of apparent inconsistencies is to mistake the nature of such performance and of the rhetoric appropriate to it. Furthermore, too unreserved a commitment to a belief in the autonomy of character is in the end self-limiting and trivial, as Jordan (1967, p. 210) points out, since it usurps 'the autonomy of the poet's controlling viewpoint' and results in a loss of judgmental perspective. Jordan draws on an important early article by Shumaker (1951) in emphasising the importance to Chaucer of 'rationally apprehensible general ideas' rather than the exploration of the implications of per-sonality for its own sake (1967, p. 212), and sums up the technique of the Wife's Prologue thus:

> Chaucer's motivation was primarily thematic . . . he was concerned with making an entertaining and artful presentation of the traditional, authoritative, pronouncements on anti-feminism, to which end the cumulative individualization of the Wife becomes a means. (p. 211)

There is a measure of agreement between the idea of the individual as 'a means' and the idea expressed above concerning the role of the indi-vidual, in dramatic monologue, as a 'nexus of conflict', but the extent to which Jordan, in distancing himself from trivial psychologising, finds himself, like Shumaker (1951, p. 88) and the iconographers, asserting an authoritative single point of view in the manipulation of the 'means' and thus in the author's 'controlling viewpoint' is clear from a later passage:

Out of the generosity and warmth of his own spirit he endows her with certain irresistibly attractive qualities, such as candor and fidelity to her own nature. But this is only to say that Chaucer dilutes the ancient vitriol, for the controlling viewpoint, however subtly conveyed, is unmistakably antifeminist. (p. 215)

Here one would hesitate, for it seems that an essential part of Chaucer's achievement, and of the pleasure that we take in the Wife of Bath's Prologue, is that he has removed the Wife from the iconographic abstraction of the traditional antifeminist portrait, where she is 'classed and done with'.

He has done much, for instance, without seeming to do much, to relocate her in a recognisable social and English setting. Her cloth-making, which was prominent in the portrait in the General Prologue, is not mentioned again, but 'Bath' would suffice to remind any fourteenth-century reader of what she was famed for,[9] and the ambience of a small-town business enterprise is suggested in the absence of her husband on an apparently regular visit to London (550) and the presence of an apprentice (303). She refers not only to her five husbands but also to her father and his kin (301), her mother (576), her maid (241, 300), nurse (299), niece (383), her 'gossyb dame Alys' (236, 239). The church to which she follows her fourth husband's bier, her eyes meanwhile on young Jankyn's fine legs (593), is where she earlier told us he was buried 'under the roode beem' (496) in a not too expensive tomb. Her mention of the Dunmow flitch (218) brings to mind a world of English village-custom relating boisterously to marriage, and her account of her activities while her husband was away in London suggests vividly the life of the bourgeois wife:

> Therfore I made my visitaciouns
> To vigilies and to processiouns,
> To prechyng eek, and to thise pilgrimages,
> To pleyes of myracles, and to mariages,
> And wered upon my gaye scarlet gytes. (555–9)

Her language and imagery, as Muscatine (1957, pp. 205–6) has pointed out, are full of references to bread and pans and bacon and mice, and she even threatens to absorb into her own literalism the wooden bowls and barley bread of the biblical texts she alludes to (101, 144). Her attitude to marriage seems rather conventional, strange to say, and she waits politely for her fourth husband to die before she makes any more plans with the clerk Jankyn. Her sexual language is full of euphemisms (*instrument, bele chose, quoniam, chambre of Venus*, as well as *queynte*, the register of which is ambiguous), and she hesitates ostentatiously over the story of Pasiphae (733–6).

Her portrayal of herself as a majestic voluptuary, of voracious and undiscriminating appetite, strikes a slightly comic note in such a homely context:

> For God so wys be my savacioun,
> I ne loved nevere by no discrecioun,
> But evere folwede myn appetit,
> Al were he short, or long, or blak, or whit;
> I took no kep, so that he liked me,
> How poore he was, ne eek of what degree. (621–6)

This may be regarded as a bit of posing, though it is odd to recall that this very passage is one of those not present in the Hengwrt manuscript (see note 5 to Chapter 1) and therefore presumably added in revision. The extravagance of the passage, and its return to the style of nymphomaniac frenzy that Jean de Meun satirises in La Vieille,[10] could well be an example of the kind of adjustment of narrative tone that we can sometimes detect in Chaucer's revisions (as for instance in the Franklin's Tale, V.1493–8). Here the intention would be to cool the ardour and whet the sceptical appetite of those who have perhaps been growing too warm in their response to the Wife's persuasive rhetoric. An interesting and somewhat similar argument has been put forward in connection with the Latin glosses that accompany the text in the Ellesmere manuscript. Graham Caie (1975–6) suggests that some of these glosses can be interpreted as attempts to point to her 'false logic and her persuasive misinterpretations of Scripture and Jerome' (p. 351), and thus to counteract the provocative temptingness of her view of life. They adjust the balance, and prevent the Wife being 'classed and done with' in another way, as an example of 'rich humanity' (Speirs, 1951, pp. 141). It is rather curious to find that the passage quoted above (lines 621–6) as an example of dehumanising extravagance is used by Ruggiers (1967) to support the contrary case. He finds in it, and in the Wife of Bath generally, 'a vigorous love of life untouched by contempt or hatred' (p. 200). A great deal turns upon the ambiguity of *liked* ('liked' or 'pleased') in line 626 (see Harwood, 1972), as Chaucer no doubt knew.

Throughout the Wife of Bath's Prologue, in addition to domesticating her and relocating her in a recognisable social environment, Chaucer works to maintain in us, in our response to her, a constant dialogue. No character in the *Canterbury Tales* is richer in texture or in contradiction, no character both repels and demands sympathy in such a bewildering way. She bursts upon us right at the beginning with strident affirmation:

> 'Experience, though noon auctoritee
> Were in this world, is right ynogh for me
> To speke of wo that is in mariage.' (1–3)

Her tone is so confident that we are taken aback, and look uneasily around, sure that it is our fault that we have somehow missed the earnest preceding discussion of the 'wo that is in mariage' to which she adverts. As she juggles biblical texts to prove that no-one ever positively said that she could not have been married five times (14–34), the colloquial rhythms of her speech, the intimate verbal cajolery, the sarcastic play with the long words (*diffinicioun, octogamye*) that her opponents use to disguise their absence of matter are irresistible. We know, with one part of ourselves, that she is mischievous and 'wrong', but her gaiety and energy is such that we feel we might happily go to the devil with her.

She has an attractive way, in her further arguments about marriage and virginity (not the case she set out to argue, incidentally, but certainly a safer one), of appealing to down-to-earth practical common sense, and identifying her scholarly opponents as killjoys, out of touch with reality. She generously grants them the privilege of virginity, suggesting more than once that such views are merely the product of lack of means or capacity (cf. 707–10), and scornfully playing with the polysyllables that imply the impotence of abstraction:

> Virginitee is greet perfeccion,
> And continence eek with devocion. (105–6)

As she says, God created men and women with sexual organs and presumably he must have intended them for use:

> Telle me also, to what conclusion
> Were membres maad of generacion,
> And of so parfit wys a wight ywroght?
> Trusteth right wel, they were nat maad for noght. (115–18)

There seems no doubt of it, as we listen to the decisive slamming of the
door on any alternative opinion in that final line. Likewise, virginity is all
very well, but nowhere is it commanded as necessary to the good life,
only to those who seek perfection:

> He spak to hem that wolde lyve parfitly;
> And lordynges, by youre leve, that am nat I. (111-12)

Indeed, if it had been commanded, then obviously the supply of virgins
would itself have dried up:

> For hadde God comanded maydenhede,
> Thanne hadde he dampned weddyng with the dede.
> And certes, if ther were no seed ysowe,
> Virginitee, thanne wherof sholde it growe? (69-72)

Our minds, in all this, register a stammering demur, for we know that the
argument has been twisted for personal reasons from its original course,
but we are swept along on the torrent of her pragmatism, and when she
speaks of virgins, ascetics, Christ and his saints, as *them*, and all-embrac-
ingly of *us wyves*,

> I nyl envye no virginitee.
> Lat hem be breed of pured whete-seed,
> And lat us wyves hoten barly-breed (142-4)

we know, whether we are wives or not, that we have a hankering to be
associated with the healthy, life-giving sexuality of *us wyves* rather than
with the pallid and sterile asexuality of *them* virgins.

It is a great rhetorical performance. If we fall for it, then we shall be
dead to the very complexity that Chaucer seeks through this assault on
our own judgement and sensibility. We shall find ourselves talking about
the abundant life-affirming sexuality of the Wife of Bath, about the
'profoundly religious' nature of her 'sexual prodigality' (Whittock, 1968,
p. 124), as if she were some Lawrentian heroine. If we can draw breath
for a moment, we may remember that all the Wife's talk of pullulating
and productive sexuality is a little beside the point, since there is no
mention here or anywhere else of her actually having any children.
Sometimes, too, her trickery rebounds upon her, as for instance when
she gets into a tangle with two recalcitrant biblical texts (99–104). There

are similar exegetical howlers in her references to Solomon (35–43) and *barly-breed* (144), all of which Robertson (1962, pp. 323–9) analyses very effectively, so that there is some encouragement to read the Wife in his terms as Chaucer's endorsement of traditional attitudes, as an iconographic figure symbolising the heresy of the flesh. But the encouragement is momentary, only one of a number of stimuli to which the reader is exposed; the vitality with which she flings together her scraps of learning remains unimpaired.

The Pardoner's interruption is a nice dramatic touch in itself, and it sets the Wife off on her autobiographical reminiscences. The dusty commonplaces of anti-feminism are absorbed into her characteristically colloquial and breathless recital and given a new zest and ambiguity, and her own perceptions and judgements flow into all that she describes and recounts in such a way as both to arm and disarm criticism. Her frankness in the confession of her bad habits and the trickery to which she has resorted may seem at times like a rhetoric of ingratiation, at other times a spontaneous reaction to something that, curiously, she has discovered in herself, but it never seems to be the product of the convention of the confessional monologue from which her own Prologue takes its ultimate origin. There, is, furthermore, a dynamic of growth at work within the Prologue, a process of change in the speaker's perception of herself as the monologue unfolds and in us as we witness it, something like the process that Browning tried to suggest in *Mr Sludge the Medium*. What she has planned to emerge from the discourse is a creed of financial and sexual supremacy, in which she will be seen to manifest her delight in the assertion of self and the bending of the world, and particularly husbands, to her will. What we come to realise is that this is a picture of reality that she has imposed, heroically, upon her own perceptions. The notions of 'good' and 'bad' that were asserted in her first categorisation of her five husbands –

The thre were goode men, and riche, and olde (197)

– begin to be subverted, and it becomes clear that the judgement of 'good' and 'bad' made there was merely a tactical debating-point. A change is signalled with the entry of the fourth husband, and the nostalgic lament that the Wife gives expression to as the springs of reminiscence begin to flow more freely:

But, Lord Crist! whan that it remembreth me
Upon my yowthe, and on my jolitee,

It tikleth me aboute myn herte roote.
Unto this day it dooth myn herte boote
That I have had my world as in my tyme.
But age, allas! that al wole envenyme,
Hath me biraft my beautee and my pith.
Lat go, farewel! the devel go therwith!
The flour is goon, ther is namoore to telle;
The bren, as I best kan, now moste I selle;
But yet to be right myrie wol I fonde.
Now wol I tellen of my fourthe housbonde. (469–80)

This famous passage has many relatives in 'the literary tradition of the randy old woman' which Matthews (1974, p. 443) describes, of which Villon's balades of *La Belle Heaulmière* are perhaps the best-known, and it draws directly on the discourse of La Vieille in the *Roman de la Rose*. Chaucer has worked a profound change on his borrowed materials, however, compressing the cycle of emotional experience, of relaxed, affectionate reminiscence, regret and sense of loss, and reassertion of will, into a single homely aria, sharpening the bitter sweetness of sentiment as well as the styptic to sentimentality. It is a passage whose power all readers have recognised, both those who have been encouraged by it to view the Wife of Bath as a figure of pathos, or even tragedy (Coghill, 1949, p. 142), and those who, seeing it as a threat to a moralised reading of the Wife, have concentrated on defusing the charge of emotion and explaining the lament away, as 'a jocular little complex of scriptural iconography designed to fill out the implications of the inversion represented by the Wife' (Robertson, 1962, p. 381).

In itself the passage can be read with neither kind of simplicity: it provokes both laughter, at the image of tickling, and pathos, at the expressive repetition of 'my world' and 'my tyme'; both criticism, at the materialism of selling, and admiration, at the determination to be cheerful, the one response following hard on the heels of the other so that we are given no chance to settle into a determined posture of judgement. In its context, the passage acts as a bridge to an extraordinary reverie (525–86), so self-absorbed as to appear completely spontaneous, in which the Wife recalls the wooing of her fifth husband. The manifesto of female sovereignty seems almost forgotten in the flood of reminiscence, in which Chaucer creates so powerfully the illusion of spontaneous mental activity that we have the impression of penetrating to a layer of consciousness usually concealed. The sense of life, of memory bringing forward 'the facts from within', is irresistible – and not merely the facts, but the facts tangled in the judgements she makes out of her own keen and partial moral awareness:

> Allas! allas! that evere love was synne! (614)

To assure ourselves that she is 'wrong', we must dwell on one element in the equivocation on 'love' to the exclusion of others. If she is wrong, then there is a truth in her wrongness which acts as a distorting mirror, parodying but also testing and implicitly criticising the values that supply quick and easy judgement.

The last scenes of the Prologue return to a rougher world of knock-about farce. Muscatine (1957, p. 213) comments on the comically symbolic aptness of the Wife's final actions where she is 'the embodiment of experience ripping out the pages of the book of authority, and of militant feminism, fetching traditional masculine domination a healthy blow on the cheek'. At the end there is a passage that provokes some reflection:

> And whan that I hadde geten unto me,
> By maistrie, al the soveraynetee,
> And that he seyde, 'Myn owene trowe wyf,
> Do as thee lust the terme of al thy lyf;
> Keep thyn honour, and keep eek myn estaat' –
> After that day we hadden never debaat.
> God helpe me so, I was to hym as kynde
> As any wyf from Denmark unto Ynde,
> And also trewe, and so was he to me. (817–25)

It is not easy to see this as an unambiguous demonstration of the truth of her manifesto, though she seems to wish it to be so interpreted. The words *kynde* and *trewe* in themselves carry weight, and draw on a richer range of significances than can readily be accommodated, ironically, to mere perversity. Yet an area of patronising contempt is left vacant, even by *kynde*, in which the Wife's assertiveness can still operate, so that it is not possible to convert, as we might wish, the search for *soveraynetee* into the quest for love, or even the more modest demand for the recognition of her identity, being a woman, as a person. David (1976, pp. 143–7) gives an excellent description of the way in which the Wife's generous and loving impulses, her craving for love (p. 144), are continually thwarted by the social and sexual regime under which she lives, and channelled into aggressive exploitation. The Wife may have brought her man to where she wants him, but she has not brought herself to where we want her. Chaucer is as unwilling to dissolve the conflict in the familiar bromide of love as in the tokenism of 'recognition'. The painful – and comic – realities of power remain.

The enigmatic ending of the Wife of Bath's Prologue, and the unresolved state of the reader's relationship with her, give a special interest to her forthcoming tale. Chaucer cunningly coils the spring of expectation, introducing the argument of the Friar and the Summoner which prepares for their tales later in Fragment III. When the Wife begins her tale, the change of mood is total:

> In th'olde days of the Kyng Arthour,
> Of which that Britons speken greet honour,
> Al was this land fulfild of fayerye. (857–9)

It is a very well-known story that she tells, universal in the annals of folk-tale, where it is known as the tale of the Loathly Lady. There are several analogues in Middle English, including a version of the story in Gower's *Confessio Amantis* and two short romances on the wedding of Sir Gawain and Lady Ragnel. It has as its affiliates fairy-tales like those of Beauty and the Beast, and the Frog Prince. Essentially a tale of transformation, it has its roots, like many folk-tales and fairy-tales, deep in the psychic experience of humanity: the way in which writers, even in sophisticated times, return again and again to such stories is a demonstration of the argument of Brewer (1980) that 'stories', so far from being unfortunately necessary pegs on which writers have to hang their more important concerns, are precious inheritances, treasured from generation to generation because they embody understandings that are not accessible in any rationally expository form. The understanding embodied in the tale of the Loathly Lady and its affiliates is that human beings who do not receive love cannot give love, and are crippled. This is expressed in imagery similar to that of dreams, emotional states, for instance, being recorded in terms of physical conditions, so that emotional mutilation is represented as physical deformity of some kind, usually the product of enchantment, and the gesture of love in some apparently trivial act, like kissing a frog.

The story as the Wife of Bath tells it is not quite so readily interpreted, for Chaucer has introduced some significant changes. It is useful to compare his version of the story with the version told by Gower (ed., Macaulay, 1900) in the tale of Florent (*Confessio Amantis*, I.1407–1861): Gower's narrative may be taken to represent the story in its 'normal' form and any major deviations that we observe in Chaucer be similarly taken to have been introduced by him for presumably specific artistic purposes.

At the start, Gower introduces us to the noble youth Florent. In battle, fair and square, he kills his opponent Branchus, but is later taken prisoner by Branchus's father, who wishes to revenge his son's death. Chivalric ethic forbids him to slay Florent out of hand, and so he takes the suggestion of his mother-in-law and sets him an impossible question: What do women most desire? If he does not provide the right answer within a twelve-month he will forfeit his life. In this way the father can get his revenge under seeming pretence of fair play.

It is worth noticing, first of all, how the Wife of Bath has changed the initial motive of the tale, for her knight is put in jeopardy not by the accident of battle, and the machinations of others, but by his own offence in committing an act of rape. It is described most casually: the knight is riding through a wood, sees a *mayde*, and ravishes her, almost, so to speak, *en passant* (885–8). To him it seems to be a matter of little moment, and he seems to be following the letter of the old mocking courtly ethic, as expressed in the *De Amore* (*De Arte Honeste Amandi*) of Andreas Capellanus (ed. Walsh, 1982, p. 222), that words and long wooing are necessary with ladies of the upper classes but a waste of time with common women. Many a courtly *pastourelle* will assume, rather more politely, the same. To the Wife of Bath, though, the knight's action is an assault on the whole of womankind, and the country is in an uproar. Significantly, when he is brought to judgment at Arthur's court, it is the ladies who pray for some mitigation of the sentence of death that is passed upon him, and who suggest the device of the question. The knight, who has done an offence against women, is indebted to women for the very chance to save his life.

In Gower, again, when Florent comes across the old hag, she tells him straightaway what she will require of him in return for the answer to his question. Florent is thrown into a torment of indecision:

> Tho fell this knyht in mochel thoght,
> Now goth he forth, now comth ayein,
> He wot noght what is best to sein,
> And thoghte, as he rod to and fro,
> That chese he mot on of the tuo,

Or forto take hire to his wif
Or elles forto lese his lif. (1568–74)

When he decides to accept the proffered exchange, she tells him the
answer and he goes off to court alone, promising to return. The Wife of
Bath changes all this: the hag does not tell him what the terms of the
exchange are to be, merely makes him promise to grant what she asks.
She does tell him the answer (1021) but she does not allow him to go off to
court by himself. She goes with him, and makes sure that she has the
sanction of the law, and the moral support of the ladies of the court, when
it comes to keeping the knight to his promise. The Wife of Bath is determined that the knight is not going to get any credit for keeping his word,
or for behaving honourably in any way: he is trapped, and controlled
throughout by superior womanly knowledge, grace and virtue.

With the wedding-night, the old hag's honeymoon homily, and the
husband's choice, everything is again radically changed in Chaucer.
What the Wife of Bath is doing, in the long homily (1109–1216), is systematically to shred away the last vestiges of recalcitrant maleness in the
knight and reconstitute him in her own image, which is, paradoxically,
his own true image too. As they lie in bed, with the knight groaning to
himself as he tries to get as far to the other side of the bed as he can, his old
wife, who 'lay smylynge everemo' (for she knows *everything*, of course),
asks him, politely enough, the reason of his unhusbandly conduct. If it is
any fault in her, she says, it may be amended:

'Amended?' quod this knyght, 'allas! nay, nay!
It wol nat been amended nevere mo.
Thou art so loothly, and so oold also,
And therto comen of so lough a kynde,
That litel wonder is thogh I walwe and wynde.
So wolde God myn herte wolde breste!' (1098–1103)

Patiently, the old hag explains to him that if she is of low birth, it is not to
her discredit or his, since true virtue and *gentillesse* is not a matter of
birth; if she is poor (he did not mention poverty, but no matter, it is all
grist to her mill, and at least she mentioned it herself, in line 1063), then
poverty too is a state of life more to be admired than shunned; if she is
old, she is worthy of the respect that goes with age; and if she is ugly, then
he has the assurance that other men will not go chasing after her. The
logic of her argument is impregnable, and if the knight, or any remnant

of him, considers that she has perhaps missed the precise point of his objections, he nevertheless remains silent, reduced to speechlessness by her unanswerable exposition of the nature of true virtue. She has turned the tables on him, if fact, by forcing him to recognise the importance of higher things when his whole natural being was concentrated on lower things. How can he resist this appeal to higher values, when those higher values of courtesy and *gentillesse* are the very basis of his existence as a knight?[11] The situation is unusual, of course: a knight is conventionally equipped to deal with fair damsels in distress, but in this case the damsel is ugly, and it is the knight who is in distress.

The hag, having talked him into tacit submission, offers him the choice of having her, in the future, fair and free or foul and faithful. Here a last comparison with Gower suggests itself. In Gower the question is asked after the old hag has shown her potential beauty, not before, and the choice offered is the one that is usual in the folk-tale of the Loathly Lady: foul by day and fair by night, or vice versa. This not a trivial conundrum, for it implies much about the relative weight that will be attached, in a man's view of marriage, to private and to public satisfactions; and it is unanswerable. But it is essentially man-related, and it is unanswerable only because the man cannot decide in what way to exercise his power. The Wife of Bath's question, however, makes him powerless, and gives him the choice only of acknowledging one or the other kind of power his wife has to make him miserable. It is, as Schlauch (1946) explains, an old and familiar antithesis of antifeminist writing: 'deformis facile fastiditur, formosa difficile custoditur'. The knight seems to recognise the triumph of virtue, and his reply, made, it is important to recall, while she is still an old hag, is less that of one who has been battered into insensibility than that of one who has won through to his own higher nature:

> This knyght avyseth hym and sore siketh,
> But atte laste he seyde in this manere:
> 'My lady and my love, and wyf so deere,
> I put me in youre wise governance;
> Cheseth youreself which may be moost plesance,
> And moost honour to yow and me also.
> I do no fors the wheither of the two;
> For as yow liketh, it suffiseth me.' (1228–35)

Thus it is not merely that the Wife of Bath proves that it is a good idea to concede sovereignty to wives: the whole tale is a demonstration of the wife's inalienable right to that sovereignty. There really is no alternative.

If this were all, the Wife of Bath's Tale would be a brilliant display of militant femininity in operation, and we should know where we were. But the enigma of the Wife of Bath, so interestingly unresolved at the end of the Prologue, persists, and the tale has an undertow, a flow of meaning which is not completely in accord with the doctrine it purports to exemplify. Part of the resistance may lie in the very nature of the tale itself, and the judgement on human relationships which lies embedded in it. In Gower, the hag is able to be released from the spell cast on her by her stepmother because she has found a knight who grants her sovereignty and love. In Chaucer the hag *chooses* to be transformed because she has got what she wanted, a knight who grants her sovereignty. Florent is able to rescue the bewitched creature because of what he is, because of his knightly virtues of loyalty and courtesy. In the Wife of Bath's Tale the hag subjects the knight to a course of education which enables him to understand what is good for him. The real transformation has been effected in the knight, not in the old hag. Yet, stubbornly, as the tale has it, it is *his* transformation that makes possible *her* transformation. The suggestion must be that, though the old hag (who is also the Wife of Bath) speaks the language of sovereignty, what she really seeks is the recognition by the man of the individuality, the inward reality of her existence, separated from all the trappings of youth, beauty, breeding and riches which act as the conventional communications of desirability. When that recognition has been made – and it seems to be a mere token, a formal, quasi-legal statement (1236–8), that is required – then the fullness of her own love is released and she is transformed. The knight meanwhile must be brought to the point where he can understand the necessity of this recognition, in terms of the claims of inward beauty and *gentillesse*, and be prepared formally to abnegate his power. When he does that, his life too is transformed, and the inference to be drawn from his address to his wife in line 1230 –

My lady and my love, and wyf so deere (1230)

– is that the transformation is effected by the claims of inward virtue, not of outward beauty.

The ideal is thus one of trust, the mutual surrender of power which we shall find called 'patience' in the Franklin's Tale (V.773). The tentative hints of a more generous notion of human relationships which can be discerned at the end of the Wife's Prologue are here advanced more confidently, perhaps because story-telling itself encourages a greater freedom of expression, or even compels it. Chaucer's way, however, is not to leave such sentimental satisfactions unalloyed: the contradictions of life are not so fully resolved in fiction as David (1976, p. 153) suggests. The Wife's own concluding remarks, as she returns to her own person, are a resumption of comically monstrous aggressiveness, as might have been expected. But even the ending of the tale itself is fraught with ambiguity:

> And whan the knyght saugh verraily al this,
> That she so fair was, and so yong therto,
> For joye he hente hire in his armes two,
> His herte bathed in a bath of blisse.
> A thousand tyme a-rewe he gan hire kisse,
> And she obeyed hym in every thyng
> That myghte doon hym plesance or likyng. (1250–6)

If the last two lines mean what they seem to mean, then the implication would be a pleasing and tender one, that the gift of sovereignty is returned in the gift of obedience, and the very notion of sovereignty dissolved in mutual love and recognition. If, however, the lines mean simply that she was sexually obliging once she had got what she wanted, then the raucous comedy of power reasserts itself.

THE PARDONER'S PROLOGUE AND TALE

It is appropriate that discussion of the Pardoner's Prologue and Tale should follow immediately upon the preceding discussion of the Wife of Bath's Prologue and Tale, since the two pilgrims are the supreme examples in the *Canterbury Tales* of Chaucer's interest in the portrayal of character 'in performance'. In some respects, indeed, the Pardoner's Prologue and Tale show an even fuller commitment on Chaucer's part to the exploration of the dramatic mode. The description of the Pardoner in the General Prologue is entirely and in detail consistent with the Pardoner's account of himself in his Prologue, where he gives a more extended description of the ways in which he can 'wel affile his tonge/To wynne silver' (General Prologue, I.712–13) from his simple-minded audiences, particularly by the use of false relics. The tale that he tells grows directly out of his autobiographical Prologue, being in its entirety a specimen of the kind of moral tale that he is wont to use in his preaching (VI.460–1). At the end of the tale, the dramatic framework is completed

with an extended 'epilogue' in which the Pardoner explicitly signals the
ending of his recital,

> And lo, sires, thus I preche (VI.915)

and turns again to the pilgrims, his primary audience:

> But, sires, o word forgat I in my tale. (919)

The exchange that follows, between Pardoner, Host, and Knight, is one
of the very few occasions where Chaucer allows the pilgrimage frame to
admit a conversation between more than two persons (the Introduction
to the Tale, with the expostulation of 'thise gentils', 323, is another). For
good measure, there is the intrusion of the Pardoner into the Wife of
Bath's Prologue.

With all this, it may seem that there is here a uniquely consistent
exploitation of the dramatic potentialities of the pilgrimage framework,
and irresistible encouragement from Chaucer to read the Pardoner's
Prologue and Tale as an elucidation of character in action. This encouragement has by no means been resisted by modern readers, who have
been variously eloquent concerning the hints they have found of profound psychological self-revelation, and the discoveries they have made
of the key to the Pardoner's inner being. Kittredge (1893), for instance,
though acknowledging that the Pardoner is 'a lost soul', clearly wished to
find in him some traits of disfigured humanity, and he read the *explicit*
of the tale –

> – And lo, sires, thus I preche,
> And Jhesu Crist, that is oure soules leche,
> So graunte yow his pardoun to receyve,
> For that is best; I wol yow nat deceyve. (915–18)

– as a paroxysm of agonised sincerity, a moment of moral convulsion, 'an
ejaculation profoundly affecting in its reminiscence of the Pardoner's
better nature, which he had himself thought dead long ago' (p. 123).
Curry (1926), prompted by the same instinct of sympathy, and the same
desire to humanise the Pardoner, found more specific grounds for a
psychological explanation in the physiognomies. Basing his argument on
the physical features attributed to the Pardoner in the General Prologue –

his long fair hair, his glaring eyes, his thin high-pitched voice, his beardlessness – and the hint in line 691 –

I trowe he were a geldyng or a mare

– he revealed 'the Pardoner's secret' and pronounced him to be a congenital eunuch, or *eunuchus ex nativitate* (p. 59). Curry detects a wistful sadness in the Pardoner's talk of his plans to get married (in the Wife of Bath's Prologue), and declares that he is more to be pitied than censured:

> Born a eunuch and in consequence provided by nature with a warped mind and soul, he is compelled to follow the urge of his unholy impulses into debauchery, vice and crime. Being an outcast from human society, isolated both physically and morally, he satisfies his depraved instincts by preying upon it. His character is consistent throughout both with itself and with nature as described in the physiognomies. (p. 70)

This has proved a very influential reading of the Pardoner's nature, and provides the basis for the standard iconographic interpretation of the Pardoner, as expounded by Miller (1955). According to this interpretation, which derives from patristic distinctions between good and bad eunuchs (distinctions required for both congenital and voluntary or involuntary castrates by the contradiction between Deuteronomy 23:1 and Isaiah 56:3), the Pardoner is the type of the perverse cleric who is sterile in good works, impotent to multiply the number of the faithful, lacking in 'the organs of spiritual generation and fertility' (Miller, 1955, p. 226). More clinically, and equally irrefutably, the Pardoner has been declared to have the character of 'a testicular pseudo-hermaphrodite of the feminine type' (Rowland, 1964, p. 58; also 1979–80).

But the outspokenness of our age has allowed attention to dwell also on the neglected second term of equine comparison applied to the Pardoner –

I trowe he were a geldyng or a mare

and for him to be identified as a practitioner of 'the love that dare not speak its name', or, as the Parson puts it, 'thilke abhomynable synne, of which that no man unnethe oghte speke ne write' (X.910). The association of effeminacy (the *mare*) with homosexuality is traditional, and several of the physical features attributed to the Pardoner concur in suggesting that he is a homosexual. The powerful association between homosexuality and inveterate wickedness and heresy, to which Mc-Alpine (1980) refers in her important essay, fits well here, of course, as does every other circumstance once the secret is out: the Summoner's 'stif burdoun' (General Prologue, 673) becomes an obscene double entendre, indicative of the nature of the association between the Summoner and the Pardoner;[12] the Pardoner's claim 'to have a joly wench in every toun' (VI.453) becomes a pathetic and ludicrous attempt to cover up his sexual deviancy; and the Host's threat to seize his *coillons* and have them enshrined 'in an hogges toord' instead of a reliquary (951–5) comes to have an even more singular pointedness. Likewise, psychologically, we can recognise that his boasting of 'normal' depravity, especially avarice, is a kind of screen for his tortured sense of abnormal depravity, and a hidden plea for acceptance (McAlpine, 1980, p. 14). For all readers there seems to be the consciousness of a challenge to rescue the Pardoner from moral responsibility for his depravity, to enter psychological pleas in mitigation, and to re-enroll him in the margins of humanity.

These that have been described are the main lines on which the Pardoner has been 'psychologised', though there have been many other incidental lines of speculation, usefully summarised in Sedgewick (1940), Calderwood (1964) and Halverson (1969–70). The various apparent inconsistencies in his performance have been particularly fruitful in stimulating critics to produce psychologically and dramatically realistic explanations of his conduct. The unlikely nature of his 'confession', for instance, and the manner in which he gives away all the secrets of his trickery to a crowd of strangers has been explained in various ways: he is on holiday and does not expect to meet these people in the future course of business; he is dazzled by the chance to show off in such comparatively distinguished company; he is drunk and does not know what he is doing; he is offended by the unwillingness of the *gentils* to allow him to tell a tale of *myrthe* and therefore deliberately gives them an exaggerated version of the diabolical degenerate of their imaginings so that they will realise their mistake and see him as a good-natured rogue by contrast. Calderwood (1964), Halverson (1969–70) and Manning (1980) all see the Pardoner's discourse as a 'put-on' that misfires. Equally prolific have been the explanations of the Pardoner's apparently inconsequential behaviour in attempting to sell pardons to the pilgrims (919–45) after having earlier told them that he is a fraud: he is joking wildly because he is ashamed of having given way to a momentary spasm of sincerity; he is in earnest; he is momentarily in earnest, having been carried away by his own tale; he sees the pilgrims carried away by his tale and seizes the chance to make the most spectacular and unlooked-for *coup*.

Some of these explanations are of course naive by any standards, and look for a literalness in the rendering of dramatic situation which would be inappropriate in most literary contexts, and which is specially inappropriate in the context of a 'performance' like the Pardoner's. In terms of literary convention, the Pardoner's monologue, like the Wife of Bath's, derives from the kind of self-revealing 'confessional' discourse employed for didactic and satirical purposes by Jean de Meun in the *Roman de la Rose*.[13] There need be no implication, in the recognition of such a debt, that Chaucer's ambition to create complex and rounded characters was frustrated by the convention of self-revealing discourse, but we have already seen, in discussion of the Wife of Bath, that there are certain kinds of interpretative reading that are irrelevant to such discourse. It may be thought, too, that the monologue of La Vieille was more readily capable of adaptation to the needs of Chaucerian character-portrayal, since the old harridan has a generalised literal existence rather than allegorical existence, whereas the Pardoner, in so far as he can be traced back to the *Roman*, is closest to Faux Semblant, an allegorical personification (10976–11980). The odds against Faux Semblant becoming a psychologically realistic character are carefully assessed by Kean (1972, pp. 98–100) and described thus by Rosemond Tuve:

> Such self-revelation, by Faux Semblant for example, is not the unrealized self-betrayal novelists use to make fine points about rationalization or projection, nor is it the introspection which dramatists use in soliloquies supposedly unheard, nor the novelist's device of allowing the flow of consciousness to be observed. Faux Semblant must instead be incredibly false – that is just what is true about him. (1966, p. 255)

There is much here that is relevant to the reading of the Pardoner's Prologue and Tale, though one might take issue with the implied attitude to the interpretation of soliloquy in drama, at least as it relates to certain kinds of drama. A resemblance between the Pardoner's monologue and the soliloquys of Richard III and Iago springs readily to mind, and has often been noted, and can be referred to here as a further example of the dramatically persuasive yet inherently unpsychological handling of first-person discourse. There is a closer connection, for just as the Pardoner is derived from an allegorical personification in a moral poem, so the Shakespeare villains take much of their dramatic character and role-playing from the 'Vice' of the morality plays. The Pardoner's relation to the pilgrims, as Peterson (1975–6) shows, is remarkably like that of the Vice to the audience of a morality play: the Vice courts the favour of the audience, lets them into his secrets, conspires with them against 'humanum genus', and, as part of the scheme of the morality play to implicate the audience in the Vice's liveliness, tries to get them to treat the whole business of contrition and penance as a joke. The Pardoner's concluding address to the pilgrims (923–40), seen in this context, has much the same character of impudent and mischievous mockery, with its ludicrous picture of sins being committed, and instant pardon being available, 'at every miles ende'. Interpretation of the Pardoner as a 'Vice' figure allows some necessary scope, too, for the enjoyment of his pulpit rhetoric, and his repertoire of sensationally effective tricks, such as the warning that anyone who is in mortal sin will not have the power or grace to come up and make offering to his relics (377–84). The laughter is of course morally 'contained', since the limitations of the dramatic conspiracy into which the audience enters with the Pardoner as Vice figure are well recognised.

The difficulty with pushing the Pardoner back into the conventional frame of moral allegory or drama is that he will not altogether fit into it. Chaucer, as usual, gives such dramatic vitality, such individuality of expression, and so many suggestions of autonomous motivation to the Pardoner that he tends to burst through the cardboard of convention. Some of the explanations that have been offered of his conduct, as they have been outlined above, are clearly a response to those suggestions of consistent inner life: their tendency, as a consequence, is to locate everything that the Pardoner says as emanating from his own psychologically real consciousness, and to view all his 'games' as part of his own personally motivated strategy. This is the view implied throughout the elaborate account of the Pardoner given by Howard, where the performance is analysed as a piece of histrionic exhibitionism and self-parody, a 'charade of evil',[14] and the temptations to which Howard so fully and ingeniously responds are clearly there. Even Muscatine, who is uncommonly aware of the conflicting demands – and richly conflicting demands – of conventional artifice and psychological drama, accepts a dominant trend towards the latter in the portrayal of the Pardoner. As he says, speaking of the inconsistencies that were present in self-revealing discourse such as that of Faux Semblant: 'Chaucer, in creating his Pardoner, did not withdraw from this simple inconsistency. He accepted it and made it dramatically operative by drawing it into a secure and complex characterization' (1957, p. 92). He goes further, and follows Speirs (1951, p. 173) in finding the style of the Pardoner's homily on the sins of the tavern itself expressive of the Pardoner's consciousness, especially his cynicism and hypocrisy in the manipulation of the tricks of the preacher's stock-in-trade and in his exaggerated tone of outrage:

> The high-flown rhetoric of the sermon, in the context of the self-revelation in the monologue, produces a mock-effect which satirises the canned fireworks of the professional preachers. (1966, p. 112)

Muscatine recognises here the pressure of context, and the way in which our consciousness of the Pardoner's presence as speaker encourages us to see further psychological self-revelation in what would, in other contexts, be mere Chaucerian or medieval mannerisms.

There are, of course, many reservations that one would have about the kind of interpretation that treats the Pardoner as a freestanding and autonomous character, and that takes every aspect of his performance to be an outward manifestation of his inner consciousness. The danger of trivialisation, as it was described in relation to interpretation of the Wife of Bath, remains, and the extremes to which psychologising readers may be driven are frequently in evidence, as in the extended analyses of the consequences of his sexual deviancy that have been already mentioned (the suggestions of deviancy are there, but as a shocking and scandalous insinuation, rather than as the clue to the understanding of his whole nature and performance); or as in the attempt of one critic (Leicester, 1982) to demonstrate that the sense of strain and confusion in the interplay of literal and spiritual meanings in the Pardoner's Tale (strain and confusion largely created, one must interject, by the imposition of spiritual meanings that are clearly not there) is the product of the Pardoner's consciousness, and specifically the precipitation of his twisted and hyperactive 'typological imagination' (p. 48).

At the same time, the impact that the Pardoner makes as a character, and as an individual, must be acknowledged. Convention has its place, and psychologically realistic interpretation its excesses, but a special quality of power, of evil, of death, is too strong in the Pardoner, and too universally apprehended, to allow him to be easily fitted into a set medieval literary convention. The 'historical' argument, advanced by

Morgan (1976) as well as Robertson (1962, pp. 269–70), that medieval poetry is interested in external action, its nature and moral interpretation, and not in individual consciousness and subjective motive, seems here, whatever its merits elsewhere, particularly inadequate. Perhaps the clues to a fuller and more specific understanding of the character of the Pardoner may be elicited from a comparison with the pilgrim with whom he seems to demand to be compared, the Wife of Bath.

The Wife of Bath is the prime example in the *Canterbury Tales* of Chaucer's interest in the literary portrayal of the workings of the individual consciousness. She speaks constantly of her thoughts and feelings, her hopes and regrets; she does not always speak consistently or honestly, but the inconsistencies and dishonesties are maintained by Chaucer within the orbit of the consciousness that he so powerfully suggests. Her discourse embodies, in its tone, rhythms and processes, the movement of her mind, both planned and spontaneous, and will sometimes imply the existence of simultaneous contrary movements. She reacts to what she herself says, loses track of what she is saying, and is at times aware of the larger moral world in which she has her being, even though she does not much like it. She has a present, in which she lives, and a past and a future within which that present exists coherently.

The Pardoner, by contrast, has no thoughts or feelings (except for the anger aroused in him by the Host's speech, which has the effect of making him speechless), no hopes or regrets. He never talks about his motives, except to reiterate monotonously that his purpose is ever one. He does not describe what he thinks or feels but only what he has done and will do, things that exist in the eternal present of his will:

> I wol nat do no labour with myne handes,
> Ne make baskettes, and lyve therby,
> By cause I wol nat beggen ydelly.
> I wol noon of the apostles countrefete;
> I wol have moneie, wolle, chese, and whete . . . (444–8)[15]

Without soul, feeling or inner being, he is a creature of naked will, unaware of its being but in the act of will. In transforming the kind of exposition he found in the *Roman de la Rose* into the context of a discourse by a realised individual, Chaucer is not so much writing unpsychologically as creating, as the phrase has it, zero-psychology. There is one flicker of awareness of a world which is not an extension of his will:

> But though myself be gilty in that synne,
> Yet kan I maken oother folk to twynne
> From avarice, and soore to repente.
> But that is nat my principal entente;
> I preche nothyng but for coveitise.
> Of this mateere it oghte ynogh suffise. (429–34)

There is a momentary unease here, part ludicrous embarrassment at having to admit to doing something good, part consciousness of an irony of which he is the victim, not the controller:

> What is more ironical than a will supposed free, freely struggling to attain pre-ordained doom, the opposite of its intention? . . . God is not mocked. (Coghill, 1949, pp. 161–2)

The partial consciousness fades, or is beaten back with insistent narcotic repetition:

> For myn entente is nat but for to wynne (403)

> I preche of no thyng but for coveityse. (424)

> I preche nothyng but for coveitise. (433)

To say that he 'relishes the irony' (Howard, 1976, p. 352) is to misinterpret this hollow juxtaposition.

The Pardoner thus creates in us a powerful reaction to his character, and yet as a character he has no capacity for change or self-awareness, and no insight into himself. There is no inner consciousness, no 'facts from within', because there is no within. He puts on a brilliant performance, as he takes pains to tell us (395–9), but it is like that of a marionette, or a clockwork toy, which once wound up goes through its motions mechanically. This image of automatism is explicitly evoked by the existence of the tale as a performance within a performance: the Pardoner does not actually tell a tale, but merely reproduces verbatim his habitual performance, even to the extent of including the homily and peroration, which have no place in the tale-telling framework. It is as if he exists only in the act of performance.

The horror, therefore, is the horror of vacuity. The Pardoner is not a rotten apple, but, rather, like one of those apples that are described in the poem *Cleanness* (line 1048) as growing near the Dead Sea, that look like true apples but turn to 'wyndowande askes' (ashes that scatter on the wind) when touched. His moral being has undergone a total atrophy, and in this state he exists, speaking but not understanding. Pittock (1974) describes the state well. It could be seen as the psychological effect of persistent lying: like many of those who traffic in words for profit, the Pardoner has lost the sense of the relation between the words he uses and the reality to which they refer. It could be seen further, Taylor (1982) argues, like Harwood (1971–2) on the Manciple's Tale, as related to the realist/nominalist debate about the nature of language, and the tendency of concentration on effect to corrupt intent. Whatever the case, the association of his atrophied state with his profession is the real secret of the Pardoner's nature.

As a Pardoner it is his job to distribute indulgences: these indulgences are granted by the Pope out of the Treasury of Merit, a kind of spiritual budgetary surplus created by Christ and added to by his Saints, out of which a bonus or dividend can be paid to the truly repentant. By it they are released from the pain of punishment in purgatory for a certain period, the pardon being specifically *a poena* (from pain) but not *a culpa* (for guilt), which only the sacrament of penance can afford. The indulgence is granted to those who are truly penitent: they in turn make a voluntary contribution to the Church in order to enable it to pursue its good works. Such an invitation to malpractice could hardly be resisted, and it was a customary abuse, as Kellogg and Haselmayer (1951) point out, for pardoners to present the exchange not as one of indulgence for repentance but as one of pardon for money; they also claimed that indulgences gave remission of guilt as well as punishment, or even that they would guarantee a place in heaven. The grotesque further excesses of the indulgence-vendors sent round Europe in 1517 to raise money for the building of St Peter's, who claimed to offer pardon not only for sins already committed but also for sins that might be committed in the future, are well known.

The reduction of the system of indulgences, conceived of first as a solace to man in his sinful state, into a form of mercantile exchange not only encourages but actually requires an atrophy of moral sensibility on the part of its professional practitioners. In this respect it is like all forms of human activity which substitute monetary values for human values: it leads to an unawareness of and an inability to distinguish between good and bad, true and false, real and illusory. Even the Pardoner's cynicism is only skin-deep, since his mockery of those who are gullible enough to be taken in by his tricks is merely, for him, a demonstration of the triumph of his will. He is, both theologically, as Miller (1955, p. 231) describes, and in terms of a human understanding that needs no patristic gloss, dead.

The mention of death brings us at last to the Pardoner's tale of the three rioters, which is about death. It is a brilliantly told tale, the stark narrative economy of which has often been praised, and it would satisfactorily defy all attempts to find flaws in it that would reveal the inadequacy of the Pardoner. In essence, it is the type of tale, favourite in folk-lore, which depends on a trick, in this case a double meaning for *death* which we understand but the rioters do not.[16] They go in search of Death in order to kill him, and they find death and die:

No lenger thanne after Deeth they soughte. (772)

The tale bears a strange affinity, as narrative, to Langland's dream of the search for Dowel: just as they find death in dying, so Langland's dreamer finds Dowel in doing well. The mixture of planes of reality, the way in which real people (including the boy and the innkeeper) behave as if they were characters in an allegory, as well as the austere yet allegorically suggestive landscape, create the same almost surrealistic effect as in Langland.

But the neat trickery of the narrative is only the most obvious level on which it works. The context provided for it by the Pardoner's Prologue and homily, and by our continuing consciousness of the Pardoner's presence as narrator, makes it resonant with suggestions of a much deeper significance. For the death that the rioters find is no more than the physical correlative, an allegorical enactment, of the death that they (and the Pardoner) have already undergone:

For if you live according to the flesh you will die, but if by the spirit you put to death the deeds of the body you will live. (Romans 8:13)

The rioters' decision to go out in search of Death in order to slay him is made in a spirit of drunken bravado: it is not the act of public-spirited vigilantes but, in the context of Christian understanding that presses imperatively for recognition in the tale, a sign of moral deadness, as well as a grotesque parody of Christ's struggle to overcome Death, which brought about of course not the elimination of physical death but the release of man from the certainty of eternal damnation. Physical death is by no means to be regarded, by the true Christian, as an enemy: in *Piers Plowman* (C.XXII.76–109) Conscience calls on *Kynde* (Nature) to send Death to help man in his battle against the Seven Deadly sins led by Antichrist, since Death, with Old Age and Disease, is a reminder of necessary mortality and therefore a stimulus to the life of the spirit. Likewise, in Lydgate's *Danse Macabre*, or *Dance of Death*, the Carthusian and the hermit, in contrast to all other estates of society, both welcome death as a manifestation of God's grace, almost as a long-awaited friend. Death in this sense is thus the physical enactment of the death to the world which is the life of the spirit:

> You must consider yourselves dead to sin and alive to God in Christ Jesus (Romans: 6:11)

Death is the only means to life, whether considered as the dying into life which is the act of abnegation of sin, or the dying into immortal life which is physical extinction.

Some of these underlying meanings are focused in the figure of the Old Man, to whom Chaucer has given some of his most unforgettable lines, and a part in the story much expanded from that of the corresponding figure in the analogues (where he most commonly represents Old Age as the messenger of Death),[17] and quite gratuitous if we consider only the needs of the narrative:

> Thus walke I, lyk a restelees kaityf,
> And on the ground, which is my moodres gate,
> I knokke with my staf, bothe erly and late,
> And seye 'Leeve mooder, leet me in!
> Lo how I vanysshe, flessh, and blood, and skyn!
> Allas! whan shul my bones been at rest? . . . (728–33)

The Old Man seeks death, and is prepared for death, but he does not seek death in any spirit of presumption. He recognises that he must live out his days,

> As longe tyme as it is Goddes wille (726)

but his weariness of the world and of his great age makes him see life as an exile, an imprisonment in which his soul is 'lyk a restelees kaityf' (728), again echoing Paul (Romans 7:24), as translated by Chaucer in the Parson's Tale (X.344):

Allas! I caytyf man! who shall delivere me from the prisoun of my caytyf body?

There is also an echo of the description of the state of man in the last days of the world in the Book of Revelation (9:6), again translated by Chaucer in the Parson's Tale (X.216):

They shullen folwe deeth, and they shul nat fynde hym; and they shul desiren to dye, and deeth shal flee from hem.

On the other hand, the Old Man, though he is conscious of the misery of his existence, is not a truly contemplative figure, and there is some ambiguity about him: his misery is not the product of a spiritual contempt of the world but of horror at the decrepitude of advancing age, and his regret at his inability to find any young man to exchange his youth for his age (721–6) hints at some unappeased yearning after life – or maybe, obscurely, after spiritual life, since it is by putting off the old man, crucified with Christ on the Cross (Romans 6:6), that he may be reunited in life with the new man (Colossians 3:9, Ephesians 4:22).

How can a man be born when he is old? said Nicodemus. Can he enter a second time into his mother's womb, and be born? (John 3:4)

The Old Man knocking with his staff upon the earth, his mother, seems to seek release from age in re-entering a more literal kind of womb.

There is, in the portrait and words of the Old Man, a powerful suggestion of the stirring of spiritual life within the Pardoner. In the discussion above, the possibility was disallowed that the Pardoner's Tale is, in mode and manner of expression, a simulation of the Pardoner's consciousness. The controls for such a reading are simply not there, and it is hard to see how they could be, in an extended and independent narrative. But it is still the Tale told by the Pardoner, and it is impossible for us to forget the context in which it is told, or our brooding consciousness of the person who tells it. The effect of this continued awareness is to strike a chill in us at the gulf that exists between his words and his understanding. The smoothness of his performance, though it may compel a reluctant admiration of the power of his will, is all the more shocking in relation to his reptilian deadness to all that he says. Yet the consciousness of that deadness, as we saw long ago in Kittredge's account of the poem, seeks relief, and longs for the opportunity of some movement of sympathy which will restrain or suspend final judgement. Browning spoke thus of the conflict:

> I have been all my life asking what connection there is between the satisfaction at the display of power, and the sympathy with – ever-increasing sympathy with – all imaginable weakness.[18]

Final judgement on the Pardoner, in which he would be for ever 'classed and done with', snags on the gratuitously and suggestively extended portrait of the Old Man, through which, conscious as we always are of his potential presence, we glimpse the Pardoner.[19] It is appropriate that this obscure and ambiguous movement of inner life should be made apparent not in his own words about himself, since these after all are part of the shell of oblivion that performance has substituted for true self-awareness, but in the self-revelation prompted by the imaginative act of telling a story. Only thus can the Pardoner uncover his consciousness of his outcast state.

THE CANON'S YEOMAN'S PROLOGUE AND TALE

The Wife of Bath and the Pardoner are both of them examples of Chaucer's profound and innovative interest in the portrayal of individual character. Their autobiographical monologues are extensive enough to establish them as speaking out of a more or less autonomous consciousness, and their tales, placed in the context of the consciousness so disclosed, take on an added dimension of significance as self-revelation. Chaucer seems to give us 'the facts from within', without interference and without explicit authorial comment. The activity of the author, however, in stimulating a multiplicity of conflicting responses to the character that he portrays, is intense, and a similar kind of activity is expected of the reader. The subjects which preoccupy the two pilgrims – women and marriage in the case of the Wife of Bath, sin and death in the case of the Pardoner – are themselves of such a nature as readily to provoke conflicting responses in the reader, and Chaucer encourages no easy acquiescence in sympathy with the pilgrim, nor in uncritical admiration of his or her 'power', nor in summary moral judgement. The whole relationship between pilgrim-performer and audience is further complicated by an ambiguity that exists in the nature of their performance. The monologues of both the Wife of Bath and the Pardoner trace their origins to the conventionally self-revealing monologues of allegorical or semi-allegorical characters in the *Roman de la Rose*, and it is at times difficult to be certain whether what the pilgrims say is to be construed as unconscious self-revelation or as part of the convention of the character 'in performance'. They remain to some extent enigmatically suggestive, and one would suppose this to be an important element in the fascination they exert, as much a fascination with the complexities of the art of portrayal, and the different modes of reading and interpretation it may call for, as with the complexities of character. It is possible, I think, to see in the Canon's Yeoman's Prologue and Tale a further experiment by Chaucer in the art of the dramatic monologue, and one in which, initially at any rate, he was seeking to grant a greater degree of autonomy to the speaker.

The Canon's Yeoman's Tale is constructed on the same model as the Prologue and Tale of the Wife of Bath and the Pardoner, that is, with an extended autobiographical monologue preceding a tale which grows out of and further illustrates the subject-matter of the monologue. The dramatic naturalism of the Canon's Yeoman's discourse is, however, further enhanced by the more elaborate manner in which it is introduced, with the long and subtly developed conversation between the Host and the Yeoman (the 'Prologue', as it is commonly called) contrasting with the relative brevity of the Introduction to the Pardoner's Prologue and Tale and the total absence of introduction for the Wife of Bath. The arrival of the Canon and his Yeoman upon the scene is itself one of the most dramatically realistic moments in the *Canterbury Tales*: totally unexpected and unprepared for, it is yet, in the context of the journey, perfectly naturalistic, and the reasons given by the Canon and his Yeoman for hastening to overtake the company (VIII.583–92) are none the less plausible for being probably untrue. The Canon himself is only briefly sketched, but the Yeoman from the beginning has that kind of authenticity which derives from being someone whose existence could not have been predicted. Most of the pilgrims have a preliminary existence in estates satire and other kinds of literature: they are representatives, some more sharply individuated than others, of types, their portraits based on the expectations attached to certain professions and trades. Even the Wife of Bath and the Pardoner, though they are given distinctly individual traits, are to a large extent the predictable products of their 'profession'. The Yeoman, however, is *sui generis*, and would have appeared very incongruously in the list of pilgrims in the General Prologue, all identified by trade and vocation, as 'The Sorcerer's

Apprentice'. There are not enough of these to constitute a profession or to make a type. His monologue, furthermore, takes its inspiration not from the convention of literary 'confession' that Chaucer adapted from the *Roman de la Rose* for the Wife of Bath and the Pardoner, but from the stimulus of a particular situation on the journey that we see dramatically arise and develop and to which the Yeoman responds quite spontaneously and naturalistically.

The introduction of the two new characters could hardly be more dramatic. Their sudden irruption, the specification of place and distance, the detail of horses, clothing and lack of baggage, all have the character of observed reality, recorded for no other reason than that it was observed. Chaucer speaks of himself explicitly (as in the General Prologue, but not usually in the links) as the observer who tries to piece together an explanation of things from what he sees:

> It semed as he had priked miles three. (561)

> And in myn herte wondren I bigan
> What that he was, til that I understood
> How that his cloke was sowed to his hood;
> For which, whan I hadde longe avysed me,
> I demed hym som chanoun for to be. (569–73)

It is as if they have taken the narrator by surprise, broken in upon what he thought he was narrating, and this fiction is kept up during the long conversation between the Yeoman and the Host, so that we only learn finally what the Yeoman is – though in retrospect there are hints in the references to sweating, to the 'stillatorie' (580), and to the paving of the streets with gold (626) – when he uses the word 'multi-plie' in line 669. This impression of deduction from observation contributes much to the dramatic immediacy of the scene, which of course is further sharpened by the contrast with what has just been occupying our attention, the pious 'lyf of Seinte Cecile' (554):[20] from the immense and abstract meaningfulness of the death of the saint in the service of Christ through martyrdom we move to the gratuitousness of the visual detail of the Canon and the Yeoman and the horses, from joy at Cecilia's lack of sweat in the burning bath (522) to joy in observing the Canon's sweat –

> But it was joye for to seen hym swete! (579)

– from remote imperial Rome to the here and now of 'Boghtoun under Blee' (556), the morning's hostelry (589), the road to Canterbury 'on which we been ridyng' (623).

The Canon is swiftly sketched, all blustering confidence that the effort he has made to join the company will be properly appreciated (583–6), and the Yeoman, though more modest, more matter-of-fact in his explanations, more ingratiating (587–92), goes on to give dramatic and pregnant hints of his master's ability to take on great enterprises. He may be playing the part of the 'setter' (Robinson, 1957, p. 760), whose simple-seeming honest admiration plants the conviction that the Canon is something out of the ordinary, but one can also see the satisfaction that he takes and has been accustomed to take in being associated, in however humble a capacity, with such a great man. The Host's down-to-earth common sense, which prompts his quizzical observation concerning the Canon's 'overslope', 'al baudy and totore' –

> 'Why is thy lord so sluttissh, I the preye,
> And is of power bettre clooth to beye,
> If that his dede accorde with thy speche?
> Telle me that, and that I thee biseche.' (636–9)

– seems to prick this bubble of satisfaction, as if the Yeoman had been concealing from himself, in the cultivation of these vanities, his real dissatisfaction and disillusion. The Host's next question, 'Where dwelle ye?' (656), prompts him to a frank recognition, and a wonderfully evocative description, of the life they actually lead, as opposed to the roads paved with gold of their dreams:

> 'In the suburbes of a toun,' quod he,
> 'Lurkynge in hernes and in lanes blynde,
> Whereas thise robbours and thise theves by kynde
> Holden hir pryvee fereful residence,
> As they that dar nat shewen hir presence;
> So faren we, if I shal seye the sothe.' (657–62)

In what follows the Yeoman expresses vividly the conflict within him – the half-understanding that the science in which he is a servant is an 'illusion' (673), the realisation that he does not fully understand what he is talking about, the strength still of the fever of hope:

> Yet is it fals, but ay we han good hope
> It for to doon, and after it we grope ... (678–9)

The departure of the Canon, however, acts to remove any lingering hesitation or inhibition on the Yeoman's part, and, prompted by the confidence he gets from the Host's support, by his annoyance at the Canon's parting threats, and by the stimulus to his vanity given by the prospect of an audience eager for a scandalous *exposé*, he decides to tell all. It is not so much that the scales have fallen from his eyes as that he does not think it worthwhile, on balance, to try to put them back again.

His autobiographical account of his life as an alchemist's assistant (the *Prima Pars* of the Tale, as it is commonly called, though it should more properly be called the Prologue) is rich in its expression of continued inner conflict. He tells the pilgrims that what he says will be a warning to others, so that they will not be cheated of their money and good name, but he is not averse to letting them understand that he knows a good deal about the technicalities of the racket he now so despises. He pours scorn on the 'termes', 'so clergial and so queynte' (752), that alchemists use to impress people, but nevertheless introduces a great many of them under pretence of passing them over (754–72). His disarming confession of ignorance (784–90) does not stop him reeling off long lists of technical terms, while at the same time commenting that there is no need to do it and that it is all a waste of time (796, 801). Having given a scathing account of the futility of the whole enterprise (834–5) he finds he has forgotten some more of his garbled scientific names and he pours them forth,

> Yet forgat I to maken rehersaille
> Of watres corosif, and of lymaille ... (852–3)

like an examinee who tries to cram all he knows, relevant or not, into a final emetic paragraph. In one sense it is indeed a form of purgation, even a quasi-sacramental form of confession (Ryan, 1973–4) for the Yeoman, who feels that he may expel the fevered instinct by utterance of the words associated with it, like a charm or exorcism, and who belatedly finds some of the technical matter still lying like an obstruction upon his stomach. In another sense, it is an indication of incomplete parturition from the illusion upon which his sense of self-importance and vanity have fed, and itself a form of vanity: like the Franklin, who has a similar outburst of technical jargon (V.1264–96), he wants to be thought an honest simple fellow, but not simple-minded.

There is further conflict within the Yeoman in his emotional attitudes towards his erstwhile profession. He is still drawn by and manages to

convey vividly and even poignantly the compulsive power of the alchemical science, the mystery, the sense of treading on forbidden ground,
the inextinguishable hope, the everlasting frustration:

> For sorwe of which almoost we wexen wood,
> But that good hope crepeth in oure herte,
> Supposynge evere, though we sore smerte,
> To be releeved by hym afterward.
> Swich supposyng and hope is sharp and hard;
> I warne yow wel, it is to seken evere. (869–74)

In his account of a failed experiment, he seems to grow absorbed again in
the passion of the search: the atmosphere is not that of rehearsal for a
cynical confidence trick, but that of a graduate seminar, with students
gathered excitedly around the master, whose resilience, determination
not to be cast down by failure, and eagerness to find rational and
manageable explanations, are admiringly described:

> As usage is, lat swepe the floor as swithe,
> Plukke up youre hertes, and beeth glad and blithe . . .
> Although this thyng myshapped have as now,
> Another tyme it may be well ynow. (936–7, 944–5)

In conflict with this, though, is the strength of condemnation that derives
from the pent-up disillusion that is now finding expression, and which
leads him to dismiss the whole science as 'oure elvysshe craft' (751), 'this
elvysshe nyce loore' (842). The force of feeling is given even stronger
impetus by his decision to turn away from his old life and by his natural
desire, therefore, to condemn it utterly and prove to himself and others
that his decision was the right one.

There is no sharp division between the autobiographical account given
in the *Prima Pars* and the narrative of alchemical trickery that constitutes the Tale proper, or *Pars Secunda*. The one blurs into the other,
and the Yeoman, conscious of this, has to assure us that it is not his
master who is the villain of the Tale, even though he too is a Canon, and a
real person, drawn from the Yeoman's experience:

> This chanon was my lord, ye wolden weene?
> Sire hoost, in feith, and by the hevenes queene,
> It was another chanoun, and nat hee,
> That kan an hundred foold moore subtiltee. (1088–91)

The Yeoman's difficulty in separating the real from the fictional is psychologically realistic as evidence of the pressure he is under to re-examine his life and disentangle his former from his preferred self; it is also appropriate in terms of the general dissolution of the distinction between appearance and reality which is in the nature of alchemical science. But the comparative degree of distancing which is made possible by the movement away from autobiography enables the Yeoman to focus more clearly the conflicting elements in his attitude, to objectify his perceptions, as Herz (1960–1) puts it. The almost lyrical sense of hope and excitement that was present in the Prologue and *Prima Pars* becomes identified as ludicrous self-deception when it is attached to the deluded priest of the Tale (1341–8). The ambiguous attitude to his master, where the Yeoman was drawn in opposite directions by his memory and by his determination to exorcise that memory, is able, when it is released into non-autobiographical narrative, to harden into a more unequivocal picture of diabolical knavery. The associations of alchemy with hell and the devil are earlier more indirect, as when the Yeoman commits his master to the devil (705), or says that you can recognise alchemists by the 'smel of brymstoon' (885). In the Tale, the identification of the Canon as a devil becomes more direct and explicit (984, 1071, 1158), and he is also represented as a type of Judas (1003). The Yeoman pursues the Canon of the Tale with a venom that derives much from the displacement of the ambiguously personal into the ostensibly and unambiguously impersonal, and which is intensified by the satisfaction that he takes in condemning outright what he was previously only half-ashamed to be associated with (1172–3, 1259, 1273–5). He speaks of his desire to warn others:

> It weerieth me to telle of his falsnesse,
> And nathelees yet wol I it expresse,
> To th'entente that men may be war therby,
> And for noon oother cause, trewely. (1304–7)

but one suspects that there is less altruism in his concern for others than a vindictive desire to revenge himself vicariously on the person and the profession that he now feels have exploited him.

The Tale is throughout informed by the liveliest sense of the Yeoman's presence. His apostrophe to the 'chanons religious' (992–1011) reveals his consciousness of the possibility of causing offence; his direct and personal hatred of the Canon of the Tale comes through in many narrative asides, including the moment when he steps completely outside the narrative to explain that the Canon is not his master; his references to his own experience and knowledge of the man make his Tale almost an extension of his autobiographical monologue. There is also throughout the Tale a constant barrage of imprecation and warning admonition (e.g., 1189, 1201, 1225, 1265) that keeps the speaker firmly in our consciousness. This is not to say, of course, that the manner of the telling is adapted to his 'personality' in any psychologically consistent manner. His apostrophe to the priest (1076), and many other features of his discourse, would be felt to be quite out of place if Chaucer were expected to observe strictly realistic criteria of speech and behaviour. Hints and suggestions, as with the Wife of Bath and the Pardoner, are sufficient to create successfully the dramatic illusion of character 'in performance'.

The centre of consciousness remains, therefore, the Yeoman's, and the author does not insist in any way, in the body of the narrative, upon his own presence. At the same time, that centre of consciousness is recognised, as with the Wife of Bath and, to a lesser extent, the Pardoner, to be not sufficient in itself but to be also a nexus of conflict, where the Yeoman's judgements of his life and the alchemical profession, themselves in a state of disturbance and change, intersect with the larger judgements we are encouraged to invoke. The Yeoman's portrayal of the Canon as a kind of devil, for instance, implies a more philosophical and theological interpretation of alchemy as a form of diabolism, an attempt to arrogate to man powers to change the nature of things and to create anew that are God's alone, and a direct challenge to God's authority. This view is stated explicitly in the non-dramatic coda to the Tale, but is implied elsewhere within the Yeoman's discourse and without violating the dramatic integrity of the consciousness from which that discourse is derived. The ubiquity of the Canon, for instance, and his lack of a home in the world, are strongly suggestive of the devil or a diabolical agent:

> On his falshede fayn wolde I me wreke,
> If I wiste how, but he is heere and there;
> He is so variaunt, he abit nowhere. (1173–5)

The commitment of the foolish priest to the service of the Canon is likewise expressed in terms reminiscent of the selling of the soul to the devil (1248, 1288–9). There are further, as Muscatine (1957) has brought out in his powerful exposition of the poem, many suggestions of the way in which alchemy, with its immersion in the world of material reality, of

things, its 'soulless striving with matter' (p. 216), directly challenges
religion, with its emphasis on the pre-eminence of the spiritual, and
even parodies religion, by claiming to effect transformations of base
metal into gold which are a grotesque travesty, as Grennen (1965)
describes, of the Christian vision of the transformation of the corporeal
into the resurrected body. The sense of the solid and immovably
unspiritual nature of the world of matter is vividly present in the
Yeoman's catalogue of the substances required by the alchemist:

> Unslekked lym, chalk, and gleyre of an ey,
> Poudres diverse, asshes, donge, pisse, and cley,
> Cered pokkets, sal peter, vitriole,
> And diverse fires maad of wode and cole;
> Sal tartre, alkaly, and sal preparat,
> And combust materes and coagulat;
> Cley maad with hors or mannes heer, and oille
> Of tartre, alum glas, berme, wort, and argoille. (806–13)

The manner of presentation itself suggests the tumbling together of
nature's 'germens' into an unnatural confusion. As Muscatine, following Speirs (1951, p. 197), says, 'this chaos of matter, refuse,
excrement, represents the universe of technology' (1957, p. 220).
Against this view of science, and still entirely within the capacities of
the Yeoman's consciousness, there is the suggestion that empirical
science (which is what is adumbrated in the experimentations of the
first Canon, however unsuccessful and ill-conceived) may exercise a
powerful hold on the human mind, not as a denial of Christian revelation and the only true 'Science', but as a form of exploration of the
unknown.

It is noteworthy that at the end of the Tale Chaucer steps outside the
Yeoman's character, and delivers with complete seriousness, and with
confident reference to learned authorities[21] quite beyond the experience of the Yeoman as a dramatic character, a verdict on the nature of
true alchemy. It is something, he says, that is knowable only to those
who are divinely permitted or inspired, and to pursue it otherwise is
against God's will:

> For whoso maketh God his adversarie,
> As for to werken any thyng in contrarie
> Of his wil, certes, never shal he thryve,
> Thogh that he multiplie terme of his lyve. (1476–9)

The undramatic nature of this conclusion is something of a puzzle. The most obvious explanation is that Chaucer thought that the matters raised in the dramatic context of the Yeoman's discourse were too serious to be left in a state of irresolution, and therefore stepped in with an authoritative final statement. This seems something of a denial of what we have recognised to be the integrity and potentially intense seriousness of his technique of dramatic monologue, and a more persuasive interpretation would be that the Canon's Yeoman's Prologue and Tale are in an incomplete state of revision or adaptation. A very late date for the whole production is suggested by its absence from the Hengwrt manuscript, the earliest attempt at a collection of the *Canterbury Tales* (see Chapter 1): its presence in the Ellesmere manuscript, the next such attempt, would seem to be due to the discovery of certain late-added material and revisions after the copying of Hengwrt. The alternative explanation, that the Canon's Yeoman's Prologue and Tale are missing from Hengwrt because they are not by Chaucer, cannot be seriously entertained:[22] quite apart from any subjective judgement that may be made on the quality of the work and on the likelihood, on internal evidence, that Chaucer wrote it, there is the argument against scribal authorship that there is no reason for a scribe to write it, no observed lacuna in the *Tales* that it has to be created to fill. The hypothesis of a late date for the work is supported by the sophisticated expectation of the pilgrimage framework that it exploits, in intruding so unexpectedly upon it, and by everything that has been said about its more advanced experimentation with the technique of dramatic monologue already established in the Prologues and Tales of the Wife of Bath and the Pardoner. A late date would help to explain the unrevised state of the work which is presumed to be evident in the dramatically undigested nature of the coda, as also in certain roughnesses of versification described by Skeat (1894, vol. 3, pp. 492–3).

A particular explanation that has been offered of the genesis of the Canon's Yeoman's Prologue and Tale is that the Tale (*Pars Secunda*) was originally designed as an independent production, perhaps for an independent occasion,[23] and was later only imperfectly adapted to the scheme of the *Canterbury Tales* and the character of the Canon's Yeoman, whence the doubling of the role of the Canon and the out-of-character ending. The first of these apparent discrepancies is capable of being interpreted as a quite exceptionally successful stroke of dramatic realism, as we have seen. The coda remains something of a puzzle: perhaps it is better to assume that the Tale is in its original 'unlicked' shape than that Chaucer lost his nerve.

CHAPTER 4

Romances

The four tales that are grouped here under the heading 'Romances' – the Knight's Tale, Squire's Tale, Franklin's Tale, and Tale of *Sir Thopas* – may seem at first sight to have little in common. In terms of length and treatment this is so. In terms of subject-matter, however, they are essentially related, and the differences they exhibit are chiefly meaningful in so far as they are observed to be differences within a common pattern of expectation. The general character of the medieval romance is that it is, first, a narrative of the life of an idealised warrior aristocracy, in which prowess in feats of arms and dedication to the service of women are the principal subjects. Such narratives may or may not be morally edifying: since this is the Middle Ages, and England, they usually are. But this is not an essential condition of their existence. What is essential is the function of such narratives as demonstrations of an ideal code of conduct in operation.[1] The demonstration may be in the form of a quest, a battle, a love-affair, but what it will always contain is a test and proof of the code. The values by which the characters of romance live are exposed to some threat, some conflict, often itself of a fantastic or ritualised kind, and are shown always to triumph. The threat in the Knight's Tale is the awkward circumstance by which two young knights fall in love with the same lady; in the Franklin's Tale, a rash promise which requires one or other of two ignoble acts whether it is kept or not; in *Sir Thopas*, with extreme typicality, a giant, who interrupts the hero in his quest for his (so far unknown) lady-love. The Squire's Tale, unfinished, was certainly promising something traditional of the kind. All four tales take as their basic assumption that the motive of existence is the conduct of life according to high-minded secular chivalric values. This is the total extent of the characters' understanding, and it is offered for our admiration.

It is not difficult to understand the strength, integrity and persistence of such a genre in the Middle Ages, despite local variations, Nor is it difficult to see how readily the genre will reject tales like those of the Merchant or the Clerk, even though they deal with the lives of knights, or better. The differences between the four tales here grouped together are of course more than mere local variations. One, indeed, is a complete spoof, and another, the Squire's Tale, may have elements of parody. But the reflexive nature of their relationship to the genre is only properly understood in terms of the genre. The Knight's Tale is a less typical romance than the Franklin's Tale, and there is much in it that carries the impress of its special origins and the special interpretation that Chaucer has given to it; but it cannot be understood, in its essential nature, except in terms of the generic expectations of romance. Finally, it is worth remarking that the four romances are specifically characterised as a group in that all exhibit, in its most explicitly developed form, the narratorial style and mode of address that Chaucer took over from the English popular romances.

THE KNIGHT'S TALE

It is appropriate that the Knight should tell the first tale, since he is the highest in rank among the Canterbury pilgrims, but it is by chance that he comes to do so, drawing the shortest 'cut' in the Host's lottery. This happy coincidence of chance and desert is unobtrusively alluded to by Chaucer:

> Were it by aventure, or sort, or cas,
> The sothe is this, the cut fil to the Knyght (I.844–5)

Chaucer has a habit, on more serious occasions, of hanging a question mark over the causes of events in this way,[2] thereby expressing his own and his characters' preoccupation with matters of destiny, fortune and chance. 'Aventure' and 'cas' are not readily distinguished, but 'sort' has more association with that which is destined to be, and suggests to us that it is no accident that the man who is most worthy and proper to tell the first tale, were chance not invoked, is the man decreed by 'chance' to tell it. The relevance of all this, of course, is that chance and desert are the central themes of the Knight's Tale.

The tale is appropriate to the Knight in a broad and obvious way. The Knight's life, as we have seen it described in the General Prologue, has been mostly spent fighting, and the portrayal of his character is devoted to an exhibition of the typical traits of the chivalric ideal of the fighter:

> He was a verray, parfit gentil knight. (I.72)

His tale contains more formal fighting, both hand-to-hand combat

(1649–60) and ceremonialised mêlée (2599–651), than all the rest of Chaucer's poetry put together, and the values associated with chivalry in the description of the Knight,

> Trouthe and honour, fredom and curteisie (I.46)

are the values embodied in Theseus, forgotten by Palamon and Arcite, and formally acknowledged by Arcite in his dying speech:

> . . . trouthe, honour, knyghthede,
> Wysdom, humblesse, estaat, and heigh kynrede,
> Fredom, and al that longeth to that art. (I.2789–9)

The poem begins with glory in battle, with Theseus's victorious return –

> What with his wysdom and his chivalrie,
> He conquered al the regne of Femenye (I.865–6)

– and it ends with Theseus's commendation of Arcite's good fortune in dying at the very moment of winning glory by victory in battle.

Beyond this obvious congruence of tale and teller, however, it would be unwise to go. We know nothing of the Knight's 'character', and there is nothing in the telling of the tale to induce us to believe that it is intended to express the point of view or feelings or ideas of a particular 'character'. Attempts that have been made to argue otherwise, and particularly the attempt by Jones (1980) to argue that Chaucer's portrait of the Knight is ironically conceived as an exposé of the cold-blooded professional mercenary, and that his tale is a perversion of the values of chivalric romance and a glorification of tyranny and violence, are ill-directed. Such arguments are essentially the product of a desire to have Chaucer share modern views on the undesirability of fighting and killing people, and to recruit him to worthy liberal causes. It is true that Chaucer seems to have had little interest in fighting, or in the older heroic values attached to it, and that some indifference or scepticism concerning those values was current in his day,[3] but critical questioning of an established code of values is not at all the same thing as refutation, and as a historical phenomenon needs altogether subtler handling. In any case, arguments concerning the ironically self-revealing nature of the narrative are more than usually far-fetched in the case of the Knight's Tale, since the tale was written, as we have seen in Chapter 1, before the scheme of

The Canterbury Tales was devised, and probably as early as 1381–2, and allocated to the Knight with only cursory efforts at adaptation, certainly with no signs of the revision that would be needed to indicate character-revelation in the whole manner of the telling.

Chaucer probably became acquainted with the poem that provides the *matière* of the Knight's Tale, Boccaccio's *Teseida*, and with other works by the same writer, such as the *Filostrato* and the *Decameron*, in the late 1370s, perhaps as a result of his second visit to Italy (1378). The impact of the Italian writer upon Chaucer was profound, and for a number of years he worked under his stimulus and inspiration. The *Teseida* is used in the *Parliament of Fowls*, *Anelida and Arcite* and *Troilus and Criseyde*, as well as in the Knight's Tale, while the *Filostrato* provides the matter of *Troilus and Criseyde*, and the *Decameron* at least the suggestion of the *Canterbury Tales*. Dante seems to have existed somewhere nearer the periphery of Chaucer's consciousness, and was used for specialised purposes rather than as a general quarry. Boccaccio's work was more congenial to the predominantly secular English poet, and in its reflection of a brilliant and sophisticated urban culture and a wide classical learning it must have been a revelation to him after the English romances and French love-visions which had been his principal secular reading-matter in the vernacular up till now. Boccaccio is a spirited and wide-ranging writer, receptive to many influences and open to many points of view, a model of urbanity. As to poetic 'purpose', he is content to write, in the *Teseida* and the *Filostrato*, within the autobiographical convention of the despised and rejected lover, who hopes that his Fiammetta will see from his suffering lovers how much he himself suffers. We should not take this too seriously. To Chaucer it must all have been as refreshing as a Mediterranean holiday, with the further advantage that Boccaccio is not so great a poet as to deter imitation. He must have been drawn especially, in the first place, to the *Teseida*, as the very model of the new kind of English poetry he wished to write, since Boccaccio himself proclaims that his is the first poem in the vernacular to challenge the classics in portraying the deeds of Mars:

> ma tu, o libro, primo a lor cantare
> di Marte fai gli affanni sostenuti,
> nel volgar lazio più mai non veduti[4]

(But thou, O book, art the first ever to be seen to bid them [the Muses] sing in the vulgar tongue the deeds undertaken in the service of Mars.)

This pride and confidence in the vernacular is surely what inspired
Chaucer to believe that he could extend the range of English poetry and
his own poetic ambition in the same way, and truly come to the European
inheritance.

Boccaccio's *Teseida delle Nozze d'Emilia* was begun towards the end of
his long youthful sojourn in Naples and finished in Florence (1339–41).
It is an epic poem in twelve books, with exactly the same number of lines
(9896) as the *Æneid*. Its story is as follows:

> Theseus makes an expedition against the women of Scythia, wins
> victory in battle against them, and is married to their queen Ipolita
> (Book I). He returns to Athens, and immediately departs for Thebes,
> at the entreaty of the Greek widows, the bodies of whose husbands the
> new ruler of Thebes, Creon, will not permit to be buried: Thebes is
> sacked, and two royal Theban cousins, Palemone and Arcita, who are
> found nearly dead on the battlefield, are taken back to Athens and
> imprisoned (Book II). From their prison-window both see Emilia,
> Ipolita's younger sister, and both fall in love with her; Arcita is
> released from prison at the intercession of Teseo's friend, Peritoo, and
> leaves Athens (Book III). After many wanderings he returns to
> Athens, sufficiently disguised by his sufferings, and serves in Teseo's
> court under the name of Penteo (Book IV). Palemone hears of this,
> escapes from prison, and confronts Arcita in a grove where he is
> accustomed to sigh out his love; they fight, but are interrupted by a
> hunting party under Teseo, who decrees that they must join battle in
> the lists for the hand of Emilia in a year's time, with a hundred knights
> each (Book V). The year passes; the champions arrive, and are
> described at length (Book VI). The lovers and Emilia pray to their
> respective deities, and the battle is prepared for (Book VII). The battle
> is described at length; Arcita has the victory (Book VIII). Arcita is
> accidentally hurt, but nevertheless celebrates his victory and weds
> Emilia (Book IX). Arcita dies, with much circumstance (Book X). He
> is given an elaborate funeral (Book XI). Teseo recommends that
> Emilia and Palemone marry; they are married (Book XII).

Chaucer, whose general debt to the *Teseida* is well analysed by Pratt
(1941, 1947), reduces the poem to about a quarter of its original length.
He alludes only briefly to the events of Book I, reduces the battle against
Creon from over 250 lines (Book II, stanzas 51–83) to a mere fifteen
(985–1000), describes two representative champions, Lygurge and Emetreus (2128–78), instead of the whole concourse of Greek warriors (Book

VI), and does the battle as a comparatively brief general mêlée (2599–651) instead of as a series of individual combats in the epic manner (Book VIII). The traditional heroic and martial content of Boccaccio's epic is thus reduced to its bare essentials. Chaucer also removes nearly all the mythological allusions with which Boccaccio had larded his narrative. Boccaccio introduced these as part of his imitation of the classical epics of Virgil and Statius (the latter's *Thebaid* is his principal source and model), and, as further evidence of his desire to dress his poem in the trappings of antiquity, provided an elaborate series of glosses ('Chiose') and annotations, in which he explains allusions and moralises the mythological content of the poem in the manner of a medieval commentator. The relation between the poem and its moralising glosses, and the relevance of the latter to the interpretation of the poet's meaning, are matters of some interest and debate (see e.g. Hollander, 1977). Boccaccio was medieval enough to believe that the moralising commentaries on the classical poets elicited meanings that were actually there, though enough of a humanist to respond with delight to the grandeur, colour and spectacle of classical epic for its own sake. The poem is thus by the poet Boccaccio, and the glosses by the scholar Boccaccio: though the *Chiose* are more self-consciously moralistic than the commentary within the narrative, there is no essential conflict between the two. The very long explanations of the significance of Mars and Venus as supernatural 'figures' that are given in the *Chiose* to Book VII argue in traditional medieval terms that man's appetites, whether 'concupiscibile' (Venus) or 'irascibile' (Mars), are destructive unless ruled by reason. There are thus two Venuses, one residing in the impulse of sexual love when it is rationally directed towards marriage and procreation, the other residing in irrational passion or infatuation.[5] Likewise, there is a righteous anger governed by reason, out of which may grow the just war, and this is to be contrasted with the anger which is a kind of madness (*Chiose*, VII.30). The poem is mostly concerned with the ill effects of these different kinds of madness. The actions of Palemone and Arcita in loving where there is no hope of a happy outcome, and in fighting for such a love, are explicitly described as 'atti insani' ('mad deeds', Book III.2), and contrasted with the actions of Teseo, which are characterised throughout, in love and war, as those endorsed by reason. His battle against Creon is not taken up for vainglory nor to the neglect of his proper responsibilities,

ma a ragion rilevare in sua gloria. (II.47)

(but to elevate reason again in its glory)

These hints, reinforced as they are in the *Chiose*, are sufficient to secure the poem, despite its panoply of classical allusion, within a medieval moral framework.

There is no certainty that Chaucer knew the *Chiose* (they do not appear in all manuscripts), and though Boitani (1977, pp. 113–16) contests the view of Pratt (1945) that he did not know them there is every reason to believe that Chaucer would have found their systematic pigeon-holing of human behaviour unsatisfactory even if he had known them. In fact, his enthusiastic and energetic response to Boccaccio's two long poems, the *Teseida* and the *Filostrato*, has certainly something to do with their pagan and classical setting, and the opportunity they give for the exploration of the operation of chance, destiny and freewill in the affairs of men who live in a world without God.[6] Like Shakespeare in *King Lear*, he recognised the poignancy and power that were brought to this exploration if man were placed naked before the realities of his existence and the forces that seem to control it, and without the consolation of the faith that answers all such questions –

> What is this world? What asketh men to have? (2777)

– with the assertion of a higher state of understanding in which they are irrelevant. Boccaccio concedes to this higher understanding not only in his moralised glosses but also in depicting the ascent of Arcita's soul, after his death, to the eighth sphere. From there he looks down with scorn upon the littleness of the world, and condemns the vanity of its creatures, who, in the blindness of their souls,

> seguon del mondo la falso biltate,
> lasciando il cielo. (XI.3)

(pursue the false beauty of the world, unmindful of heaven).

Chaucer quite deliberately omits this passage, covering the omission with some brusque remarks concerning the possibility or propriety of predicting the destination of pagan souls (2809–14). He used the passage, subsequently, in *Troilus*, where he found it more difficult to hold to a view of events which was not explicitly Christian. Troilus's ascent to the eighth sphere is followed, inevitably it seems, by the Christian palinode to the poem. In the Knight's Tale, by contrast, the whole story is conducted according to the premises of pagan and classical belief.

Palamon's remarks about the pain that men may suffer after death (1319–21) and Theseus's description of the work of 'the Firste Moevere' (2987–3040) are entirely in accord with this system of belief.

Chaucer's model for these and other similar additions to Boccaccio's narrative is Boethius, whose *Consolation of Philosophy* is likewise an attempt to consider man's life within the context of classical beliefs. Boethius, though himself a Christian, chose to exclude the consolations of faith from his enquiry, and to concentrate on those qualities within man's will and reason through which he could choose to ally himself to a higher good, rise above the miseries incident to human life, and understand the dispensation of a benevolent providence in which all fortune and misfortune was, to the higher reason, alike good. Chaucer fell deeply under the influence of Boethius, and made his own translation of the *Consolation* at the same time that he was working on the Knight's Tale and the *Troilus*. He was drawn to the work because it asked serious questions about man's life, and about the freedom he has to choose his destiny, and answered those questions in terms of man's life, without invoking the mysteries of the scheme of salvation. It was not for him, of course, an alternative form of understanding, and there is nothing in the *Consolation* which is contrary or alien to Christian belief; but it was a philosophical system which he may have thought more fitted to his own preoccupations as a poet, and their predominantly secular cast. Like Dr Johnson he seems to have felt that the mysteries of the faith were a matter for the private man, not for the public poet.

It was with these considerations in mind that Chaucer turned to Boethius for help in the reshaping of Boccaccio's poem, and in so doing moved away from the moral physiology of human action, which is incipient in the narrative of the *Teseida* and fully explicit in the *Chiose*, towards a more philosophical sense of man's predicament. He gives long speeches to Arcite, exiled from the sight of Emelye, and to Palamon, left solitary in prison, in which they lament their fate in the manner of the exiled and imprisoned Boethius, or in the manner of those prisoners of Fortune whose obscured understanding of the higher providence is related by the Lady Philosophy.[7] Arcite, who finds that his apparent good fortune in being released from prison is really the misfortune of being deprived of even the sight of Emelye, comments bitterly on the reversals to which man, in his state of ignorance, is subject:

> Allas, why pleynen folk so in commune
> On purveiaunce of God, or of Fortune,

> That yeveth hem ful ofte in many a gyse
> Wel bettre than they kan hemself devyse? (1251–4)

This contrasts with the rather easy consolations he earlier offered to
Palamon (1081–91) when no occasion pricked him with a sense of his
own misfortune. Palamon himself has a grander and more eloquent
speech in which he questions the benevolence of the order of the
world:

> Thanne seyde he, 'O crueel goddes that governe
> This world with byndyng of youre word eterne,
> And writen in the table of atthamaunt
> Youre parlement and youre eterne graunt,
> What is mankynde moore unto yow holde
> Than is the sheep that rouketh in the folde?
> For slayn is man right as another beest,
> And dwelleth eek in prison and arreest
> And hath siknesse and greet adversitee,
> And ofte tymes giltelees, pardee.
> What governance is in this prescience,
> That giltelees tormenteth innocence?' (1303–14)

There is a power in this speech, both in the solemn and weighty
manner of expression and in the convincingly bleak picture of a world
ruled by a harsh determinism. The awareness granted to Arcite and
Palamon of their existence in a larger world of superhuman forces is
quite different from the various complaints offered by Boccaccio's two
young men, which centre on the thwarting of their hopes of love, with
only brief and conventional allusions to fortune, as in III.75–9, 84, IV,
5–17, 23–4, 80–88, V.9–12. Chaucer's effort here is to carry us into the
passion of such questioning, not to make us laugh at youthful folly (as
suggested by Robertson, 1962, pp. 105–10, 466). It is true that from a
lofty philosophical point of view they are showing a regrettable short-
sightedness in not recognising that everything is for the best, or at least
that everything is inevitable, but that point of view is something to be
come to through the experience of the poem, and through its embodiment of the wisdom of experience. Without that sense of process, of passionate challenge to the received order of things, and of growth of understanding that derives from suffering and blighted hope, the poem would
be an unmemorable lesson in conduct. Like Boethius, Chaucer knew
that the consolations of philosophy, and of a philosophical view of the

order of existence, were meaningful only to those who had struggled to them out of the need for them.

It is appropriate, therefore, that the young men should speak with the vehemence and passion of youth, and that Theseus should speak with maturer understanding of their folly,

> Who may been a fool, but if he love? (1799)[8]

He even finds something comic, 'the beste game of alle' (1806), in the spectacle of their fighting to the death for a lady who does not know they exist. But Theseus's maturity does not cause him to deny the reality of their passion, which he recognises as part of his own experience:

> A man moot ben a fool, or yong or oold, –
> I woot it by myself ful yore agon,
> For in my tyme a servant was I oon. (1812–14)

It is further appropriate that the wisdom of age, the battered resignation that comes from the surcease of passion, should be given, after Arcite's death, to Aegeus, the father of Theseus, in a speech which Chaucer, in a moment of inspiration, transferred from Teseo:

> 'Right as ther dyed nevere man', quod he,
> 'That he ne lyvede in erthe in some degree,
> Right so ther lyvede never man,' he seyde,
> 'In al this world, that som tyme he ne deyde.
> This world nys but a thurghfare ful of wo,
> And we been pilgrymes, passynge to and fro.
> Deeth is an ende of every worldly soore.'
> And over al this yet seyde he muchel moore . . . (2843–50)

We know how 'muchel moore' he would have said, and have an idea as to its content, and there is some temptation to smile at his vacuous logic (though it is taken directly from the *Teseida*, XII.6) and his toothless sense of the futility of life (surely life's pilgrims should be going somewhere, not passing *to and fro*?) in face of the easy release of death. The temptation is as natural as should be the stern effort to resist it, for Aegeus speaks out of an even greater wisdom of experience: he 'knew this worldes transmutacioun' (2839), just as cold Saturn 'knew so manye of aventures olde':

As sooth is seyd, elde hath greet avantage;
In elde is bothe wysdom and usage. (2447–8)

But Aegeus's wisdom does not have the last word in the poem, any more
than Saturn's solution to the conundrum of the plot provides the last act.
In his last major Boethian addition to the poem, Chaucer gives to
Theseus a final speech in which the problems of life and death, of chance
and destiny, are to be resolved.

There is no real dilemma for Chaucer here in the providing of the
philosophical resolution. The providential scheme approved by Boethius
(IV, prose 6, V, metre 1) and Dante (*Inferno*, vii. 72–96) has already been
outlined in a brief digression introduced to explain how Theseus, by
'chance', came upon the lovers fighting in the grove:

The destinee, ministre general,
That executeth in the world over al
The purveiaunce that God hath seyn biforn,
So strong it is that, though the world had sworn
The contrarie of a thyng by ye or nay,
Yet somtyme it shal fallen on a day
That falleth nat eft withinne a thousand yeer.
For certeinly, oure appetites heer,
Be it of werre, or pees, or hate, or love,
Al is this reuled by the sighte above. (1663–72)

What he has to do, it appears, is to present these traditional arguments in
a poetic form which will match in loftiness and serenity the vehemence
and passion of the counter-arguments that have been put forward, and
match too in logic the logic of events as they have unfolded. Chaucer's
answer is to graft on to the consolatory platitudes of Teseo (XII.7–19) an
opening address in which he calls upon Boethius (II, metre 8, III, metre
9, IV, prose 6 and metre 6) for his noble Platonic vision of a universe
bound by 'the faire cheyne of love' (2988, 2991). Within this universe, all
the elements unite in harmony, and all things bear witness, though in
their corruptible temporal form, to the incorruptible divine being from
which they are derived and to which they will be recalled in the due cyclic
process. Chaucer's grafting operation, though there have been many
opinions on it,[9] is not successful. The graft does not take: 'all things must
die', which is the theme of lines 3017–34, largely taken from the *Teseida*,
is not at all the same as 'all things derive from and return to the divine
being', which is the ostensible theme of 2987–3016 and 3035–40. Nor

does Chaucer seem to respond to the grandeur of the Platonic vision of
existence: he is content to speak of the 'progressiouns' and 'successiouns'
(3013–14) of the cycle of being in relation to things or to nature, but not
in relation to man. For man, the Platonic vision offers only the certainty
of a divinely ordered and eternal universe and the certainty of death at the
appointed time. The imperatives of the Christian scheme of redemption
inhibit any larger acquiescence in the Platonic-Boethian scheme, and the
language of consolation betrays an eschatological rather than a cyclic
view of things – 'this wrecched world' (2995), 'this foule prisoun of this
lyf' (3061). Chaucer's hesitancies and inconsistencies are entirely understandable, given that he is writing a serious poem – and therefore a poem
that inevitably seeks some place in the only intelligible scheme of things,
that is the Christian scheme – and not a classical charade. The recon-
ciliations and resolutions that he seeks are not easily achieved, and there
is a certain philosophical pathos in the evasions to which he resorts. It
may be a mark of his uneasiness that the speech, after its solemn and
pregnant opening lines, declines to occasional prosiness and chatter,

> Ther nedeth noght noon auctoritee t'allegge,
> For it is preeved by experience,
> But that me list declaren my sentence . . . (3000–2)
>
> Wel may men knowe, but it be a fool . . . (3005)
>
> This maystow understonde and seen at ye (3016)

as if Chaucer were retreating for security behind his usual barrage of
colloquial mannerisms, even though the context demands impres-
siveness and unbroken decorum above all else. It would be the modern
fashion to attribute the weaknesses of the speech to Theseus, as a
'dramatic' exhibition of his philosophical incapacities,[10] or to agree that
it is, like the 'degree' speech of Ulysses in Shakespeare's *Troilus and
Cressida*, a primarily political speech, designed to pave the way for the
grand alliance of Athens and Thebes with some rotund and impressive
platitudes. But the questions that the tale has raised, in Chaucer's
handling of it, make such interpretations seem something of an evasion.
    The seriousness of Chaucer's engagement with the narrative of the
Knight's Tale is what places so much strain on Theseus's speech, and it is
demonstrated in other ways than those that have already been discussed.
His handling of the 'supernatural machinery' of the *Teseida* is striking

testimony to his desire to stake out the story in an intelligibly ordered world. Boccaccio treats the classical deities in the classical way in the narrative, and then allegorises them, or some of them, in the *Chiose*. Chaucer throughout blurs the Mediterranean clarity of this treatment, and allows the classical deities to be understood as figures for planetary influences (Curry, 1926, pp. 119–63; Wood, 1970, pp. 62–76). The influence of the planets was well accepted in medieval lore as part of the agency of providence, and of destiny, its 'ministre general':

> Astrological reading of the power of the planet-gods is universally present in books of interpretation ... Belief in the stars' powers over men's destinies gave complete meaningfulness and often frightening truth to innumerable stories and conceptions of the power of pagan deities, which would otherwise have glanced off the shield of a different religious faith. (Tuve, 1966, p. 226)

The hierarchy of instrumentality placed the planets, in particular conjunctions and stellar configurations, as the causes of certain 'accidents', and the causes of certain dispositions in man through which he was induced though not compelled to certain acts. When Saturn is first mentioned, it is as a planetary influence rather than as a god, an influence which Arcite interprets as fully deterministic:

> Fortune hath yeven us this adversitee.
> Som wikke aspect or disposicioun
> Of Saturne, by som constellacioun,
> Hath yeven us this, although we hadde it sworn;
> So stood the hevene whan that we were born.
> We moste endure it; this is the short and playn. (1086–91)

Chaucer makes a major change in the representation of the temples of Mars and Venus so as to make a planetary interpretation possible. Where in Boccaccio they are described as the actual places to which the prayers of Arcita and Palemone ascend (VII.29, 50), in Chaucer the temples are represented as painted on the walls of the oratories dedicated to the respective deities and built into the circumference of the tournament-theatre. They remain, that is, part of the world in which the characters believe themselves to exist, but not one to which we are required to give assent. The recurrent emphasis on the temple-paintings as something seen ('Yet saugh I ... Yet saugh I ...') may be quite out of keeping with the long-forgotten 'dramatic' character of the narration, and quite at odds with the magnificent poetic realisation of an actual temple of Mars, full of noise and tumult (1975–94), but it is an important part of Chaucer's strategy here. So too, in the description of the temple of Mars, he adds to the traditional images of war, violence, and sudden death, which are themselves evoked in poetry of horrific power, a string of more homely misfortunes:

> Yet saugh I brent the shippes hoppesteres;
> The hunte strangled with the wilde beres;
> The sowe freten the child right in the cradel;
> The cook yscalded, for al his longe ladel.
> Noght was foryeten by the infortune of Marte
> The cartere overryden with his carte;
> Under the wheel ful lowe he lay adoun.
> Ther were also, of Martes divisioun,
> The barbour, and the bocher, and the smyth,
> That forgeth sharpe swerdes on his styth. (2017–26)

An astrologically minded audience would have recognised immediately the technical references to astrological influence ('infortune', 'divisioun') as well as the allusion to the pictures of 'the children of Mars' that commonly appeared in astrological treatises and other sources as mnemonics of planetary influence (Kean, 1972, pp. 25–6; Salter, 1983, p. 164). The one scene in which the gods actually appear in conversation, that in which Saturn offers to stint the strife of Mars and Venus (2438–78), is dominated by the similar description of the planetary influence of Saturn:

> My cours, that hath so wyde for to turne,
> Hath moore power than woot any man.
> Myn is the drenchyng in the see so wan;
> Myn is the prison in the derke cote;
> Myn is the stranglyng and hangyng by the throte,
> The murmure and the cherles rebellyng,
> The groynynge, and the pryvee empoysonyng;
> I do vengeance and pleyn correccioun,
> Whil I dwelle in the signe of the leoun. (2454–62)

All this is new in Chaucer, as is the entire role allotted to Saturn (in Boccaccio, Venus herself, with Mars' agreement, fetches Furies from the underworld to unseat Arcita, IX.4), and the effect here is to turn the conversation into a figurative account of the operation of planetary influences, rather like Chaucer's own *Complaynt of Mars*.

It is Saturn, therefore, who brings about Arcite's fall (2684–5), and Saturn too whose influence takes him to his grave. The extended account of the process of his death has often been castigated as improperly or even ludicrously technical:

> The vertu expulsif, or animal,
> Fro thilke vertu cleped natural
> Ne may the venym voyden ne expelle.
> The pipes of his longes gonne to swelle,
> And every lacerte in his brest adoun
> Is shent with venym and corrupcioun.
> Hym gayneth neither, for to gete his lif,
> Vomyt upward, ne dounward laxatif. (2749–56)

There is not, to be sure, much to smile at here, though something to ponder on in the reference to the inactivity of the 'vertu expulsif' if we recall that this 'vertu' was, in astrological medicine, under the power of Saturn.[11] There are it seems, no accidents, and the fates of men are determined by forces to which they unwittingly subject themselves.

Throughout the poem, Chaucer removes Boccaccio's many references to the classical cosmos, to Hades, Dis, Styx, and the rest of the pagan paraphernalia, and substitutes allusions to Fortune or to the influences of the planets. He does not in this way change the fabric of the story, nor explicitly assert an interpretation which will be more intelligible to a medieval reader, but he does impregnate the story with the hints of a deeper meaning, at the same time that he eschews allegory completely. Chaucer does not rush to deny the reality of the story as he receives it from Boccaccio. On the contrary, it is the strength of the story as a 'machine' for the demonstration of man's power, or lack of power, over his destiny that draws him irresistibly towards it. He invests himself, as a poet, fully in the action, and gives majestic expression to its ceremonies and pageantry – the heroic chivalry of Theseus setting out for Thebes (975–84), the beauty of Emelye (1033–55), the temples of Venus, Mars and Diana, into which he gathers much new material from the *Roman de la Rose*, Ovid, and Statius (1918–2088), the preparations for the tournament (2483–598), the battle (2599–651), and the funeral of Arcite (2913–66), to which he draws added attention by his pretence of hurrying over it. Much of this writing is in a declamatory or panegyric or otherwise heightened style which we have grown used to not expecting of Chaucer, but the energy of his engagement with his unaccustomed matter is undeniable, and the Knight's Tale, as a poem, is perhaps Chaucer's *tour de force*.

At the same time, Chaucer's innovations in the handling of the narrative hint at deeper meanings, at an 'argument' that lies behind the celebration of the ceremony and rituals of 'the noble life'.[12] It is important to observe the infiltration of astrological significances into the accounts of the classical deities, and important also to notice the care with which Chaucer identifies the propitious planetary hour (2217, 2271, 2367) at which the three petitioners attend with prayer their tutelary deities (see Curry, 1960, pp. 124–6, 138–9). The sense is not one of appropriate dedication, as it is in Boccaccio, where Arcita and Palemone, after general religious observance, pay special respects to Mars and Venus (VII.23, 42); but one of special and innate relationship. Their gods figure their destiny, but in a very real sense too they figure their character.[13] Palamon has a gift of love, which is early recognised and derided by Arcite as 'affeccioun of hoolynesse' and contrasted with his own 'love, as to a creature' (1158–9). Arcite thus chooses a lesser good, yet claims it as a greater good, and his prayer shows a similar boldness and rashness. He asks for victory, and victory alone,

> 'Yif me victorie, I aske thee namoore' (2420)

and demands of future events that they be constrained to his will by this victory in granting him Emelye. Palamon is more far-sighted, more conscious of the greater goal which he seeks, and of the unpredictable means by which it may be achieved:

> 'I kepe noght of armes for to yelpe,
> Ne I ne axe nat tomorwe to have victorie,
> Ne renoun in this cas, ne veyne glorie
> Of pris of armes blowen up and doun;
> But I wolde have fully possessioun
> Of Emelye, and dye in thy servyse.
> Fynd thow the manere hou, and in what wyse'. (2238–44)

He is, in the poem's terms, the more likely postulant; in terms of its argument, he shows a consciousness, albeit only fitful, of a 'divinity which shapes our ends', where Arcite thinks he alone may 'rough-hew' them.

The distinction in the prayers of the two is part of a quite profound pattern of change that Chaucer has wrought throughout in Boccaccio's story. One purpose has been to isolate Palamon and Arcite as emblematic or exemplary characters, suitable for a demonstration of the workings of providence. The 'realism' of the Knight's Tale has often been remarked upon (e.g., Robertson, 1915), and one can certainly point to many ways in which Chaucer has 'realised' the events of the tale in terms of medieval life. It is Chaucer who has Palamon and Arcite discovered by 'pilours' (1007) on the battlefield, and who speaks of 'raunsoun' (1024) being denied. His accounts of the feast before the tournament (2197–2205), and of the tournament itself, with the bustle and business of the heralds (2533, 2599), are packed with detail of the most vividly realistic kind, detail that his audience would be struck by from their experience of the feasts and tournaments they had been to or had read about. In this way the story is drawn within the context of idealised medieval experience. In other ways, though, the events of the story and the behaviour of the characters are made more distant, more remote from everyday experience: above all, the characters are remote from each other, almost like elemental beings propelled by forces beyond themselves. Muscatine (1950, pp. 61–2), who recognises the absence of 'characterisation', in the usual sense, in the Knight's Tale, and recognises too the bewilderment of earlier critics at its absence, finds himself here in unexpected agreement with Robertson (1962), who sees the characters functioning as exemplars and their speeches as 'revelations of moral character or statements of principle rather than psychological revelations' (p. 270). Boccaccio, by contrast, is consistently attentive to the literal circumstances of his narrative, and his characters respond to events and make decisions in a natural and human way. Palemone escapes from prison because his servant Panfilo has come across Arcita complaining of his love in a grove near Athens; he fears Arcita may have stolen an advantage, and he knows where to find him. All this attention to the why and the how is passed over by Chaucer, in favour of sudden and unexplained impulse, and the operations of chance or destiny on mysteriously momentous days (see McCall, 1961):

> It fel that in the seventhe yer, in May,
> The thridde nyght, (as olde bookes seyn,
> That al this storie tellen moore pleyn)
> Were it by aventure or destynee –
> As, whan a thyng is shapen, it shal be –
> That soone after the mydnyght Palamoun,
> By helpyng of a freend, brak his prisoun. (1462–8)

The meeting in the grove is a complete coincidence. Earlier in the poem, when Boccaccio's Arcita leaves Athens, he makes various peregrinations through Greece, and it is when a boat from Athens comes into the harbour, and he hears of the death of Theseus's son Achates, who was to marry Emilia, that he decides to return to Athens. In Chaucer, Arcite returns to Thebes, which of course is now a merely symbolic place, having been razed to the ground in the late wars, as Boccaccio reports (IV.12), and he stays there, suffering the ravages of a love which is explicitly described as an affliction, 'rather lyk manye' (1374), until visited in a dream by the god Mercury. The command he is given is cryptic, and fraught with fateful irony:

> 'To Atthenes shaltou wende,
> Ther is thee shapen of thy wo an ende.' (1391–2)

The arrival of the Greek warriors for the tournament is described by Boccaccio with an enormous wealth of circumstantial detail. He even tells us why certain famous heroes are not there. In place of this, Chaucer gives two extended portraits of the champions Lygurge and Emetreus, who have been convincingly shown by Curry (1960, pp. 130–7) and by Brooks and Fowler (1970, pp. 130–4) to be quasi-symbolic represen-tations of Saturnalian and Martian types, with the characteristic physiog-nomy and colouring associated in astrology with the influence of the two planets. Everywhere there are signs, symbols, portents, and a constant current of allusion to forces at work that lie beyond mere circumstance. The action of the poem takes place on certain days of evident but unexplained significance, and Chaucer makes every effort to give a similar significance to the locus of action[14] of the poem. Thebes is miraculously renewed as a symbolic place of exile and despair, and Theseus makes a point of having the lists built in the very grove where the lovers were found fighting, as if to assert by that act the civilised and ceremonial ordering of ungoverned animal impulse. 'In the middle of the wilderness an area is set off to be devoted to a ceremonial activity of civilized society' (Halverson, 1960, p. 615). It may be observed, inci-dentally, as not entirely uncharacteristic of Chaucer that, having made this striking innovation, he seems unfortunately to forget about it when he follows Boccaccio later in having Theseus assign Arcite's funeral to be held in the self-same grove (2860).

As to the characters, Chaucer removes from them almost every trace of the mundane and familiar. Emelye, especially, is reduced to a cipher, a

mere trigger for impulse in others. In Boccaccio, Emilia plays a full part
in the action. She knows that she is being gazed at by the two young men
in prison and returns to the garden frequently to enjoy their attentions
(III.19); she takes a compassionate farewell of Arcita when he goes into
exile (III.83); recognises him and communicates with him when he
returns disguised (IV.54); spends the whole year in the company of the
two lovers in the Athenian court while they await the great tournament
(VI.9) – where Chaucer has them return for the year to Thebes, 'with his
olde walles wyde' (1880); laments the blood shed on her account at the
tournament (VIII.94–110); prefers Arcita (VIII.127); courteously frees
Palemone when he is made her prisoner after his defeat (IX.65–75); has a
long conversation with the dying Arcita (X.52–85), and a discussion with
Teseo about the proposed marriage with Palemone (XII.39–42).

By contrast, Chaucer throughout systematically depersonalises
Emelye. Her appearance in the garden, where she is first seen by the
young men, is described by Chaucer almost explicitly as a paradisal
vision of innocent sexuality surrounded and hallowed by the images of
springtime:

> Hir yelow heer was broyded in a tresse
> Bihynde hir bak, a yerde long, I gessc.
> And in the gardyn, at the sonne upriste,
> She walketh up and doun, and as hire liste
> She gadereth floures, party white and rede,
> To make a subtil gerland for hire hede;
> And as an aungel hevenysshly she soong. (1049–55)

But Emelye herself, in this superb poetic realisation of the power of her
beauty, is unaware of anything but her 'observaunce' (1045).
Throughout the poem, she knows nothing, feels nothing, wants nothing,
except to remain a virgin, and the only time she is shown actually
speaking is when she makes her prayer to Diana. She exchanges not a
single word with either lover, and at Arcite's death simply shrieks in
company.

Such systematic reshaping is not the result of mere economy,
especially when other parts of the poem, such as the temple scenes, are
rendered in full or expanded. The effect is deeply impersonal: Emelye is
not a woman with whom Palamon and Arcite fall in love, but the agent
through which powerful forces are released and find their way to
destruction or resolution. 'Love' is not the subject-matter of the poem,
rather the fuel that drives the machine of its plot.

The subordination of Emelye has its effect too in shaping our response to the two lovers. There have been many attempts (e.g., Fairchild, 1927; Frost, 1949, pp. 295–7) at an interpretation and differentiation of the two, but one of the dominant impressions we have, as French (1949) and Muscatine (1950, pp. 61–6) point out, is that they are not to be differentiated. In Boccaccio, Arcita is the hero, the centre of the action, and both he and Palemone are portrayed with the greatest generosity. Arcita sees Emilia first, but nothing is made of this, and there is harmony between the two lovers during the summer they spend gazing at Emilia out of the prison window. A touch of jealousy affects Palemone when Arcita is released (III.60), but they take a tender farewell. Though Palemone occasionally suffers renewed pangs of jealousy (V.2), he says explicitly that he means Arcita no harm (V.8). Their reunion in the grove is initially joyful, and it is only when Palemone insists on precedence in loving Emilia that the quarrel starts. Arcita points out how futile it is to fight over something neither can possess (remarks given to Theseus by Chaucer), but unwillingly agrees to Palemone's demand for battle, lamenting how all Thebes is brought to an unhappy end. He sorrows over Palemone when he thinks he has killed him, but Palemone behaves very churlishly on recovering (V.73). Arcita wants peace, is respectful of his commitment to both love and friendship, is prepared to let time find a solution. Palemone, by contrast, is said to be driven by the madness and wild fantasies of his jealousy (VI.3). As the tournament begins, the relationship between them, and their place in the reader's estimation, is well communicated in the contrast between Arcita's long speech of love for Emilia (VII.122) and his address to his followers, claiming his prior right of love and asserting his own desire to have solved things peacefully (VII.136), and, on the other hand, the passing remark that Palemone spoke to much the same effect (VII.128, 145). The poem is the tragedy of the noble Arcita, struck down by the arbitrary dictates of fate.

The changes wrought by Chaucer are striking, and in some respects quite shocking. The behaviour of his Palamon and Arcite has little of nobility or generosity to commend it. Their vows of sworn brotherhood are forgotten as soon as they are aware that they are rivals, and the remark made when they are arming for battle –

> Everich of hem heelp for to armen oother
> As freendly as he were his owene brother (1651–2)

is ironic in its obliviousness that they are indeed more than brothers. There is little to choose between them, and Arcite's sophistries in arguing that he should have precedence, or that there is no such thing as precedence,[15] are as deplorable as Palamon's second thoughts about the order in which he would have Theseus slay them:

> But sle me first, for seinte charitee!
> But sle my felawe eek as wel as me;
> Or sle hym first, for though thow knowest it lite,
> This is thy mortal foo, this is Arcite. (1721-4)

On occasions their fortunes are deliberately placed in the balance of the reader's judgement, the implication being that the reader will not readily be able to decide between them:

> Yow loveres axe I now this questioun,
> Who hath the worse, Arcite or Palamoun? (1347-8)

As the story moves to its climax, the impression is created, in the account of the prayers in the temple, that the equality of Palamon and Arcite in desert and merit is an impasse which only a trick of fortune will circumvent. It seems that Chaucer has deliberately levelled the two in the reader's opinion, so that the outcome of the story will appear not even nobly tragic but bleakly capricious. Much in the handling of the story would support this impression, and Chaucer's addition to the description of the temples of the further images of suffering and menace so vividly analysed in Salter (1983, pp. 155-68), especially the statue of Mars –

> This god of armes was arrayed thus.
> A wolf ther stood biforn hym at his feet
> With eyen rede, and of a man he eet (2046-8)

– increases the sense of a world in which man is at the mercy of unintelligible powers outside himself. Arcite's dying question seems very much to the point:

> What is this world? What asketh men to have?
> Now with his love, now in his colde grave
> Allone, withouten any compaignye. (2777-9)

The familiarity of that last line as a conventional tag has been often remarked, most interestingly by Bennett (1947, pp. 83-4), but it is put here to miraculous effect, suggesting, in its homely and rather naive memory of the nature of life, the eternal and empty loneliness of the grave.

A number of things in the poem, however, work against the starkness of this impression. One is Theseus, who is actually portrayed as more human than the other characters, despite the impersonality of his role, and who has the control of his passions to allow him to respond to the ladies' pleas for mercy. His maturity, though, even that ability to change his mind which Elbow (1973, pp. 79–89) rightly signals as a mark of mature rationality, chiefly consists in his power to view the ups and downs of other people's lives with equanimity.[16] This is not quite the answer to the questions Arcite was asking. It may be, of course, that the questions are sufficiently answered elsewhere, and by Arcite himself. 'What is this world?' he asks, and we may remember his own account of the world as the struggle of competing appetites:

> 'And therfore, at the kynges court, my brother,
> Ech man for hymself, ther is noon oother.' (1181–2)

'What asketh men to have?' is his other question, and the answer comes with the force of still more recent experience:

> 'Yif me the victorie, I aske thee namoore'. (2420)

With this in mind, it may be opportune to remind ourselves that, in the strictest sense, Arcite's fate is his own responsibility, since it was Palamon who saw Emelye first and Arcite who deliberately denied, with a barrage of false arguments, Palamon's prior claim and explicit, formal assertion of that claim. This may seem a fine point, but the law is full of fine points,[17] and it is the law of destiny, that is, the order that underlies apparent chaos, that Chaucer is deducing for us from the story. The change here from Boccaccio, whose hero Arcita it is who sees Emilia first, is not casual or whimsical. It is clearly a decisive move on Chaucer's part, and the reason for it seems obvious: it is Arcite who is made responsible for the first release of disorder through ungoverned impulse because it is Arcite who dies. Men do not die in reality beause of lapses of this kind, and even in romances they sometimes survive, like Sir Gawain; but romance stories characteristically pitch their representation of life at the extreme edge of expectation, where a man lives or dies by a single word or deed. This is not to say that the strength of the poem's argument is dependent on the single change which I have emphasised. There is much in the account of planetary influences to suggest that Arcite's act in asserting appetite and will was 'in character'.

There is, finally, after many subtle strengthenings of the thread of argument, and much to test its strength – for Chaucer gives full force to the impression of blind fortune – a momentous confirmation of it in Arcite's dying speech, which can best be called a heroic act of penitence. He prefaces it, after his more traditionally rhetorical outburst on the sorrows of life and the stern appearance of death, with some deliberateness (2780–2), and then continues:

> I have heer with my cosyn Palamon
> Had strif and rancour many a day agon
> For love of yow, and for my jalousye.
> And Juppiter so wys my soule gye,
> To speken of a servaunt proprely,
> With alle circumstaunces trewely –
> That is to seyen, trouthe, honour, kynghthede,
> Wisdom, humblesse, estaat, and heigh kynrede,
> Fredom, and al that longeth to that art –
> So Juppiter have of my soule part,
> As in this world right now ne knowe I non
> So worthy to ben loved as Palamon,
> That serveth yow, and wol doon al his lyf.
> And if that evere ye shul ben a wyf,
> Foryet nat Palamon, the gentil man (2783–97)

Arcite here acknowledges that the fault is in him, and that the 'strif and rancour' have been due to his 'jalousye' in love. He rehearses the qualities of the true servant of love and chivalry, attributing them to Palamon, but associating himself again with them, after long neglectfulness, through his act of renunciation, as if in a litany of commemoration. By adjuration and prayer, not by claim of right, he commends his soul to the higher power of Jupiter,[18] not Mars, recognising in this act the existence of a providential power which lies beyond the immediate instrumentality of passion and circumstance. Finally, in the most moving line of the poem, he gently commends the noble Palamon to Emelye:

> 'Foryet nat Palamon, the gentil man'.

This of course is what Boccaccio's Arcita, amidst much wordy compliment and self-congratulation, also does. Chaucer has brought Arcite to the same point: the difference is that he has brought him there the hard way. He shows us too the act of will by which Arcite finally asserts man's power over circumstance and his ability to rise above the claims of his appetite. Theseus speaks later of the wisdom of making virtue of necessity (3041–2), which sounds like a form of pragmatism. Arcite here demonstrates the true nature of that virtue in its voluntary and willed activity. Theseus provides a mere epilogue to the poem's action, which effectively ends with Arcite's last words, and his long speech has something of the quality of a chairman's closing remarks after the main speaker has had his say. There is nothing very comforting about Arcite's sudden acquisition of wisdom in the face of death, but nevertheless his act of will has a quite different exemplary significance from the gift of posthumous vision which is granted to Boccaccio's Arcita and Chaucer's Troilus. It gives to the 'argument' an essentially positive conclusion.

There is much more in this great though somewhat uneven poem that deserves exposition and comment, but a final word may be reserved for the style of narration. Many opinions have been expressed concerning the frequent lapses into colloquialism and triviality which apparently mar the decorum of the high style of romance. The use of homely images and proverbs (e.g., 1261, 1522, 1533, 1809–10, 1838, 2759–60) has been castigated as incompetence or applauded as subtle irony at the expense of the narrator's incompetence. There are moments of apparent levity, in the midst of serious matter, such as the remarks about the destination of Arcite's soul, already quoted (2809–15), or the aside concerning the rites of Diana's temple,

> But hou she dide hire ryte I dar nat telle,
> But it be any thing in general;
> And yet it were a game to heeren al.
> To hym that meneth wel it were no charge;
> But it is good a man been at his large[19]

which have been similarly interpreted as incompetence or irony, or as part of the clash of styles through which Chaucer disrupts conventional expectation and embodies in his poem a fuller vision of reality. Those who find such lines and passages incongruous usually detect some satiric or ironic purpose on Chaucer's part, as does Baum (1958, pp. 84–104), but Muscatine (1950), speaking of the lightness of tone in the two passages flanking Arcite's death-speech (2759–60, 2809–15), warns the critic to be on his guard 'not to convert a deftly administered antidote to tragedy into an actively satiric strain' (p. 77). Over-alertness to irony, and unfamiliarity with rhetorical modes of narrative, has probably led to misinterpretation in certain other passages (e.g., 1459–60, 2273, 2835), and many modern readers may find obtrusive the constant chatter of *abbreviatio* (e.g., 994, 1000, 1188, 1210, etc.) and *transitio* (e.g., 1334, 1449, 1488, 1661, etc.). It is hard to think of such empty lines contributing anything significant, in themselves, as Kean (1972, pp. 63–8) argues, to the narrative, but they are so much part of Chaucer's characteristic style of narrative in romance, as well as dream-vision, that they cannot be dismissed as a peculiarity of the Knight's Tale, or a mark of its incompetence, or as in some way appropriate to the character of its teller. What we have here, rather, is Chaucer's version of the familiar and unbuttoned style of narrative that he learnt early from the English popular romances,[20] and habitually used with his own modifications from the *Roman de la Rose* and other works, when he wished to distance himself as author from the matter of a narrative, and to take on the role of mere reporter of other men's stories. It is not a mark of inadequacy on his part, or of insufficiency in the literary language, but part of his strategy of indirection. Chaucer assumes no role of responsibility in relation to the content or interpretation of his story, but meanwhile, under the guise of innocence, he works to elicit the full meaning of the story, as story, and to impregnate it with the seeds of argument.

THE SQUIRE'S TALE

The story that the Squire tells, or begins to tell, is one of pure romance, and is the kind of story one would have expected of an amorous bachelor-knight. It seems to have been concocted by Chaucer from his miscellaneous reminiscences of tales of the East, such as the legends of Prester John, and other sources. It tells of the present delivered to Cambyuskan, King of Tartary, and his daughter Canacee on his birthday feast – a magic horse, a magic mirror, a magic ring, and a magic sword – and of the first use to which the ring is put, in enabling Canacee to understand the complaint of a lovelorn lady-falcon and to comfort the bird in her distress. The only connection between the two episodes is the magic ring, though the Squire's enthusiastic proposals for the continuation of his story, which he presents just before he is interrupted by the Franklin, show that the episodes will eventually be woven into a longer narrative, as was the custom in the longer medieval romances, with their 'interlaced' or 'polyphonic' structure (Vinaver, 1971, pp. 68–98). The story celebrates the nobility of the king, the beauty of his daughter, the courtesy of the ambassador, the richness and refinement of court-life, and, in the episode of the falcon, delicacy of feeling and the importance of 'trouthe' in love. There is also much emphasis on marvels and the sense of wonder, and there were to have been some battles.

In all these respects, the Squire's Tale affirms its kinship with the Knight's Tale and the Franklin's Tale, as indeed one would expect, since the former is told by his father and the latter by the man who would like to be his father (see V.682–6). The values implied and presented for our admiration are the same, namely those of romance. There are similarities of treatment, too, reflecting Chaucer's own individual reception of the genre. The setting is again pagan (see lines 17–18), and the handling of the supernatural or supposedly supernatural machinery again, as in Knight's Tale, I.2807–8, and Franklin's Tale, V.1139–51, 1261–96, betrays an inclination to scepticism and rationalisation. The ambassador himself explains the 'magic' horse, in a rather unromantic way, as a piece of advanced technology (128–31), and the explanation of the horse offered by one of the curious bystanders is strikingly reminiscent of the Franklin's Tale:

> '. . . for it is rather lyk
> An apparence ymaad by som magyk,
> As jogelours pleyen at thise feestes grete.' (217–19)

This later description (189–262) of the crowd that swarms round the presents, debating how they work and how they were made, is one of the two finest and most characteristically Chaucerian passages in the Tale, full of bustle and vitality and cleverly contrived allusion to horses, mirrors, swords and rings of the past. The hubbub of conversation and speculation is vividly conveyed,

> 'Myn herte,' quod oon, 'is everemoore in drede;
> I trowe som men of armes been therinne,
> That shapen hem this citee for to wynne.
> It were right good that al swich thyng were knowe.'
> Another rowned to his felawe lowe,
> And seyde, 'He lyeth . . .' (212–17)

and recalls the similar scene before the tournament in the Knight's Tale (2513–22). The narrator's general attitude to this speculation is rather like the Franklin's – dismissive, suggestive of superior knowledge yet doubtful of any value that can be attached to so-called 'modern science':

> They speken of sondry hardyng of metal,
> And speke of medicynes therwithal,
> And how and whanne it sholde yharded be,
> Which is unknowe, algates unto me. (243–6, cf.258–61)

The tone of 'algates unto me' (246) implies the valuelessness of what is not known to the speaker, rather than the modesty of ignorance.

In another respect, too, the Squire's Tale has a distinctively Chaucerian narrative tone, or mode of address, characteristic of the Knight's Tale and to a lesser extent of the Franklin's Tale, though not confined to them. This is the habit of passing over or purporting to pass over some opportunity for narrative amplification, whether by apologising for the speaker's inadequacy to describe something (34–41), or by stating that something is impossible to describe (61–74), or by stating that the one man who might describe it is dead (278–87). There are a number of other devices of a similar kind that are used by Chaucer, deriving from rhetorical figures like *occupatio* (Faral, 1923, pp. 233, 354) and from what Curtius (1953) classifies as *topoi*, or 'topics', of modesty and inexpressibility (pp. 83–5, 159–62). They are not uncommon in medieval literature, and Chaucer seems to have had a fondness for them, principally as ways of making us conscious of the act of narration and thereby complicating our response to what is narrated.

The Squire, therefore, does no more than his father did, and as we pointed out there, consciousness of the act of narration is not the same as interest in the character of the narrator. However, there is a temptation in reading the Squire's Tale, and one which the present writer has not resisted in the past, to see something more in these confessions of inadequacy – to see them, namely, as signs, ironically planted by Chaucer, of real inadequacy on the Squire's part.[21] The clues to this irony are supposed to be in the unusual concentration of such modesty formulae in the first part of the Tale, and in the aptness of the Squire, as a young man (and the only youngster on the pilgrimage), to be portrayed as a greenhorn in such matters. Once the clue to the presence of irony has been detected, of course, everything starts to seem a sign of the Squire's incompetence or stupidity, and a joke at his expense. The elaborate emphasis on the proper behaviour and sense of decorum of the ambassador (89–109) shows the Squire self-consciously rehearsing the elementary principles of etiquette he has painfully memorised as part of his recent education. The extensive use of astronomical periphrasis, another form of rhetorical dilation, shows him not the expert he thinks he is:

'This has to be parody ... The Squire wanders in his maze of astrological detail ...' (Wood, 1970, pp. 98–9). There is a very unnecessary account of why people need sleep and have bad dreams after drinking heavily (347–59), as if the Squire could not resist dragging in his little knowledge of medicine. And just as his expressions of modesty show that he has a good deal to be modest about, so his remarks about the need to get to the point of a story betray his own labouring consciousness that he has not got to the point of his, or maybe that he has not got one:

> The knotte why that every tale is toold,
> If it be taried til that lust be coold
> Of hem that han it after herkned yoore,
> The savour passeth ever lenger the moore,
> For fulsomnesse of his prolixitee;
> And by the same resoun, thynketh me,
> I sholde to the knotte condescende,
> And maken of hir walkyng soone an ende. (401–8)

So it could go on.

Reservations are expressed throughout this book about the validity and value of such an approach, especially when it is designed to make a tale conform to modern tastes by 'ironising' the narrator. Even when the motive is no more than to give interest to an otherwise not very interesting tale, the approach must be suspect on every methodological ground. The temptation to salvage a wreck must be recognised as a mere reaction to the dispersive tendency of Chaucer's style in tales that lack a commanding centre of attention. In other words, those features of style that are held and made effective within the orbit of the narration in tales with a dominant theme or point, like the Knight's Tale, may slip out of focus and seem directionless, or independently directed, in a tale like the Squire's Tale (or the Physician's Tale, or the Manciple's Tale, and perhaps one or two others). The drift of this argument, of course, is towards accepting that Chaucer sometimes nods, as is recognised in a sensible recent pronouncement on the matter in general:

> It must be conceded that the layered narration of the *Canterbury Tales* invites this dramatic ironic reading ... The problem in the *Canterbury Tales* is that the critic's convenience quickly develops such a potency as to become a universal solvent. All is irony and negation. (Lenaghan, 1974, p. 34)

The awkwardnesses that have been described would, on this reading, be laid more appropriately at Chaucer's door than at the Squire's, as well as certain definite signs of drowsiness (e.g., 305–8).

Resistance to a 'dramatic ironic' interpretation is easier in the second part of the Tale, where the story of the falcon betrayed in love is told with sympathy and poignancy. It is a 'silly' story, of course, and the modern reader may be excused his smirk at the picture of Canacee circling the tree apprehensively with the lap of her skirt extended to catch the bleeding falcon (441), or at the falcon's opening words:

> 'That pitee renneth soone in gentil herte,
> Feelynge his similitude in peynes smerte,
> Is preved alday, as men may it see,
> As wel by werk as by auctoritee.' (479–82)

But anyone who cannot sternly suppress such inappropriate reactions is unlikely to get any appropriate pleasure out of medieval romance, which is full of things like this. To have faith is to be rewarded with a touching story of woman's true love, and a beautifully observed portrait of the philanderer:

> As I best myghte, I hidde fro hym my sorwe,
> And took hym by the hond, Seint John to borwe,
> And seyde hym thus: 'Lo, I am youres al;
> Beth swich as I to yow have been and shal.'
> What he answerde, it nedeth noght reherce;
> Who kan sey bet than he, who kan do werse?
> Whan he hath al wel seyd, thanne hath he doon. (595–601)

The theme of the woman betrayed in love is one to which Chaucer frequently recurs, but nowhere is there quite such an effective combination of tenderness and bitterness as in the falcon's story, which at one or two points, for all its simplicity, strikes as keenly to the heart as the tale of another departure and betrayal in *Troilus and Criseyde:*

> Wher me was wo, that is no questioun;
> I kan nat make of it discripsioun;
> For o thyng dar I tellen boldely,
> I knowe what is the peyne of deeth therby. (579–82)

It is hard to see how Chaucer could have returned to the world of the first part of the Tale after this. In the absence of any other explanation, perhaps this will do to explain why he left the Tale unfinished. Neverthe-less, he does allow the Squire to end with a promise of what is to come:

> But hennesforth I wol my proces holde
> To speken of aventures and of batailles,
> That nevere yet was herd so grete mervailles.
> First wol I telle yow of Cambyuskan,
> That in his tyme many a citee wan;
> And after wol I speke of Algarsif ...
> And after wol I speke of Cambalo ...
> And ther I lefte I wol ayeyn bigynne. (658–63, 667, 670)

It is still difficult to take this ending seriously, and Kean (1972, p. 64) allows the possibility of a joke 'against the Squire's literary ambition'. That Spenser (*Faerie Queene*, IV.ii.32) and Milton (*Il Penseroso*, 109) felt able to take it seriously ought to act as a restraint on a humorous response, one must admit. But the language of the promises is so extravagant, the future of the tale so remote from our experience of its past, that one is reminded irresistibly of the student who, in the absence of the promised essay, produces a hopeful and elaborately tabulated 'plan'. It seems likely that Chaucer, in the whole passage, is portraying the Squire as somewhat confused about the future development of his story. Returning to the story he had left unfinished, Chaucer adapted it to the *Canterbury Tales* by adding an impossible scenario for its continu-ation and then having it 'dramatically' interrupted. He seems to have used a similar technique with the unfinished Monk's Tale, and the late addition to the Clerk's Tale shows how little worried Chaucer was by discontinuities of mood between tale and frame.

The Franklin now emerges in a new and rather engaging light. Having listened with something approaching dismay to the Squire's sketch of his threatened epic, he decides to rescue himself, the rest of the company, and the Squire by pretending that he thinks the story is over:

> 'In feith, Squier, thow hast thee well yquit
> And gentilly. I preise wel thy wit,'
> Quod the Frankeleyn, 'considerynge thy yowthe,
> So feelyngly thou spekest, sire, I allow the.' (673–6)

As Coghill says, 'the Squire, gathering himself for an almost endless recital, is choked by the praises of the Franklin'.[22] It takes some confidence on the Franklin's part to do this, as well as some public spirit, for he runs the risk of being thought either an ignoramus (for not realising the tale was not finished) or a boor (for interrupting it). The Franklin relies on the good opinion others have of him, which is not a bad preparation for the spirit of the Tale that follows.

THE FRANKLIN'S TALE

The basic story of the Franklin's Tale is well-known to folklorists as the tale of 'The Damsel's Rash Promise'. It is a favourite type of folk-tale, that in which the influence of alien, inhuman or 'bad magic' (an image of forces at work in human life which appear to be beyond human power) is reversed and defeated by the 'good magic' of human love, fortitude or fidelity. (The Wife of Bath's Tale belongs to a closely related type.) Chaucer may have known the story before he came across it in Boccaccio's *Decameron* or *Filocolo*, but there are a number of parallels between the Franklin's Tale and the latter versions which suggests that they may constitute a direct source.[23] The occasion for the telling of the story in Boccaccio's romance is a courtly gathering where various questions of love are presented in the form of stories and debated under the presidency of Fiammetta, who acts as 'queen'. Menedon tells the story of a beautiful and loving wife who is so pestered by the attentions of an unwelcome suitor, Tarolfo, that she decides to put him off for ever by asking him to do something for her – a request he is bound to agree to – which will be impossible. She will grant him all her love, she promises, if he can make a garden bloom in January. Much to her dismay, he manages to do this, with the help of Tebano, a plant expert. Not knowing what to do, she confesses everything to her husband, who calmly tells her that she should keep her promise: it will be a warning to her not to make such promises in the future. She adorns herself for the assignation, but Tarolfo is so impressed by the husband's generosity that he gives up his claim on her. Tebano, in his turn, foregoes the rich reward he had been promised. Which of the three, asks Menedon, at the end of his story, showed the greatest generosity? The husband, answers Fiammetta, since he gave up what was most to be prized, his honour, where Tarolfo and Tebano gave up only lustful desires and wealth, respectively. Menedon disagrees: the husband gave up nothing voluntarily, because he was bound by the terms of the promise; Tarolfo gave up something he had yearned and laboured for; but Tebano gave up more, the wealth which would have rescued him from the grinding misery of poverty. Fiammetta, in conclusion, points out that the husband was under no obligation, since his wife's promise was invalidated by her previous marriage-vow. What he gave up, furthermore, was a man's most precious possession, the honour that comes from having a chaste wife. Tebano, meanwhile, if he were a sensible man, would have welcomed a return to virtuous poverty.

Chaucer keeps the question,

> Which was the mooste fre, as thynketh yow? (V.1622)

but abandons the debate about the answer. The Canterbury pilgrims are perhaps not quite the company for such a debate, and in any case his treatment of the story makes it something quite different from Boccaccio's conundrum. Boccaccio tells the story, in the *Filocolo*, as an elaborate anecdote, designed principally to provide the occasion for the high-flown casuistry that follows. No-one is much moved by what happens: the calm and businesslike manner of the husband and the lady's thoughtfulness in beautifying herself for the meeting with Tarolfo are nicely contrasted with the near-speechless grief of Arviragus and Dorigen at the same points in the Franklin's Tale. The debaters do not in any sense take the story seriously: though Fiammetta argues that the husband showed the greatest generosity, she comments also in passing that 'he behaved less than prudently' (Havely, 1980, p. 159), thus demonstrating that the terms in which she commends his action are purely those of the game that is being played. Chaucer, by contrast, gives to the three main characters a full and at times quite moving emotional response to the predicament in which they find themselves, especially Dorigen, and shows all three acting from the noblest and most high-minded motives. Even Aurelius seems to be seeking release from a mortal torment rather than following out his lustful desires. Furthermore, the nature of the promise is changed in a most significant way. In a word, Chaucer makes the story into a 'romance', and in so doing releases again some of its traditional powers.

The Franklin introduces his tale as a 'Breton lay' (709–15), a type of medieval romance characterised originally by the delicacy of its treatment of love-relationships, the presence of magic, and the absence of any very strenuous engagement with strictly moral issues (such as the marital status of lovers). Marie de France established the form in her collection of *Lais*, claiming to have drawn her *contes* from the *lais* made by the Bretons:

Les contes ke jo sai verrais,
Dunt li Bretun unt fait les lais,
Vos conterai assez briefment.[24]

The claim may be partly true, but her chief reason for making it is to distance the tales from their contemporary audience and to explain how such excursions into a world of fantasy and enchantment come to arise. The Breton lay, its features somewhat coarsened, became popular in England, and the name was often attached to short romances of independent origin but similar type – or what the authors hoped would look similar. Chaucer's knowledge of the form is derived from English examples, and perhaps from two in particular, *Sir Orfeo* and *Lai le Freine*, the latter taken directly from Marie de France's *Le Fresne*. Both appear in the Auchinleck manuscript (c.1330–40), a famous literary miscellany which may even at one point, as Loomis (1941) suggests, have been in Chaucer's hands, and they have a common prologue which states the origins and nature of the Breton lay in a manner quite like Chaucer's. There is no need to assume, as is often assumed, that the Breton lay was 'old-fashioned' in Chaucer's time, and the idea that it was thereby suited to the 'noble but old-fashioned tastes of the white-bearded Franklin' (Loomis, 1941, p. 16) is pure fantasy. However, Chaucer's insistence on the antiquity of the form, if not of the taste for it, is important. In telling the tale, he takes care to emphasise the remoteness of the time in which the story is set. It is a pre-Christian era, as is shown by the prayer of Aurelius to Apollo (1031–79) and by the Franklin's comments on the astrological magic of the Clerk of Orleans, which he characterises as

swich folye
As in oure dayes is nat worth a flye, –
For hooly chirches feith in oure bileve
Ne suffreth noon illusioun us to greve. (1131–4)

He later speaks of the deceitful and mischievous operation of such magic,

As hethen folk useden in thilke dayes. (1293)

Aurelius's name suggests Roman or immediately post-Roman times, but Chaucer would be content with 'a long time ago' and not much worried about the anachronistic university of Orleans. We are, it will be seen, in the same twilight world as within the Knight's Tale, where the characters behave in a high-minded, quasi-Christian way (Dorigen's address to 'Eterne God', 865, is entirely ambiguous), but without the immediate moral constraint on their actions, or upon the evaluation of those actions, that comes with 'doctrine'.[25] Chaucer's emphasis on the location of the tale in Brittany is also unusually prominent, both in personal names (Arviragus, Dorigen) and in place-names (Armorik, Pedmark, Kayrrud), and seems similarly intended to create a sense of distance and remoteness, of happenings in the world of high romance.

Chaucer's careful arrangements for the reception of the tale might seem to set it on course as a demonstration of the idealised values of truth and *gentillesse* in operation in the traditional romance style. But the course of romance, in Chaucer anyway, never did run smooth, and there are a number of interesting complications that hinder a simple and straightforward reading, some of them concocted by modern critics, some of them real enough. One problem has been the debate about the extent to which the character of the Franklin informs the telling of the tale, the degree to which its opinions and values are to be attributed to him as a character, and the effect of this on our acceptance or rejection of them. For Kittredge (1915, p. 207), the Franklin is the one who brings the 'marriage-debate', begun by the Wife of Bath, to a close, telling a tale which demonstrates that wedded happiness rests not on the sovereignty of either one party or the other but on 'mutual love and forbearance'. It is his character as a practical, sensible, experienced man of the world that compels acceptance of his views:

He is no cloistered rhetorician, but a ruddy, white-bearded vavasour, a great man in his neighbourhood, fond of the good things of life and famous for his lavish hospitality ... When *he* speaks of mutual forbearance and perfect gentle love between husband and wife, we listen with conviction. The thing is possible. The problem need puzzle us no longer. (Kittredge, 1915, p. 210)

For Robertson (1962, pp. 470–2; 1974), on the other hand, the Franklin is a pleasure-loving, self-seeking upstart, whose famous hospitality is simply a way of impressing prospective clients and patrons. He prates on in the introduction to the Tale about his admiration for the Squire and his *gentillesse*, but he has no understanding of what *gentillesse* really means, and only talks about it so as to cut a dash with his social superiors. He gives himself away by comparing his desires for his own son's better 'discrecioun' with his desires for 'twenty pound worth lond' (683). His idea of marriage is a thing of appearances only, a typical bourgeois-sentimental compromise which tries to combine passionate love with the institution of marriage, as if you could eat your cake and have it too, and the Franklin is too stupid to realise how the tale collapses his illusion about his ears. To his final question a tart reply may be returned: Arviragus's 'freedom' consists in being 'free' with what he has no right to be free with anyway, namely the honour and chastity of his wife, who is bound to him, as Gaylord (1964) argues at length, by prior and inalienable vows; Aurelius's 'freedom' consists in being 'free' with what he had no right to make a claim to in the first place, namely, the honour and virtue of another man's wife (and who can suppose that there is much to admire in his giving up a pleasure from which all savour must have been extracted once the husband had ratified it and assigned a place and time thereto?); and finally the clerk's 'freedom' consists in being 'free' in waiving his right to a sum of money he had won by a trick – for we are never told that the rocks were actually removed, only that they 'semed' to be away (1296).

There is little historical support for the view of the Franklin as a member of a class of bourgeois *parvenus*, as Pearcy (1973–4), Specht (1981) and Coss (1983) make clear, and it will be seen that the interpretation outlined above derives chiefly from a very jaundiced reading of the description of the Franklin in the General Prologue (especially 'Epicurus owene sone' – surely a hyperbolical little jest), and the application of this reading, without sense of context, to his Tale. It is a good example of the excesses of a thoroughgoing 'dramatic' reading of the *Tales*, where every tale becomes primarily an act of self-revelation on the part of its teller, and where the whole apparent meaning of a story is reversed once we recognise how the tale is intended to expose some inadequacy in its teller. Gaylord (1964), for instance, comments on the 'finesse' that enables Chaucer to create a tale 'exceeding its ostensible teller's capacity to understand' (p. 332), and congratulates Chaucer on having reached a point 'where a whole tale can be turned back against its teller to comment satirically on his character and the values he represents' (p. 334). Some objections to this kind of reading have already been entered (as at note 12 in Chapter 2), but it may be stressed again that the weakness of systematic ironisation is that it simplifies the text in an intolerably reductive manner, and substitutes meanings that derive from the critic's own specialised views for the free and complex play of the author's mind.

Nevertheless, one must acknowledge in the Tale the presence of a narrative 'voice', essentially a variation on Chaucer's characteristic style of narration in romance. It is, principally, the voice of the plain man, the 'burel man' (716), whose disclaimers of skill in rhetoric (716–28), themselves a figure of rhetoric, serve to endorse the truthfulness of the tale-telling and to expose the simplicity of the narrator's relationship to his material. The brusque explanation of the content of a periphrasis (1015–18), paralleled in the rhetoricians and in Chaucer's own *Troilus and Criseyde* (ii.904–5), serves likewise as a disarmingly self-conscious indication that the narrator knows the difference between rhetoric and plain speech, and that he has his feet on the ground.

Another aspect of the narrative voice is a certain impatience or amusement in dealing with extravagant emotion. This is how Dorigen's grief at her husband's absence is described:

> For his absence wepeth she and siketh,
> As doon thise noble wyves whan hem liketh.
> She moorneth, waketh, wayleth, fasteth, pleyneth . . . (817–19)

There is no mistaking the heaping-up of synonyms, and the inevitable effect created that she is overdoing things. But this is felt as a reaction to events of the story by the teller of the story, not as a criticism of Dorigen which is embedded in those events. Likewise, there is a rather impatient reaction to the narrative of Aurelius's love-stricken grief:

> He was despeyred; no thyng dorste he seye,
> Save in his songes somwhat wolde he wreye
> His wo, as in a general compleynyng;
> He seyde he lovede, and was biloved no thyng.
> Of swich matere made he manye layes,
> Songes, compleintes, roundels, virelayes,
> How that he dorste nat his sorwe telle,
> But langwissheth as a furye dooth in helle;
> And dye he moste, he seyde, as dide Ekko
> For Narcisus, that dorste nat telle hir wo. (943–52)

The juxtaposition of Aurelius's speechlessness with his torrential poetic output (the listing, again, of specific verse-forms is stylistically important), the disingenuous *he seyde*, are not without a certain mischievousness. So too the dismissive remark with which the narrative of Aurelius's grief is concluded:

> Lete I this woful creature lye;
> Chese he, for me, wheither he wol lyve or dye. (1085–6)

It must be stressed that these are not authoritative moral judgements upon a would-be adulterer – nothing of the kind is ever said, and in fact Aurelius is loaded with admiring epithets (931–4) – but passing reactions to the matter of the story as given. It is not the Franklin's Tale, but a tale that the Franklin happens to be telling.

A third characteristic of the narrative voice is the bluff scepticism concerning astrological magic, which is dismissed, as we have seen, as pagan mumbo-jumbo and 'supersticious cursednesse' (1272). Associated with this are protestations of ignorance concerning such matters.

> I ne kan no termes of astrologye, (1266)

and a fair display of the appropriate technical terms (1273–96). The rhetorical effect of such disclaimers has already been described, and it can be seen that they contribute too to the sense of a difference between the narrator's time and the time of the story. They serve here an additional purpose. The disappearance of the rocks is the one unaccountable event in the Tale: did they disappear, or did the clever clerk simply look up the tide-tables and predict the next spring tide? The Franklin's smoke-screen of disbelief covers Chaucer's tracks well. It does not *matter*, but one of the great arts of narrative is in dealing unobtrusively with the things that do not matter.[26]

The problems of the Franklin's Tale, therefore, do not reside in the Franklin. The Tale is what it is however conscious we may try to make ourselves of his presence. The difficulty is more intrinsic, and has to to do with the discrepancy we are aware of between the story, as story, and the ideal values of truth and *gentillesse* that it purports to be a triumphant vindication of.

There are some apparent awkwardnesses which can readily be disposed of. It is no objection, for instance, to the idealism of the opening account of the marriage to say that there is something radically wrong about an arrangement which one of the parties does not wish to acknowledge in public:

> And for to lede the moore in blisse hir lyves,
> Of his free wyl he swoor hire as a knyght
> That nevere in al his lyf he, day ne nyght,
> Ne sholde upon hym take no maistrie
> Agayn hir wyl, ne kithe hire jalousie,
> But hire obeye, and folwe hir wyl in al,
> As any lovere to his lady shal,

Save that the name of soveraynetee,
That wolde he have for shame of his degree. (744–52)

Marriage is both a public and a private contract, and the former is
nothing without the latter. Arviragus respects the former and cherishes
the latter, and does not wish to change the world. (Maybe the world is
changed by a multitude of private acts such as his.) The modern reaction
to *shame* as an unworthy motive for action, something one is 'ashamed
of', is out of place; *shame* is the spur to honourable acts, and honour is not
the same as honesty, if honesty be understood to include telling the truth
whether or not you are asked. (Agravain's accusations against Lancelot
and Guenevere, in the *Morte D'Arthur*, are true, but there is no sense that
he is behaving anything but maliciously or dishonourably in making
them.) The account of the marriage, generally, is clearly intended to be
recognised as an account of an ideal marriage. Jill Mann (1982, p. 136)
points to the use of generalisation in the passage (e.g., 768–70) and
comments:

'The use of the plural, the appeal to the general, is indeed an invitation
to readers to bring their own experience and feelings to bear, but it
invites them to an identification with the narrative, not to a critical
dissociation from it.'

Likewise, it is not to Arviragus's discredit as a loving husband that he
leaves his wife after a year or two of wedded bliss to go off to England,

To seke in armes worshipe and honour. (811)

Though it may not mean much to a modern reader, this is his obligation
as a knight, and if he neglected it, it would be as much to Dorigen's
dishonour as his own, as Brewer (1973b, p. 6) points out. Chrétien de
Troyes, in his romance of *Erec*, make it clear that the wife whose husband
goes off on 'adventures' has nothing to complain about: it is the wife
whose husband does not go off on adventures who has the problem.

No: the substantial difficulty in the way of a simple reading of the
story, as a demonstration of an ideal marriage in action, is the *dénouement*, where Arviragus commands his wife to go off and commit
adultery because of a rash and foolish promise she has made, and in so
doing denies a great truth in order to serve, as we may feel, a petty truth,
in addition to behaving in a wholly ridiculous and unlikely manner.

There are many things that a decent and sensible man in his situation could have done, and this is not one of them. An intolerable strain is placed on any straightforwardly naturalistic reading of the Tale by Arviragus's action, despite the resounding generalisation with which he concludes:

'Trouthe is the hyeste thyng that man may kepe'. (1479)

We do not need to be told what St Augustine said about the sanctity of the marriage-vow or about the nullity of rash promises that involve sinful conduct (Gaylord, 1964, p. 351), nor that 'under canon law a man who consents to the adultery of his wife is to be denied Holy Communion perpetually' (Robertson, 1974, p. 77), for we appreciate perfectly clearly that Arviragus's act is not that of a sensible man, not even a sensible pagan, and we understand that the world in which such acts are admired is not the world of ordinary reality.

Yet we do understand that his act is to be admired, that it is the demonstration in action of some ideal code of behaviour. There appears to be, therefore, a conflict between the general 'feel' of the story and the creakiness of the hinge on which it turns. It is a not uncommon experience for the reader of Chaucer. What Chaucer often seems to be doing is to take a conventional form of story and to render it with an intense quality of imaginative engagement, so that the enigmatic nature of the story as a representation of the matter of experience and reality is brought into sharp focus, and the reader is stimulated to unexpected feats of perceptual tolerance. What he does here is to give to a romantic fairy-tale a degree of dramatic realisation which takes us at least momentarily out of the realm of romance into that of domestic tragedy – rather as *Cymbeline* and *The Winter's Tale* inhabit for a time the world of *Othello*.

There is, throughout the early part of the Tale, dramatic realisation of a high order. The account of the marriage of Arviragus and Dorigen, and particularly of the patience and mutual forbearance that make it so successful and harmonious (761–90), is so close to what we recognise as the realities of such a relationship that we are drawn to share in the narrator's pleasure in it, in a manner quite different from our response to superficially similar lines in the Merchant's Tale (IV.1337–41):

Who koude telle, but he hadde wedded be,
The joye, the ese, and the prosperitee
That is bitwixe an housbonde and his wyf? (803–5)

Dorigen's grief at her husband's absence seems natural and understandable in this context, and her obsession with the black rocks, which she
can only see as a threat to her husband's safe return, takes root in a most
convincing way. What she says is not 'reasonable', if looked at from the
point of view of the higher reason:

> But, Lord, thise grisly feendly rokkes blake,
> That semen rather a foul confusion
> Of werk than any fair creacion
> Of swich a parfit wys God and a stable,
> Why han ye wroght this werk unresonable? (868–72)

but it is 'in character', and is communicated with the power of felt
experience, like the outbursts against destiny from Palamon and Arcite
(I.1251, 1303), and from Troilus (IV. 958–1082), at similar moments of
personal crisis. Chaucer would expect us to be aware of the philosophical
context for and corrective to such an outburst, but he does not encourage
us to see Dorigen as sinful, or even as silly and hysterical, which is what
Robertson (1974) and others argue. It is an aberration which she gives
way to under the stress of emotion, a failure of self-discipline, a proud
impulsiveness, which makes her momentarily forget the order of things
(see Benjamin, 1959) which man must accept, and live by: we understand it as such, and of course she herself sees it for what it is when the
rocks are, apparently, removed:

> 'Allas,' quod she, 'that evere this sholde happe!
> For wende I nevere by possibilitee
> That swich a monstre or merveille myghte be!
> It is agayns the proces of nature.' (1342–5)

The scene in the garden, again, is done with perfect fidelity. Dorigen's
answer to Aurelius comes from the deep simplicity of truth and loyalty:

> But now, Aurelie, I knowe youre entente,
> By thilke God that yaf me soule and lyf,
> Ne shal I nevere been untrewe wyf
> In word ne werk, as fer as I have wit;
> I wol been his to whom that I am knyt. (982–6)

The ten monosyllables of that last line are as starkly and honestly
assertive as they could be. But the obsessive nature of her preoccupation
with the black rocks leads her to promise her love to Aurelius if he can

remove them. She does this 'in pley' (988), the kind of playfulness, that is, in which we find some release for our deepest anxieties, like Criseyde's remark about her fear of the Greeks (*Troilus*, ii.124). Chaucer's change in the terms of the promise, his most brilliant single stroke in his rehandling of the narrative, gives to it a poignant irony, for Dorigen's promise allows momentarily for the destruction of all that she holds most dear. Her lack of 'patience' makes her mistake illusion for reality (the rocks were never, in reality, evil) and gives the illusion power:[27] Aurelius seizes on the letter of the promise, acquiesces in the illusion, reinforces it by invoking the further power of illusion (1139–64), and forgets the reality of human love and loyalty which it is left to Arviragus to reassert. Dorigen anticipates none of this as a consequence of her promise, of course, and immediately after making it she declares that it is meaningless:

> For wel I woot that it shal never bityde.
> Lat swiche folies out of youre herte slyde.
> What deyntee sholde a man han in his lyf
> For to go love another mannes wyf,
> That hath hir body whan so that hym liketh? (1001–5)

Her question is rather unexpected: in its naïveté, it reveals something of the depth and transparency of perfect fidelity, and is a good example of Chaucer's power of giving imaginative pressure to conventional situations, of realising, making *real*, aspects of behaviour which are usually, and necessarily, taken for granted in medieval romance.

There is much else that one could point to as demonstrating the quality of dramatic realisation in the Tale. The portrayal of the magician's skill in proving himself a skilful magician, and the right man for the job in hand, is an example, an almost gratuitous exhibition of Chaucer's delight in his own poetic powers. The young clerk greets the two brothers 'in Latyn' (1174) – a very potent sign – knows what they have come for before he is told, and whets Aurelius's appetite with a show of illusions, of the stage-tricks of the 'tregetour' (1143), which ends with Aurelius dancing with his lady. Best of all, this is done casually, with no apparent effort, for at the end he claps his hands to dispel the illusion like an early Prospero –

> And farewel! al oure revel was ago (1204)

– and calls his attendant to ask whether supper is at last ready, as if he has been merely passing the time while waiting for his dilatory kitchen staff to get the dinner on the table. Who could resist such careless mastery?

But of course this kind of vivid dramatic reality cannot be offered to the final scene of the story, since Arviragus's actions are by any standard of normal realistic behaviour quite preposterous. Danger threatens:

> The greater the air of naturalness such a story is given, the greater the risk of exposing its unnaturalness. (Baum, 1958, p. 129)

What Chaucer does, recognising the danger, is to shift course back to romance, to modulate from the ominous key of impending tragedy to the optimistic harmonies of romance. It is something he does with consummate skill, as does Shakespeare when faced with similar problems in *The Merchant of Venice* or *The Winter's Tale*. The transition is effected stylistically, through Dorigen's long *compleynt* (1355–456). Instead of treating Dorigen's plight, now that the rocks have (apparently) been removed, with the sense of dramatic verisimilitude given to earlier phases of the story, Chaucer drops her back into the flat plane of conventional romance in this elaborate and wholly improbable complaint. The complaint is isolated, as a rhetorical set-piece, and done in a formal rhetorical manner, and thus tends, as Sledd (1947) argues, to draw the reader away from any close emotional participation in the action: the effect is rather similar to the effect created by the insertion of the three formal portraits of Diomede, Criseyde and Troilus in *Troilus and Criseyde* (v.799–840). Furthermore, no-one can read the complaint, as it develops over 'a day or tweye' (1457), with twenty-two *exempla* of 135 ladies, without at least a twinge of amusement. Dorigen has long had a tendency to dramatise herself, and there is nothing unreal or psychologically implausible about that: but now she behaves like the melodramatic heroine of a bad Italian opera. She even seems to lose track of what she is talking about: as she rifles through her repertoire of examples she gets further and further from wives and maidens who preferred death to dishonour, which is her ostensible theme, and at the end she is simply talking about faithful wives, ending with the imperishable three:

> The same thyng I seye of Bilyea,
> Of Rodogone, and eek Valeria. (1455–6)[28]

There may be some vestigial psychological plausibility in this, Dorigen's meditation tracing the process, illogical but inevitable, by which she comes to her decision to tell her husband about everything,[29] but what Chaucer is doing here, essentially, is to distance us from Dorigen, so that we think more and more of her as a character in a story. She was always this, but not so much so.

Chaucer completes this subtle modulation from impending tragedy to romantic fantasy with his reminder to the reader that nothing untoward is going to happen:

> Paraventure an heep of yow, ywis,
> Wol holden hym a lewed man in this
> That he wol putte his wyf in jupartie.
> Herkneth the tale er ye upon hire crie.
> She may have bettre fortune than yow semeth;
> And whan that ye han herd the tale, demeth. (1493–8)

There is evidence that these six lines were introduced in revision (they are in Ellesmere but not in Hengwrt), as if Chaucer became aware of the need to make this slight change in the 'tuning' of the tale, to add something to the enigmatic optimism of Arviragus's consoling line,

> It may be wel, paraventure, yet to day. (1473)

This view of the telling of the story as a matter of 'tuning' and 'modulation' is a way of being true to the strong sense of *performance* in Chaucer, the sense not of resolved positions being demonstrated and exemplified, but of difficult feats brilliantly accomplished. This is how it is *this time*. He is a virtuoso narrator, who loves taking stories to the brink of expectation. Henry James, of course, criticises writers who interrupt a narrative with comments about what might or might not happen, and what the reader should think,[30] but he was looking for a different engagement of the reader with the story, and one which seems to have been, on the whole, unmedieval. What happens to the reader here is that he receives an assurance of the genre of the story, and how all will end happily, and how he can admire, in the manner proper to romance, the principles on which Arviragus so high-mindedly grits his teeth, and settle to share in the delight of a world in which good nature and generosity seem to spread like an infection. Happy endings are important, especially when there are tales like the Merchant's in our mind.

Whether this account of the *dénouement* of the story in terms of narrative technique is quite satisfactory I am not sure. It seems to explain how but not why, and the story, with the resonances it has set up, is more than this explanation allows, more than a skilfully brewed storm in a teacup. David Aers (1980, pp. 160–69) takes the story seriously, in a way that may be helpful. For him the Franklin's Tale is an exploration of the gulf between utopian aspiration (concerning marriage) and the actual emergence of that aspiration in the impoverished reality of an egotistic and male-dominated society. The satisfaction at the end is all the Franklin's, who welcomes the assertion of male values of privilege and authority, even though he has enjoyed toying with the fantasy of mutuality. The difficulties in embodying that fantasy in language that makes sense are again the Franklin's.

What is unsatisfactory about this explanation is, first, the pressure placed on a literal reading of Arviragus's decision that Dorigen should keep her promise. Such a reading, as I have suggested, is not on, and Chaucer, by the detail of his handling of the story, shows that it is not. Nevertheless, romance has its own kind of access to reality, and Arviragus's action signifies something important. It is this: that the keeping of truth is a form of trust. Arviragus, like Dorigen, had a choice, and chose truth and trust: she granted to Arviragus the keeping of her love and honour, as he had given over the same to her at their marriage, while he chose truth for truth's sake alone, trusting to who knows what providence, whether that of John 8:32 ('the truth shall set you free') or that of Chaucer's own Boethian poem, *Truth*: 'And trouthe thee shal delivere, it is no drede'. Trust, the voluntary giving over of self, the hostaging of the will, breeds trust, and changes the world – in stories. It is, as Mann (1982, p. 146) calls it, a 'surrender of the self which miraculously releases power'. Arviragus seems to recognise this. It is the kind of perennial insight that traditional stories often embody: a promise kept is a reassertion of civilisation, of the primacy of human values, over the blind forces of nature,[31] of black rocks, or of the dark wintry season. As Aurelius's magician prepares his apparatus of illusion, the world, at 'the year's midnight', grows cold and lifeless:

> Phebus wax old, and hewed lyk laton,
> That in his hoote declynacion
> Shoon as the burned gold with stremes brighte;
> But now in Capricorn adoun he lighte,
> Where as he shoon ful pale, I dar wel seyn.
> The bittre frostes, with the sleet and reyn,
> Destroyed hath the grene in every yerd. (1245–51)

But even at this nadir of the year's fortunes, there is present a sense of warmth and hope and life:

> Janus sit by the fyr, with double berd,
> And drynketh of his bugle horn the wyn;
> Biforn hym stant brawen of the tusked swyn,
> And 'Nowel' crieth every lusty man. (1252–5)

The world in winter is sustained by the promise of spring, and renewal – or the hope of redemption, as Donaldson (1958, p. 926) says, making explicit the Christian undertone in this extraordinarily evocative piece of writing (prompted, be it observed, by the brief description of the garden in winter which is a mere part of the plot-mechanism in Boccaccio) – and it is similar acts of trust that constitute and preserve the fabric of human society and civilised values. The story as Chaucer tells it embodies in poetic form this perception of reality.

The other defect of Aers's interpretation is his insistence on validating his reading by ironizing the role of the Franklin. The difficulties of such an approach have been indicated: as a way of validating a preferred reading, it succeeds only by turning all readings into expressions of preferred opinion. Thus the attempt to express the equality of relationship between Arviragus and Dorigen is seen by Aers as a series of incompetent subterfuges on the part of the Franklin to keep the language of authority whilst fantasising about mutuality:

> Heere may men seen an humble, wys accord;
> Thus hath she take hir servant and hir lord, –
> Servant in love, and lord in mariage.
> Thanne was he bothe in lordshipe and servage.
> Servage? nay, but in lordshipe above,
> Sith he hath bothe his lady and his love;
> His lady, certes, and his wyf also,
> The which that lawe of love acordeth to. (791–8)

There may be problems in finding a language to describe what is being described, and perhaps line 793 is a little neat, but they are Chaucer's problems, not the Franklin's. It is perhaps not too hard to follow what Chaucer is saying: that 'equality' is, as Mann (1982, p. 139) puts it, the alternate exercise and surrender of power, where sometimes one will take the lead, sometimes the other. Chaucer may be seen as trying to write a reply to the cynical analysis of the marriage-relationship by Ami in *Le Roman de la Rose* (9391–462). And after all, a vocabulary to express a truly loving mutuality of human relationship is not so easily come by. If we wish to see Chaucer searching for a positive language of this kind, we can look to Book III of the *Troilus*, where a sense of fragile, delicate equilibrium is conveyed, with a strong sexual suggestion:

> For ech of hem gan otheres lust obeye (iii.1695)

There are echoes of this language in the Franklin's Tale – 'Thus been they bothe in quiete and in reste' (V.760) more or less repeats *Troilus*, iii.1680, 'And thus they ben in quyete and in reste' – but generally the language through which Chaucer searches here has a more traditional moral connotation: perhaps the language of emotional maturity is inevitably moral. He begins with the courtly commonplaces of the *Roman de la Rose* and of Boccaccio (761–70), and much of what he says here could be returned to the 'game of love' and to the ironic contexts from which it is derived. But the last lines (768–70), on 'wommen' and 'men', like the earlier reference to 'freendes' (762), have a different, more direct and general quality, as Chaucer embarks now on his account of the true 'civilisation of the heart':

> Looke who that is moost pacient in love,
> He is at his avantage al above.
> Pacience is an heigh vertu, certeyn,
> For it venquysseth, as thise clerkes seyn,
> Thynges that rigour sholde nevere atteyne.
> For every word men may nat chide or pleyne.
> Lerneth to suffre, or elles, so moot I goon,
> Ye shul it lerne, wher so ye wole or noon;
> For in this world, certein, ther no wight is
> That he ne dooth or seith somtyme amys.
> Ire, siknese, or constellacioun,
> Wyn, wo, or chaungynge of complexioun
> Causeth ful ofte to doon amys or speken.
> On every wrong a man may nat be wreken.
> After the tyme moste be temperaunce
> To every wight that kan on governaunce. (771–86)

'Lerneth to suffre' is the key command here: it has a steely ring. Winter, we may remember, is a traditional image of patient *suffraunce*, as when Langland speaks in *Piers Plowman* (C.XII.185–208) of the winter-sown seed which is (spiritually) tougher than the spring variety. A religious dimension is present ('Love is patient', I Corinthians 13:4) and is made explicit in the Clerk's Tale:

Lat us thanne lyve in vertuous suffraunce. (IV.1162)

But here it remains implicit, as Chaucer struggles to disentangle a human truth from a vocabulary dominated by moral and religious ideas. He also draws away from the familiar exploration of those ideas by amatory poets, for instance the recommendation in Machaut's *Dit dou Lyon*, that the lover who wishes to win his lady should suffer humbly all that she sets him to:

> Mais par souffrir l'estuet conquerre
> D'aucun bon cuer qui soit si frans
> Qu'adès soit humbles et souffrans;
> Car autrement estre conquise
> Ne puet, tant soit bien entreprise. (ed. Hoepffner, 1911, 2040–4)

These are tactics in the game of love: but Chaucer is talking about 'men' and 'women' in the conduct of their everyday lives, as Kean (1972, p. 145) makes clear: 'The Franklin places the difficulty of establishing such a relationship firmly in the day to day annoyances and inconveniences of life'. Chaucer's use of *suffre* in 'Lerneth to suffre' emphasises its intransitivity, at the same time appropriating the transitive sense of 'tolerate, allow' to the construction of the usually intransitive 'endure pain'. By this means he gives a self-existent quality to the verb, so that it expresses a state of mind rather than a response to some imposed circumstance.[32] It becomes a willing forbearance, a voluntary embrace of some constraint upon or diminution of the demands of the self. It means in fact 'be tolerant', though modern usage may have cheapened the value of this expression. *Patientes vincunt* is the usual medieval formulation: Chaucer, as often, breaks the bondage of habitual formulation, and gives a new meaning to a moral commonplace. *Suffraunce* becomes his way of talking about mutual tolerance, a positive and willing embrace of the will of another as a means to the strengthening of the bond of love.

CHAUCER'S TALE OF SIR THOPAS

When the Prioress's Tale is ended, the company is all 'sobre', a reverent tear in every eye. The Host, whose spirit of activity can abide no pause or silence or cease of busyness, tries to restore the mood of frivolity and enjoyment appropriate to a pilgrimage, and looks around for some inoffensive fellow that he can take a rise out of and make people laugh at.

His eye lights on Chaucer, whom he peruses affectionately: a shy, tubby little man, who hangs around the edge of the company, trying to avoid catching anyone's eye, an odd, amiable freak, 'elvissh', melancholy, distracted, not quite all there, but satisfactorily submissive in his response to the Host's raillery and to his request for a tale:

> 'Hooste,' quod I, 'ne beth nat yvele apayd,
> For oother tale certes kan I noon,
> But of a rym I lerned longe agoon.' (707–9)

The Host winks at the pilgrims, and composes himself with a superior smile on his face to the listening of the tale:

> 'Ye, that is good,' quod he; 'now shul we heere
> Som deyntee thyng, me thynketh by his cheere.' (710–11)

We can imagine the smile fading as the tale progresses, and as the Host gradually realises that his joke has backfired: Chaucer's 'drasty rymyng' (930) is so bad that it is not even funny.

The Host has missed the point, of course – the tale is funny because it is so ineffably, exquisitely bad – but he does not realise that he has missed the point. Dramatic comedy depends upon the immersion of the characters within the world of their limited perceptions, and it is for this reason that Chaucer, likewise, must be understood to be doing the best that he can, and to be genuinely upset when the Host interrupts him:

> 'Why so?' quod I, 'why wiltow lette me
> Moore of my tale than another man,
> Syn that it is the beste rym I kan?' (926–8)

The reader can of course enjoy the comedy and also stand outside it, for he is privileged to know the relationship between 'Chaucer', as we must now call him, and Chaucer. He takes pleasure in recognising the ironic comedy of the game Chaucer is playing with us (not with the Host), and the witty climaxing of that persistent theme of self-mockery which is present in all Chaucer's poems.

The tale itself is something to be treasured. It has been said that an appreciation of Milton is one of the rewards of a classical education, and it can be said of *Thopas* that it would be worth reading all the popular Middle English romances for no other reason than to savour the more its delicious absurdity. Chaucer knew these romances well, especially, it seems, some of those, such as *Guy of Warwick* and *Libeaus Desconus*, that appear in the Auchinleck manuscript, which may itself have been in his hands at some time (Loomis, 1941), and they helped in the establishment of his own poetic style.[33] His attitude towards these romances is one of affectionate contempt, much as one might in later life characterise an early enthusiasm for the romantic verse-narratives of Byron and Scott. He can catch their vapidity perfectly, but also their ethereal innocence:

> Heere is the queene of Fayerye,
> With harpe and pipe and symphonye,
> Dwellynge in this place. (814–16)

It seems not quite right to call *Thopas*, as Moore (1954) does, a parody of or a satire upon Middle English romance ('exceedingly abrasive and . . . penetrating criticism of oral literary art', p. 532; 'finally signals the collapse of minstrel pretensions on the literary level', p. 545). Both terms imply some critical cutting-edge, some awareness that is pressed upon us of a world of superior values or literary art, which informs our laughter with purpose. The genre of *Thopas* seems to be rather that of burlesque, which can perhaps be distinguished from parody by the glee with which it absorbs all the business of satirical puncturing and deflating into the joyful celebration of the ridiculous. It is the world of *The Knight of the Burning Pestle* (*Don Quixote* is more serious) and above all of the play of Pyramus and Thisbe put on by the rude mechanicals in *A Midsummer Night's Dream*. There too there is the lovingly absurd burlesque of a style and a literary art that Shakespeare had absorbed, learnt from and outgrown.

For these reasons, one would be resistant to the other satirical interpretations that have been offered of *Thopas*: that it is, for instance, a satire on the pretensions to knighthood of the Flemish bourgeoisie.[34] Admittedly, our hero comes from 'Poperyng, in the place' (Poperinghe, in Flanders), but that is a funny enough name in itself and already ludicrously inappropriate to the exotic romantic promise of a 'fer contree . . . al biyonde the see' (718–19). Maybe one should recognise something innately humorous in the idea of a noble chivalric knight coming from Flanders, that land of shopkeepers, but the humour is that of burlesque incongruity rather than satire. There is also the interpretation of *Thopas* as a salvo in Chaucer's campaign against the glorification of war and fighting which is the essence of medieval romance. It has been associated

by Scattergood (1981) with the tale of *Melibee* as Chaucer's contribution
to the anti-war movement of the late 1380s; it has been characterised as
an expression of Chaucer's contempt for the whole business of martial
chivalry (Brewer, 1979, p. 238). The objection to these interpretations is
not their implausibility, but the way in which they arm a tale for satiric
battle which is bound by its nature to scatter its shot indiscriminately.

Thopas is unfinished, a structural imperfection which contributes to its
artistic perfection, for in these matters it is 'ever the longer, the worse'.
Yet, though unfinished, it is recognisable as the epitome of the genre of
medieval romance. Indeed, a scrupulous survey of Middle English
romances from the point of view of the strictest definitions of the nature
of the genre concludes that *Thopas* is the only English romance that
satisfies all the criteria: '*Sir Thopas* has everything that the chivalric
romance ought to have – except sense' (Gibbs, 1966, p. 36). There are all
the expected features: the description of the hero, the hero riding forth in
search of adventures, his love for a faery mistress (though he does not
know who it is), the romance landscape, the encounter with a giant, the
feast, the arming, the mention of other romances. It almost seems to have
been made up by a latter-day Peter Quince from some list of instructions
on 'How to write a romance'. Yet everything is *wrong* – not always or
absolutely wrong, for a judicious admixture of sense is necessary to give
the nonsense its full relish, but subtly, knowingly and hilariously wrong.
Thopas (Topaz, a girl's name with perhaps some of the other associations
explored by Conley, 1978), is the wrong name, and Popering is certainly
the wrong place to come from. His complexion is described in terms
more appropriate a girl (there are many suggestions, as Camden, 1935,
points out, of effeminacy), and to compare the whiteness of his skin to
'payndemayn' is rather as if a modern advertiser should speak of a
desired whiteness as the whiteness of sliced bread. 'Saffron' too has
kitchen connotations, and is quite the wrong word to describe the colour
of his beard, which reaches, ridiculously and unfashionably, to his waist,
for all the world like some Tibetan lama. To have 'hosen' is probably
realistic enough, though to mention it is on a par with references to
thermal underwear, and to have 'hosen broun' made in Bruges makes us
think again of a shopkeeper setting up as a chivalric knight. The imagery
has a strong bourgeois flavour, which reminds us of the Flemish
connection, but also of the tendency of all popular Middle English
romances to debase the courtly sentiments and values of their originals to
the tastes of an audience whose knowledge of upper-class life was mostly
that of below stairs. So too the sports in which our hero excels are the

generally homely ones of archery and wrestling, more suited to a yeoman or a miller than a knight, and when he goes hunting he carries on his hand his 'grey goshawk', a recognised poor substitute for the aristocratic falcon.

In the 'fair forest' through which he rides there is 'many a wilde best' – buck and hare, no less – and exotic plants: liquorice, cloves,

> And notemuge to putte in ale,
> Wheither it be moyste or stale,
> Or for to leye in cofre. (763–5)

The narrator and his hero can hardly escape, it seems, the cosy domesticity of the kitchen and its familiar routines, and it is inevitable that the feasting of the hero, later, should be on gingerbread and liquorice, and that he should swear his battle vows not on peacocks and herons but 'on ale and breed' (872). The arming of the hero is a perfect example of the mixing of the plausible and the absurd, the momentary sense that sanity has been regained dissolving constantly into laughter at nonsense triumphant.

> What is ridiculous is the presentation of the details with certain modifications, exaggerations, and oddities, such as, possibly, the white surcoat [with no coat of arms]; certainly the shield of *gold*, so soft and heavy; the leathern, not steel, greaves; the sword-sheath of ivory yet no sword mentioned; the helmet of the cheap soft metal, latten . . . all splendidly absurd. (Brewer, 1979, p. 238)

At the end of it, still without sword or spurs (Linn, 1936), Thopas goes riding off on an ambling dapple-grey steed, a gentle horse, more suited to his maiden aunt.

The narrator, who, as we have said, has no intention but to do his best and to enhance the glowing images of chivalric idealism, is always putting his foot in it. Thopas's popularity with the ladies – a necessary attribute of the true knightly hero – calls forth some wholly inappropriate maternal clucking:

> Ful many a mayde, bright in bour,
> They moorne for hym paramour,
> Whan hem were bet to slepe. (742–4)

Thopas 'climbs' into his saddle, almost, we imagine, panting with the exertion (797), and when he ventures into the 'contree of Fairye' there is no-one who dare accost him,

> Neither wyf ne childe. (806)

When he meets the 'greet geaunt', 'sire Olifaunt' (Sir Elephant), who we are told in a belated aside has three heads (842), Thopas's response is to excuse himself until tomorrow, when he will return with his armour. Meanwhile, he makes off with a fair turn of speed ('fair berynge'), pursued by the giant's slingshot (a ludicrous transposition of the David and Goliath story).

Even at the most intimate level of style, metre and vocabulary, *Thopas* shows a minute observation of those qualities of the romances, especially the tail-rhyme romances, which need only the slightest exaggeration to make them seem ridiculous. The jog-trot rhythm of the tail-rhyme stanza, always potentially inane, is cruelly caught, as is the manner in which the tail-line or the two-syllable 'bob' will tend to drop off from the main stanza like a mortified limb (e.g. 793).[35] Chaucer has recaptured the superlative badness of these poems right down to their bad rhymes. The only exceptions to the rhyme-tests used to establish the canonicity of Chaucer's poems are the bad rhymes of *Thopas*. If we did not know it were by Chaucer, it would have to be by someone else: would anyone, one wonders, ever think, in such a case, that it was purposely bad?

CHAPTER 5

Comic Tales and Fables

The eight tales treated in this chapter (or nine, if one counts the unfinished fragment of the Cook's Tale) do not belong to a single well-defined literary genre, as do the romances of the previous chapter. Four – the Miller's Tale, Reeve's Tale, Merchant's Tale and Shipman's Tale – are closely related as examples of the genre of *fabliau*, which is capable of quite strict definition as a comic tale of low or bourgeois life, involving trickery, often obscene, with a coarse sexual motive. The Friar's Tale and Summoner's Tale are often associated with the *fabliaux*, but the association is only a loose one, and it is better to distinguish these two as satirical anecdotes. The Nun's Priest's Tale and Manciple's Tale, finally, are examples of animal fable, and themselves constitute variants of another quite well-defined genre.

It may seem that the grouping is arbitrary, and certainly, if one attempted to justify the grouping in terms of some familiar theory of 'the comic', one would have to make many exceptions and qualifications. The idea of comedy as socially normative, as the correction through ridicule of the follies and vices of society, is powerfully if not universally present, but also constantly undercut through recurrent questioning of both the social norms and the simpler aspects of the satiric process. The more generally current concept of 'comedy' as the alternative to 'tragedy' (that is, stories of change and reversal that end happily, or at least undisastrously, rather than with death) is too broad and abstract to be very useful. So, too, the recognition that all these tales depend for their structure upon a trick, the acting out of which constitutes the comic climax of the tale, is perhaps of less specific consequence than it seems, though Cooke (1978) writes well of the fabliaux from this point of view, and it is interesting that Boccaccio devotes a day to such tales in the *Decameron*. Even the kind and quality of the humour in the tales are very different. The Manciple's Tale is humorous only by dramatic implication, and the Merchant's Tale is so bitterly unfunny at times that it would surely qualify as a 'problem comedy'.

However, there is one very important way in which the present group of tales constitute a unity, and it is a unity of the same kind, or rather a unity derived from the observation of the same kind of phenomena, as may be discerned in the other two principal groups of tales. The romances have in common a belief and an expectation, shared by the fictional characters and understood to exist by author and reader, that there are ideal forms of behaviour, ideal secular values, to which a man must aspire and through which his existence is validated. *Sir Thopas* is funny, but even there the humour depends on the acceptance, for the purposes of the tale, of this belief and expectation. The 'religious tales', which will be dealt with in the next chapter, rely likewise upon a shared assumption, in this case that the significance of human life is to be seen in the transcending of its secular limitation. With the comic tales and fables, the 'rules' of the game are different, though equally important for those who wish to enter into the world of their fiction. In this case, the common understanding of author and reader is that there are no values, secular or religious, more important than survival and the satisfaction of appetite. The principal characters of these stories will usually live and act according to the same understanding: from time to time they may be lured away from it, by some temporary illusion of self-transcending idealism (Absolon, January, Chauntecler), but they will suffer for it, and be brought back to a proper recognition of the law of nature. Though there will be many cross-currents, and allusions to other determinants of behaviour, these are the conditions we accept in reading such stories. It must be stressed that these agreements made by author and reader do not constitute a narrative theme or purpose. Comic tales of this type do not exist in order to 'celebrate life' any more than they exist to warn us how terribly badly people behave who consult only their appetites. 'Realism' is not in question, only the conspiracy into which we enter in any fiction, and through which we expect many slanting lights to be thrown upon reality, and some aid, invigoration, enrichment or shock to be given to our perceptions of the world around us.

Fabliaux are a notably clear-cut and decisive demonstration of the mode of operation of such narrative artifice. They are widely current in France and Italy (the *Decameron* contains many examples), though for some reason rare in England, and almost unknown in English before Chaucer. It may be that clerical culture exerted a firmer hold upon writers in England, or that the taste for such tales was well satisfied, among the classes that had such a taste, by French fabliaux. This taste, it should be stressed, is an aristocratic or élite taste as much as or rather than a bourgeois or vulgar one. The belief, or pretence, that refined taste

and moral propriety go together commonly misled an earlier generation
of critics into assuming that the fabliaux, with their bourgeois or peasant
settings, and vulgarity of incident and language, were designed for an
unrefined audience. The truth seems to be, on the contrary, that the
same audience enjoyed both romance and fabliau, seeing in the one the
obverse, though not the denial, of the other. However, it is not to be
expected that the enjoyment of fabliaux, any more than that of romances,
was confined to the upper classes. Nykrog (1957), in his standard study
of the genre, asserted (pp. 66–71, 136–9) that literary fabliaux were
essentially an upper-class taste, countering the earlier argument of
Joseph Bédier (*Les Fabliaux*, 1893) that they were essentially bourgeois.
Nykrog (1974) later developed his ideas in more detail, and his argument
holds sway now, and can be supported from the evidence of well-known
collections like the *Decameron* and the mid-fifteenth-century *Cent
Nouvelles Nouvelles*. But Muscatine (1976) has made some important
qualifications to this view, pointing out that the French fabliaux are
imbued with the language, knowledge and social assumptions of non-
courtly literature, and concluding: 'We cannot speak of simple, homo-
geneous social classes, nor of simple social attitudes, in discussing fabliau
origins or audiences' (p. 18). Chaucer seems to recognise the mobility of
the genre, in attributing such tales, as Burrow (1982, p. 80) points out, to
the kind of people they are about, thus playing off the 'bourgeois' fiction
of the pilgrimage against the circumstances of the fictions it encloses.

In romance, then, the audience enjoys participating in the fantasy of
the superhuman, the idea that men may act in ways that surpass their
nature and that raise them to a higher level of moral and social and
emotional being. In fabliau the same audience enjoys equally the fantasy
of the subhuman, the idea that men will always act in accordance with
their basest appetites, untouched, or only amusingly sullied, by morality
or any form of idealism. Neither view of life is more 'realistic' than the
other: it is no more nor less true to life to be stricken inert with passion
than to be permanently on heat. The juxtaposition of the two forms of
fictional 'idealism' provides, however, an interestingly rich contrast, as
Chaucer recognised in setting the Knight's Tale and the Miller's Tale
side by side.

Though Chaucer expands the fabliau almost into a new dimension,
through elaboration of characterisation, plot and setting and through
ironic play of style,[1] yet his four fabliaux are remarkably strict in their
observance of a basic narrative structure, which may be taken to
represent his own choice from among the various available patternings of

the form. In each case, a bourgeois husband is duped or tricked into conniving at the free award of his wife's sexual favours to a clever young man. The 'riche gnof' of the Miller's Tale and the merchant of the Shipman's Tale are typically bourgeois figures; the miller of the Reeve's Tale is lower in the social scale, but his pretensions make up for it; January in the Merchant's Tale is a knight but his habits and tastes are those of a merchant. The wife of the fabliaux is younger, or at least more sexually active, than her husband: she is clearly younger in the Miller's Tale and the Merchant's Tale, where the discrepancy in age between husband and wife makes the sexual intervention of a third party almost inevitable, almost 'right', in fabliau terms. The wives in the Reeve's Tale and Shipman's Tale do not seem to be significantly younger than their husbands, but they have unsatisfied sexual potential, as is made very clear in the Shipman's Tale (VII.116–17, 161–71) and hinted at in the Reeve's Tale in a devastating aside:

> So myrie a fit ne hadde she nat ful yoore. (I.4230)

The wives, it should be stressed, are not portrayed as promiscuous. 'And, for she was of towne, he profred meede' (I.3380), referring to Absolon's attempted wooing of Alison, does not mean she was a prostitute, or anything like one; only that presents of money, unthinkable in upper-class society, were acceptable in bourgeois town society. It is not suggested that the wives' appetites are anything but newly awakened: if it were, the necessity and quality of the intrigue would be diminished. Intrigue and trickery is the central feature of the plot of fabliaux, and the instigator of the plot is the third member of the triangle. This third party is a man (it is possible to imagine a modern fabliau with a woman in this role, but not a medieval one), usually younger than the husband, or at least, again, more sexually active. The monk of the Shipman's Tale is 'yonge', we are told (VII.28), but we are also told that he was thirty years old (VII.26), which is not very young in medieval terms. He seems to be a near-contemporary of the merchant. However, what he has in abundance is that virility which is commonly associated with monks in the medieval comic imagination (and given expression by the Host in a notable burst of raillery, VII.1943–63) and attributed to that husbanding of resources which is no longer a choice for husbands, 'thise wedded men' (VII.103). Apart from youth and the spirit of activity, the distinguishing feature of the third party, the sexual intruder upon the bourgeois domestic scene, is that he does not belong to the same class as the

wedded pair. He is, characteristically, a student, as in the Miller's Tale
and Reeve's Tale, or a cleric, as in the Miller's Tale again (there is a
duplication of roles in both these tales) and Shipman's Tale, and
therefore a member of a different social grouping, if not quite of a
classless intellectual élite. The intruder can thus properly have attributed
to him whatever superior intelligence is necessary to the outwitting of the
husband and can act as a vigorous predator upon a bourgeois society that
has grown stale and old in its conventional marital and materialistic
values. Delany (1967) stresses the flexibility and mobility of the clerks, as
a class, their traditional hostility to the bourgeoisie in 'town–gown'
conflicts, and their implicit alliance with the aristocracy. The Merchant's
Tale, where the intruder is January's own squire, is of course an
exception, and one might simply accept that the Merchant's Tale is a tale
of many exceptions, but it may be worth pointing out that the principal
agent of the intrigue in the Merchant's Tale is, exceptionally, the wife
and not the 'intruder'. This gives the tale an added edge of nastiness, as
does the fact that the intruder is a member of January's own household.

The Friar's Tale and Summoner's Tale were described above as
'satirical anecdotes'. It may be wise to qualify this term, or at least to
recognise that they are satirical only from the point of view of their
deliverers and not according to any normative values expressed through
the narrative. The Friar's attack on the Summoner and the Summoner's
attack on the Friar are interesting as anthologies of the abuse traditionally appropriate to the two classes, but the point of the stories is not to
demonstrate that the person who is the object of attack is wicked, but
rather that he is stupid. There is no distinction of venality between the
Friar and the Summoner, and for the one to prove that the other is venal,
that is, successfully wicked in terms of worldly gain, would be merely to
relinquish to him a higher rung on the ladder of survival. Both tales
therefore pay conventional tribute to the victim's wickedness, but
reserve their main ammunition for his stupidity. They are not morally
normative satirical tales, except through the ironic reconstructions we
may choose to place on them, but tales told within the framework of the
assumptions common to all these comic tales, namely that the important
thing is survival and the preservation of the maximum range of opportunities for the satisfaction of appetite.

The two beast-fables, finally, clearly belong to this group in the
importance they attach, by their traditional nature as stories, to survival.
Such fables exemplify a kind of wisdom which may be found also in
proverbs or in the distichs of Cato, and which has essentially to do with

calculations of practical utility. Morality has little to do with the systems of value on which such tales are based, least of all Christian morality. 'Honesty is the best policy' is the nearest such exemplary tales will come to morality, and when circumstances change it may be equally well be that 'Honesty is not the best policy', as in the Manciple's Tale. A characteristic of the Middle Ages is the readiness of its exegetes and commentators to annex such stories, subservient as they are on their literal level to the imperatives of appetite, to the illustration of Christian doctrine. The Nun's Priest's Tale chiefly exists to enable Chaucer to share with us his amusement at the consequence.

THE MILLER'S TALE

After the Knight's Tale, the Host, pleased with the way things have gone so far, turns to the Monk and asks him to tell

'Somwhat to quite with the Knyghtes tale'. (I.3119)

He clearly intends to observe the proper order of social priority. The Miller, however, bursts in upon this prim ceremony and, in upsetting all the Host's plans, begins the unfolding of Chaucer's plans for the roadside drama. The Host, who sees that he is drunk, tries to restrain him, but to no avail, and the Miller, after he has dealt with the Reeve's choleric interruption, and after Chaucer has issued a polite disclaimer of responsibility for what follows, begins his tale.

The prologues to individual tales always give great pleasure in themselves, especially for their dramatic vitality, but they also serve Chaucer's artistic purposes in a variety of other ways. Very important here is the frame that he builds around the tale: it is the first of the low comic tales and the entry upon it is a significant moment in his public poetic career. His own disclaimer (3167–86), which takes up at the earliest possible point the similar remarks that he made at the end of the General Prologue (725–42), and which, in an amusing but not fundamentally unserious way, simultaneously rejects one kind of artistic responsibility and assumes another, has already been discussed in Chapter 2. But there are other signs, too, of a sophisticated poetic self-consciousness at work, in giving the tale its proper context as 'game' (3186). The allocation of such a tale to the Miller is a dramatic device so plausible, so flattering to the expectations of rank, that it seems natural – until one remembers the literary provenance of fabliau, and the readiness of Boccaccio's young ladies and gentlemen to swap similar stories. It is in fact a remarkable innovation, as Burrow (1982, p. 80) points out. Not only that, but the Miller himself apologises for his own tale in advance, attributing anything that may cause offence to his drunkenness (3137–40). When he has announced the subject of his tale, and has been scolded by the Reeve, he offers his own pragmatic and laughably spurious morality of the marriage-bed:

> An housbonde shal nat been inquisityf
> Of Goddes pryvetee, nor of his wyf.
> So he may fynde Goddes foyson there,
> Of the remenant nedeth nat enquere. (3163–6)[2]

And when the tale is under way, and the main characters have been introduced, the Miller justifies the story he is about to relate with an appeal to the formidable authority of Cato,

> That bad man sholde wedde his simylitude. (3228)

The Miller has, so to speak, internalised the 'morality' of survival, of pragmatism, and made it into a pattern of justice. It is all very ludicrous, and a splendid game, but it serves Chaucer's purpose well: he now sits at the heart of such a labyrinth of false trails and 'dramatic' subterfuges that he can count himself free from the traditional burdens of poetic responsibility and allow full scope to his verbal wit and dramatic imagination.

The Miller, having served his turn, plays little further part. The consciousness of his presence fades rapidly, and by the middle of the tale he has become part of the subject-matter of the narrative, as we note, with a delighted sense of alienation, that the carpenter's servant is also called 'Robyn' (3466, cf.3129) and that he too seems to have a way with doors (3469–71), if not the extraordinary versatility of the Miller (550–1). The narrative voice is totally absorbed in the narrative, and even the exchange with the Reeve has little or no function in heightening dramatic consciousness: the portrait of John the carpenter is in no way attached to the Reeve, nor is John a special target of ridicule. In fact, he is quite affectionately portrayed.

The prologue to the Miller's Tale is thus quite a complex piece of narrative engineering, serving a number of purposes in the economy of the Tales, none of them having to do with the 'characterisation' of the Miller, except in the broad sense that he is a coarse fellow. It has one other important function, to which attention needs to be drawn, and that is in the indication it gives of a link to be seen between the Knight's Tale and the Miller's Tale. Once observed, this link proves quite intriguingly suggestive, and it has been interestingly explored by Stokoe (1951–2), Owen (1954) and Kean (1972, pp. 94–6), though elsewhere pointlessly over-elaborated. Both tales tell of the rivalry of two young men in love with the same girl; the descriptions of Emelye and of Alison are nicely contrasted; Nicholas in his Oxford lodgings,

> Allone, withouten any compaignye (3204)

is just like Arcite,

> Allone, withouten any compaignye (2779)

as he goes to his eternal lodgings. John the carpenter's 'Allas, my wyf!' (3522) echoes the same poignant speech of Arcite (2775), and perhaps the striking figure of speech associated with Absolon's discomfiture,

> Who rubbeth now, who froteth now his lippes
> With dust, with sond, with straw, with clooth, with chippes,
> But Absolon ... (3747–9)

reminds us of the similar figure used in very different circumstances in the Knight's Tale:

> Who looketh lightly now but Palamoun?
> Who spryngeth up for joye but Arcite? (1870–1)

There are other parallels that might be adduced, and a good deal of amusement to be derived from the juxtaposition of romance and fabliau, and the sardonic implied comment of the latter on the lofty ideals and manners of the former. But the comedy is essentially the comedy of incongruous juxtaposition, and, despite a modern tendency to believe that stories of low life and sexual intrigue are more 'realistic', the Miller's Tale acts in no dialectical process to undercut the idealism of the Knight's Tale. The two kinds of tale are told according to different sets of rules, which may be compared but should not be confused. The Miller's promise to 'quite' the Knight's Tale has often been misinterpreted: it does not mean that he is going to put down or satirise the Knight's Tale, any more than the Host meant this in making the same suggestion to the Monk. 'Quite' means 'repay' ('make return for with something of equivalent value'), and the Miller is speaking of the tale-telling competition and not about the contents of the tales. The amusement that we have in the juxtaposition of the two tales does not affect interpretation of either. Arcite's question,

> What is this world? what asketh men to have? (2777)

may have an interesting further resonance when it is remembered in the Miller's Tale, where the world is a simpler place and what men ask to have very obvious, likewise what they get, but the invitation to compare the deep and near-impenetrable justice of the Knight's Tale with the very obvious 'justice' of the Miller's Tale should not induce us into thinking that the one is more 'real' than the other.

The courtly idealism of love, initially a theme picked up from the Knight's Tale, is present throughout the Miller's Tale as an implied and ludicrously inappropriate standard of conduct, and contributes much to the richness and exuberant literariness of this most brilliant of the *Canterbury Tales*. Nicholas, we are told, is an expert in 'deerne love' (3200), and when he makes his first addresses to his landlady both he and Alison go through some pretty rituals, he playing the part of one stricken to death by love, she the disdainful mistress (3276–87). Their play-acting is accompanied by some decidedly uncourtly activities around 'queynte' and 'haunchebones', some very improper language ('lemman' is from popular poetry,[3] and 'spille' is an obscene double entendre), and the suggestion that Alison's cries for help may be sufficiently muted, but it is engaged in none the less earnestly for that. When Nicholas has obtained, without too much difficulty, his promise of grace, he returns, like a true courtly lover, to his instrument, upon which he vents his unused passion:

> Whan Nicholas had doon thus everideel,
> And thakked hire aboute the lendes weel,
> He kiste hire sweete and taketh his sawtrie,
> And pleyeth faste, and maketh melodie. (3303–6)

Music plays a large part in the tale, as Rowland (1970) and Gellrich (1974) describe: Nicholas often makes his chamber ring with his singing of *Angelus ad virginem* (3216, a song that spicily foretells his own role in relation to Alison – and John's too, in old Joseph's ignorance of all those

angelic goings-on), and Absolon is armed with his 'gyterne' when he goes
serenading his lady-love in the small hours. The sweetest musical
moment is the image of the love-making of Nicholas and Alison, and
Chaucer's mischievous time-keeping:

> Ther was the revel and the melodye;
> And thus lith Alison and Nicholas,
> In bisynesse of myrthe and of solas,
> Til that the belle of laudes gan to rynge,
> And freres in the chauncel gonne synge. (3652–6)

Such allusions can be taken in a very heavy-handed way, as iconographic
reminders of the contrast between the 'old song' of lust and cupidity and
the 'new song' of grace (Robertson, 1962, pp. 133, 243), which the lovers
seem not to have heard of, but the poem does not insist on this, and the
general effect of such allusions is to enhance a marked lyrical quality in
the tale. The church and its activities are present in the poem as part of its
naturalistic setting, part of the texture of town-life, and not, except in
jocular way, as a reminder to us of what the characters ought to be busy
about.

Nicholas is surpassed as a would-be courtly lover by the egregious
Absolon, who has many of the epicene characteristics of Sir Thopas. His
blond curly hair, sprouting like a fan around his head, is his chief glory,
in allusion to his biblical namesake (Beichner, 1950), and his care with
his attire extends even to the 'Poules wyndow corven on his shoos'
(3318). His way of life does not, perhaps, quite live up to the legitimate
expectations of such a dashing young rake, and he has to make do with
ogling the ladies of the parish as he 'senses' them, and paying court to
flighty barmaids (3325–36). Alison is to be his *grande amour*, and for her
he is assiduous in the chewing of liquorice, the combing of his hair, and
the snatching of a few hours' sleep so that he can be wakeful at night
(3685–6). And so he comes, a jolly thriving wooer, to the 'shot-
wyndowe':

> And softe he cougheth with a semy soun:
> 'What do ye, hony-comb, sweete Alisoun,
> My faire bryd, my sweete cynamome?
> Awaketh, lemman myn, and speketh to me!
> Wel litel thynken ye upon my wo,
> That for youre love I swete ther I go.
> No wonder is thogh that I swelte and swete;

I moorne as dooth a lamb after the tete.
Ywis, lemman, I have swich love-longynge,
That lik a turtel trewe is my moornynge.
I may nat ete na moore than a mayde.' (3697–3707)

This burlesque of love-complaint is justly celebrated, and has been
analysed by Donaldson (1951) and Kaske (1962) for its witty echoes of
the language both of popular poetry ('lemman', and also 'oore' below,
3726) and of the Song of Songs ('hony-comb', 'cynamome'). It is also
intrinsically ridiculous: the insistent repetition of 'swete' turns the
metaphor into ludicrously literal reality, while the image of the lamb
seeking the teat has a prurient suggestiveness hopelessly missed by
Absolon. The joke is on these street-corner Romeos, of course, not on the
courtly idealism of love that they get so idiotically wrong. Likewise, the
allusion to the Song of Songs, though it may provoke some mirth at the
outrageous incongruity of the association, is not really intended to supply
any 'moral edge' to the poem, or give any 'implicit orientation toward a
controlling set of values' (Kaske, 1962, p. 497). To be reminded that
Absolon is not the spiritual wooer of the bible, nor Alison his *sponsa*, is
not to be reminded of what the tale is 'really' about: it is a gratuitous and
very pleasing extra.

The burlesquing of courtly idealism plays an important part, with
both Nicholas and Absolon, in that enrichment of character-delineation
which is one of Chaucer's most significant additions to the basic matter of
fabliau. Alison, too, is a kind of courtly heroine *manquée*, with her
genteel protestations and her appeal to Nicholas's 'curteisye' (3287), and
she is favoured with an elaborate introductory description, modelled on
the *descriptio feminae* which would traditionally, by rhetorical precept,
introduce the heroine of a romance.[4] The description of Emelye, in the
Knight's Tale, is a typical example. Alison, though, is a heroine with a
difference, the queen of a sailor's dreams, if not quite a queen of curds
and cream. She is surrounded with dairymaid and pastoral imagery,

A barmclooth eek as whit as morne milk . . . (3236)

She was ful moore blisful on to see
Than is the newe pere-jonette tree,
And softer than the wolle is of a wether . . . (3247–9)

Hir mouth was sweete as bragot or the meeth
Or hoord of apples leyd in hey or heeth . . . (3261–2)

She was a prymerole, a piggesnye (3268)

but she is essentially a town-girl, a 'popelote', a 'wenche' (3254), with 'a likerous ye' (3244), who knows how to dress in the height of sophisticated vulgarity, and how to deck herself out, all in black and white, in the most slyly seductive way. The touches of extreme vulgarity, like the brooch she wears on her collar,

As brood as is the boos of a bokeler (3266)

would not be recognised as such in the local *palais de danse*, in the medieval equivalent of which she has her true being. She is lively, accessible, with an irresistible hint of lasciviousness, but she has an instinct of self-preservation too, and is certainly no pushover. She has the lithe grace of a 'wezele' (3234), but the image suggests too a sharp nip for any who try to take unwelcome advantage. She would not be disturbed by any thought of the sexual imperatives of her class, to which Chaucer makes brief sardonic allusion in passing:

She was a prymerole, a piggesnye,
For any lord to leggen in his bedde,
Or yet for any good yeman to wedde. (3268–70)

The patrician mode of fabliau is obvious enough.

Alison plays no part in the intrigue, once she has indicated her availability. She shows a cool and almost disinterested self-command in her reply to her husband's expostulations about Absolon's midnight serenading:

'Yis, God woot, John, I heere it every deel.' (3369)

and of course she manages the episode of 'the misdirected kiss' (as it is delicately called by the folk-tale analysts) with gaiety and aplomb:

'Tehee!' quod she, and clapte the wyndow to. (3740)

She is the one character who wins out in the end, who escapes scot-free, while the male characters suffer various painful and cruel indignities:

> Thus swyved was this carpenteris wyf,
> For al his kepyng and his jalousye;
> And Absolon hath kist hir nether ye;
> And Nicholas is scalded in the towte.
> This tale is doon, and God save al the rowte! (3850–4)

This brief concluding eschatology is very precise in its appeal to a kind of poetic justice, but Alison's being 'swyved' is of course John's punishment, not hers. We may ask, and it is often asked, why she is spared. She is surely just as worthy of punishment, if 'justice' is in question? Intuitively, though, we know that the reason she does not suffer the consequences of her actions is that she behaves throughout in accordance with her nature as an animal, without pretence or affectation. She understands the world in which she lives, the world of fabliau, of appetite and survival, and she lives according to its rules. The emphasis on animal comparisons in the description of Alison is thus very significant, especially the comparisons with young, spirited animals (3259–60, 3263, 3282). Absolon, by contrast, has fantasies of an animal-relationship with Alison:

> I dar wel seyn, if she hadde been a mous,
> And he a cat, he wolde hire hente anon. (3346–7)

which are contrary to his nature. The image of the lamb seeking for its mother's teat is perhaps truer for him, though no help in this assertive and competitive world.

Nicholas has the qualities of instinctive animal vitality that liberate Alison, as well as the further qualities of intelligence, cleverness, smartness, or, best, animal cunning that are required of men (in accordance with medieval sexual stereotyping) in fabliaux. Nicholas is indeed more than merely cunning: he has something of a connoisseur's relish for intrigue, and takes genuine imaginative delight in the acting out of his fantastic plot. It might even seem that he desires intrigue more than Alison, since he could presumably have had his way with her on that Saturday when her husband was away all day (3400) rather than lay the plans for Monday night: but it seems to be one of the rules of the game, one of the challenges, that he must contrive some way of spending the night with her. His plot, anyway, is a magnificent one, and in expounding his prophecy to John, Nicholas seems almost to be carried away on the flood-tide of his imagination:

> Thanne shaltou swymme as myrie, I undertake,
> As dooth the white doke after hire drake.
> Thanne wol I clepe, 'How, Alison! how, John!
> Be myrie, for the flood wol passe anon.'
> And thou wolt seyn, 'Hayl, maister Nicholay!
> Good morwe, I se thee wel, for it is day.'
> And thanne shul we be lordes al oure lyf
> Of al the world, as Noe and his wyf. (3575–82)

Nicholas is certainly here, as he has been throughout, 'our hero', and he has all those qualities – youth, sexual vitality, smartness – which are the means to success in the world of fabliau. One admires with special relish the moral obligations he places upon John in order to secure his own immoral appetites:

> Thy wyf and thou moote hange fer atwynne;
> For that bitwixe yow shal be no synne. (3589–90)

How, then, does Nicholas so forfeit our esteem as to end up as one of the victims, with poor John and Absolon? The satisfaction we have in his come-uppance, cruel and painful as it is, is complete, and is only partly due to that love of reversals, of 'the biter bit', which is built into the structure of fabliau. Nicholas's fall pleases us and makes us laugh because he betrays his nature: in trying to play Alison's trick a second time he shows himself less than smart, less than his true animal self, and he pays the price. Perhaps his wits are dulled by sexual euphoria: these are dangerous moments for the fabliau hero.

The principles according to which fabliau works are very clearly revealed in this reversal. It demonstrates, perhaps, how irrelevant it is to attach moral considerations to Nicholas's actions, or indeed to those of any of the other characters. The idea that Nicholas suffers because he has committed adultery is the last thing that we have in mind, and the method used by Robertson (1962, pp. 382–6), Bolton (1962) and Olson (1963) of interpreting the Miller's Tale as a paradigm of the punishments awarded to lechery (Nicholas), avarice (John) and pride (Absolon) is irrelevant to the expectations of the genre. A number of writers have used Bakhtin (1965) in order to explain and understand the principles and mode of working of such comic tales, and the nature of 'festive comedy'. David quotes him (1976, p. 94), and comments:

> It is possible to take festive comedy seriously without turning it into inverted morality ... The Miller's Tale has its own truth, different

from the Knight's – what Bakhtin calls 'the people's unofficial truth'. The Knight's truth means fidelity to higher principle; the Miller's truth is fidelity to the vital principle of life. (1976, pp. 104–5)

These are persuasive arguments, and attractive in their suggestion of Chaucer's espousal of an alternative non-establishment ideology. It would be as nice to recruit Chaucer to the radical people's party as it is tempting to others to have him join the conservative neo-Christian establishment. But to succumb to such temptations would be simply to acquiesce in another form of ideological reconstruction. There is no 'truth' to which the Miller's Tale is faithful, no alternative principle of life which it celebrates, only a set of assumptions about life which we are asked to agree to as part of the narrative treaty. The seriousness of the work, its relation to life, arises from the place of these assumptions in relation to a whole series of other assumptions that we are asked to make in other kinds of narrative fiction, the place of the genre in the interlocking and overlapping map of genres. To make the Miller's Tale, or any other tale, the vehicle of 'a view of life' is to break this treaty.

A return to the tale, and to the characterisation of John the carpenter, may enable us to map out one other quarter of the territory of fabliau. John is set up as the butt of the tale at the beginning – old men should not marry young wives – and most writers would have been content with the licence this gave for a moral holiday. Chaucer, however, enriches the portrait of the old husband with a greater variety of observation than with any of the other characters. The expression of 'bourgeois complacency', of that reliance on old saws and shibboleths that masquerades as homespun philosophy and simple faith, of that suspicion of learning which takes the greatest pleasure in the discomfiture of the learned, could hardly be bettered:

> This man is falle, with his astromye,
> In some woodnesse or in som agonye.
> I thoghte ay wel how that it sholde be!
> Men sholde nat knowe of Goddes pryvetee.
> Ye, blessed be alwey a lewed man
> That noght but oonly his bileve kan!
> So ferde another clerk with astromye;
> He walked in the feeldes, for to prye
> Upon the sterres, what ther sholde bifalle,
> Til he was in a marle-pit yfalle;
> He saugh nat that ... (3451–61)

Yet when his vanity and concern for his (and his wife's) survival are appealed to, John succumbs immediately to the mysterious learning he was so scornful of, and takes an eager part in Nicholas's farcical charade. The association Nicholas encourages him to make between himself and Noah shows the total absence, in his simple faith, of any notion that the Flood was anything more than a nasty accident. This is another of Chaucer's literary references, for he alludes clearly to the episode of Noah's termagant wife (3540) that was familiarly expanded in the English mystery plays, and mischievously intends us to understand that the grasp John has of the grand design of Christian history is about as much as the average citizen would get from the mystery plays. The background in town life of these plays is reinforced by further references to the mystery plays, as Harder (1956) shows, such as the mention of the Miller speaking 'in Pilates voys' (3124) and of Absolon who, 'to shewe his lightnesse and maistrye', often played Herod 'upon a scaffold hye' (3383–4).

Chaucer adds, though, a still richer colouring to his characterisation of John in the frequent suggestion that he is a good-hearted old fellow. Cooper (1980) notes the recurrent use of the epithet 'sely' for John, and the way Chaucer plays upon its contemporary range of meanings, from 'silly' through 'simple-minded' and 'pitiable' to 'innocent'. John's concern for Nicholas, whom he has not seen all weekend, is genuine, though he makes a maundering empty morality of it:

> God shilde that he deyde sodeynly!
> This world is now ful tikel, sikerly.
> I saugh to-day a cors yborn to chirche
> That now, on Monday last, I saugh hym wirche. (3427–30)

Most notable is his reaction to the news of the coming deluge, where his first thought is of his wife:

> This carpenter answerde, 'Allas, my wyf!
> And shal she drenche? allas, myn Alisoun!' (3522–3)

He seems sincerely upset. In the analogues, it may be noted (see Benson and Andersson, 1971, p. 61), the husband only makes a tub for himself. Chaucer is not averse to giving us an emotional twinge or two, and sometimes more, as we shall see in the Merchant's Tale, and he seems prepared here, with his easy mastery of the genre, to encourage us to a spasm of fellow-feeling and emotional participation before he allows it to be swallowed up again in the general exuberance and gaiety of fabliau, making us feel embarrassed that we even gave way to it. As Brewer says, John the carpenter is

> real enough for the stratagem to have point, but not enough to make us think in terms of real life about the true pathos and bitterness of his situation. A story such as this has to be told without forcing us back on our normal moral feelings ... *The Miller's Tale*, for all its realism, is not real life. It is comic fantasy ... (1973, p. 120)

In his treatment of the characters, then, Chaucer blends a tempting realism within an overall structure of fantasy. In one respect, though, the realism of the tale is uninhibited: the density of detail of town and domestic life is quite unparalleled in Chaucer and indeed in medieval literature. Muscatine (1957, p. 226) speaks of the tale's 'overpowering substantiality', and indeed wherever one looks the eye can follow out material reality continuously to a seemingly infinite depth of perspective, like a fifteenth-century Flemish painting. Much of this detail is on a small scale, and prompted by the needs of the plot. The breast-high 'shot-wyndowe', for instance, which is so vital a part of the plot-mechanism, is deeply implanted in our visual consciousness (3358, 3676, 3696) by the time it comes to be needed: this kind of planting of necessary detail in inconspicuous places is part of Chaucer's consummate artistry in the tale, as is the witty irony, well described by Birney (1960), in the early mention of Nicholas's skill in predicting 'droghte or elles shoures' (3196), or of Absolon's fastidiousness about 'fartyng' (3338), or his certainty, from the itching of his mouth, that this night he will kiss Alison 'at the leeste wey' (3680). More substantial than this, beyond the needs of the plot yet not gratuitous, is the filling in of the background that Chaucer engages in at every opportunity: Alison's visit to the church,

Cristes owene werkes for to wirche; (3308)

the cloisterer that Absolon interviews concerning John's whereabouts, and the banal and prosaic authenticity of his reply (3664–70); the little scene with Gerveys the blacksmith, working, as was a blacksmith's wont, at night at the repair of the ploughshares and other implements that would be needed by day. We could find our way blindfold about old John's house, with its cat-flap in Nicholas's bedroom-door (3440), or the gable-end over the stable from which the three tubs will come triumphantly floating (3571) – and Bennett (1974, p. 28) in a book packed with data such as only the Miller's and Reeve's Tales could sustain, has been confident enough to offer a three-dimensional plan of the house – though we might find ourselves stumbling into some unexpected obstacles. That door, for instance, crashed off its hinges into Nicholas's bedchamber with such a deal of heaving from Robin (3470), is back in position without a word a few lines later (3499) so that Nicholas and John can have their *tête-à-tête*.

Comic fantasy, unfolded for us with an exuberant gusto of the imagination, is in the end the dominant mode of the Miller's Tale. The richness of characterisation and setting, the witty allusiveness, the versatility of style – from blunt colloquialism (e.g., 3772–5, 3820–3) to high passion, with special delights like the contrived play on *hende* (courteous, clever, at hand, handy – with his hands) as an epithet for Nicholas (Beichner, 1952) – are all in the service of this marvellously engineered ridiculous plot. Chaucer interweaves the different phases of his two plots, the 'flood' plot and the 'misdirected kiss' plot, with unobtrusive cunning, absorbing us into the development of each in turn, so that when the climactic cry comes from Nicholas,

'Help! water! water! help, for Goddes herte!' (3815)

it is with the purest delight that we recall the long-forgotten carpenter, and what the cry will mean to him.

> The surprise, the sudden union of the two themes, is sublime. It is as if, for a fraction of a second, the heavens opened and we saw all the gods watching the trivial and ridiculous human comedy below. (Tillyard, 1934, p. 90)

THE REEVE'S TALE

The Reeve, as anticipated, duly takes offence at the Miller's Tale, which he believes to be a personal attack upon himself (3913–15), since he, like John, was 'of carpenteris craft' (3861). The Reeve is by this act isolated from the rest of the pilgrims, who are said to have generally enjoyed the Tale: by contrast, only the Cook is said to have responded in any way to the Reeve's Tale. This isolation is in accord with the impression created in the description of the Reeve in the General Prologue, that he has no great love for his fellow-men, and wishes to be separated from and singled out from them. Where the Miller rides at the head of the company, playing on his bagpipes (I.565–6), the Reeve brings up the rear:

> And evere he rood the hyndreste of oure route. (I.622)

The suggestion is of a narrow-eyed suspicion, of a desire always to place himself in a position of calculated advantage. The impression is confirmed as his introduction to his Tale unfolds, and the prologue here can be seen performing a different function from that of the prologue to the Miller's Tale. There, the Miller spoke generally and quite genially, hardly at all about himself (except to acknowledge that he was drunk), and what he said mostly served Chaucer's purposes in establishing the nature of the type of tale he was about to tell. The Reeve, however, speaks entirely about himself, and provokes a concentration upon himself as a person which is bound to have an effect upon the way we regard his Tale. It is noteworthy, too, that he speaks constantly, here and later (3864, 3916, 4324), about 'quiting' the Miller, where the Host and the Miller spoke of 'quiting' the Knight's Tale (3119, 3127). His suspicious and retentive nature is unlikely to allow him to enter into the spirit of a tale-telling competition.

His own words in the prologue provide a vivid series of images for the predicament of old age, pricked by lust yet unable to satisfy it, sexually ripe yet physically rotten (3869–80). The decline into old age is described in terms of an image which disturbingly associates life, being alive, with sexual potency, almost as if the Reeve himself were a character in a fabliau:

> For sikerly, whan I was bore, anon
> Deeth drough the tappe of lyf and leet it gon;
> And ever sithe hath so the tappe yronne
> Til that almoost al empty is the tonne.
> The streem of lyf now droppeth on the chymbe. (3891–5)

The world has changed from that of the Miller's Tale, and with it the suggestiveness of the poetic imagery: David (1976, p. 111), in his excellent account of the Reeve's Tale, shows how the 'open-ers' (3871), or medlar, has replaced the 'newe pere-jonette tree' (3248), the leek (3879) the primrose, the 'coltes tooth' (3888) the colt in its 'trave' (3282).

The contrast between the world of youthful vitality and the world of obscene senescence is sufficiently interesting in itself, and of course a favourite medieval and Chaucerian theme, but there seems to be something more personal here, more specifically associated with the Reeve. The Reeve claims to be too old to 'pley', that is, to tell a coarse tale to cap the Miller's,

> But ik am oold, me list not pley for age. (3867)

This turns out to be untrue, but meanwhile he has turned the meaning of 'pley' to sexual play, and made a frank acknowledgement of impotence in order to ingratiate himself with the pilgrims by his modesty, and to gain their sympathy. He claims a position of weakness in order to win a position of strength. This can be related, again, as Olson (1962, pp. 2–3) points out, to his character as described in the General Prologue, where we see a man who is used to making acts of self-interest look like acts of justice:

> His lord wel koude he plesen subtilly,
> To yeve and lene hym of his owene good,
> And have a thank, and yet a cote and hood. (610–12)

Something else emerges, too, in his fondness for proverbs and legal maxims expressive of a harsh kind of retributive justice,

> For leveful is with force force of-showve (3912)

and his use of biblical texts as a sanction for straightforward vindictiveness:

> I pray to God his nekke mote to-breke;
> He kan wel in myn eye seen a stalke,
> But in his owene he kan nat seen a balke. (3918–20)

We remember that his first words were of unsolicited morality (2144–8), and remember too the hints of a priest *manqué* in the General Prologue description:

> His top was dokked lyk a preest biforn . . . (590)

> Tukked he was as is a frere aboute . . . (621)

He is a man, it is suggested, who puts on moral airs as a form of self-advancement and self-gratification, an early Malvolio ('a kind of Puritan') or Blifil. He is a hypocrite, whose moral rectitude shows itself all warped, and whose view of life is of the kind that curdles all experience.[5] When we find that his ideas of 'justice' are embodied not only within the narration of the Tale,

> Lo, swich it is a millere to be fals!
> And therfore this proverbe is seyd ful sooth,
> 'Hym thar nat wene wel that yvele dooth';
> A gylour shal hymself bigyled be. (4318–21)

but also in the motivation acknowledged by the characters (e.g., 4178–86), we may properly recognise, though we may find it insufficiently identified in other tales, a 'dramatic' role for the Reeve in the telling of his tale.

The Tale itself has many of the qualities of the Miller's Tale. It is, quite deliberately, a Cambridge counterblast to the Miller's Oxford tale, and has the same technical brilliance as narration, and the same kind, if not the same degree, of substantiality of characterisation and setting. The carefully located mill (3921–4), the practices and problems of provisioning a large Cambridge college (3987–4001), the fens surrounding Trumpington, 'ther wilde mares renne' (4065), the bedroom which forms the scene of the dénouement, are all brought before us with full authenticity:

> And this is verray sooth that I yow telle. (3924)

Yet, despite this, everything is changed. Everything is directed and concentrated to a satirically destructive purpose, and in a way that makes us conscious both of the destructive effect and of the vindictiveness of purpose. At the head of the tale, where the Miller's Tale exuberantly evokes youthful high spirits and animal vitality in the itchily seductive portrait of Alison, there stands the portrait of the Miller. Unmistakably modelled on the 'real' Miller, it is a systematically vituperative portrait, barely pausing to establish him as real in the determination to present him as a target for attack. His own vanity and his ridiculous pride in his high-born wife, his bully-boy violence, which sends him abroad festooned with weapons, and his outrageous thievery, are set before us without pretence of neutrality, and the tale, as Olson (1962, pp. 11–14) and Copland (1962, pp. 16–17) show, is shaped and organised to destroy him. His pride in his daughter's lineage, which derives from the fact that her mother is the daughter of a parson (and therefore, of course, strictly speaking, illegitimate) of whom she has high expectations if she marries well, is grotesquely dismayed when she is 'swyved' by Aleyn and thus 'disparaged' by a lad of no repute:

> Who dorste be so boold to disparage
> My doghter, that is come of swich lynage? (4271–2)

His dangerous violence is made ridiculous when he goes down to the crucial blow in the final mêlée, struck on his bald pate with a stick wielded by his own wife; and his thieving gets its reward when he is robbed of his ill-gotten cake of flour at the instigation of his own daughter.

Even when he has qualities in common with old John the carpenter, they emerge differently. Both are dismissive of book-learning and complacent about their own good sense, but where in John it is the innocent expression of genuine ignorance, and quite good-hearted, with 'deynous Symkyn' it is a practised and self-conscious presumption, in which he adopts for himself the role taken by Nicholas in the Miller's Tale (3299–300):

> But by my thrift, yet shal I blere hir ye,
> For al the sleighte in hir philosophye. (4049–50)

Such a man is evidently riding for a fall.

The venom directed against the Miller spills over onto his wife and daughter, who are no part of the Reeve's revenge nor traditional victims of fabliau. The pride Symkyn takes in his wife is openly abused in her too (3963–5), and the daughter is contemptuously dismissed, in a few lines totally without Chaucerian affection:

> This wenche thikke and wel ygrowen was,
> With kamus nose, and eyen greye as glas,
> With buttokes brode, and brestes rounde and hye;
> But right fair was hire heer, I wol nat lye. (3973–6)

Even the old parson comes in for some gratuitous sarcasm, and the cynicism at the church's expense (3981–6) is very different from the bland recognition of the Church's role in life (opportunities for the 'sensing' of wives and histrionic display by ambitious parish clerks, employment for carpenters in roof-building, early morning musical interludes) in the Miller's Tale. The latter has a kind of largesse in the conception and handling of characters, and John is no worse treated than the others in the end. Here, the vindictiveness issues constantly in a bitter and narrow view of life.

The students, of course, escape scot-free, as the story demands, but here too, at every turn, there is some twist given to the original story in order to heap further abuse and ridicule upon the Miller. They come from the north (4014–15), and Chaucer's originality in having them speak in a fair imitation of northern dialect has often been noted, and is the subject of a classic essay by Tolkien (1934). The effect is egregious – this is the beginning of a long tradition in English literature where northerners have been made to sound thick and oafish for the amusement of metropolitan audiences – and of course the net result is to humiliate Symkyn even further. To be tricked is bad enough, but to be tricked by such rustic buffoons is absurd.

The story has also been emptied of all affection, even that tingling of sexual desire that operates as a motive for action in nearly all fabliaux. In the nearest analogue, which is actually a good deal closer than anything that can be found for the Miller's Tale (see Benson and Andersson, 1971, pp. 101–15), one of the students conceives a pressing attachment to the Miller's daughter while they eat together at dinner, and arranges to come to her at night. The other, left without solace in his lonely bed, observes the Miller's wife tripping out to piss, all naked, and it is this sight that prompts him to move the cradle. In the Reeve's Tale there is no movement of affection or lust. The two students are kept awake by the symphony of snoring from the family trio, and it is this alone that prompts Aleyn to think of revenge and 'esement'. The act is described with utter blankness:

> And up he rist, and by the wenche he crepte.
> This wenche lay uprighte, and faste slepte,
> Til he so ny was, er she myghte espie,
> That it had been to late for to crie,
> And shortly for to seyn, they were aton. (4193–7)

The other student, not wishing to be thought 'a daf, a cokenay' (4208) by contrast with his fellow, moves the cradle *before* the wife gets up. He is not prompted by any natural animal impulse awakened by seeing her naked – and of course, as Chaucer remembered, he could not have seen her anyway, since the whole point of the plot is that the bedroom must be very dark – but rather by one-upmanship, a motive that the Reeve understands very well. There is about the act this time a kind of animal violence:

> Withinne a while this John the clerk up leep,
> And on this goode wyf he leith on soore.
> So myrie a fit ne hadde she nat ful yoore;
> He priketh harde and depe as he were mad. (4228–31)

The reason for this is not that John is more virile or the wife more receptive, but that here there is another opportunity to strike a blow at the Miller, in the suggestion that his own sexual performance was unsatisfactory.

It is all a very long way from the carefree lyricism of the Miller's Tale, 'the revel and the melodye' (3652). There is no musical imagery here, except for the snoring:

> His wyf bar hym a burdon, a ful strong;
> Men myghte hir rowtyng heere two furlong;
> The wenche rowteth eek, *par compaignye*. (4165–7)

Nor is there any hint of the presence, even by its absence, of any courtly idealism of love. Coupling is all that is described, not much different from the clerks' horse wehee-ing after the mares, which, interestingly enough, Kolve (1974, p. 309) selects as the governing visual image of the tale (4064–6). The one hint of affection comes in the morning scene between Aleyn and the daughter, Malyne:

> Aleyn wax wery in the dawenynge,
> For he had swonken al the longe nyght,
> And seyde, 'Fare weel, Malyne, sweete wight!
> The day is come, I may no lenger byde;
> But everemo, wher so I go or ryde,
> I is thyn awen clerk, swa have I seel!' (4234–9)

The parody, however, of the delicacies of the traditional *aube* scene of the parting of the lovers (see Kaske, 1959) is so grotesque as to stifle in coarse laughter any temptation to tender feeling. Malyne, having told John where the stolen cake of meal is to be found, almost has a twinge of feeling:

> And with that word almoost she gan to wepe. (4248)

But the 'almoost' has a typically sardonic edge to it.

Chaucer draws attention to the character of the Reeve quite deliberately in the prologue to his Tale, and the bitterness and single-minded vindictiveness of the Tale seem dramatically continuous with what was there displayed. He encourages us to read it as a dramatic exposition of the Reeve's character in action, and some of the best readers have responded to this encouragement:

> The tale's special naturalism goes beyond factual description to contribute to the rendering of a particularly bilious view of life. (Muscatine, 1957, p. 204)

Such views, though, are not universally held, and have been resisted by Brewer (1973, pp. 121–2, 175) and Craik (1964, pp. 30–47), and in an excellent article by Glending Olson (1974), who stresses the 'normality' of the Reeve's Tale.

Certainly, one must recognise that there are limitations to the reading of the Tale which finds in it chiefly revelations of the character of the Reeve. There is so much else to the Tale, so much enjoyment of the 'game', the battle of wits, which is not rendered as part of our response if we read the Tale as a condemnation of the Reeve, and the recoil upon him of all the judgements he makes on others. The comparison that Paul Olson (1962) makes with *Measure for Measure* is instructive, but chiefly so in reminding us, as Olson reminds himself (p. 17), that neither Shakespeare nor Chaucer was teaching lessons in Christian morality. Rather, Chaucer is seeking by non-dramatic means the complexity, the multiplicity of points of view, the indirection, that Shakespeare achieved by dramatic means. The method here, as in the Merchant's Tale, is to incorporate satire from a fixed but not central point of view, so that our laughter has an edge of uneasiness, our moral sense not completely tuned out. Part of Chaucer's larger purpose, also, is to tell the Reeve's Tale in such a way as to make it an interesting and effective contrast to the Miller's Tale.

Some such accommodation is necessary if full praise is to be given to the final scene of the poem, where the *allegro con brio* of the narrative of the comic climax is as purely a matter of aesthetic delight as anything in the Miller's Tale. Chaucer's acute visual realisation of that darkened bedroom has already been applauded: the slow build-up of suspense, as the wife gropes with her hand and finds the bed and wonders with wicked primness on the fate worse than death that she thinks she has narrowly averted:

> 'Allas!' quod she, 'I hadde almoost mysgoon;
> I hadde almoost goon to the clerkes bed.
> Ey, benedicite! thanne hadde I foule ysped.' (4218–20)

The tempo increases as Aleyn goes through the same labyrinth of wooden bed-ends to a different wrong bed, and we realise with delighted anticipation where he will land up:

> 'By God', thoughte he, 'al wrang I have mysgon.
> Myn heed is toty of my swynk to-nyght,
> That makes me that I ga nat aright.
> I woot wel by the cradel I have mysgo;
> Heere lith the millere and his wyf also.'
> And forth he goth, a twenty devel way,
> Unto the bed ther as the millere lay. (4252–8)

The explosion of recognition that follows is as pure a source of pleasure, in its way, as the *anagnorisis* of a tragic drama. Aleyn and Symkyn struggle 'as doon two pigges in a poke', Symkyn falls back on his wife, who now finds that she has two bodies on top of her instead of the customary one. Though it was just now too dark for her to find her own bed, she manages to find a staff, and, with further help from Chaucer, who temporarily dislodges a tile to allow the moon in, homes in with unerring instinct upon the wrong target:

> And by that light she saugh hem bothe two,
> But sikerly she nyste who was who,
> But as she saugh a whit thyng in hir ye.
> And whan she gan this white thyng espye,
> She wende the clerk hadde wered a volupeer,
> And with the staf she drow ay neer and neer,
> And wende han hit this Aleyn at the fulle,
> And smoot the millere on the pyled skulle,
> That doun he gooth, and cride, 'Harrow! I dye!' (4299–307)

There are still to come the Reeve's sour and self-congratulatory *obiter dicta*, but this paragraph, with its brilliant chiaroscuro, its tumble of coordinating conjunctions matching the breathless helter-skelter of events, makes that bedroom in Trumpington one of the unforgettable places of English poetry.

THE COOK'S TALE

Chaucer, it seems, can hardly hold back the dramatic impetus he has created in Fragment I, and the Reeve's Tale prompts another spontaneous intervention, this time from the Cook, who is in ecstasies over what he very aptly calls this 'jape of malice in the derk' (4338). He also refers rather specifically to the 'argument of herbergage' (4329) in the Tale, the dangers of taking in lodgers or guests for the night, and there is a link here to the last lines of his own fragmentary tale, where the hero, the apprentice 'Perkyn Revelour', after being turned out by his master, goes to stay with

> ... a compeer of his owene sort,
> That lovede dys, and revel, and disport,
> And hadde a wyf that heeld for contenance
> A shoppe, and swyved for hir sustenance. (4419–20)

Before this 'little jape' gets under way, though, there is further dramatic interweaving and anticipation, as the Host takes the opportunity to compliment the Cook on his twice-warmed-up meat pies, on his 'pilgrims' special' – goose cooked with parsley – that has sent many of them on their way to Canterbury at a run, and on his flyblown premises. The Cook acknowledges that the Host speaks truth with the licence of 'game and pley', but says too that he does not find it very funny, and promises to tell a tale 'of an hostileer' before they part, though not yet. There is some allusion here to a traditional enmity between innkeepers and cooks, who were in competition for the same trade, and the attribution of specific and traceable names to both Host ('Herry Bailly', 4358) and Cook ('Hogge of Ware', 4336) – the only occasion when Chaucer does anything of the sort in all the *Canterbury Tales* – suggests that he intends to be understood to be referring to contemporary persons and events, and maybe in the tale too.

The tale itself gets under way swimmingly, with a lively description of Perkyn, vivid evocation of London street life, and some characteristically Chaucerian use of proverbs (4406–7) and passing gnomic wisdom (4391–8). Then it stops, on its famously provocative last line. It may be that it was left accidentally unfinished, like the Squire's Tale and the Monk's Tale, but that in this case Chaucer never got round to integrating it in the framework of *Tales* by treating it as if 'interrupted'. Beyond this, one can only speculate on the intriguing question of why he might have deliberately dropped the Tale. Perhaps it was simply that he realised, on maturer consideration, that three such tales in a row, as Brewer (1973) says, 'would be too much of a good thing' (p. 122). Muscatine (1957) takes a more serious position: for him, there are signs in Chaucer of late Gothic decadence – pointless elaboration, sentimentality, pessimism, empty ceremonialism and empty realism – and 'The unfinished *Cook's Tale* promises to have been the rawest of Chaucer's works'. But he recognised 'the possible dangers of his artistic and moral position', and in the *Tales* as a whole, while he 'explores the outermost limits of the medieval moral order', he still 'proclaims the integrity of that order' (pp. 246–7). That is to put it perhaps rather too portentously, but it seems possible that Chaucer saw the tunnel that realism might go into.

THE MERCHANT'S TALE

The amplification, elaboration and enrichment of narrative, to which Chaucer was inspired in his handling of fabliau-form in the Miller's Tale and Reeve's Tale, are seen in their most advanced stage of development in the Merchant's Tale. The basic fabliau is still there, in the form of the 'pear-tree episode', a story of sexual intrigue in which an old husband is cuckolded and then – a favourite twist in such stories – talked into disbelieving the evidence of his senses by his clever wife, even though he has caught her *in flagrante delicto*. However, the story, or at least the trick upon which it turns, is the mere dessert to a great feast, occupying only, as to its essentials, the last hundred lines (IV.2320–418) of a 1173-line story (the Miller's Tale has 667 lines and the Reeve's Tale 403). The expansions of the narrative leading up to the dénouement are in certain ways comparable with the two shorter tales, especially in regard to the attention given to characterisation, here principally in the presentation of the old husband January. But there is less attention to setting, and what there is, such as the account of the garden in which the climactic events take place, has a symbolic rather than a realistic significance. The major expansions are of a kind unique to the Merchant's Tale – an extended mock-encomium of marriage (1267–392), a debate about marriage between January and his advisors, Placebo and Justinus (1399–577, 1617–95), an elaborate description of the wedding, wedding-feast and wedding-night (1700–865), and a mythological interlude in which Pluto and Proserpina argue the case of the husband and wife, respectively, and explain how they will intervene to assist their *protégés* (2225–319). Much attention is given, it will be seen, to the preparations for and the nature of the marriage between the old husband and his young wife, a subject which is usually not mentioned or else dismissed quite briefly in fabliau. Additional, too, and very prominent in the latter half of the tale, is a good deal of ostentatious rhetorical elaboration, including exclamation, apostrophe and periphrasis, of a kind specifically associated with the high style of romance. Finally, the story is told in a tone of voice that persistently expresses bitterness, cynicism and sardonic humour. There are reminders of the Reeve's Tale in this, as there are reminders of the Reeve in the portrayal of January (1461–4), but the Reeve's voice is not nearly so profound and persistent a part of our experience of his tale as is the voice of the narrator here.

The tale is hardly under way before January, a sixty-year-old philanderer who thinks it high time he got married, is in a cross-fire of snide remarks, some of them seemingly of the kind that a cleric might make, such as the attribution of an interest in women to 'thise fooles that been seculeer' (1251), which goes with a number of other remarks in the mock-encomium of marriage that reinforce the same suggestion (e.g., 1322, 1383–4, 1389–90). There is perhaps less profit in using these passages to debate what pilgrim Chaucer might originally have intended the tale for[6] than in recognising the dyspeptic tone of voice of the clerical satirist, a tone of voice that Chaucer may have caught first from his principal source in the early part of the tale, the *Miroir de Mariage* of Deschamps. Basically misogynistic, this type of satire is even more contemptuous of men who allow themselves to fall into the power of women, and the general effect is one of cynicism about all aspects of human sexuality. The vehement denunciation of women which is the apparent object of such writing is thus constantly revealed to be the expression of a self-lacerating disgust, specially virulent in a society in which both writing and attitudes to sexuality were dominated by celibate clerics but powerful also in other male-dominated cultures. The voice can be heard in Shakespeare, sometimes strident, as in the venomous outbursts of Timon or of Thersites in *Troilus and Cressida*, sometimes contained within a higher art, as with many passages in *Hamlet*, *Othello* and *The Winter's Tale*. The great imaginative writers seem to be able to go

beyond the tempting rhetoric of male cynicism, to recognise the cause of
disorder in a disordered consciousness, and to isolate this consciousness
through the power of their art. Chaucer is one such, and the Merchant's
Tale, with the Wife of Bath's Prologue, his great achievement in this
respect.

The cynical voice is well established in these opening lines of the
Merchant's Tale. The sneering offer of a choice between 'hoolynesse'
and 'dotage' as explanations of January's desire to get married, the
implication of suicidal haste in his 'greet corage' to become 'a wedded
man', the bitter ironies of 'esy' and 'clene' in January's description of
wedlock ('*esy*', 'full of ease', but also 'without obstacles to the practice of
lechery'; '*clene*', 'chaste', but also 'clearly defined as exempt from
constraint'), the drawling contempt of 'this olde knyght, that was so wys'
– all attempt to draw us into a narratorial conspiracy. In such a context,
remarks that might otherwise appear innocent, like the reference to

> thilke blisful lyf
> That is bitwixe an housbonde and his wyf, (1259–60)

take on a sardonic undertone. The latter line appears also in the
Franklin's Tale, but in a context of genuine approbation, and the
contrast between the two Tales, all the sharper because of certain
structural similarities (the triangle of relationships, the role of Aurelius/
Damyan), expresses well Chaucer's power of 'colouring' narration in a
manner suitable to the different generic expectations of romance and
fabliau and the consequently different expectations that the characters in
such stories have of themselves. This power is more fully displayed than
usual in the Merchant's Tale, and comparison with the Reeve's Tale
obliges recognition of how much less pervasive the sense of the narrator's
voice is there, and how relatively strictly confined within the narrower
psychology of vindictiveness. The further contrast with the Miller's
Tale, where the misfortune of the old carpenter in marrying a young wife
is dismissed with genial perfunctoriness –

> But sith that he was fallen in the snare,
> He moste endure, as oother folk, his care (I.3231–2)

– is even more profound.

The mock-encomium of marriage reinforces our sense that it is a
special, intrusive voice, not Chaucer's voice, that is responsible for the

conduct of the narrative.[7] The matter of the encomium is orthodox, but there is an intermittent counter-current of irony which occasionally breaks the surface, in a manner uncharacteristic of Chaucer's own voice, in open sarcasm or in venomous asides. The first open lapse into sarcasm comes at the end of a discussion of the superior longevity of a wife, 'Goddes yifte', over 'yiftes of Fortune':

> A wyf wol laste, and in thyn hous endure,
> Wel lenger than thee list, paraventure. (1317–18)

Again, God's decision to provide Adam with a mate, when he sees him 'al allone, bely-naked' (1326), is described in such a way as to suggest a kind of embarrassment or even 'cynical pity' (Donaldson, 1970, pp. 38–40) on God's part, while the exaggerated panegyric of these lines –

> A wyf? a, Seinte Marie, *benedicite!*
> How myghte a man han any adversitee
> That hath a wyf? Certes, I kan nat seye. (1337–9)

– with the deflating effect of rhetorical question lamely answered, comes to seem as ludicrous, in context (contrast Franklin's Tale, V.803–5) as the little dialogue of wifely obedience (contrast Clerk's Tale, IV.355):

> She seith nat ones 'nay', whan he seith 'ye'.
> 'Do this', seith he; 'Al redy, sire,' seith she. (1345–6)

The encomium ends with another sardonic aside:

> Housbonde and wyf, what so men jape or pleye,
> Of worldly folk holden the siker weye;
> They been so knyt ther may noon harm bityde,
> And namely upon the wyves syde. (1389–92)

The general effect is that the narrator is agreeing with and encouraging January, whom he seems to be apostrophising, whilst letting slip stray hints and innuendoes to us as an audience of superior understanding.

January, from this point on, is the centre of the tale's attention, and the centre of its imaginative potency. The portrait of the *senex amans* here takes on a lurid physical reality. January offers a good many reasons for getting married, including all the usual ones – procreation, the eschewing of lechery, the payment of the marriage-debt (1448–52) – and in fact shows a well-developed though totally perverted consciousness of the moral implications of his decision. It is this parody of the operation of moral consciousness that provides much of the intensity of the Merchant's Tale. January knows that he wants a young wife, but he also wants to explain why he should, properly, want such a wife. His first image is of the Wife of Bath, and how well he can do without 'thise olde wydwes' (1423) and their argumentativeness: the alternative is expressed, aptly enough, in tactile images,

> But certeynly, a yong thyng may men gye,
> Right as men may warm wex with handes plye (1429–30)[8]

and, more powerfully, in the imagery of eating:

> 'Bet is,' quod he, 'a pyk than a pykerel,
> And bet than old boef is the tendre veel.
> I wol no womman thritty yeer of age;
> It is but bene-straw and greet forage.' (1419–22)

It is notable, here, how January thinks of himself as a horse, the traditional image of unbridled virility, as we saw in the Reeve's Tale (I.4066), but ludicrously, and pathetically too, of a horse quietly at its fodder. The topsy-turvy justification of his decision to take a young wife that January finally arrives at is equally comical:

> I wol noon oold wyf han right for this cause.
> For if so were I hadde swich myschaunce,
> That I in hire ne koude han no plesaunce,
> Thanne sholde I lede my lyf in avoutrye,
> And go streight to the devel, whan I dye. (1432–6)

Here is morality, and the traditional sanction of matrimony, in a distorting mirror.

It is lust, of course, or the thought of it, that drives January to these feats of moral prestidigitation. The precepts of marriage he accepts, in his own way, but the recommendation to chastity within marriage he brushes aside, much as the Wife of Bath did the counsel of virginity (III.112):

> But sires, by youre leve, that am nat I.

> For, God be thanked! I dar make avaunt,
> I feele my lymes stark and suffisaunt
> To do al that a man bilongeth to;
> I woot myselven best what I may do. (1456–60)

He creates out of his fantasy an object upon whom his lust can descend
(1580–7) – 'an excellent example of the danger of *delectatio cogitationis*',
it is called by Robertson (1962, p. 110), whose iconographic analysis of
the passage is much to the point – and, once decided, can brook no delay.
He is in haste to be married (1409–11, 1613), to fix the wedding day
(1694), to end the wedding-feast (1767), to get to bed (1805), but then,
sustained by aphrodisiacs (1807–12) and long feeding of his lechery in
contemplation, he looks for the long night of the epithalamion:

> The bryde was broght abedde as stille as stoon;
> And whan the bed was with the preest yblessed,
> Out of the chambre hath every wight hym dressed;
> And Januarie hath faste in armes take
> His fresshe May, his paradys, his make.
> He lulleth hire, he kisseth hire ful ofte;
> With thikke brustles of his berd unsofte,
> Lyk to the skyn of houndfyssh, sharp as brere –
> For he was shave al newe in his manere –
> He rubbeth hire aboute hir tendre face,
> And seyde thus, 'Allas! I moot trespace
> To yow, my spouse, and yow greetly offende,
> Er tyme come that I wil doun descende.
> But nathelees, considereth this,' quod he,
> 'Ther nys no werkman, whatsoevere he be,
> That may both werke wel and hastily;
> This wol be doon at leyser parfitly.
> It is no fors how longe that we pleye;
> In trewe wedlok coupled be we tweye;
> And blessed be the yok that we been inne,
> For in oure actes we mowe do no synne.
> A man may do no synne with his wyf,
> Ne hurte hymselven with his owene knyf;
> For we han leve to pleye us by the lawe.'
> Thus laboureth he til that the day gan dawe;
> And thanne he taketh a sop in fyn clarree,
> And upright in his bed thanne sitteth he,
> And after that he sang ful loude and cleere,
> And kiste his wyf, and made wantown cheere.
> He was al coltissh, ful of ragerye,

And ful of jargon as a flekked pye.
The slakke skyn aboute his nekke shaketh,
Whil that he sang, so chaunteth he and craketh. (1818–50)

This superb passage is as full of wit and amusement as it is of horror and
disgust: perhaps it is really disgust under the disguise of a contemptuous
amusement, like much salacious writing. The unremitting concentration
upon the physicality of the event draws us into the experience of it, and,
in an extraordinary and perverted way, as Donaldson (1958, p. 922) first
described, into the experience of May especially, both tactile (1825) and
visual (1849). The numbness of bridehood ('as stille as stoon') is as vivid
as January's cavortings and yodellings. Still, though, and more ludicrously than ever, January tries to give his actions the sanction of
matrimonial morality: for him there is some divine but welcome mystery
in the way sexual activity, hitherto forbidden, is now somehow not
merely permitted but almost a matter of moral and legal obligation
(1841). The irony of his knife-image (explicitly used in the Parson's Tale,
X.859, as the illustration of the sin that a man *can* do with his own wife) is
lost on him.

January's blindness, his self-deception, his lack of understanding of
himself and of his actions, make him a figure of ridicule and contempt.
His age adds to his ridiculousness: the not-too-successful close shave, 'al
newe in his manere' (1826), the contemptuous 'laboureth' (1842), the
gleeful performance that follows his success (1843–50), the abrupt
collapse into exhausted sleep (1855–7) with its cruel echo of the traditional aube (Kaske, 1960) – are all set before us with great explicitness.
The extraordinary consequence of this vividness of portrayal, however,
is to draw us into a participation in January's experience which creates
quite strong feeling. There is no need to emphasise how improper such
feeling is in the context of the genre of fabliau, and we have already seen
how deftly Chaucer suggests and withdraws the suggestion of emotional
participation in the Miller's Tale and Reeve's Tale. The violation of the
expectation of the genre is deliberate, and deeply shocking: it is rather as
if someone telling a dirty story had begun to dwell upon the actual nature
and consequences of events that had been accepted to be fantasy. The
effect here in the Merchant's Tale, in the materialisation, the making
concrete and explicit, of the world of stock innuendo that attaches to the
wedding of 'tendre youthe' and 'stoupyng age' (1738), is comparable in
its power of disorientating response.[9]

It is not only January, however, who is made the object of the
narrator's contempt:

> But God woot what that May thoughte in hir herte,
> Whan she hym saugh up sittynge in his sherte,
> In his nyght-cappe, and with his nekke lene;
> She preyseth nat his pleyyng worth a bene. (1851–4)

'God woot', it is said, what May thought, but then, quite explicitly, we are told, and the image used expresses a cold appraisal on her part of the night's doings. Bridal chastity never appeared a more sordid commodity: she has sold herself cheap, it seems, and with Damian sickening off-stage determines to raise some further profit on her capital. The progress of their adulterous liaison is described with much of the language appropriate to a romantic love-affair, but also with sneering interventions on the part of the narrator that declare his valuation of 'this gentil May, fulfilled of pitee' (1995):

> Heere may ye se how excellent franchise
> In wommen is, whan they hem narwe avyse. (1987–8)

There are moments in the realisation of the narrative, too, gratuitous invasions of the characters' privacy, which have the same shocking effect in materialising the fantasy of romance that we observed earlier with the fantasy of fabliau. The narrator's insistence on telling us exactly what May did with Damian's love-letter (1953–4) has about it the sour disillusion of one who is determined to tell the truth about this squalid business of sex. The delivery of May's letter in return is a masterpiece of salacious suggestiveness, with the 'thrusting' and 'twisting' (2003, 2005) anticipating the *twiste* and *throng* of the dénouement (2349, 2353). Damian is, if anything, more unspeakably degraded than May.

> And eek to Januarie he gooth as lowe
> As evere dide a dogge for the bowe.
> He is so plesant unto every man
> (For craft is al, whoso that do it kan). (2013–16)

The comment betrays the spitting malice with which the narration is imbued, for all its high-flown phrases, and the cynical reduction of all human behaviour to lust and greed. It may be thought that this is nothing more than we expect in fabliau: the difference is that we have been made to think and feel about this story in a way that takes it far beyond the limited expectations of the genre.

These revelations about May and Damian, and about the 'real' nature of young love, have the bewildering effect of changing or at least disturbing our view of January. From the first, there was about him a kind of perverted idealism, a consciousness that there was such a thing as 'love', as well as 'synne', even though he had no clear notion of either. His fantasy of marital rape ('in his herte he gan hire to manace', 1752) has a nastiness about it, but the edge of nastiness is blunted by the egregiousness of his vanity as well as by a strangely touching consideration for the victim of his all-consuming sexuality (1755–61). In the marital bed, he embarks on elaborate apologies for what he is about to do and how long he is going to take doing it (1828–30). This is revolting enough, but again there is some recognition of May's existence and of her possible feelings which, though it may not qualify as humanity or compassion, at least seems somewhat less disgusting when we find that she has not got any. The subsequent history of January, apart from demonstrating his general good nature (and extreme 'foolishness') in his care for Damyan (1897–1925), is of declining potency, of sleep overtaking all as he lapses into the comfort of the marriage-bed:

> And spede yow faste, for I wole abyde
> Til that ye slepe faste by my syde. (1927–8)

From time to time he stirs himself, by some effort of imagination, to activity:

> Adoun by olde Januarie she lay,
> That sleep til that the coughe hath hym awaked.
> Anon he preyde hire strepen hire al naked;
> He wolde of hire, he seyde, han som plesaunce,
> And seyde hir clothes dide hym encombraunce ... (1956–60)

The pathetic effortfulness of it all is made more bitter by the narrator's sleazy suggestiveness in referring to the 'precious' folk who might be offended at a long description of January's efforts (1962–3), which has about it the same prurience and mock-delicacy as the earlier lines (1950–1) describing May's visit to the privy.

January's blindness makes him a still more pathetic figure. To say that his physical blindness is the figure of his moral blindness is true enough, and it is often enough said, but the story, as it has been developed and realised, resists neat iconographic interpretation. Close attention to

January's lust and greed, especially by contrast with the lust and greed of
May and Damian, has revealed in him a kind of warmth, a kind of
humanity, albeit twisted and perverted from its natural course. His
bewilderment and pain at his blindness produces in him a new fire of
jealousy, at first insane (2075–6). His solution, as he gradually resigns
himself to his state, is to treat May like a cross between a prisoner in
custody and a guide-dog:

> He nolde suffre hire for to ryde or go,
> But if that he had hond on hire alway. (2090–1)

The picture is comical, pathetic, ridiculous: it asks to be laughed at, but
it is hard to laugh heartily. Burrow (1957) has spoken well of the
'essential intelligibility' of January's behaviour, of the 'lyrical expan-
siveness' of treatment in parts of the Tale (p. 207), of the generosity of 'an
irony which does justice to its victims' (p. 201), and of the 'generalising'
tendency of the poem (p. 203), which relates January's fantasies in a
meaningful way to general human weakness. The complexity of response
that is asked for is not dissimilar from that evoked by one or two of the
victims of later satirical comedy, such as Molière's Harpagon, and
McGalliard (1946) makes some interesting comparisons between the two
writers, particularly in their portraits of self-deception on the part of
those in the grip of an *idée fixe*.

The same disturbing mixture of responses is created by the garden
which January contrives for himself, before he goes blind:

> Amonges othere of his honeste thynges,
> He made a gardyn, walled al with stoon;
> So fair a gardyn woot I nowher noon. (2028–30)

The charming and idyllic description that follows, with its wealth of
literary allusion, is however no more than the preparation for further
disgusting revelations concerning January's sex-life:

> And whan he wolde paye his wyf hir dette
> In somer seson, thider wolde he go,
> And May his wyf, and no wight but they two;
> And thynges whiche that were nat doon abedde
> He in the gardyn parfourned hem and spedde. (2048–52)

There has been no difficulty for exegetical critics in identifying this garden as the garden of self-love, the perversion of the garden of love, where charity has become cupidity:

> We are, I think, in the garden of Deduit, under Tristan's pine-tree, in the garden of Jehan [in *Cligés*], in Amoenitas [in the *De Arte Honeste Amandi* of Andreas Capellanus], and beside Grendel's pool. Ultimately, we are back at Eve and Adam's *in medio ligni paradisi* ... (Robertson, 1962, p. 44)

The iconographic significances of the garden can be unrolled almost *ad libitum*: the poem has been full of references to marriage or a wife or the sexual act as 'paradise' (1265, 1332, 1647, 1822, 1964), which prepares for the scriptural parody present here. The 'laurer alwey grene' in the garden (2037) recalls January's earlier description of himself,

> Myn herte and alle my lymes been as grene
> As laurer thurgh the yeer is for to sene. (1465–6)

and suggests to us that the garden is the projection of his fantasy of perpetual lust. The double entendre of the *clyket* is well developed: January alone has the *clyket*, or key, to his *hortus conclusus*, but May has a print of it made 'in warm wex' (2117) – the sort of 'wex' January wanted his wife to be – so that Damian can counterfeit it:

> Som wonder by this clyket shal bityde,
> Which ye shul heeren, if ye wole abyde. (2123–4)

So Damian now has January's 'clyket' to get through the 'wyket' into January's own private paradise. Bleeth (1974) develops these points with force and subtlety, and comments too on the hint of an allusion to Satan gaining entry to the Garden of Eden, which is thereby turned from a *hortus conclusus* into a *paradisus voluptatis* (pp. 58–9).

At the same time, though, that we enjoy this rich feast of allusion and parody, it is worth recalling the circumstances in which it is being served up. January is a butt for every gibe:

> Who may been a fool, but if he love? (I.1799)

And of course there is no fool like an old one. But the eagerness to laugh at senile folly, especially sexual folly, should not obliterate completely the recognition, again, of a quality of perverse romantic idealism in

January. The outstanding example, and a comment which is inexplicable except in terms of Chaucer's intention to isolate his narrator as an embittered cynic, comes at the end of January's lyrical address to May as they enter the garden:

> Swiche olde lewed wordes used he. (2149)

The phraseology of January's love-song (2138–48) is from the Song of Songs, again, as in the Miller's Tale (I.3697–3703), though in this case uncorrupted by incongruous elements. Exegetes such as Wimsatt (1973, pp. 84–8) have had a good many laughs at the grotesque figure January cuts in this parody of the mystical union of *sponsor* and *sponsa*, but the dramatic effect of such a passage of unsullied poetic lyricism is to absorb us into the reality of the emotion, so that the narrator's cynical comment sets up a violent opposition within us. The comment is unfair to January, and it is also wrong, for these are not, whether the narrator is to be understood as realising it or not, 'olde lewed wordes'. If he does not realise it, he is a fool; if he does, he is a foolish cynic. In this way, as throughout the tale, Chaucer opens up a trap beneath his narrator.

Perhaps the most unequivocal demonstration of the power of the story to tell itself, despite the efforts of the narrator to turn it to dust and ashes, is January's more serious speech to his wife as they enter the garden, which ends thus:

> I prey yow first, in covenant ye me kisse;
> And though that I be jalous, wyte me noght.
> Ye been so depe enprented in my thoght
> That, whan that I considere youre beautee,
> And therwithal the unlikly elde of me,
> I may nat, certes, though I sholde dye,
> Forbere to been out of youre compaignye
> For verray love; this is withouten doute.
> Now kys me, wyf, and lat us rome aboute. (2176–84)

The whole speech again reveals what a fool January is, to bestow such goods and such trust upon his wife. It thus serves the purposes of the narrator, who shows himself more and more closely identified with May's point of view. But, as a speech, it has a soberly meditative quality, and brings January to a point of self-awareness where he seems to understand, truly, himself and the nature of the contract into which he is entered. The echo of his earlier inanities ('dyen on a knyf', 'offende,'

2163-4) is quite touching, and there is a pathetic recognition on his part now of what he has to give in what he knows is a commercially based relationship. It is the voice of the Wife of Bath's old husbands, unmediated by her own strident contempt. It was never to be expected that the *senex amans* of fabliau tradition would speak with such frankness of his own 'unlikly elde', and create in us what Kean (1972) recognises as a kind of sympathy, though not, as she says, without 'ambiguities and ironies' (pp. 162-3). The contrast with May's petulant posturing, as she keeps an eye on Damyan, sitting now, ridiculously, 'in' his bush (2208), is profound enough. Chaucer's humanity, in other words, asserts itself even when the mode of narration that he had originally opted for seemed to deny it.

That mode of narration spoke from the start, as we have seen, of a corrupted understanding. It emerges starkly in the description of the wedding-ceremony:

> Forth comth the preest, with stole aboute his nekke,
> And bad hire be lyk Sarra and Rebekke
> In wysdom and in trouthe of mariage;
> And seyde his orisons, as is usage,
> And croucheth hem, and bad God sholde hem blesse,
> And made al siker ynogh with hoolynesse. (1703-8)

Every line drips contempt for this mumbo-jumbo which fools accept as making licit what was hitherto illicit.[10] Nothing escapes the narrator's passion to demonstrate that everything is false and hollow, and since nothing escapes it everything escapes it in the end. The hollowness is at the heart of the narration: the glittering lines that describe the wedding-feast, with their wealth of classical and mythological allusion (1709-49), are a rhetorical charade, detached from any reality to which they might refer, and the flurry of apostrophes and exclamations and sententious comments that accompany the action have no centre. At one time the narrator will apostrophise January, warning him of the snake in the grass, or at least the 'fyr . . . in the bedstraw' (1783-94), that threatens him; at another he will ask God's help for Damyan (1866-74); destiny is pointlessly invoked (1967-76), and Fortune apostrophised, again on January's behalf (2057-68). It is the high style of *Troilus*, but meretriciously applied, like a coat of gloss paint on a damp and decaying wall. It is itself a parody and perversion of rhetoric, a 'dyspeptic' rhetoric, as Muscatine (1957, p. 233) calls it, and it issues, not from a heightened consciousness like the Nun's Priest's Tale, but from a disordered consciousness.

The dénouement is handled in a rather different way. As often, for instance in the Franklin's Tale, Chaucer has his eye on the end of the tale, and prepares now for the restoration of some equilibrium, the reestablishment of a more light-hearted mood, after the exploration of the dark corners to which his narrator's peculiar preoccupations have given him access. The method is similar to that employed in the Franklin's Tale, that is, the rendering in explicit form of some blatant artifice in the narrative, so that participation is discouraged. The particular technique used here – the introduction of mythological deities conversing about the fortunes of the characters and the way in which they will intervene to engineer the 'right' conclusion – is strikingly reminiscent of Shakespeare's technique of using similar kinds of creaky supernatural machinery as he moves from potentially dark and disturbing events to relatively sunny endings in his comedies and romances. The darkness is not entirely dissipated in the Merchant's Tale, any more than it is at the end of *Measure for Measure* or *Cymbeline*, but there is a perceptible change.

The lightening of mood is apparent in the lovely opening to the final garden scene:

> Bright was the day, and blew the firmament;
> Phebus hath of gold his stremes doun ysent,
> To gladen every flour with his warmnesse. (2219–21)

The conversation that follows, between Pluto, 'king of Fayerye', and his queen, Proserpina, has a touch of Oberon and Titania about it, in the suggestion of unscrupulous passions at work in the government of human affairs, but the two of them sound more like the Wife of Bath and Jankyn than mythological deities, and the general effect is one of deflation and domestic comedy, rather than of any weighty addition to the 'doctrine' of the poem such as has been derived by Dalbey (1974) and others from Christian iconographic interpretation of classical mythology. Having heard how the two deities are to engineer the final climax, we witness the ridiculous farce that ensues with no great feeling of anxiety or disturbance. It is, indeed, narrated with the greatest brilliance and brevity, the swift tying-up of events so well prepared for needing only a few deft manoeuvres from Chaucer. May's desire to get up into the pear-tree, to pluck 'the smale peres grene', is amply accounted for by her *plit* (2335), or 'interesting condition', and of course the thought that he has been able to get her into this interesting condition is very pleasing to

January. Her explanation that the tree is the one place where he can be sure she is not up to any mischief, since he embraces its trunk and forbids all access as she uses his bent back as a step-ladder, is similarly satisfying to him. The description of the coupling in the pear-tree catches the tone of prurient mock-delicacy, of fascinated disgust, that has pervaded the telling of the tale:

> He stoupeth doun, and on his bak she stood,
> And caughte hire by a twiste, and up she gooth –
> Ladyes, I prey yow that ye be nat wrooth;
> I kan nat glose, I am a rude man –
> And sodeynly anon this Damyan
> Gan pullen up the smok, and in he throng. (2348–53)

The word 'throng' is an extraordinarily repulsive one, and the subsequent descriptions of January's reaction, with its reminiscence of the Massacre of the Innocents, shows a familiar sardonic mockery as well as salaciously suggestive mock-delicacy (2360–7). The tale ends in a kind of harmony, with May promising herself, on the strength of her success here, a few more adventures of the same kind (2405–10) and January remembering how pleased he is that she is pregnant (perhaps she really is, now, as Miller, 1950, pertinently remarks), and contenting himself with the thought that it is better to see and be blind than be blind and not see. Illusions must be cherished, for happiness, as Swift said, 'is a perpetual possession of being well deceived' (*A Tale of a Tub*, Sect. IX).

The ending is a mockery, of course, but it is well in accord with the mock-morality that is conventional in fabliau, and in that respect quite undisturbing. The disturbance created by the tale, however, still lingers in one's consciousness and seems to call for some explanation. The mood of savagery and cynicism, the Thersitean disgust, which has been felt to permeate the tale by all but a few of the commentators,[11] is so unlike what we are used to in Chaucer that one inevitably asks what he was up to. A crucial problem is that the tale, having violated the expectations of the genre to which it apparently belongs, establishes no consistent new set of expectations: the high style of romance is as meretricious as the low style of fabliau. There is no centre to the poem, no literary convention within which it has its place in relation to reality, no body of moral values to which it refers. The character who should, according to his name, embody the morally normative values to which the actions of the others might be referred, is himself a distorting mirror. The two speeches of

Justinus have the wisdom of experience, but the only wisdom that experience has taught Justinus is the wisdom of not getting married:

> But I woot best where wryngeth me my sho. (1553)

His later speech, where he is assuaging January's anxiety that married bliss here may deprive him of bliss hereafter, is bitterly serious, and there is not much mockery in the way he twists the question so as to speak, not of the bliss that may be lost by bliss, but of the salvation that may be missed if the strait way of marriage is not kept (1674–81). Throughout, Justinus speaks of marriage in terms of the purchase of a commodity: his only wisdom is to recognise that it is a commodity which never gives satisfaction. Marriage is a deal, and always a bad deal, or at best only marginally profitable (1540–2). To think of this as the way in which Chaucer thought, or the Middle Ages thought, is to neglect the evidence of what is said in the Franklin's Tale or even the Wife of Bath's Tale. The voice of Justinus is the voice of the clerical establishment, and it is only this narrator who would give such a man such a name.

We must recognise, I think, that the Merchant's Tale is deliberately set off-centre, and is Chaucer's way of exploring some dark corners of consciousness and especially that horror of sexuality which is as much part of human experience as awe and gladness. It is an artistic experiment or exercise, or perhaps, as David (1976, p. 181) says, 'an act of exorcism'. The disgustingness of being human, of growing old, of having sexual instincts, was felt similarly by Swift, and precariously brought under control by him in Book IV of *Gulliver's Travels* through the distancing from the author of the misanthropic voice of Gulliver. Chaucer works in a comparable way in the Merchant's Tale, establishing a narrator who is obsessed with the vileness of human sexual relationships, the sham language in which it is concealed, the lies that are told about it:

> The storyteller means to strip away the illusion of beauty and sanctity with which Christian and courtly traditions have, so he thinks, disguised the animal lust and economic interest that are the only basis he can conceive for intercourse between man and woman. (David, 1976, p. 173)

David concludes:

> The Merchant's Tale shows us a portrait of the artist as he might have become except for the saving grace of his affection for the objects of his

satire ... There is a danger for every satirist that his observation of mankind may sour his imagination, that his judgment of man will wear away the last drop of his charity, that he will come to despise his own kind ... It is like an act of exorcism. (David, 1976, p. 181)

The only demur that might be made from this excellent account of the tale, and of Chaucer's motives in writing it, is in the suggestion that has been made, throughout the above account, that Chaucer does indeed, perhaps even despite himself, express his humanity, his 'affection for the objects of his satire', within the tale itself, in the portrayal of January.

Whether we should seek to embody this understanding of the Merchant's Tale by speaking of it as the revelation of the character of its teller, the Merchant, is a familiar though not in the end an important question.[12] Something of the intensity of the tale may be lost if it is thought of as an act of such deliberate calculation on Chaucer's part, and certainly nothing is gained. The Merchant of the General Prologue is not a person in whom we might properly suspect such depths, and the interpretation of the generally 'mercantile' values of the tale as generally appropriate to a Merchant is rather trite. We do not need the Merchant to enable us to understand the tale, for the narratorial voice, and the judgement we should make of it, is fully established from within. The Merchant's two-month-old disastrous marriage to a 'shrewe' (1222) can be seen in this light as a convenient accommodation on Chaucer's part, and the voice of the *mal marié* as a convenient one for the purposes of integrating the story within the framework of the *Canterbury Tales*. There is reasonably good evidence that the Merchant's Prologue was written after the Tale (Manly and Rickert, 1940, vol. 2, p. 266), which would certainly affect its status in the interpretation of the tale.

THE SHIPMAN'S TALE

The original teller of the Shipman's Tale is generally agreed to have been the Wife of Bath. This deduction is based on the feminine pronouns of lines 11–19, where wives' views on the allocation of the household budget are put forward. Not everyone agrees with the deduction, as was noted in Chapter 1 (see Chapman, 1956; Copland, 1966, pp. 24–7), but it matters little to interpretation. There is little to make us think further of the Wife of Bath, and nothing to make us think of the Shipman, to whom the tale seems to have been assigned in a rather perfunctory manner. It is not even very coarse, except for the raucous last line, which is probably better suited to a (rather rude) woman.

The tale with its 'beautifully machined plot', as Burrow (1977, p. 201) calls it, is a version of a widely known story called 'The Lover's Gift Regained'. It is a genuine fabliau, with the characteristic narrative structure and structure of values, but the trickery involved is, on the face of it, unusually mild. There is no scene of confrontation and reversal: the husband never gets to know that he has been deceived, and the wife swallows her humiliation, at the realisation that she has been deceived, very quickly. The sexual act which is the point of the plot is led up to in a scene of quite arch and mannered comedy (89–211) and described with the utmost brevity (314–19). There is no violence of any kind, not even to anyone's feelings – or at least to the feelings that are available to the characters in this kind of story – and no-one 'suffers' or is treated satirically. The characters have no obsessions or fantasies, as does January, no lusts that cause them to move heaven and earth to gain their desires, as does Nicholas, no passions of rage and revenge such as motivate the action in the Reeve's Tale. The tale is remarkably free from the amplifications and rhetorical extravagances that characterised the other three fabliaux, and there is no moment in it when courtly values are invoked or parodied. The style of the narrator in the Shipman's Tale is quite plain and bland, and in fact Chaucer uses here, in the strictly narrative portions of the tale, his homely reportorial manner –

> ... but herkneth to my tale (23)

> ... this monk, of which that I began (34)

> Na moore of this as now, for it suffiseth (52)

> This noble monk, of which I yow devyse (62)

> And thus I lete hem ete and drynke and pleye (73)

> ... and there I lete hym dwelle (306)

> ... namoore of hym I seye (324)

– in contrast to the rather high-flown and brilliant artifice of the other three tales. The narrator seems to be a contented member of the world he reports with such fidelity, and to share its calculations of what is worthwhile.

The evocation and minute description of this world and its *mores* is the principal business and glory of this minor masterpiece, especially in the central scene of double intrigue (75–298), in which unity of place, time and action is maintained almost inviolate, and in the final pillow-scene (377–432). The absence of any overt satirical point of view or comment – except what is present in the very fact of reporting such a world without comment – allows full scope to Chaucer's gift for close-textured dramatic writing, and the scene between the monk and the wife in the garden has the same quality, in little, as the scene between Pandarus and Criseyde in Book II of *Troilus*.

The first character in this scene, the monk 'Daun John', has been introduced as an amiable enough fellow,

> Oure deere cosyn, ful of curteisye. (69)

The effect here of what Tatlock (1921, p. 425) calls 'the domestic "our"' is familiar, homely and quite friendly. If his popularity in the merchant's establishment is due to his success in judging gifts and tips –

> Free was daun John, and namely of dispence (43)

– as much as to his general affability, then it is left to us to think ill of him for that. His monastic profession hardly seems to have any bearing on our judgement of him, except in so far as we recognise the opportunity it gives to a man of such 'heigh prudence' to 'ryde out' (64–5). At least, to his credit, he is up early, saying 'his thynges' as he strolls in the garden, and 'ful curteisly' too (91). The monk has no other design in being in the garden, but the wife is there by premeditation: she arrives 'pryvely', bringing with her, for form's sake, the 'mayde child' that she has under governance, that is, someone else's daughter that she is bringing up. This girl is 'yet under the yerde' and probably therefore about twelve years old. She is present throughout the following scene, and acts as a kind of chaperone, inhibiting any too free physical intimacies and encouraging euphemism. Chaucer's care with small but significant dramatic details is thereby well illustrated. The monk is pleased to be thus sought out, and ventures some rather saucy remarks concerning the somnolence of 'thise wedded men' compared with his own friskiness (the virility of monks was a stock motif of fabliau), and concerning the wife's fortunes abed:

> 'But deere nece, why be ye so pale?
> I trowe, certes, that oure goode man
> Hath yow laboured sith the nyght bigan,
> That yow were nede to resten hastily.'
> And with that word he lough ful murily,
> And of his owene thought he wax al reed. (106–11)

There is a conspiratorial quality about 'oure goode man', an invitation to
intimacy in sharing this patronising condescension and in sharing the
secrets of the marital bed. There is nothing so open, though, that it could
not be concealed under the cover of general raillery if the wife proves
unresponsive, and the monk has the decency to blush at the implications
of his remarks – a rare reaction in a fabliau and rather an endearing one.
The wife, though, is more than ready to respond to the hint of intimacy,
which she takes up with her reference to 'that sory pley', at the same time
protecting herself from any accusations of forwardness by setting the
reference in a context of general lament. The monk recognises the signal,
and gives the green light to further revelations by promising to reveal
them to no-one else and swearing thereto on his 'porthors', or breviary
(prayer-book, or book of 'thynges'). The wife swears likewise on 'this
porthors' and we must imagine her reaching out to touch it in a pretty
gesture of most sacred intimacy. Her promise not to betray a word of
what he tells her is of course a new idea, and a very encouraging one for
the monk, though in the context seemingly prompted only by the
laudable desire to return good for good.

They are brought thus to a new plateau of understanding, and mark
their progress with an exchange of kisses. The wife proceeds to a
declaration of the 'legende' of her life that she might tell if she did not fear
to offend the monk, who is after all her husband's 'cosyn'. The tone is
still that of saintly martyrdom and extreme delicacy and reticence, as if
the wife were only emboldened to speak by the confessor-like manner of
the monk. The monk takes the opportunity to disclaim kinship with the
husband, and to make a much more flattering claim:

> I clepe hym so, by Seint Denys of Fraunce,
> To have the moore cause of aqueyntaunce
> Of yow, which I have loved specially
> Aboven alle wommen, sikerly.
> This swere I yow on my professioun. (151–5)

That the monk should prove the truth of his profession of love by swearing on his 'professioun' is a nice irony. The barriers to a full and free exchange are now down, the opening gambits have all been satisfactorily answered, and the wife, who has taken the initiative throughout, addresses the monk in frankly affectionate terms,

> 'My deere love,' quod she, 'O my daun John' (158)

and embarks on a tirade against her husband (161–72), the striking quality of which is the constant ambiguity of her references to her husband's unsatisfactoriness. The 'yet' of line 172 suggests that she wishes to be understood to have been referring to her husband's niggardliness in bed, though there is no explicit statement to that effect. All is suggestion and innuendo. An interesting quality of the passage is in the way the language of money, of financial generosity and meanness, is used to give respectableness and outward propriety to a discourse that also concerns sexual generosity and meanness. The wife wants the money, primarily, and the promise of sex is a means to that end –

> For at a certeyn day I wol yow paye (190)

– but there seems little difficulty for either of them in recognising the overriding importance of a financial obligation. A sexual liaison is thus justified, rather than perverted, by being made part of a financial exchange. This 'identification of sex with money' is an important element in the meaning of the Tale, and is well analysed by Silverman (1953) and Owen (1977, pp. 115–18).

The monk accedes to her request for a loan with a good grace:

> 'I wol delyvere yow out of this care;
> For I wol brynge yow an hundred frankes.'
> And with that word he caughte hire by the flankes ... (200–2)

The delicious rhyme on *frankes/flankes* epitomises the theme of convertibility, while the monk's concern about his dinner (203–6) suggests how unprofoundly he has been stirred up by the morning's events. The wife, though, is very pleased with herself, and a little excited, and it is natural that she should go back to her dull old husband, sitting in his 'countour-hous', with a certain impatience:

> 'Com doun to-day, and lat youre bagges stonde.
> Ne be ye nat ashamed that daun John
> Shal fasting al this day alenge goon?
> What! lat us heere a messe, and go we dyne.' (220–3)

The ease and speed with which she converts her own offence into a cause of complaint against her husband is nicely observed.

The merchant, who now speaks and comes to the front of the stage for the first time, is one of Chaucer's more unexpected creations. One might have anticipated a type-figure of avarice, and a suitable gull for the tale's ridicule, but the merchant has not been set up so: his generosity and hospitality seem genuine enough, and there appear on his part to be no advantages in cultivating the monk such as the monk obtains by cultivating him. His speech to his wife now is a long disquisition on the life of the businessman and the responsibilities of capital (224–38) which is patient – he sounds as if he has tried to explain the matter to his wife more than once – serious, a little boring, entirely worthy.[13] Chaucer, as often, surprises us with his readiness to take a stock-response and turn it inside-out. It is not, of course, that Chaucer wants to talk seriously about 'chapmanhede', only that he wants to stretch us and test us in our responses to the merchant, rather as he did with the old husbands in the Miller's Tale and the Merchant's Tale, suggesting for a moment that we might think of them as human beings. The merchant's response to the monk's request for a loan – which we might remark in passing as a masterly 'touch', with its concern for the victim's health, assurances of service, casual introduction of the subject of a loan (for some 'beestes' that he must buy – a mischievous little irony), and mention of a good large round sum as if it came only then into his head – is more subtle; and more subtly qualified:

> But o thyng is, ye knowe it wel ynogh,
> Of chapmen, that hir moneie is hir plogh.
> We may creaunce whil we have a name;
> But goldlees for to be, it is no game.
> Paye it agayn whan it lith in youre ese;
> After my myght ful fayn wolde I yow plese. (287–92)

The movement here between the proprieties of generous behaviour, of being seen to be and thinking oneself generous, and the instinctive caution of the professional financier is beautifully observed. The open and unqualified offer of the loan is followed by the explanation of why it is so difficult for a merchant to make over such large sums of ready cash and the firm but tactful reminder of the obligation to repay. The explanation of the nature of capital investment and of the problems of cash-flow is perfectly sound and serious, and we are certainly not meant to see the merchant as 'mean'. Chaucer has in a way transcended the familiar stereotype of the avaricious merchant, and shown us the man as he would like to think himself to be – a favourite technique in the General Prologue – and shown us some of the inner springs, therefore, of what is familiarly called virtue.

It is this wish to be regarded and to regard himself as a generous man – which we can now see as the underlying motive of the merchant's hospitality, as it was described at the beginning of the tale – that prompts the merchant to rebuke his wife when he returns from Paris. That return was described with a combination of reassuring sentimental propriety and acid observation:

> His wyf ful redy mette hym atte gate,
> As she was wont of oold usage algate,
> And al that nyght in myrthe they bisette;
> For he was riche and cleerly out of dette. (373–6)

The little word 'for' links the two activities of money-making and love-making in the coolest possible way, alluding lightly to the relative priority that they are accorded in a bourgeois marriage, and reinforcing the equation of sex and money. The merchant, however, his first ardour abated on the morrow, reproves his wife for not having told him, on his earlier brief return home (326), that the monk had repaid the loan to her. He is upset that the monk might have thought that he had gone to visit him in Paris to remind him, in speaking of his need to 'make a chevyssaunce' (raise a loan), of the hundred francs outstanding,

> . . . and heeld hym yvele apayed,
> For that I to hym spak of chevyssaunce;
> Me semed so, as by his contenaunce. (390–2)

This was far from his intention, so far, in fact, that the narrator made a special point of saying so:

> Unto daun John he gooth first, hym to pleye;
> Nat for to axe or borwe of hym moneye,

> But for to wite and seen of his welfare,
> And for to tellen hym of his chaffare,
> As freendes doon whan they been met yfeere. (337–41)

The narrator's special point is of course a clue to the merchant's special point in not speaking of the loan, and the flattering tribute he pays to his own generosity in refraining from doing so (one of the richer ironies of the Tale, as Dempster, 1932, p. 40, points out). Now his wife has spoilt it all.

The wife, in the final neat working out of the sex-money equation, sees at once where the hundred francs came from, but she decides, after some glancing references to her contempt for the monk's 'tokenes' (another word ironically caught up from earlier in the poem, lines 359, 390) and his 'monkes snowte' (405), to make the best of a bad job. She proposes now to repay her husband for the hundred francs she got from him via the monk in exactly the same coin that she paid the monk:

> I am youre wyf; score it upon my taille (416)

So the hundred francs has gone the rounds, and the wife has notched up another debt on her *taille* ('tally' or 'tail'), and no-one is much the wiser, or indeed much put out. The neatness of the tale is appallingly satisfactory.

> The reduction of all human values to commercial ones is accomplished with almost mathematical precision ... Within the tale neither the cheating nor the cheated perceive any significance in their actions beyond the immediate financial gain or loss that is incurred, and since there is no real financial loss, the events cause hardly a ripple on the surface of their lives. Sensitivity to other values besides cash has been submitted to appraisal and, having been found nonconvertible, has been thrown away. (Donaldson, 1958, pp. 931–2)

Donaldson, as always, puts things extremely well, but Chaucer, I suggest, could not be quite content with a such a closed system of narrative or such a comprehensive demonstration of amorality. There is something quite exhilarating, as Copland (1966, p. 23) says, in the impudence of the wife's totally materialistic challenge to familiar pieties and decencies, and throughout the Tale an interest in the characters and their relationships that goes far beyond the needs of the plot

(McClintock, 1970–1). Chaucer introduces, furthermore, in his characterisation of the merchant, hints of the operation of motives more subtle and more profound than those of mere gain, motives that have to do with the accommodating of the world, and of the circumstances and experiences that it throws up, to the image of the self that is present to the self as its evidence of a satisfactory identity. Criseyde is the fullest working out of this psychological insight.

THE FRIAR'S TALE

The Friar's Tale and the Summoner's Tale were isolated, at the beginning of the present chapter, from the fabliaux as more strictly defined, and identified as 'satirical anecdotes'. The absence of the sexual motive and of the familiar triangular pattern of relationships seems sufficient reason to make such a distinction, though there is no need to press it too hard. The lyricism, rhetorical extravagance, and parodic romantic idealism of the Miller's Tale and the Merchant's Tale are missing, but the idea of sex as a commodity for profit, in the Shipman's Tale, or as an instrument of revenge, in the Reeve's Tale, brings those two tales closer to the Friar's and Summoner's Tales, in which rapacity is the principal motive assigned to the victim (there is a flutter of sexuality in the Summoner's Tale, III. 1804–5, but it is soon superseded by more pressing concerns), and in which the vindictive motive of the narrator is, as in the Reeve's Tale, the *raison d'être* of the story. Broadly speaking, too, the Friar's and Summoner's Tales operate, as narratives, according to the assumptions and systems of values appropriate to comic tales generally, including fabliaux. The point of the attacks is not that the victims are wicked but that they are stupid. Their wickedness is sufficiently exposed, of course, but there is nothing for a knave to be ashamed about in being shown to be successful in wrongdoing, as long as he makes it pay. The real force of the satire comes from showing the Summoner and the Friar to be gullible fools, both of them, what is more, gullible in the same way, in mistaking the surface for the reality, the literal for the inward meaning. An implication of puppet-like emptiness, even of spiritual deadness, can thus be left to attach to them, as well as stupidity.

The quarrel begins, and the nature of the two combatants is first revealed, at the end of the Wife of Bath's Prologue, where the temperamental difference between the two is communicated with characteristic dramatic sharpness and economy by Chaucer. When the Wife of Bath has finished her tale, the dispute, so carefully seeded and prepared, bursts out. The Friar compliments the Wife on her tale in unctuously and emptily polite terms, alluding airily to the 'scole-matere' she has touched upon, and intimating with patronising condescension that she has done well to speak at all on a subject she knows nothing about. He appeals to the decorum of 'game', and it is as 'game' that he introduces his tale of a summoner, whose profession he sums up with wicked finality:

> A somonour is a rennere up and doun
> With mandementz for fornicacioun. (1283–4)

The Friar knows what profit and general approval accrue to the man who can represent his spite and vindictiveness as light-hearted raillery.

The tale begins with a comprehensive exposure of the system of blackmail and extortion operated by Summoners. The historical accuracy of this account is well illustrated by Hahn and Kaeuper (1983). Interestingly, the Friar does not explicitly criticise the larger system of extortion of which it is part, that is, the commutation for money-payment, or 'pecunyal peyne' (1314), of the penance due for offences (such as fornication and adultery) against the ecclesiastical jurisdiction of the archdeacon's court. The archdeacon is simply represented as ruthless: all the opprobrium attaches to the Summoner, for operating the system for his own personal profit (1345, 1352). The manner of the attack and the crisp dismissive use of the couplet –

> He was, if I shal yeven hym his laude,
> A theef, and eek a somonour, and a baude (1353–4)

– are reminiscent of parts of the Merchant's Tale in mordancy. The relation between the summoner of the tale and 'this Somonour' (1327) is shrewdly hinted at, and we are encouraged to imagine the Summoner visibly fuming as the tale gets under way. He actually breaks in after a few lines, to cap the Friar's complacent assertion of his order's exemption from ecclesiastical jurisdiction with the remark that the brothels are similarly exempt. The Friar makes a similar interruption at about the same point in the Summoner's Tale, further indication, with the interruption by the Pardoner of the Wife of Bath's Prologue and the anticipation at the end of that Prologue of the Friar/Summoner altercation, of the quality of dramatic life consistently sought by Chaucer in Fragment III.

With the beginning of the narrative part of the tale (1375), a change is noticeable: 'As always', says Craik (1964, p. 98), 'the tale soon begins to tell, or rather act, itself.' The unfolding of the plot absorbs more and more of our attention, and creates its own delight, so that we cease to be so conscious of 'this Somonour', and hardly conscious at all of the Friar-narrator. Towards the end of the tale, when the summoner suggests that the old widow has some 'frere or preest' with her (1583), the dramatic impropriety – for impropriety it is, not 'irony' – hardly registers.

The attack, though, is maintained with undiminished vigour, and every aspect of the treatment of the story exposes the stupidity, the shallow cunning, the inane vanity of the summoner.[14] The significance of the 'gay yeman' that he meets, with his 'courtepy of grene' and black-fringed hat, is suggestively diabolical, as Robertson (1954) points out, but it quite escapes the summoner in his delight at having found what looks to be a ready source of supply (1400) as well as a perfect soulmate. We alone are conscious of the rich ironies of which he is the victim: the idea of the hunter, 'evere waityng on his pray' (1376), now at the mercy of the hunter of souls, ready to ride to the world's end 'for a preye' (1455); the identification of the work of the devil, living 'by extorcions' (1429), whether 'by sleyghte or by violence' (1431), with the work of the summoner. The yeoman's sly hints of his nature, as in his references to 'oure shire' (1401), 'fer in the north contree' (1413), where he is sure he will see the summoner soon, are quite lost on the summoner, who tries his best to claim an equal reputation for villainy (1441–2) at the same time, ludi-crously, that he tries to conceal what he really is, as if recognising that to confess to being a summoner would turn anyone's stomach:

> 'Artow thanne a bailly?' 'Ye,' quod he.
> He dorste nat, for verray filthe and shame,
> Seye that he was a somonour, for the name. (1392–4)

The summoner goes on with this inane pretence (1524) long after the yeoman has addressed him as 'leeve sire somonour' (1474).

The yeoman finally declares, in language that no-one could misunder-stand, what he is:

> 'Brother,' quod he, 'wiltow that I thee telle?
> I am a feend; my dwellyng is in helle.' (1447–8)

Here is the most delightful twist in the story, for the summoner, far from expressing any natural revulsion or fear, is provoked only to insistent, naive questioning about diabolical shape-changing, which he clearly regards as a superior kind of conjuring trick:

> 'A!' quod this somonour, '*benedicite*! what sey ye?
> I wende ye were a yeman trewely.
> Ye han a mannes shap as wel as I;
> Han ye a figure thanne determinat
> In helle, ther ye been in youre estat?' (1456–60)

The devil, who had hoped for better things and who might be forgiven for thinking that some souls are not worth winning, grows increasingly outspoken and impatient in his contempt for the summoner. It takes no great effort to deceive someone like the summoner, he says –

> A lowsy jogelour kan deceyve thee,
> And pardee, yet kan I moore craft than he (1467–8)

– and he assures him, in response to another question, that the summoner has not the brains to understand the answer (1480–1). His impatience, his eagerness to be finished with this tedious assignment, are palpable:

> 'What maketh yow to han al this labour?'
> 'Ful many a cause, leeve sire somonour,'
> Seyde this feend, 'but alle thyng hath tyme.
> The day is short, and it is passed pryme.' (1473–6)

However, he does offer a quite serious explanation of the activities of devils, and the licence allowed to them by God (1482–503). He need not have bothered, for the summoner hardly seems to hear, and returns immediately to his questions about shape-changing, about the material nature of devils (1504–6). The devil's promise that he will soon, for certain, know all about hell, and be an authority on it (1513–20), ends with an ambiguous invitation:

> '... Now lat us ryde blyve,
> For I wole holde compaignye with thee
> Til it be so that thou forsake me.' (1520–2)

He invites the summoner, in the manner approved for the penitencer, to repent: 'Forsaketh synne, er synne yow forsake' (Physician's Tale, VI. 286; cf. X.93). The tale is nothing if not fair, and the summoner is to be given every chance of redemption, as also later when the old widow offers him the opportunity to repent (1629). But the summoner is impregnable to all sense: nothing has reality for him except materiality, and nothing is present to him but what is presented to his eyes and ears. His failure to see any difference between the carter's curse on his horses and the old widow's curse on himself shows him to be, as Robertson (1962, pp. 266–9) says, dead to all but the most literalistic understanding, and utterly stupid.

At the same time, there is, in the summoner's vow of undying fidelity to his promise of sworn brotherhood with the 'yeman', 'a kind of wild bravado', as Havely (1975, p. 14) calls it, an engaging dottiness, which is brought out over and again in the brilliant dialogue of the closing scenes of the two curses. The Friar's Tale, like the Summoner's Tale, has been compared unfavourably by Burrow (1957, pp. 206–7) with tales like those of the Merchant, as having something of their 'destructive wit' and 'farcical popular humour', but lacking their 'solidity'. As Copland (1966) says,

> It is not the individuality or idiosyncrasy of the characters that counts here, but the inordinate expansiveness of the demonstration provided of the extent to which they consistently *are* the types they represent (p. 15)

It might be possible to make some slight objection here, and suggest that there is, even in this comparatively small squib, a quality of engagement with and absorption in the narrative which makes it more than mere 'demonstration'. Chaucer was delighted to find in the scheme of the *Canterbury Tales* an opportunity to write satirically without asserting a satirical centre, but here, as in the Reeve's Tale and the Summoner's Tale, satire in the end was not quite sufficient to satisfy his appetite. His imagination was drawn irresistibly to assert the vitality of his creatures, and to do justice, or more than justice, to the objects of his satire. The summoner, in his wide-eyed childish wonder at the devil's power to change his shape, grows interested in something outside himself, something that is irrelevant to his profession as a summoner, or to any attack upon his profession. His evident admiration for the devil, and pleasure in his company, have little to do with the motive of profit, which was only perfunctorily stated, and more to do with what seems to be genuine *camaraderie*. He becomes curious and interesting, rather than simply reprehensible. Satire and irony give way to humour.

The Friar's voice, which has been absorbed into the narration for virtually the whole action of the tale, resumes at the end, with some

solemn-sounding warnings about hell, and a pious prayer that even
summoners may repent. It is his way of getting a last jab in at the
Summoner, and Chaucer's way of returning to the surrounding fiction of
the pilgrimage.

THE SUMMONER'S TALE

The Summoner's response to the Friar's venomous civility is one of
violent anger, and he stands high in his stirrups, trembling like an aspen
leaf with rage. This anger is not, however, converted into an angry or
distempered story, if one can imagine such a thing. The Tale, which,
from a literary point of view, is a rich anthology of anti-mendicant
writing with exempla added from Jerome and the preachers,[15] is not an
open attack on friars or a tirade against them, but a coolly and wittily
observed demonstration of a friar in action. The greed and hypocrisy of
friars is exposed in a long and pervasively ironical scene[16] which has a
high degree of dramatic realism and plausibility, and in which the friar
himself is the principal speaker (he speaks 315 of the 391 lines of this
central scene, 1765–2155). It is characteristic of Chaucer to wish to
convert traditional polemic materials into more or less self-contained
dramatic form in this way, and he works similarly in the Wife of Bath's
and Pardoner's Prologues. Only towards the end of the Tale does the
ridiculously plausible give way to the openly ridiculous, as Chaucer turns
his energies to the telling of the story of the divided fart. The shifting of
point of view is again characteristic of Chaucer in a number of stories,
such as the Merchant's and Franklin's Tales, where the point or 'knotte'
(Squire's Tale, V.401) of the story is some traditional anecdote. The
Summoner by this time is virtually forgotten.

At the beginning of the Tale, and in the brief Prologue, we are
certainly very much aware of the Summoner. The little story he tells of
the special place that friars have in hell (up 'the develes ers', 1694) seems
to be the sort that a coarse mind might particularly relish, and the
incivility of his general benediction –

> God save yow alle, save this cursed Frere! (1707)

– contrasts with the Friar's correct and pious hope that summoners may
repent (1644, 1663). The opening of the tale itself, however, is generally
bland, and already distanced from the Summoner, for it is the reported
words of the friar's own sermon which proclaim the benefits of giving

money to friars. The narrator chiefly emphasises the speed and vigour with which the friar goes about his business of winning souls and money:

> And whan this frere had seyd al his entente,
> With *qui cum patre* forth his wey he wente. (1733–4)

The lines have an airy freedom, the friar giving a cheery wave, perhaps, as he hastens to his next engagement. The narrator makes little comment, and resumes unperturbed after the Friar's interruption (1761), with no addition of malice (the Friar's Tale is again a contrast, 1338), indeed with no apparent malice at all.

It is worth stressing this point, because of the tendency there has been (e.g., Lumiansky, 1955, p. 140) to read the Summoner's Tale, in the light of his character, as an angry and vituperative and ugly tale, the sort that a man might tell who lived on a diet of garlic and onions. Indeed, it is true, there is a kind of absurd aptness in having such a man tell such a tale – one that has a fart as its great climax, that begins with a vision of 'the develes ers', and that contains so much verbal flatulence and so many allusions to the subject-matter of the dénouement. The poem is a minefield of ironic anticipations and echoes: the quotation, in a context thick with suggestiveness (see Beichner, 1956), of Psalm 44.2, 'Cor meum eructavit' (III.1934); the deliciously premonitory 'What is a ferthyng worth parted in twelve?' (1967), with its hint, too, it has been suggested (Whitesell, 1956), of the pilgrim Friar's lisp (General Prologue, I.164); the friar's reference to the unfinished state of the 'fundement' (2103) of their cloister; the proposal to solve the problem of dividing the fart by the use of 'ars-metrike' (2222); and other subtler allusivenesses and puns, described by Baum (1956), Birney (1960b) and Richardson (1970, pp. 147–58), such as the memory of *grope*, line 1817, in *grope*, line 2148. Chaucer would not want us to miss the nice congruity of all this with the Summoner's habits; but it would be dreary to press it further, to argue, for instance, that the tale is specially repulsive because it 'has about it the odor of his sewer-like mind' (Huppé, 1964, p. 201). The witty and indecent word-play to which the subject matter of the plot gives rise is quite in Chaucer's normal vein, as we see it elsewhere exploited in the Miller's and Merchant's Tales, and the whole tale is told with cool urbanity. Distancing the tale from the Summoner is not to deny the importance of the dramatic feud which Chaucer deliberately invents to motivate it, but to recognise that it was through this dramatic

strategy that he won the freedom to write in his own manner, uncon-
strained by the tyrannies of moral satire.

The opening of the central scene, with the arrival of the friar at
Thomas's house, shows why this freedom was worth winning:

> 'Thomas,' quod he, 'God yelde yow! ful ofte
> Have I upon this bench faren ful weel;
> Heere have I eten many a myrie meel.'
> And fro the bench he droof awey the cat,
> And leyde adoun his potente and his hat,
> And eek his scrippe, and sette hym softe adoun. (1772–77)

Those who have responded to the mention of the cat as an inimitable bit
of Chaucerian realism (e.g., Bennett, 1947, p. 74) have not picked on
something gratuitous and trivial. That action tells us more of the friar
than a quantity of exposition: the cat is sitting, as is the wont of cats, in
the most comfortable seat in the place, and the one therefore that the friar
has his eye on and naturally appropriates as his own; his actions, further,
have the easy and insinuating assumption of privilege, the unhurried
deliberateness, the gentleness, of a cat's, and withal the ruthlessness, and
obliviousness of all but physical advantage.

His mastery of the situation is complete. His manner is easy and
affable, and he deals adroitly with the social niceties – asking after
Thomas's wife, greeting her with something more than the conventional
kiss (1802–5) and ordering his dinner with a care for his conscience as
delicate as his care for his palate:

> 'Now, dame,' quod he, 'now *je vous dy sanz doute*,
> Have I nat of a capon but the lyvere,
> And of youre softe breed nat but a shyvere,
> And after that a rosted pigges hed –
> But that I nolde no beest for me were deed –
> Thanne hadde I with yow hoomly suffisaunce.' (1838–43)

One can even see why friars were so successful with their bourgeois
customers: they brought a touch of class, with their learning and their
French phrases; they were clean, amiable, and had good manners; they
licensed a little mild flirtatiousness, and could be the recipient, without
prejudice, of intimate confidences of the marriage bed in the form of
expressions of anxiety (1823–31). Meanwhile, the friar has his eye on the
main chance, and returns to the theme of money ever and again. He tells

Thomas of the sermon he has just been preaching, the theme of which
was that friars know how to 'glose' the scriptures (i.e., interpret them so
that lay people can understand them) and the conclusion of their
'glosynge' is that people should be charitable in giving, and give their
money 'ther it is resonable' (i.e., to the friars).

The news of the death of the couple's child is something of an
embarrassment to the friar. Perhaps Thomas had been eyeing him
narrowly when he asked him where he had been for the last fortnight
(1783), since it is during that time that the child has died (1852) and
presumably been buried in the friar's church, of which Thomas was a
'brother' (1944).[17] But, Falstaff-like, the friar recovers immediately,
and turns the little awkwardness into another triumph for himself and
his order:

> 'His deeth saugh I by revelacioun,'
> Seide this frere, 'at hoom in oure dortour.
> I dar wel seyn that, er that half an hour
> After his deeth, I saugh hym born to blisse
> In myn avision, so God me wisse!' (1854–8)

He is shrewd enough to remember to emphasise that they celebrated the
child's passing without a lot of noise,

> And up I roos, and al oure covent eke,
> With many a teere trillyng on my cheke,
> Withouten noyse or claterynge of belles;
> *Te Deum* was oure song, and nothyng elles (1863–6)

since he knows the parents would have expected to hear it. He goes on to
explain how efficacious the prayers of friars are, since they live in
poverty and abstinence; his concluding image of those who, unlike the
friars, 'swymmen in possessioun' (i.e., the possessioners) is most mem-
orable:

> Me thynketh they been lyk Jovinyan,
> Fat as a whale, and walkynge as a swan,
> Al vinolent as botel in the spence.
> Hir preyere is of ful greet reverence,
> Whan they for soules seye the psalm of Davit;
> Lo, 'buf!' they seye, '*cor meum eructavit!*' (1929–34)

This is witty and vivid in itself: it also anticipates a later eructation.

Thomas's reply to all this, that he has spent a mint of money on different friars over the years, but never felt any benefit, is both ungrateful and awkward, but the friar bounces back with great vigour:

> The frere answerde, 'O Thomas, dostow so?
> What nedeth yow diverse freres seche?
> What nedeth hym that hath a parfit leche
> To sechen othere leches in the toun?
> Youre inconstance is youre confusioun.
> Holde ye thanne me, or elles oure covent,
> To praye for yow been insufficient?
> Thomas, that jape nys nat worth a myte.
> Youre maladye is for we han to lyte.
> A! yif that covent half a quarter otes!
> A! yif that covent foure and twenty grotes!
> A! yif that frere a peny, and lat hym go!
> Nay, nay, Thomas, it may no thyng be so!
> What is a ferthyng worth parted in twelve?' (1954–67)

There is much to take delight in here, in the spectacle of a skilled rhetorician in full spate (the scornful mock-imperatives of 1963–5 are particularly effective), and also in the sharing of the pleasure that the friar takes in having hit upon a successful line of argument. The artistic and dramatic power of the lines almost overwhelms our moral consciousness, as Chaucer, in a characteristic vein, draws us to a delighted assent in the vitality of his creations, in the teeth of our objections to their vicious greed and hypocrisy. As Kean (1972, pp. 88–9) says, the whole portrait of 'the maddening friar' is 'made enjoyable and so far, in a sense, sympathetic by the very perfection and completeness of its self-consistency'. It becomes, in this respect, far more than what Robertson (1962, p. 249) calls it, a mere 'compendium of charges which had been leveled at friars'.

The friar now turns to the rebuke of Thomas's ire, immediately prompted by the wife's complaints that her husband is 'as angry as a pissemyre' (1825), but more profoundly by the need to talk Thomas out of his evident truculence and soften him to acts of charity (to friars). He begins like a marriage guidance counsellor, but soon the professional preacher takes over, and he embarks on his long series of *exempla* against ire in men of high degree. The comedy of watching the two main stories (2017–73) appropriated to the exemplification of a theme which is nothing to the friar's purpose is crowned in the gloriously earnest immorality (truly, 'glosynge is a glorious thyng') of his moral conclusion:

> Beth war, therfore, with lordes how ye pleye.
> Syngeth *Placebo*, and 'I shal, if I kan,'
> But if it be unto a povre man.
> To a povre man men sholde his vices telle,
> But nat to a lord, thogh he sholde go to helle. (2074–8)

Anything better calculated to make Thomas 'as angry as a pissemyre', whether he thinks of himself as a 'lord' or 'povre man', or neither, it is hard to imagine. The friar has evidently gone into automatic: the dramatic context of his sermon, the sense we have that it grows out of his character and the situation in which he finds himself, are strong encouragements to such an interpretation, and the arguments that the inadequacies of the sermon are signs that 'the economy of the story is yielding to the Summoner's anger at the Friar' (Owen, 1977, p. 166) or clever indications of the Summoner's lack of art (Coghill, 1949, p. 164) seem ingeniously to miss the principal impetus of the Tale. Merrill (1962–3, p. 349) seems to think that the sermon can be understood as 'comic self-exposure' on the part of both: but surely the one would spoil, not enhance, the effect of the other? Interpretation of narrative, like interpretation of language or metaphor, needs to select from among different possibilities, not pile them up together.

Thomas is unmoved, as he is entitled to be, by the friar's oratory, and he begins the procedures for the unleashing of the final *coup de tonnerre*. This climactic episode of the narrative is too brilliantly ridiculous for words, or at least any words but Chaucer's. The long-maintained and tightly wound up drama of the situation, 'stif and toght/As any tabour' (2267–8), explodes in hilarity, and there is only a moment to glimpse the friar's anger giving way to his wonted obsequiousness towards a 'lord' –

> 'Now, maister,' quod this lord, 'I yow biseke, –
> 'No maister, sire,' quod he, 'but servitour,
> Thogh I have had in scole that honour.' (2184–6)

– before we are engaged in the fantastic problem of 'ars-metrike' (2222) posed by Thomas's unexpected gift, a new kind of glorious 'glosynge'. The friar seems as much put out by the impossibility of the condition laid upon the gift –

To parte that wol nat departed be (2214)

– as by nature of the gift itself. This shows him up as a great fool, of course, rather like the summoner of the Friar's Tale; but, honestly, a man would have to be not a fool to be so taken in, but a being from another planet. Any serious possibility of satire seems to be swallowed up in the purer comic delight of 'this posing of a creative exercise and its fantastically imaginative solution' (Thro, 1979, p. 97). The proposed contrivance of the cart-wheel must also, surely, contain some allusion, as Levitan (1970–1) argues, to the manner in which the pentecostal descent of the holy spirit was portrayed in illustrations, with the apostles attending earnestly to the spoke-ends of a cartwheel-like figure so that they receive the inspiration simultaneously; and such an allusion defies exegesis, or interpretation in relation to any moral or satirical theme in the tale such as Szittya (1974) has tried to elicit. The endings of the Miller's and Reeve's Tales move similarly into this realm of what may be called 'pure' comedy. It is, on Chaucer's part, 'complicity' of a kind in the world of his creation.[18]

The quality of dramatic realisation in the Summoner's Tale, and the fireworks of the conclusion, make it a better tale than it has often been allowed to be. Burrow assigns it this modest place, in relation to the Merchant's Tale:

> The tone of the poem never modulates from the ironic and critical; the method is exclusively mimetic. It is 'poetry of the surface' . . . The particularity of the *Summoner's Tale* is invigorating . . . but in the end the poem does not add up to much. It remains an extended anecdote. (1957, p. 207)

In a sense, this is true: it does not 'add up to much'. But then, there are a great many kinds of literary and intellectual virtuosity from which we do not expect such calculable rewards but which nevertheless give delight. Like many of Chaucer's poems, the Summoner's Tale has its own unexpectedly creative line of development, which takes us on a far different imaginative journey from that which we thought we had a ticket for.

THE NUN'S PRIEST'S TALE

The Knight's interruption of the Monk's Tale is one of Chaucer's happiest inspirations. Originally, in the earlier, shorter form of the

Prologue to the Nun's Priest's Tale, as Manly and Rickert (1940, vol. 2, p. 410, vol. 4, pp. 513–14) explain, it was the Host who had made the interruption, but the subsequent development of the Host's role in Fragment VII, described by Dempster (1953), and the introduction of the exchanges between Chaucer and the Host, made his intervention here rather repetitive. His opening words are therefore transferred to the Knight, and new material introduced in which the Knight argues, reasonably enough, that folk do not wish to listen to a long string of stories of disasters, and that some report of stories with a happy outcome would be welcome. In further added lines, the Host chimes in, lowering the tone of the proceedings with some embarrassingly bluff and hearty comments of his own, comically expressive of his impatience and bewilderment in their echoing of some disjointed words and phrases from the Monk's last stanza (2780–90).

Chaucer's changes contribute much to the dramatic liveliness of the Link, but they also draw attention to some important contrasts between the Monk's Tale and the Nun's Priest's Tale, contrasts that figure significantly in the impressive account of the Nun's Priest's Tale given by Kean (1972, pp. 131–9). There is nothing intrinsically absurd about the Monk's Tale, but there is something monotonous in its unvaried diet of disasters, and no great depth of discrimination in its account of the circumstances and causes of human 'tragedie'. The Knight's distinction between stories with unhappy endings and stories with happy endings is a simple one, but it has a common-sense and quite warmly personal quality, and may gain added weight, as Kaske (1957) argues, from our memory of his own tale, where the tragedy of man's life and the unpredictability and apparent injustice of fate were tackled on an altogether deeper and more serious level. The Knight's request for something 'gladsom' (2778) is answered in the Nun's Priest's Tale, where indeed we hear of one who

> hath been in povre estaat,
> And clymbeth up and wexeth fortunat (2775–6)

in the story of the cock who escapes from the fox's mouth and flies up into a tree. It is not perhaps quite the tale that the Knight had in mind, but in the course of the telling there is more wit and wisdom, a more truly philosophical reflection of the condition of man's life, and the part played in it by choice, chance and circumstance, than in a hundred 'tragedies' of the Monk's type. In this, as in other respects, Chaucer seems to have found in the comedy of the Nun's Priest's Tale the perfect medium for the expression of his view of life: it is perhaps the best and certainly the most inimitably 'Chaucerian' of the *Tales*.

It is necessary to stress, though, that the effectiveness of the contrast between the Monk's Tale and the Nun's Priest's Tale is in the juxtaposition of the two tales as tales, and not in any dramatically conceived confrontation between the Monk and the Nun's Priest as pilgrim-characters. To see the Nun's Priest's Tale, as Hemingway (1916) and others, still, see it, as a satire on the Monk's Tale, directed personally by the Nun's Priest against the Monk, and prompted by outrage at his ostentation, jealousy of his high position in the ecclesiastical establishment, or contempt for his stupidity, is to mistake the trivial for the important. The objection to such a reading cannot be theoretical or *a priori*, since the structure of the *Canterbury Tales* allows and even encourages such interpretations, and on occasions they may have merit. It is rather that the collecting of allusions and comments from within the Nun's Priest's Tale which may then plausibly be interpreted as 'personal', and as part of a dramatic conflict taking place outside the tale, leads to a reconstruction of the poem which disregards, or fails to explain, or actually neutralises the effectiveness of a great part of its matter. Such a reading is thus of no value in enhancing our understanding of the poem. The same is true of those interpretations of the poem, as by Broes (1963), which see it as the product of a desire to satirise the Prioress. There is no suggestion from Chaucer, except in the very profession assigned to the Nun's Priest, that the Prioress should be much in our minds. It may be that some amusement can be gleaned from a momentary under-image of Chauntecler surrounded by his hens as a comic reversal of the Nun's Priest's situation in a convent of nuns, or from thinking of the hurried disclaimer that follows the unfavourable comments on women's advice (3260–6) as prompted by a severe stare from his lady-superior, and it may be that such amusements can be added to all the more substantial pleasures of the Tale. But systematic pursuit of such meanings results in trivialisation, and distraction from important matters, as when, for instance, the description of the old widow's sobriety of life is seen as a satire on the Prioress's delicacy and self-indulgence. It cannot, I suggest, be seen in such a way and at the same time retain its power to function in the story according to its primary purpose.

It could be argued against the 'dramatic' reading of the Tale that Chaucer, in presenting the Nun's Priest as such an anonymous figure, has deprived its exponents of the very material for such a reading that they would normally expect.[19] He has even removed the Nun's Priest's Epilogue, which, in an earlier stage of the existence of the *Canterbury Tales*, provided more information about the Nun's Priest. A devout adherent of the dramatic principle might retort that the greatest skill of the artist is shown when he reveals character entirely through the character's own discourse, without the intervention of authorial description or commentary. This is to some extent true of Chaucer's own experiments in the genre, in the introductory monologues of the Wife of Bath, Pardoner and Canon's Yeoman, but whether such an observation could be shown to be true of narratives of events other than their own lives attributed to undescribed characters is very debatable indeed.

The principal source of pleasure in the Nun's Priest's Tale, then, is not the Nun's Priest, but the comical juxtaposition of the simplicities of beast-fable with a mass of circumstance derived from the observation of human life and with a similar mass of commentary and allusion derived from some of Chaucer's favourite encyclopaedic rag-bags, as they have been described by Aiken (1953) and Pratt (1972, 1977). The enhancement of beast-fable in the direction of burlesque and mock-heroic is something Chaucer may have learnt initially from the *Roman de Renart*, though there is a discernible difference in the handling. The narratorial tone of *Renart* is consistently superior and detached, and the absurdities are displayed for us with a knowing wink: we share the narrator's superior stance, as we do in a mock-heroic poem like *The Rape of the Lock*. There is no doubt who is in control. Chaucer, though, enriches our experience of reading by absorbing the narrator into the poem, and giving us the sense that it is being told by a well-intentioned crank, so that the comedy seems to arise naturally, without the exertion of satiric or any other kind of control on the part of the author. To call the narrator 'incompetent' is perhaps a way of identifying our experience, or part of our experience, of reading the tale, and it is not, of course, an unfamiliar experience in our reading of Chaucer. This 'incompetence' is not to be associated with the intentions, achieved or unachieved, of a dramatically conceived 'character'. Nor is it really 'incompetence': rather it is the misdirected competence of someone telling the wrong tale, or telling the right tale the wrong way. It is like a fireworks display that has got into the hands of a pyromaniac.

The effects of this obsessive over-earnestness are chiefly felt in the latter part of the tale, from line 3187 onward, the earlier part being devoted to the genuinely mock-heroic description of the farmyard and its inhabitants and to the debate on dreams, where the pleasures we take in the incongruousness of the situation are more traditional and more readily identifiable. In the latter part of the tale, however, our reaction is more complex. Here are the lines, for instance, in which the narrator moralises with exquisite melancholy upon the impending fall of Chauntecler:

> But sodeynly hym fil a sorweful cas,
> For evere the latter ende of joye is wo.
> God woot that worldly joye is soone ago;
> And if a rethor koude faire endite,
> He in a cronycle saufly myghte it write
> As for a sovereyn notabilitee. (3204–9)

The full comic effect is released here through the impression created that the person who is saying these words is not Chaucer with his tongue in his cheek, ironically, but someone who is really serious in his desire to tell the story well. The discourse on predestination that follows, and with which the narrator embellishes his account of Chauntecler's fall (3226–50), is similar. This discourse is not in itself at all confused or tortuous, but is in fact extremely clear and succinct, a model précis of current views on the theology of predestination. It could hardly have been better done. What causes laughter is that it should be done at all, in relation to a cock and fox, and this playfulness is solemnly buried if the passage is seen, as by Payne (1976), as a satire on the theology of free will and predestination. The narrator does not realise how funny he appears, and must not, if the comedy is to remain buoyed up at the highest level. He must have no intention but to tell the story to the best of his ability.

Parts of the remaining narrative are done in the more transparent manner of mock-heroic. The learned allusions made by the fox to his reading of Boethius (3294) and 'Daun Burnel the Asse' (3312), though they may contain glancing ironies, described by Chamberlain (1970–1) and Mann (1975), that enrich our pleasure in them, are chiefly comic in the context of beast-fable. The chase-scene (3375–401), the climax of the story, is a classic piece of mock-heroic writing. Still, though, the comedy of incongruity is constantly enriched by the flow of earnest moralisation, as the narrator jettisons upon us, in undiscriminating profusion, the contents of his well-stocked mind. The catastrophe is introduced with a warning against flatterers (3325–30), and accompanied by elaborately mounting apostrophes to destiny, to Venus, and to the rhetorician Geoffrey of Vinsauf, whose own apostrophe to Friday (as the day on which Richard I was slain) is invoked as the unscalable height of the narrator's ambition.[20]

> O Gaufred, deere maister soverayn,
> That whan thy worthy kyng Richard was slayn
> With shot, compleynedest his deeth so soore,
> Why ne hadde I now thy sentence and thy loore,
> The Friday for to chide, as diden ye?
> For on a Friday, soothly, slayn was he. (3347–52)

In the classical allusions that follow, Troy, Carthage and Rome are burnt in the attempt to convey to us the full dimensions of the barnyard tragedy, and at the end, after Chauntecler has escaped, we are showered with 'morals', including one from the cock, one from the fox, and two or three from the Nun's Priest (3431–7). He concludes, as if anxious that this may not be moralisation enough, with the exhortation to 'look for the moral':

> But ye that holden this tale a folye,
> As of a fox, or of a cok and hen,
> Taketh the moralite, goode men.
> For seint Paul seith that al that writen is,
> To oure doctrine it is ywrite, ywis;
> Taketh the fruyt, and lat the chaf be stille. (3438–43)

The openness of this invitation, intended by the Nun's Priest to cover all possible opportunities for moralisation that even he may not have thought of, is also Chaucer's openness. His voice merges with the narrator's, offering us his own challenge to distinguish the 'fruyt' from the 'chaf'.[21]

There are some striking parallels between the narrator of the tale and his chief character, Chauntecler, particularly in the elaborate preparation both of them make to go charging off in the wrong direction. Chauntecler is a superbly competent cock, and an excellent scholar. He puts down his wife Pertelote, with her busy little housewife's comforting diagnoses and homely remedies and her one threadbare 'auctoritee' on dreams, in majestic fashion:

> 'Madame,' quod he, 'graunt mercy of youre loore.
> But nathelees, as touchyng daun Catoun,
> That hath of wysdom swich a greet renoun,
> Though that he bad no dremes for to drede,

By God, men may in olde bookes rede
Of many a man moore of auctorite
Than evere Caton was, so moot I thee.' (2970–6)

His analysis of the oracular and significative power of dreams is a model of scholarly discourse, complete with full illustration, citation of authority, and judicious balancing of the evidence (3131). It is persuasive and – in terms of the weight of medieval authority on the subject, and in terms of the events of the tale – it is true. Within his discourse there are two *exempla* told which demonstrate the art of laconic narrative at its most starkly portentous, especially the tale of the murdered man in the dung-cart. We are close here to the excellences of the Pardoner's Tale. Pratt (1977, pp. 551–69) has shown clearly how Chaucer has adapted his sources here to reinforce Chauntecler's theme of oracular premonition in dreams and his polite repudiation of Pertelote's view of the vanity of dreams. It is all very much to the point, which is missed by those such as Broes (1963, p. 160) who detect in the discourse a deflating irony directed against Chauntecler – for rambling on aimlessly, or for forgetting his argument in stressing the theme of 'Mordre wol out' (3052) – or, more wildly still, satire on the Prioress's Tale, where this theme is also introduced. It is essential to the story, on the contrary, that Chauntecler should be doing what he does to the top of his bent: only if this is recognised is the full comedy of the situation released, which is that Chauntecler, for all his eloquence, takes no notice at all of what he says. Having proved to his own and any intelligent listener's satisfaction, in his long and eloquent discourse, the oracular power of dreams, he now sets aside all he has warned himself of, and proceeds to 'diffye' his dream in his enjoyment of the beauty of Pertelote. Indeed, it is his eloquence that enables him to enjoy her, as Dempster (1932, p. 69) and Bishop (1979, pp. 266–7) have pointed out, for his self-esteem, bruised by Pertelote's reaction to his dream –

Have ye no mannes herte, and han a berd? (2920)

needs the upholstering which it gets by proving his intellectual superiority to her. Thus the grandeur of reason serves the animal instinct, the learned scholar the randy cock. The return of virility, the flush of success and sexual enthusiasm, is what directly impels him to fly down from the beam (3172), where he would have been safe from the fox:

'For whan I feele a-nyght your softe syde,
Al be it that I may nat on yow ryde,
For that oure perche is maad so narwe, allas!
I am so ful of joye and of solas,
That I diffye bothe sweven and dreem.'
And with that word he fley doun fro the beem. (3167–72)

The reflection of human behaviour is both uncannily accurate and also totally ridiculous. Chauntecler's little joke at Pertelote's expense likewise misfires: his polite mistranslation of an antifeminist tag (3166) is a way of eating his cake and having it too, of flattering her as the occasion requires and at the same reminding himself of his own intellectual superiority. What he will find out is that his mistranslation is really a true translation: woman is man's confusion *because* she is his joy and bliss (Owen, 1977, p. 137)

There is allusion to serious matters here, and indeed the tale is shot through with such allusion, which has proved a temptation that modern interpreters, unwilling to regard laughter as an adequate reward for the effort expended in reading the tale, have found it difficult to resist, despite the wise warnings issued by Muscatine:

The tale will betray with laughter any too-solemn scrutiny of its naked argument; if it is true that Chauntecler and Pertelote are rounded characters, it is also true that they are chickens ... Unlike fable, the Nun's Priest's Tale does not so much make true and solemn assertions about life as it tests truths and tries out solemnities. If you are not careful, it will try out your solemnity too. (1957, p. 242)

Starting from the narrator's own injunction to 'take the moralite' (3440), modern exegetes have subjected the tale to moral and even to systematic allegorical interpretation in the endeavour to extract from it a lesson that will confirm a certain set of moral and religious values. Thus Donovan (1953) used the traditional iconography of the cock and fox, in bestiary and scriptural commentary, to show that the tale is 'a sermon on alertness to moral obligation' (p. 498), in which the cock is the priest or preacher, whose crowing is the sounding of the canonical hours, the call to Christians to be wakeful, while the fox is the devil-heretic. The poor widow, meanwhile, is the Church, widowhood being the model for the control of the very passions Chauntecler succumbs to, especially vanity and non-procreative sexuality (3345). Dahlberg (1954) confirmed and extended the iconographic interpretation, identifying the cock as the secular priest and the fox as the false flattering friar, and going on to identify the 'drye dych' (2848) which surrounds the farmyard as an iconographic reversal of the *fons signatus* of the Song of Songs, and an emblem therefore of the dry and desolate state of the Church in the world; to see in Chauntecler's 'paramours' (2867) a reversal of the *sponsa*, or holy bride of Christ; and to associate the colours of Chauntecler's plumage with liturgical colours and priestly vestments. Robertson endorses these readings:

> The Nun's Priest's Tale is a story of a priest who falls into the clutches of a friar but who escapes just in time when he discovers the essential weakness of the friar's evil nature. (1962, p. 252)

Another essay builds on the early work of Speirs (1951) and Holbrook (1954), in which the Tale was seen as an allegory of the Fall, and the farmyard chase at the end as a burlesque version of the chaos and violent disorder which followed on the Fall. In the hands of Speirs, the interpretation was quite nicely judged, responsive to the allusions which are undoubtedly there, but conscious always of the informing spirit of comedy and the mock-heroic. In this later essay, the 'moralite' of the Tale is quite categorically stated to be

> the recapitulation by Chauntecler of man's fall and redemption, and the theological meanings inherent in Chauntecler's repeating Adam's expe ience. (Levy and Adams, 1967, p. 178)

So Chauntecler and Pertelote have their debate about dreams on a *beem*, which represents the Forbidden Tree and typologically the Cross; the flying down from the safety of the *beem* symbolises the Fall, while flying up for safety into the *tree* at the end symbolises the Resurrection. There is hardly a single piece of timber in the Tale that is not used in the construction of this interpretation. Meanwhile, the barnyard represents paradise, ruled over by a series of symbolic trinities – the widow and her two daughters, the three cows, the three sows – and the ram, which signifies Christ. To point out that the ram is in fact a ewe (called Molly) might seem an intrusion upon some act of private self-communion, and would certainly be countered by the invoking of 'irony', or at least that peculiar version of irony which asserts as its basic premises that (1) nothing means what it says and (2) everything means the same thing.

With all this said, it must be recognised that moral and allegorical interpretation of the Nun's Priest's Tale has contributed significantly to the fuller understanding of the tale. Those critics, for instance Ruggiers (1965, pp. 184–95) and Hieatt (1970), who have analysed the aptness of the portrayal of Chauntecler as an image of male vanity, or of the temporary triumph of the lower nature of man over his higher, have certainly hit upon an important element in our enjoyment of the tale. The consistent, witty and generous observation of human nature is one of the characteristically Chaucerian excellences of the tale. But there is no lesson to be learnt from this, no little nugget of 'moralite' which we can hoard away for our better edification. For one thing, Chauntecler escapes from the plight his folly has brought him to by the exercise, not of his higher reason, but of his low cunning, of a technique of flattery that he has learnt from his deceiver. There is no moral lesson to be learnt from this. Likewise, the presentation of Chauntecler's folly is not true satire, since it is not done from the point of view of a standard of values that could be called morally normative. Moralistic interpreters (e.g., Donovan, 1953, p. 505) often comment on Chauntecler's uxoriousness and his fondness for non-procreative love-play ('Moore for delit than world to multiplye', 3345) as the cause of his downfall. But it will be seen that there are no moral standards by which we can judge this matter in relation to cocks and hens – a reasonably continent cock, as Mann (1975, p. 275) says, would be no cock at all. Here, as often in the tale, Chaucer employs the juxtapositions of the beast-fable, the constant switching to and from awareness of the animals as animal, to deflate pompous interpretations and snag morality. The embarrassing surfeit of 'morals' we are offered at the end of the tale hints at the inadequacy of easy moralising.

Exegetical interpretation has also been valuable in alerting us to allusions and levels of meaning which do indeed need recovery. The idea of the cock as preacher, or of the fox as diabolical seducer, is certainly present in the tale by implication, as is the quite explicit series of allusions to the Fall. But the effect is not to set out for us a diagram of salvation, but to take us deeper into the comedy of the tale, and particularly to allow us to enjoy there the rich humour of the comedy of survival converted to the comedy of salvation. The inspiration for Chaucer's laughter here has been well documented in a series of essays, by Manning (1960), Allen (1969), Scheps (1970) and Shallers (1975), on Chaucer's debt to the preachers' use of beast-fables. It is only in the knowledge of this characteristically medieval exemplary material that we can appreciate how exactly Chaucer caricatures the absurdities of allegorised fable, of stories that have one point matched with allegories that have another.

The manner in which the Nun's Priest's Tale recoils upon all systematic attempts at interpretation is not a sign that more efforts should be made to find one that works. Its machinery is designed to defy such attempts: that is the point of the tale. Language and rhetoric and learning are noble arts, but they are constantly shown in the tale being used, by expert practitioners, to conceal the world from themselves, and themselves from themselves. They become, not means to understanding, but a series of reflecting mirrors in which we can be satisfied we shall see only those things that preserve our high opinion of ourselves.[22] Chauntecler's great advance in wisdom is to learn that language is a form of trickery, and how to use it; the Nun's Priest, surrounded by the debris of his grandiose narrative, suggests we look around to see if we can find something useful. The laughter has an edge, but it is salutary, not satirical: it implicates the reader, and the critic.

THE MANCIPLE'S TALE

The Manciple's Tale is in many respects a peculiar performance. Chaucer has removed or not exploited those elements in the tale which might have given it human interest as a story, or poignancy, or sense of reality or meaningful conflict; and he has amplified the tale with some pragmatic moralising of perfectly respectable pedigree but no intrinsic depth or interest. The tale is, on the one hand, bleak and vacant, devoid of atmosphere, yet by no means low-spirited; and on the other hand, digressive and rambling and lacking the pointedness, the remorseless drive towards the moral, of an effectively told fable. These peculiarities require some explanation.

A beginning can be made with Chaucer's portrayal of Phoebus's wife. In the analogues, described by Severs (1952), and in the closest of the analogues, the *Ovide Moralisé*, which is possibly Chaucer's source, she is given a name, Coronis, and some sympathy attaches to her, especially in the moment of her death, when she reveals that she is pregnant with Phoebus's child: 'Duo nunc moriemur in una', she says, in Ovid (*Metamorphoses*, II.609). In Chaucer, she is introduced in a most offhand way, almost spitefully. Chaucer tells us:

Now hadde this Phebus in his hous a crowe (130)

and then, nine lines later:

> Now hadde this Phebus in his hous a wyf. (139)

This reverses the natural order of events, as narrated in the *Ovide Moralisé*:

> En Thesale ot une pucele . . .
> Phebus l'ama moult longuement . . .
> Phebus ot lors un sien oisiau . . . (Bryan and Dempster, 1941, p. 703)

Her adulterous liaison is dismissed as a squalid affair with

> A man of litel reputacioun. (199)

She sends for her lover when Phoebus goes out, like the cheap trull of a fabliau, and the narrator tells us bluntly about the goings on:

> Whan Phebus wyf had sent for hir lemman,
> Anon they wroghten al hire lust volage. (238–9)

The effect is quite different from that of the analogues, where the adultery is briefly reported, the lover represented simply as 'un autre damoisiau', and where there is a suggestion of the complexity of events, the possible causes of extenuation, which make Phoebus's action seem hasty and his regret understandable.

Chaucer's treatment of the story, by contrast, makes the crow's report, though maybe a little abrupt in its wording –

> For on thy bed thy wyf I saugh him swyve (256)

– seem like the action of an honest and faithful servitor, not a trouble-making 'jangler'. All the potential of a narrative to demonstrate how 'telling the truth' can be much less than an unmitigated good – how it can indeed be a way in which malice vents its spleen, as with Agravaine's tale-telling in *Le Morte D'Arthur* – is thus squandered, and Phoebus made to look like a petulant fool who wants to find a scapegoat for his action. The 'moral' for the story, therefore, when it comes, is vile, not because it is essentially untrue that silence is golden, nor that keeping your mouth shut always causes less trouble than shooting it off, or even that it is wrong to be an

> auctour newe
> Of tidynges, wheither they been false or trewe. (359–60)

but because the way in which the story has been told makes the recommendation to discretion in speaking so obviously an act of policy. Chaucer may well have been sceptical about the value of proverbial wisdom such as that of the *Distichs* of Cato, which he draws upon here (see Hazelton, 1960), and may have seen the essential difference between the morality of survival, which, like beast-fable, teaches man to be a successful animal, and the higher morality of chivalric or spiritual idealism. We have seen him mockingly exposing this discrepancy in the Nun's Priest's Tale, and in the friar's ludicrous moralising of his sermon on Ire in the Summoner's Tale. But Chaucer is likely to have been more interested in and amused by the comically reductive effects created when proverbial moralising of this kind was applied, as it customarily was, to stories. In the string of wise saws concerning the virtues of taciturnity which the narrator says he learnt from his mother, and with which he concludes his story (318–62), there may be, in the constant repetition of 'My sone', some specific and gently ironic reminiscence of Gower's *Confessio Amantis*.[23] The stories told there by the shrift-father Genius, who constantly addresses Amans as 'My sone', are all *exempla* of various sins against love, and they demonstrate the habit of fitting stories into set moral schemes. Of course, Chaucer is being unfair, since Gower's moralising is not glib or self-centred, nor are his narratives always or even often constrained by their moral function, but his unfairness is, I suppose, a way of blunting the edge of his satire and making it more a form of humour. The general relevance of Gower's use of exemplary narrative for the purposes of moralising is clear.

All the Manciple's earlier moralising interventions are expressive, to a greater or less extent, of a kind of moral quietism, of that shrewdness in the calculation of personal profit and loss which is characteristic of proverbial wisdom. Phoebus's attempts to keep his wife faithful are dismissed as futile. If she had been good, he shouldn't have, and if she had been bad he couldn't have. This is the labour-saving conclusion:

> This holde I for a verray nycetee,
> To spille labour for to kepe wyves. (152–3)

Nothing, in fact, can change nature: human beings will always follow their natural instincts, just as does a bird, or a cat, or she-wolf. The immediate relevance of the last example –

> A she-wolf hath also a vileyns kynde.
> The lewedeste wolf that she may fynde,
> Or leest of reputacioun, wol she take,
> In tyme whan hir lust to han a make (183–6)

to the story of Phoebus's wife as it is told here is sneeringly underlined in the sardonic disclaimer which follows:

> Alle thise ensamples speke I by thise men
> That been untrewe, and nothyng by wommen. (187–9)

When he comes to deal with the adulterous liaison, the Manciple finds himself calling the wife's lover her 'lemman'. He immediately pulls himself up:

> Hir lemman? Certes, this is a knavyssh speche!
> Foryeveth it me, and that I yow biseche. (205–6)

He embarks on an extended explanation, however, of why he was right to use the word, claiming that there is no essential difference between an adultress of high birth and one of low birth, except that the one is called the lover's 'lady' and the other 'his wenche or his lemman' (220):

> And, God it woot, myn owene deere brother.
> Men leyn that oon as lowe as lith that oother. (221–2)

He continues with some further remarks in the same vein concerning the 'tirant' and the 'outlawe': they are only different names for the same kind of predator. Language is a form of trickery, a sham, a way men have of dressing up their acts of animal instinct in a fancy guise.[24] The thing to do, the Manciple implies, is to learn the tricks (to learn how to call black white) and use them for one's own advantage, and not to be carried away by passion or idealism or that shibboleth called truth. Life is to be seen through, and recognised for the warfare of self-interest that it is, and, in calling himself 'a boystous man' (211) and one who is 'noght textueel' (235, 316), the Manciple makes the further claim that he speaks nothing but the plain unvarnished facts of the matter. Such is the reductiveness of viewpoint, the mean-spiritedness, that diminishes the tale.

Chaucer's fascination with the matter of narrative, and the relation it may have to the kind of interpretation that is imposed upon it and the morals that are drawn from it, is sufficient to sustain the Manciple's Tale and give it interest as a footnote to the Nun's Priest's Tale. It will be seen, though, that the narrative takes on a further dimension when it is seen in the context of the Prologue to the Manciple's Tale. There, in one of his most vivid and completely realised pieces of pilgrimage drama, Chaucer portrays the quarrel that flares up between the Cook and the Manciple. The latter, whose opinion no-one has asked for, takes advantage of the Host's jesting at the expense of the drunken Cook to enter the lists on his own account. Declaring that he for one will speak plainly in the matter –

> Of me, certeyn, thou shalt nat been yglosed (34)

– he rudely upbraids the Cook with his drunkenness and foul breath. The cook is so angry that he falls off his horse –

> This was a fair chyvachee of a cook!

– and there is great pushing and heaving needed to get him back in the saddle. The Host accepts the Manciple's offer of a tale, chiefly having in mind, it seems, that the Cook may find it too much both to tell a tale and also stay on his horse –

> And if he falle from his capul eftsoone,
> Thanne shal we alle have ynogh to doone (65–6)

– but he also remarks on the Manciple's foolishness in being so out-spoken with the Cook. The Cook might get his own back, suggests the Host, by niggling at the Manciple's accounts back in London and getting him into trouble – a reminder that a manciple, as steward of a lawyers' lodging-house, would have had much to do with cooks, in 'byynge of vitaille' (General Prologue, I.569), and probably expected to co-operate with them in making a little extra money on the side. The Manciple is quick to see the force of the Host's remarks, and he extracts himself from his awkward situation by claiming that his own outburst had been a joke, and then offering the Cook a draught from his own personal hip-flask. The Cook is 'wonder fayn' and the Host much amused at this triumph of

Bacchus. In the light of this encounter, the Manciple's Tale can readily be seen, and has often been seen (e.g., by Severs, 1952; Birney, 1960c; Scattergood, 1974), as a dramatic expression of the truth of the lesson in human nature that the Manciple has just learnt: talking too much, and especially telling the truth, can get you into difficulties. The relation of the moral to the tale is as queasy in its recommendation of self-interest as the Manciple's own behaviour just described.

The parallels are certainly there, and intended to be observed: they add something, though nothing indispensable, to the Tale. It would detract from their effectiveness to look for further signs of the Manciple's intention or consciousness at work in his tale – to argue, for instance as do Spector (1957) or Fulk (1979), that he incorporates into it an attack on the Host, or on the Cook. Temptations of this kind are constantly present in the *Canterbury Tales*, and to succumb to them is generally to substitute some superficial illusion of vitality for the real energies of narrative. It may be, as Diekstra (1983) says, that 'the elaborate characterizations that critics have produced of the narrators are remarkable namely as indirect attempts to describe the variety of Chaucer's stylistic inventory'. This is a generous and positive view, and may stand as a commentary on the possibility of a modestly 'dramatic' interpretation of the Manciple's Tale that I have suggested. At the same time, there does seem something quite striking, and not requiring 'elaborate characterizations', about the 'fit' between Prologue and Tale in this case.

CHAPTER 6

Religious Tales

The tales grouped here as 'Religious Tales' are very varied in form, though all have in common the assertion or the implied assertion (in the Monk's Tale) of Christian values as their essential motive and reason for existence. This sets them unequivocally apart from those other groups of tales where the controlling concepts are those, respectively, of romantic and chivalric idealism and of comedy, and from the three tales which are represented to us specifically as extensions of a pilgrim's own acts of self-revelation.

The religious tales fall into four groups. The most obviously identifiable is the group consisting of the two saints' legends, the Prioress's Tale and the Second Nun's Tale. These are true saints' legends, in that both move with complete single-mindedness towards the *passio sancti*, which is the narrative climax and also the point of such stories. It is death, and the manner of death, that sanctifies. The Prioress's Tale is not about a named calendar-saint, and it belongs strictly to the well-defined genre of 'Miracles of the Virgin', but the mention of Hugh of Lincoln at the end makes clear that we should understand the little boy to be one of her unnamed martyr-saints.

A second group consists of the three exemplary tales of virtuous women, the Man of Law's Tale, Clerk's Tale and Physician's Tale. They are closely associated with the Prioress's Tale and Second Nun's Tale as examples of what Payne (1963, p. 164) calls Chaucer's 'sentimental experiment', an interest in effects of pathos in tales of affective piety, in which he may have been participating in or observing certain specifically late fourteenth-century developments in religious sensibility, as a number of writers (e.g., Weissman, 1979) have noted in relation to particular tales, and Stugrin (1980–1) in relation to the group as a whole. The three tales of virtuous women all demonstrate the order of God's providence and its beneficence towards those who are constant in virtue; all have a strong suggestion of allegory, though largely unrealised in the narrative. Two, the Man of Law's Tale and the Clerk's Tale, are very long, and each deals with an extended and unified series of episodes in the life of a married woman. They are both drawn directly from known literary sources, in which they have already been subject to interpretation in terms of Christian values. Both, however, have affiliations with a larger group of tales, called 'Eustace-Constance-Florence-Griselda Legends' in the revised *Manual* of Severs (1967, p. 278), which may be described as narratives of tribulation constantly borne, ending happily. The sufferings are always those of domestic separation and alienation. Some of these narratives, such as *Emare* and *Sir Isumbras*, present themselves as 'romances' and are so described in all modern accounts of them.[1] This may argue that 'romance' is an over-capacious generic term, and that the special pleading of medieval didactic writers is responsible for making it so. However, the term 'romance' has its less confusing specialised value in relation to the tales discussed in Chapter 4, and it is clear that no useful purpose would be served by a discussion of why the Man of Law's Tale, being like the 'romance' *Emare*, is nothing like the Franklin's Tale.

The third tale in this second group, the Physician's Tale, is there because it is likewise a pious *exemplum* of a virtuous woman. It is different from the other two in that it relates a single episode in her life and ends in death. This makes it very different, though it is not in any sense a *passio sancti*: Virginia's death is not a martyrdom but a rescue from a fate worse than death. The difficulty of saying exactly what the Physician's Tale is may reflect some confusion or even complexity in its design.

There is no such confusion or suggestion of complexity in the Monk's Tale, which has a place on its own among the religious tales. As a string of 'tragedies', resulting from pride or the fickleness of fortune or merely the passage of time that eventually brings death, it may be presumed to belong to the genre of writings that, in pointing to the unstable and unsatisfactory nature of worldly rewards, recommend the heavenly alternative. The Monk, however, never actually gets round to the alternative, so that his tale, when it is interrupted, remains a pointless account of the pointlessness of existence. Chaucer perhaps wanted it that way.

The fourth group comprises the Tale of Melibeus and the Parson's Tale. Both are in prose, and neither is strictly speaking a 'tale' at all, though the former has a narrative peg on which the allegorical discourse is hung. The Parson's Tale is straight exposition. They are drawn directly from treatises of, respectively, moral and penitential instruction, and are perhaps chiefly remarkable as reminders of how very 'medieval'

Chaucer could be. Since they are not cast as stories, and therefore do not draw upon the imaginative power that resides in stories, and since they are in prose, and demonstrate little interest in the imaginatively self-aware and generative use of language most commonly associated with poetry,[2] they are not, according to certain quite useful distinctions, 'literature' at all.

The religious tales are generally lacking in the qualities that modern readers expect to find in Chaucer, and their insistent and pervasive doctrinal emphasis makes them uninteresting or even repugnant to many. They are much less frequently read than the other tales, and even less frequently enjoyed. They offer little, at first sight, to the devotee of the dramatic principle. However, modern critics have not been deterred by the preliminary resistance offered by the tales to their favoured methods of interpretation, and it would be now true to say that every one of the eight tales has been subjected to 'ironisation'. Even tales that stood out long against such reading, such as the Parson's Tale and the Second Nun's Tale, have now been annexed, and shown to be ironically flawed accounts of what they were hitherto thought to be accounts of, and demonstrations of the inadequacy of their narrators or perhaps even of the Middle Ages as a whole. This new scrutiny has often drawn attention valuably to certain kinds of discrepancy within the narratives, certain kinds of strain to which they are subject in Chaucer's hands, and obliged readers to recognise and confront the complexities that they are aware of in their experience of some at least of these stories. But appropriation through irony (see Chapter 2, note 12) tends to substitute one kind of simplicity for another, a new kind for an old one, and it will perhaps have to be rather doggedly repeated in the following pages that reconstruction is not the same as interpretation, and that finding what one wants to find is not the same as seeing what is there.

THE PRIORESS'S TALE

The transition from the Shipman's Tale to the Prioress's Tale, one of the most breathtakingly abrupt in the 'big dipper' sequence of Fragment VII, is effected by means of the Host's exquisitely polite little request to the Prioress, and her one-word reply, 'Gladly'. Her involvement in the frame-narrative is thus minimal, and the isolation of her tale from its surroundings is further emphasised by the invocation to God and to the Virgin with which she begins, and the prayer to the Virgin to guide her in the telling of her tale. Her Prologue serves to encapsulate and elevate the tale that follows, and to transport us into the world of devout and pious sentiment. It is done as an act of worship and humble observance, in a semi-liturgical style full of echoes of the offices of the Church, especially the services dedicated to the Virgin and to the commemoration of the Massacre of the Innocents. It is compact of reverence, dominated by devotion to the Virgin yet unexaggerated in tone and loftily orthodox in its statement of her role in the Trinitarian scheme (467–73). None of this, it will be seen, awakens any specific recollections of the charming lady of the General Prologue, though there is no essential conflict. The portrait there was of what was visible of the lady from the outside: what this implied about her inner life was left to be inferred by the observer, as if it depended on his own good or ill-nature.

The Prologue to the Prioress's Tale nevertheless conveys a deeply personalised sense of its speaker, as does the tale itself. The Prologue is not an independent effusion, but is directed by the speaker's humble consciousness of presumption in telling a tale in praise of the Virgin. It also expresses the reverence for motherhood and childhood which is the source of emotional power in the tale and its telling. The special sweetness of childish piety is announced as a theme as soon as the Prioress begins to speak (455–9), and she returns to the story of St Nicholas in a brief digression during the tale, which comes unbidden, almost as if she were overwhelmed by the sweetness of the recollection:

> But ay, whan I remembre on this mateere,
> Seint Nicholas stant evere in my presence,
> For he so yong to Crist dide reverence. (513–15)

She herself assumes the innocence and ignorance of

> ... a child of twelf month oold, or lesse,
> That kan unnethes any word expresse (484–5)

when she wishes to lay secure claim to help and guidance. The appropriateness of these expressions of feeling to the Prioress, who is a woman, and also, in her own profession, a 'mother', is obvious, and to speak of 'the sublimation of frustrated maternal feelings' would only be to put what is obvious in a rather condescending modern way.

The reverence for childish piety and for maternal love is strongly brought out in the tale. The 'litel clergeon' is made somewhat younger than he is in the closest analogues, as Brown (1941, p. 465) and Statler

(1950, p. 898) remark, and the repetition of 'litel', not only in reference to the boy but also in reference to everything connected with him – 'A litel scole . . . A litel clergeon . . . hir litel sone . . . This litel child, his litel book lernynge' – creates a sentimental pathos so piercing as almost to verge on mawkishness. Equally touching is the child's purity of devotion in learning the opening words of the antiphon in praise of the Virgin, *Alma redemptoris mater*, even though he does not understand what they mean, and his determination to learn the whole thing, come what may:

> Though that I for my prymer shal be shent,
> And shal be beten thries in an houre,
> I wol it konne Oure Lady for to honoure! (541–3)

By contrast, there is no trace of sentimentality in the portrait of the mother as she searches for her lost child (586–602), not a word too much nor a word out of place in the description of her mother's feelings as they grow through anxiety and fear to desperation and desperate acts of courage and self-abnegation. It is, some time, the experience of all parents, and Chaucer has caught both the homeliness of the experience and the grandeur of the mother's emotion in language of the greatest simplicity. To call the passage Wordsworthian would be to characterise if not to praise it sufficiently. Beyond Wordsworth, too, there is the typological significance of the old widow, who expressed her deepest love of her son in teaching him the worship of the Virgin (511), and who becomes the type of Rachel as she mourns her son in this 'post-figuring' (Burrow, 1982, p. 102) of the Massacre of the Innocents (627). Yet she herself is superseded, as a type of maternal love, by the Virgin, to whom the child offers a higher love and devotion, and who makes to him this promise:

> 'My litel child, now wol I fecche thee,
> Whan that the greyn is fro thy tonge ytake.
> Be nat agast, I wol thee nat forsake.' (667–9)

Throughout, the Prioress is present to us as the emotional consciousness through which the tale is mediated. The sense of her presence is communicated partly through little asides which seem to have been deliberately planted, like the emphatic 'hym meene I' of line 670, and the slightly prim comment on monks (perhaps inspired by the part played by the monk in the Shipman's Tale, immediately preceding):

> This abbot, which that was an hooly man,
> As monkes been – or elles oghte be . . . (642–3)

On occasions, there are more striking reminders of the Prioress, and the activity of her mind and feelings in narrating the story. The death of the little child provokes from her a little aria (579–85), in which she celebrates the special reward of heaven promised to virginity, expressing herself in terms that go beyond the immediate confines of the story and in a manner explicitly differentiated ('quod she') from the surrounding narrative. Also, the emphasis on the repulsive details of the child's death –

> I seye that in a wardrobe they hym threwe
> Where as thise Jewes purgen hire entraille (572–3)

– has the air of a deliberate act of self-discipline, inspired by a determination not to be mealy-mouthed about the full horror of an event which must have been specially distressing, we may remind ourselves, to a lady who found the death-agonies of mice caught in traps so upsetting (General Prologue, I.145).

The authenticity of the tale's pathos and pity is difficult to resist and yet at the same time easy to be embarrassed by. Some understanding of late medieval affective piety is required, as Hirsh (1975–6) and Collette (1980–1) suggest, and surely it is mere embarrassment and lack of contact with the conventions of such piety that prompts readers like Baum (1958, pp. 75–8) to find humour or satire in the echoing of the child's song throughout 'al the place' (613, i.e., the 'wardrobe'), or in the phrase interpolated into the child's speech, 'as ye in bookes fynde' (652), or in the dogged insistence on the nature of the 'pit' (571), or in the tentative observations of the abbot:

> Tel me what is thy cause for to synge,
> Sith that thy throte is kut to my semynge? (647–8)

More attractive still to modern readers have been those interpretations of the tale that avoid the embarrassment of its appeal to the feelings by blaming the Prioress for so meretriciously arousing them. She is the kind of person, we are told, whose shallow piety permits a flood of sentimentality about children – children being as easy to love and feel sentimental about as mice and lapdogs – but who has none of the truly deep Christian charity that demands painful and difficult acts of loving self-discipline. In particular, her attitude to the Jews shows a pitiless and mindless hatred which can be shown to be at odds with certain moves towards a more charitable view of the Jews that were being taken by the Church at the time.[3] They are described as foul usurers, hateful to Christ (491–2), right at the beginning of the story; identified with Satan (558); constantly referred to as 'cursed' folk (570, 574, 578); and finally dismissed, more cruelly than in most of the analogues, to torture, drawing and hanging, with the contemptuous allusion to their own Law:

> 'Yvele shal have that yvele wol deserve'. (632)

The view of the tale as a satire on the shallow sentimentality and mindless bigotry of the Prioress has been characterised at length, since it is so widely and respectably held.[4] It can be seen as an example of ideological appropriation, whereby stories that seem to promote attitudes or ideas distasteful to modern readers are shown, through dramatic irony or ironic reconstruction, to promote the opposite. Chaucer, by this means, can be recruited to good modern liberal causes: here, Chaucer expresses his opinion of anti-Semitism by locating it within and as a natural part of the consciousness of a mindless, shallow and thoroughly inadequate woman. The appeal of such an interpretation has to be admitted, since it is difficult for those who admire Chaucer to acknowledge that he might have shared the Prioress's uncomplex view of the Jews. However, it cannot be allowed in this simple form, and Chaucer's views on the subject must remain a matter for generous speculation. His integrity resides rather in his truth as a writer, his truth to the nature of the story he is telling and the conventions according to which it exists. Legends and miracles of this kind require the existence of an 'opposition', an inhuman enemy, whether Roman, Saracen or Jew, that provides the opportunity for martyrdom. To treat such an enemy as human would deny the very purpose of such legends and miracles as witnesses of faith and providential reward and turn them into conflicts of interest, or even tragedies. In this story there is in addition the typological presence of the Jews in the Gospels, in the description of the Asian Jews as the 'cursed folk of Herodes al newe' (574), and a reminder of the responsibility of the Jews for the Massacre of the Innocents and, ultimately, for the Crucifixion. This does not mean that the literal level is subsumed in the allegorical, and that the Jews become mere 'symbols', as Hawkins (1964, p. 604) argues, but it does mean that all historical and human understanding is absorbed in this stereotype, even such as might have been evoked by the story of St Hugh of Lincoln, 'but a litel while ago' (686). The 'cursed Jew' is part of the grain of the story that the Prioress tells, and Chaucer, in being true to it, is true to the character of emotional religious exaltation and those elements in it that are repugnant and embarrassing as well as those that are expressive of pity and love.

So far from being a satire on the Prioress, or an ironic act of self-revelation on her part, the Prioress's Tale is Chaucer's tribute to her. Without her, to put it naively, it could not have been written. It is not an 'exercise', if by that term is meant some self-conscious act of self-discipline within a certain genre, and perhaps Payne goes too far in that direction in identifying the Prioress's Tale thus, in his excellent account of this and the other tales of affective piety (Man of Law's, Clerk's, Physician's and Second Nun's Tales):

> The Prioress's Tale is the summation of an effort, running through five of the twenty-three tales, to write a purely affective narrative in which irony, characterization, and complexity of action all give way to a very rigidly controlled stylistic artifice. (1963, p. 169)

The Prioress's Tale is rather a genuine exploration of a mode of thought and feeling perhaps alien to Chaucer himself and perhaps only accessible to him through the opportunity for the exercise of 'negative capability' given by the dramatic framework of the *Canterbury Tales*. Specifically, it is an exploration of that kind of piety that takes its roots in the appeal to feeling – love of mother for child, of child for mother or Virgin-mother, of child for child-Jesus – rather than in intellectual argument or moral certainty. It is not religion, but religiousness, or religiosity, the activity of human affection or emotional attachment under the sanction of religion. David, comparing the Prioress's Tale with *An ABC*, stresses also the self-conscious cultivation of beauty in the artefact, of aesthetic satisfaction, in coming to a broadly similar conclusion:

> The poem and the Prioress help explain one another. They reveal between them a new and fashionable religiosity that combines gentility and emotion, decorousness with enthusiasm. Still dressed in the forms and symbols of orthodox Christianity, it is a sentimentalized religiosity that worships beauty as a version of truth. (1982, p. 157)

It has perhaps the same relation to religion as contemporary decorated Gothic sculpture and window-tracery has to the church: the one contributes nothing to the moral life of the individual, nor the other to the structure of which it is part. It is the response of a certain kind of temperament to the stimulus of religious feeling. Chaucer stands both within and apart: like a dramatist, he is fully committed in imagination to the realisation of the story, and yet uncommitted to any endorsement of its attitudes. As Whittock says, 'With his dramatic skill he draws the reader into the heart of medieval belief, and at the same time, by means of one or two slight touches, he invites an objective appraisal' (1968, p. 202).

THE SECOND NUN'S TALE

Chaucer made no attempt to adapt his early 'lyf of Seynt Cecile', which he refers to as already written in the Prologue to *The Legend of Good Women* (F 426), to the framework of the *Canterbury Tales*. The references to the 'feithful bisynesse' that the author has done in 'translacioun' of the legend (VIII.24–5), and to himself as an 'unworthy sone of Eve' (62), and the plea for indulgence, from those who read what he writes, for his lack of skill in composition (78–84), are all inappropriate to a pilgrim-narrator.[5]

The tale is a conventional saint's legend, complete with the usual introductory apparatus: author's statement of formal intent, to eschew idleness; invocation to the Virgin; *captatio benevolentiae*, or author's plea for indulgence; and etymological interpretation of the name of the saint. The etymology (all of it, of course, edifying and 'wrong') is drawn from the same source as the legend, that is, from some version of the very popular thirteenth-century legendary known as the *Legenda Aurea*, conflated or not with other sources;[6] the rest of the prologue is drawn from a variety of sources, including the address to the Virgin which Dante gives to St Bernard in Canto 33 of the *Paradiso*, which accounts for lines 36–56.

The earnest homiletic tone of the prologue is entirely characteristic: such prologues, as Jones (1937) remarks, are often used in sermons of the *de sanctis* type, where the life of the saint is told as the form of sermon appropriate to the day of the saint. The work of translation, which is taken on to avoid the 'roten slogardye' of idleness (17), is specifically described as a form of penitential exercise, in a manner reminiscent, if it is reminiscent of anything in Chaucer, of the close of the Parson's Tale.

The *Invocacio ad Mariam* is comparable with the invocation at the beginning of the Prioress's Tale, but the differences are noticeable. The speaker is not the trusting child, seemingly unaware of sin, who asks for help and guidance in the telling of the tale, as in the Prioress's Prologue, but a sinner,

> Me, flemed wrecche, in this desert of galle, (58)

who begs that the tale, and the effort of telling it, may be an earnest of his humble intention to be penitent, and so lighten the affliction of his soul (72–4). The tone of the address to the Virgin is more sober than in the Prioress's Prologue, less intimate, less exalted, and, in the stanzas drawn from Dante, more highly intellectualised and given to paradox:

> Thow Mayde and Mooder, doghter of thy Sone . . . (36)

> Thow humble, and heigh over every creature. (39)

It is also less fully absorbed poetically (Pratt, 1946, considers that the later Prologue was actually worked up from the earlier), as can be seen from a comparison of the stanzas where both prologues draw on the prayer of St Bernard in Dante:

> Assembled is in thee magnificence
> With mercy, goodnesse, and with swich pitee
> That thou, that art the sonne of excellence
> Nat oonly helpest hem that preyen thee,
> But often tyme, of thy benygnytee,
> Ful frely, er that men thyn help biseche,
> Thou goost biforn, and art hir lyves leche. (VIII.50–6)

> Lady, thy bountee, thy magnificence,
> Thy vertu, and thy grete humylitee,
> Ther may no tonge expresse in no science;
> For somtyme, Lady, er men praye to thee,
> Thou goost biforn of thy benyngnytee,
> And getest us the lyght, of thy preyere,
> To gyden us unto thy Sone so deere. (VII. 474–80)

It is in particular worth noting the literal and rather affectingly homely interpretation given in the latter passage to 'goost biforn', whereby the Virgin seems to run before to beg a candle of her Son to light the way for us. This contrasts with the flatly stated and undeveloped image of 'the sonne of excellence' in the Second Nun's Prologue, which is quite independent of the following image of the Virgin as physician. Comparison, of course, needs to be qualified by the recognition that the essential quality of poetic language in a tale like the Second Nun's Tale is that it should be remote and un-affecting, opening up a realm of supra-verbal reality rather than embodying experiential reality. 'The world of ordinary meanings splits apart like a husk to reveal the realm of Divine truths'.[7] There is a suggestive contrast here with the overwhelming sense of the 'materialness' of words in the Canon's Yeoman's Tale, and also with the Manciple's idea of language as a form of trickery.

The tale likewise is told without any sense of involvement on the part of the narrator, or any invitation to involvement on the part of the reader, except as co-celebrant in the majesty of the Church Triumphant. Asides that might have meant mischief elsewhere in Chaucer –

> The nyght cam, and to bedde moste she gon
> With hire housbonde, as ofte is the manere (141–2)

– are here transparently unironic. The one touch of humour, where the prefect Almachius congratulates himself on his power to suffer Cecilia's rebukes 'as a philosophre' (490), shows up the speaker contemptuously as a fool. The processes of change and conversion are instantaneous and inexplicable: Cecilia's bridegroom, Valerian, is immediately 'corrected as God wolde' (162), and his brother Tiburce, who brings with him a breath of the real world when he arrives –

> And seyde, 'I wondre, this tyme of the yeer,
> Whennes that soote savour cometh so
> Of rose and lilies that I smelle heer' (246–8)

– is likewise instantly transformed:

> 'The sweete smel that in myn herte I fynde
> Hath chaunged me al in another kynde.' (251–2)

Kean (1972, p. 206) contrasts 'the grand, flat stylization of Cecilia's offer to her husband of a choice between love and death, as tranquilly accepted by him as it is offered', with the 'minute attention to motivation and the logical development of the action' in the Prioress's Tale. This is very well observed and the sense of contrast might be compared to the similar impression of contrast that we have in looking at pictorial representations of the Crucifixion in the early fourteenth-century Peterborough Psalter and in the early fifteenth-century Sherborne Missal:[8] in the one, 'grand, flat stylization', with the emotion of the scene distanced and made transcendent through the static nature of the composition and the subdued, even calm poses of the figures; in the other, restless compositional rhythms, and an attention to the actuality of the emotions of the participants which verges on the sentimental, even hysterical.

There is little or no human feeling in the Second Nun's Tale, and no sense of pain or fear. The processes of change that take place are all brought about by the exercise of irresistible power. Cecilia exerts her power over Valerian in converting him from a 'fiers leoun' into a meek lamb (198–9), and she addresses the two brothers and the company of newly christened former executioners, as they go to their death, in the language of militant Christianity (383–7). The climactic interview between Almachius and Cecilia is briskly developed by Chaucer, with some original material that makes it more one-sided, with Cecilia more belligerent than in the analogues and Almachius more obtuse, as Beichner (1973–4) and Hirsh (1977–8) observe. Cecilia is virginity triumphant, even rampant, and her sharp retorts to her inquisitor –

> 'Ye han bigonne youre questioun folily,'
> Quod she, 'that wolden two answeres conclude
> In o demande; ye axed lewedly.' (428–30)

make him seem a simpleton or a dummy. The behaviour of the virgin-martyrs of the early thirteenth-century 'Katherine Group' of legends (St Katherine, St Juliana and St Margaret) is very comparable. The final torments of the 'bath of flambes rede' (515) and the botched execution are quite briefly recounted, and the tale ends abruptly, without any narratorial comment. Cecilia finds the bath quite comfortably cool –

> It made hire nat a drope for to sweete (522)

and it has not escaped the notice of critics that the next character who appears in Fragment VIII, the alchemical canon, sweats, by contrast, a lot:

But it was joye for to seen hym swete! (579)

This sets up some quite interesting lines of communication between the tales, since the Canon's Yeoman's Tale has much to do with getting overheated in the practice of another kind of 'conversion',[9] but the suggested associations are of an extraneous and gratuitous kind, such as often arise in the juxtaposition of the tales, and are not essential or even relevant to the interpretation of the individual tales. Indeed, the association made by Grennen (1966) between the ideal chaste marriage of Cecilia and Valerian and the ideal 'alchemical wedding' of elements in the Canon's Yeoman's Tale, though it may enliven our view of the latter, may actually distract attention from the primary iconographic significance of the Second Nun's Tale, which is more centred, as Kolve (1981) explains, on the flaming bath as a demonstration of chastity and on Cecilia's martyrdom as the means by which she becomes, spiritually, procreative.

The Second Nun's Tale has some virtues of quiet grandeur and simplicity, and demonstrates Chaucer's power to write well in an un-Chaucerian and maybe even uncongenial vein. It is itself one of the best examples of late medieval saint's legend, flawed only by the undigested matter from St Ambrose's 'preface' (270–83). At times it strikes the authentic note of pure and transparent faith:

> Tiburce answerde, 'Seistow this to me
> In soothnesse, or in dreem I herkne this?'
> 'In dremes,' quod Valerian, 'han we be
> Unto this tyme, brother myn, ywis.
> But now at erst in trouthe oure dwellyng is.' (260–4)

It was, however, to 'dremes', rather than 'trouthe', that Chaucer was to make his most lasting dedication, to the world in which people fail in such interesting ways to live the truth that Cecilia drives towards so single-mindedly.

THE MAN OF LAW'S TALE

The Introduction to the Man of Law's Tale has the character of a new beginning. The astronomical calculation that is made by the Host of the date and time of day (10 a.m. on April 18) is introduced with remarkable deliberateness, and may be compared with the similar calculation made in the Prologue to the Parson's Tale by the narrator, as the evening shadows begin to lengthen. The existence of an early and more formal 'envelope' for the *Tales* has been suggested (Owen, 1977, pp. 25–31).

The Man of Law replies to the Host's sober request for a tale in legal-sounding language, his second word, *depardieux* (39), being appropriate to a man who would have spent much of his time pleading in the courts in Anglo-French. Immediately, though, he falls into the role simply of a person who has to tell a story, not a Man of Law who has to tell a story, and there is nothing that can be discerned in the remainder of the Introduction, or the prologue, or the Tale, that has specifically to do with a lawyer, not even one who has been further characterised, in the General Prologue, as shrewd and pompous and ostentatiously full of business. His amusing comments on Chaucer are directly prompted by his remarks on how difficult it is to find a story to tell that Chaucer has not already told, and mangled in the telling (46–52). The comments are relevant to the thread of his discourse, but they cannot usefully be regarded as a way of characterising the Man of Law.[10] The Man of Law's benevolent acknowledgement that Chaucer, though he writes too much, does not write filthy tales of incest, such as those of Canacee and Appollonius, is likewise a literary jest sufficient in itself. The grand comedy of the gross misrepresentation of Gower, who tells both stories with complete sobriety and decorum and much tender detail in the *Confessio Amantis*, is quite ruined if one assumes that the Man of Law is aware of it, or that it is he who, in the excessive zeal of prurience, has inserted the detail – not present in Gower – that the king Antiochus raped his daughter 'upon the pavement' (II.85). One hopes that Gower appreciated the humour, and did not need the satire to make it palatable.

The Man of Law is still thinking about the problem of telling a tale:

But of my tale how shal I doon this day? (90)

He hates to be thought a poetic pilferer, and so he decides to do something plain and simple, and speak in prose. The stage seems set for a solid and worthwhile piece – something like the *Melibee*, which is often assumed (e.g., Brown, 1937) to have been originally intended for the Man of Law – that will contrast nicely with the playful literary comedy of the Introduction. It comes as something of a surprise, therefore, when he immediately embarks on a rhetorically elaborate apostrophe, in rhyme royal, against the hateful condition of poverty. It is drawn directly from the *De Miseria Condicionis Humane* of Pope Innocent III, which Chaucer claims on another occasion to have translated in full (*Legend of Good Women*, Prologue G.414–15). It is perfectly orthodox in sentiment, though rather repugnant to modern sensibilities. At the end, the Man of Law introduces a glowing tribute to merchants, who avoid all the nastiness and bad effects of poverty by being prosperous:

> O riche marchauntz, ful of wele been yee,
> O noble, o prudent folk, as in this cas! (122–3)

They are also, by their profession, the 'fadres of tidynges and tales' (129–30), and the Man of Law concludes by expressing his gratitude – since otherwise he would have been 'of tales desolaat' – to the merchant who told him, long ago, the tale that he is now about to tell. The tale begins, to compound this bizarre articulation of the essentially disarticulate, with a warmly appreciative account of the Syrian merchants whose journeyings to Rome provided their Sultan with the news of the beauty of the Emperor's daughter Constance, with whom he immediately falls in love. The merchants have no further part in the story, which is not about poverty, nor in prose.

It is hard to know what to make of these odd proceedings. The thread of consistency is there, in the Man of Law's repeated concern at not having a tale to tell, but it seems a small peg to hang such a weight of discourse on. The praise of merchants seems bound to be ironical, since the correct alternative to the 'hateful harm' of poverty is of course not wealth but the patience which makes poverty a good (Wife of Bath's Tale, III.1177–1206); it could be tied in with an ironical view of the apostrophe to poverty as an exposure of the Man of Law's materialism and admiration of those who are successful in business. The whole tale can now be interpreted as an exposure of the Man of Law's inability to understand the kind of tale he is telling, and his habit of casing it in bombastic rhetoric and over-stressing the element of material misfortune. The rhetorical embellishment, which Wurtele (1976) sees simply as appropriate to a lawyer, is viewed as meretricious by Scheps (1974), and the mark, with the excessive interest in rank and wealth, of a charlatan. The heightened emotionalism of the telling is 'as though the poet were deliberately raising his voice to conceal an emptiness of feeling' (Baum, 1958, p. 118), or, as Manning (1979, p 21) puts it, 'the Narrator's emotional and intellectual intensities cover up a lack of depth'. The sentimentalised piety, which Weissman (1979) sees as part of a general critique of 'the publicly sentimentalizing sensibility' of the age, 'the self-displaying sentimentality' (p. 134), is taken to be specially and pejoratively appropriate to a bourgeois *parvenu* by Duffey (1947, p. 193). Wood (1970, pp. 242–3) considers that the ignorance of the proper nature of divine providence reveals the Man of Law's 'central concern for worldly prosperity' and his tendency to regard Christ as 'a kind of super-astrologer, who not only knows the future, but can change it for our immediate pleasure'.

All this is extremely far-fetched, though pleasing to modern tastes that despise both the rhetorical high style and passive virtue, and therefore a way of rescuing the tale by 'ironising' the narrator. To use the Introduction and Prologue (and the General Prologue) in this way is not impermissible, and there are several occasions elsewhere in the *Tales* where interpretation of this kind can be seen to enhance the meaning and power of a tale. In this case, though, as in others, the tale is blighted by such interpretation. There is too the matter of the promise to speak in prose, which proves the existence of some real and unironic disjunction between Introduction and Prologue–Tale, and suggests that Fragment II remained imperfectly revised. This provides good reason for treating the tale as an independent poem rather than as a means of characterising the Man of Law as an inadequate narrator and thereby making the point of the tale to satirise him.

To refuse this easy opening is not to remove the problems of coming to terms with the tale, however, for it remains a somewhat puzzling performance. There is some clash between the piously romantic matter of the tale and the heightened rhetorical manner of treatment which seems to have been deliberately engineered by Chaucer, as if he wanted us both to participate emotionally in the tensions and reliefs of the narrative and at the same time to stand outside it. Like the other religious tales in the present sequence – the Prioress's, Second Nun's and Clerk's Tales – the Man of Law's Tale is cast in rhyme royal, the stanza that Chaucer reserved for these four of the *Canterbury Tales*, and therefore apparently for serious religious tales with a strong emotional content. Like those other tales, the Man of Law's Tale can be seen as an exploration of the narrative possibilities of a certain genre of writing, undertaken by Chaucer not to expose the limitations of that genre – though this may be a side-effect of the pressures to which he subjects it – but genuinely to explore, and at the same time test and temper, to 'prove', the powers of English as a literary language, capable of a more complex operation in its influence upon the reader than mere entertainment or edification.

The genre of the Man of Law's Tale is not easily defined. The story is widespread in folk-tale, and is known as the tale of 'the Calumniated Wife': it has the motifs (the setting adrift in a boat, the wicked mother-in-law), the structural repetitions, sudden reversals and unexplained motivations characteristic of folk-tale. Much of this translates readily into the forms of medieval romance, as Schlauch (1927) shows, and many of the literary versions of the story are familiarly classified as romance. However, the human fortitude and fidelity of the folk-tale heroine adapt so naturally to the exemplification of religious faith and of a providential guidance system that it is not surprising to find that many of the medieval retellings of the story, such as the romance of *Emare*, are more religious *exempla* than romances. This battleground of generic distinction has been frequently crossed and recrossed by armies from both sides, as mentioned in note 1 above, and one would not wish to get embroiled in an unnecessary mêlée: but it is clear that the Man of Law's Tale, like *Emare*, is much more of a religious *exemplum* than a romance, if indeed it is anything at all of the latter. On the other hand, it is not a saint's legend. The reason for asserting this, despite what Paull (1970–1) has shown of the influence of the saint's legend genre in Chaucer's adaptation of the story, is not simply that Constance is not a saint, nor even that her life is defective in not ending in martyrdom (the life of St Elizabeth of Hungary demonstrates that the *passio sancti* is not essential to sanctification). It is rather that she does not bear witness of her own will to a superhuman and transcendental scheme of values, does not deliberately create the circumstances in which her suffering, her 'martyrdom', is necessary. A saint must demand, though not with excessive importunacy, election. Constance undergoes a whole series of misfortunes with exemplary fortitude, but she never chooses them, or creates the conditions from which they necessarily follow. The conversions that accompany her marriages to the Sultan of Syria and to Alla, king of Northumberland, are the by-product of her nature, not the consequence of her will. She does not choose to go into heathendom, like the proselytising heroes of evangelical Christianity, and the tribulations that are heaped upon her are the product of more or less unexplained ill-will on the part of the two mothers-in-law. Constance bears no responsibility or credit for these actions: she is unlucky and she behaves in an exemplary fashion, but not in a way that is unavailable to ordinary mortals. The happy outcome of her life is a vindication of her faith, but the trials are not those which she chose in order to bear witness to that faith. She is a heroine despite herself: the hero of the story is God.

Chaucer has not resisted the romantic elements in the story. The immediate source from which he drew is the Anglo-Norman *Annales* of Nicholas Trivet, and it is from here that his story derives its sense of weight and historical circumstance. Yet he has not, as he might have done elsewhere, drawn out the implications of circumstantiality by any special or 'Chaucerian' attention to motivation, dramatic realisation, or generally increased density of narrative texture. Block (1953, pp. 574–81), who gives a detailed account of Chaucer's handling of his source, shows how he neglects, in fact, some of the hints of this kind he finds in Trivet, alluding only briefly to the manner in which Donegild meets her death (893–6), and abbreviating Trivet's quite circumstantial account of the wicked steward's attempted shipboard rape, and Constance's defensive measures, so that it becomes a swiftly contrived example of divine intervention:

> For with hir struglyng wel and myghtily
> The theef fil over bord al sodeynly. (921–2)

Yunck (1960, pp. 257–8) emphasises this change as an example of the way Chaucer consistently turns the tale into 'a romantic homily on the virtues of complete submission to divine providence, worked out against the harshest vicissitudes which folktale could provide' (p. 250). Chaucer's concentration is all upon Constance, whom he strives to keep 'unwemmed' by distancing her from the surrounding mass of historical and human circumstance. It is the pathos of isolation of the pure and romantic figure of the heroine that he seeks to emphasise, especially in the great tableau-scenes that he contrives of her suffering and devotion as the story rises to its climax. First, there is the prayer to the Cross when she is first set adrift (449–62); then, the prayer for deliverance when she is wrongfully condemned for Hermengild's death (638–43), and the wonderfully pathetic simile of the pale prisoner drawn to his death, with its vivid reminiscence of the picture of Christ on his way to Calvary:

> Have ye nat seyn somtyme a pale face,
> Among a prees, of hym that hath be lad
> Toward his deeth, wher as hym gat no grace,
> And swich a colour in his face hath had,
> Men myghte knowe his face that was bistad,
> Amonges alle the faces in that route?
> So stant Custance, and looketh hire aboute. (645–51)

Most striking of all is Chaucer's extended development of the scene of
her second departure into exile, with her prayers to God and to Mary, her
touching farewell rebuke to her 'housbonde routheles' (863), and the
deliberate pathos, reminiscent of the Prioress's Tale, of her address to
her child (834–40). All of this is new, and all serves to enhance the pathos
of the story, the passive suffering of the heroine. On the two occasions
when she could have acted to ease her passage through life, by explaining
who she was and the misfortunes she had undergone, she chooses to say
nothing: first, when she lands on the coast of Northumberland (523–5),
and then, when she is picked up by the senator on his way to Rome
(971–3). Her reticence is, of course, essential to the story, which would
be less interestingly prolonged if she behaved in any other way, but there
is here, in addition, a deliberate unloading onto God of the responsibility
for her fate.

The elaborated portrayal of Constance as a passive romantic heroine is
part of Chaucer's strategy for turning the tale into an extended *exemplum*
of God's grace granted to patience and constant faith. The developed
account of the operation of this grace is Chaucer's most significant single
innovation in the telling of the story. He first stresses, when anticipating
the death of the unfortunate Sultan, how man's destiny is written in the
stars (194–6). He gives examples from history, of Hector, Achilles,
Julius Caesar and others. Constance's departure for the east is accompanied by a rhetorically heightened account of the planetary conjunction
that made disaster inevitable:

> O firste moevyng! crueel firmament,
> With thy diurnal sweigh that crowdest ay
> And hurlest al from est til occident
> That naturelly wolde holde another way,
> Thy crowdyng set the hevene in swich array
> At the bigynnyng of this fiers viage,
> That crueel Mars hath slayn this mariage. (295–301)

The malevolent aspect of Mars is emphasised, as in the Knight's Tale,
and even some suggestion given of cruelty in the will of the 'firste
moevyng', the *primum mobile*, by whose power the heavens are driven
apparently contrary to their natural motion.[11] But Chaucer is not
essentially interested here, as he was in the Knight's Tale, in relocating
the causes of events in human freewill: the setting up of a malevolent
destinal power is preparation rather for the triumphant statement of
God's providence, which, as Constance embarks on her first dangerous

voyage, is shown to defy all expectation of disaster, even that decreed by destiny:[12]

> God liste to shewe his wonderful myracle
> In hire, for we sholde seen his myghty werkis. (477–8)

The transcendent power of God's 'purveiance' is not described in abstract, philosophical, Boethian terms, as it was in the Knight's Tale (I.1663–72), but through direct biblical examples, of God's care for his chosen people. It is a point of faith, not a point of philosophical principle, and in depriving Constance of all hope, all reasonable expectation of salvation, Chaucer stresses the unique power of faith. He returns to the same theme, using the same technique of emphatically reiterated question, when Constance escapes from her would-be ravisher (932–9). These passages are the central statement of the theme of submissive faith rewarded and triumphant, which is the *raison d'être* of the Man of Law's Tale.

The heightened rhetorical quality of these passages is readily observable. They may even seem strained, though they can hardly be parodic. The whole tale is told with a similar rhetorical intensity: acts of emotional participation are continually demanded of us at one level, at the same time that, on another level, the quality of intellectual and imaginative engagement and reflexivity seems remarkably, for Chaucer, thin. 'In the interests of seriousness', as Robinson (1972, p. 154) says, 'Chaucer seems to be trying to stifle his critical intelligence'. The basic style is that of the 'impersonal familiar', which Chaucer learnt from English romance (there is much in the constant barrage of imprecation and ironic foreshadowing that reminds one of *Havelok*) and which he adapted to a lofty purpose in a similar way in the Knight's Tale, perhaps there, as here, with a comparable intention of distancing himself from, writing himself out of the narration. Its characteristic features are the exposed transition (321–2, 581, 900, 953–4, 983–7), the refusal to delay the narrative with long description (232, 246–7, 410–11, 701–7, 1069–71, 1116–17, 1124–7), and the constant interventions in the narrative with apostrophes to Constance ('O my Custance . . .' 446, 803) that God may be her help and Christ her champion (245, 446, 631, 803), apostrophes to noble ladies to have pity on her (652) and to God to save her (907), and apostrophes to the Sultaness and Satan (358) and to the messenger and Donegild (771). Ominous warning notes are sounded (261, 420), and opportunity taken for digressive dilation on the speed with which woe

follows joy (421), or the punishment for lechery (952), and again on the
transitoriness of joy (1132). These last three passages, as well as the
apostrophe to the messenger ('O messager, fulfild of dronkenesse', 771)
are all taken from the *De Miseria* of Innocent III, which also provided the
apostrophe against Poverty in the Prologue to the tale. The tone here is
less that of the Knight's Tale, or of romance, than that of the preacher
amplifying his matter from conventional sources, and is inevitably
reminiscent of the Pardoner, whose homily also draws on the *De miseria*
(e.g., VI.535, 551–2, 557–61). The trite reflections on the transience of
worldly joy are likewise, in their turn, reminiscent of the Nun's Priest's
Tale (VII.3205, 3355–73), as are the epic comparisons for Constance's
grief at leaving Rome (288) or for the splendour of the wedding with the
Sultan (400). But the existence of these resemblances does not necessarily provide a clue to the reading of the Man of Law's Tale, however
strong may be our desire to seize on them as such and escape from the
embarrassingly unironic operation of the narrative. The kinds of rhetorical amplification which Chaucer exposed to critical and ironic scrutiny
in other tales are here, apparently, intrinsic to the proper functioning of
the narrative. It is true too, perhaps, that Chaucer could hardly have
burlesqued these traditional techniques so successfully if he had not, on
occasions, recognised and exploited their special effectiveness.

There are moments in the Man of Law's Tale when the declamatory
and emotional mode of narration is suggestively relaxed. When Constance is about to leave home for her unknown Sultan, the narrator
comments, with heavy irony:

> Housbondes been alle goode, and han ben yoore;
> That knowen wyves; I dar sey yow na moore. (272–3)

In context, this contributes to the build-up of ominous anticipation, but
it is hard to keep such a remark in context. So, too, there seems to be
more than the narrative requires in the comment on the wedding-night of
Constance and Alla (708–14). Some similar instabilities of tone are
present in the Knight's Tale, as if Chaucer were still working at the fine
tuning of this new heightened narrative style, or as if, more frankly, he
could hardly forbear the mischievous aside. As Muscatine says, in
another context:

> We must always be prepared to tolerate, if not enjoy in him, a certain
> amiable inconsistency of tone, or of perspective, or of detail, as his
> narrative goes along . . . (1966, p. 89)

It is better, certainly, to recognise this 'inconsistency of tone' than to use such asides as the means to destroy the credibility of the Man of Law's Tale and reconstruct it as an attack on false religiosity. At the same time, the limitations of the tale are apparent. It is a full and, in artistic terms, fully committed exploitation of the emotional power of a certain kind of religious story. Like the Prioress's Tale and the Second Nun's Tale, it is a superlative example of its kind. But the distance created between reader and subject by the mode of narration is sufficient to allow a critical consciousness to continue to operate, not so much upon the events and characters of the story as upon the nature of such stories, and the simplicities upon which they rest.[13]

THE CLERK'S TALE

At the end of his tale of patient Griselda, the Clerk explains how the story is to be understood (IV.1142–62). It does not, he says, recommend how wives should behave towards their husbands, since Griselda's 'humylitee' would be intolerable ('inportable') for them, as human beings, even if they had ambitions of the kind. It is not possible nor appropriate for them, in their capacity as wives, to behave in such a way. (This seems the necessary interpretation of line 1144: it cannot mean that *we* should find it insupportable if they *did* behave so.) The story is rather an example of the patience that all men should display in adversity, and the example is the more forceful in that our obedience is due to God, where Griselda's was due only to a man. We have the greater reason as well as the greater obligation to be obedient. God, furthermore, does not test his creatures to find out how they will react – which is what Walter does to Griselda – but rather proves and tempers their will through adversity, making them strong through suffering. 'Vertuous suffraunce' is the recognition of God's will at work in all the circumstances of our lives, even though they may be contrary to our own will and may appear to be contrary to our good.

Chaucer takes this explanation of the meaning of the story, as well as the story itself, from Petrarch's Latin version of the last tale of Boccaccio's *Decameron*. He follows Petrarch's version of the story with exceptional fidelity. There are some changes, omissions and additions, some of which may be derived, as Severs (1942) explains, in his very full account of the sources, from a French translation of Petrarch's Latin which he consulted, but they stand out clearly from the surrounding quite close paraphrase. Only the prose tales are comparable in the closeness of their rendering of their sources. Chaucer's respect for the great Italian writer, and for the authoritativeness of the Latin language, may be important influences at work here (his handling of the stories he took from Boccaccio is strikingly different), but his desire to raise English poetry to new heights of dignity and seriousness should not be underestimated. His handling of the story and his style of narration are remarkably austere and restrained, with the 'fine astringency' of which Muscatine (1957, p. 191) speaks, and there are few of the human and humorous touches or narratorial asides with which he customarily stamps the narration as his.

Petrarch's interpretation of the story, as adopted by Chaucer, does not make it a thoroughgoing allegory. The distinction he draws is not between a literal and an allegorical level of meaning, in which the former exists only to communicate the latter and is in itself intrinsically meaningless, but between a humanly realistic story and a story told as an *exemplum*. In an exemplary story, it is usual for the models of human behaviour to be presented in extremely unrealistic terms: Griselda's behaviour, in allowing her children to be, as she thinks, slain, without a word of protest, is by any standards of 'real' behaviour both preposterous and repugnant. However, the customary understanding of the exemplary mode of narrative screens out these irrelevant meanings, while allowing those elements in the story that contribute to its exemplary significance to be fully exploited. Petrarch stresses that this significance is reinforced by the nature of the relationship between Griselda and Walter on the literal level – 'sith a womman was so pacient/Unto a mortal man' (1149–50) – and he makes no attempt to allegorise the relationship, as for instance by portraying Walter as a divinely guided minister of providence. There are hints of mystery and inordinate power in his actions, but no more than one would expect in this type of 'traditional' story, derived from folk-tale, where the motives and existence of characters other than the protagonist remain, by and large, in a dramatically unrealised state (Brewer, 1980, p. 23). These hints of mystery and power are sufficient to deflect any humanly realistic questioning of Walter's actions, without turning him into a representative of 'God': they establish the mode of the narrative, and allow full accommodation for the exemplary role of Griselda. Further reinforcement for the exemplary significance of the tale comes from the relationship of Griselda to Walter, not merely as 'womman' to 'mortal man', but as wife to husband. Her subordination to his will is an extreme version of the traditionally sanctioned distribution of power in marriage, and is made more absolute, in the tale, by the difference in social class and by certain explicit promises of absolute obedience made by Griselda which go beyond the promises of the marriage vow. Walter's power over Griselda is thus not something that is used in the story for mere allegorical convenience, as a way of representing God's power over man, but something that relates, in however extreme a form, to accepted social reality. The inner strength of the story, as an *exemplum* of the obedience man owes to God, and the patience and constancy he should show in adversity, derives from the cruel and poignant appropriateness of the mode of exemplification. It is, however, a precarious strength, vulnerable, in its exploitation for exemplary purposes of certain terms of a relationship both complex and deeply human, to the intrusion of other kinds of interpretation, and in Chaucer's version of the story these vulnerabilities are fully exposed.

Initially, there is little to alert us to the possibility of alternative forms of interpretation. Walter's behaviour as a lord and his treatment of his people is not that of a tyrant, or at least not tyrannical in terms of any construction that can usefully be put upon it at this stage and within the context of medieval political beliefs. There may be reason to look back sceptically on his present behaviour when his later cruelty is described, and specific reference made to the obdurate wilfulness of 'lordes' (581) and 'wedded men' (622), and better grounds for seeing the Tale as a critique of both kinds of power relationship than as an assertion of the principle of divine order and hierarchy according to which such exercise of power is justified (as Heninger, 1957, asserts), but this reading seems forced at this stage in the Tale and will later prove to be inapplicable. Walter at this stage is acknowledged to have a fault, in that he lacks the wisdom and far-sightedness to subject his present pleasure to the necessities of the future, but he quickly accepts the advice of the people's spokesman that he should take a wife, and thus ensure the succession. His youth, and natural youthful wilfulness, are soon and properly brought under the sway of wise counsel and the warning of mortality (116–26). Walter's assertion that he will marry regardless of rank, and his demand that his subjects accept his choice of bride as a condition of his promise to marry, might be construed as his means of reserving to himself his absolute freedom and power, but they are not so construed in the tale. His argument that true virtue is not associated with rank (157–8) is one of the most cherished commonplaces of the Middle Ages (e.g., Wife of Bath's Tale, III.1109). He cannot be faulted for acting upon it, nor for committing his choice of bride to God's disposition (159–61). The narrative explicitly discounts any motives on his part but those most proper to the choice of bride:

> He noght with wantown lookyng of folye
> His eyen caste on hire, but in sad wyse
> Upon hir chiere he wolde hym ofte avyse,
> Commendynge in his herte hir wommanhede,
> And eek hir vertu, passynge any wight
> Of so yong age, as wel in chiere as dede. (236–41)

Walter's courtship of Griselda has something of that mysteriously sudden exercise of power that characterises the other-worldly visitant in tales like *Sir Degarre* and *Sir Orfeo*. The formal requests to Griselda's father, Janicula (311–12), and to Griselda herself (344–7) have a deceptive softness ('quod this markys *softely*', 323). His will, beneath this formality, seems irresistible. His demand that she promise absolute obedience is part of this mysterious assumption of power (351–7). There is the suggestion that Griselda is being prepared for some test, and that each move is part of a plan. Walter's presentation of Griselda to his people

> 'This is my wyf,' quod he, 'that standeth heere' (369)

seems a preliminary part of this plan in much the same way as God's presentation of Jesus ('This is my son ...') at the Baptism was a preliminary part of the divine plan. Yet, in all this, Walter does nothing that is incapable of being understood in literal terms.

These matters of political and social circumstance provide the context in which Griselda is brought forth as a heroine of saintly virtue and purity. Like Shakespeare, Chaucer seems powerfully drawn to the imaging of such qualities in the person of a young woman, and there are anticipations of Cordelia in Griselda, especially in the emphasis on her depth and resilience of character, her 'rype and sad corage' (220). It is notable that four of the five religious tales at present under consideration centre on female saintly or exemplary figures, and the fifth (the Prioress's Tale) concerns a young boy, who has the same essential innocence and maidenliness. Griselda is portrayed in idealised terms (209–24), though it is characteristic of Chaucer to add an affectionate human touch, in his description of Griselda hurrying through her domestic chores so that she can join the onlookers at Walter's wedding (274–87). There is nothing allegorical about her – though, as with Walter, a number of biblical and figural parallels are suggested (well analysed by Speirs, 1951, p. 154). Chaucer, in referring to Griselda's lowly birth, mentions the power of God to send his grace 'into a litel oxes stalle' (207), and he recurs to this image on two further occasions (291, 398), both additions to Petrarch, in obvious allusion to the birth of Christ in similar homely surroundings. There is similar reiteration of the suggestion that Griselda is so wise and virtuous that it seems she must have been brought up 'in an emperoures halle' (399), or sent from heaven,

> Peple to save and every wrong t'amende. (441)

Walter's original demand that his wife, whoever he chooses, should be respected by his subjects,

> As she an emperoures doghter weere (168)

is significantly recalled, and the hidden divinity of Christ again clearly alluded to.

Under test, Griselda displays an inhuman self-control, and it is here, of course, that the story is under great pressure, either to dissolve into allegory or to explode into absurdity. Petrarch's technique is to have Walter explicitly remind Griselda of her promise of obedience and require her assent to the removal of her daughter (492–7); Griselda then makes a declaration of obedience which has the formal affirmative quality of a creed, and strong religious overtones:

> She seyde, 'Lord, al lyth in youre plesaunce.
> My child and I, with hertely obeisaunce,
> Been youres al, and ye mowe save or spille
> Youre owene thyng; werketh after youre wille.
>
> Ther may no thyng, God so my soule save,
> Liken to yow that may displese me;
> Ne I desire no thyng for to have,
> Ne drede for to leese, save oonly yee.
> This wyl is in myn herte, and ay shal be;
> No lengthe of tyme or deeth may this deface,
> Ne chaunge my corage to another place.' (501–11)

The majestic and measured certitude that Chaucer imparts to these lines is the surest guarantee of the seriousness of his intentions in the Clerk's Tale, whatever difficulties he may have had in working them out. This is the sober poetry of faith and voluntary *willed* submission to a will acknowledged to be higher. It is not of course the way a real wife would talk to a real husband who had fatal designs on their only daughter: the real situation rather provides the apt occasion for the exemplary demonstration of the 'vertuous suffraunce' which is man's part in freely accommodating his will to the will of God. Credulity is strained, but so it should be: 'Patience demands responses as impossible in ordinary terms as Griselda's' (Robinson, 1972, p. 168).

In addition to following out faithfully Petrarch's serious intentions in describing the first test, Chaucer also introduces a new poignancy and humanity. The sergeant who comes to fetch the child is more abrupt and brutal (533–6), and therefore more likely to awaken in us the horror, fear and indignation that Griselda must be shown to overcome. She herself has a long and touching scene with her child, far fuller than in Petrarch, and exploiting further the vein of pathos so promisingly worked in the Man of Law's Tale (554–60). It might seem that such humanisation is likely to work against the exemplary significance of the tale, widening the gulf that already exists between our response to what happens and the construction that we are required to place upon it. In part this may be due to over-literal habits of reading that we bring to such exemplary narratives, but two further points might be stressed. One is that Griselda's love for her child is what gives depth of exemplary significance to her forbearance. Petrarch makes a point of emphasising her love for her children (687–95), to counter any argument that she gave up what she had no wish to keep. Chaucer, in taking this point, and elaborating the pathos of her loss in dramatic terms, adds strength to this counterargument, though of course in 'showing' rather than 'telling' he places the story under still greater strain, as did those dramatists who expanded the stark and controlled biblical narrative of Abraham and Isaac in the more expressive and open medium of the drama.[14] The second point to be made about the 'humanisation' of Griselda is that she is not, through it, deprived of her clear-sighted recognition of the choice she is making. The last line of her address to her child,

> For this nyght shaltow dyen for my sake (560)

with its enigmatic echo of the concluding formula of Christian prayer, asserts her recognition that the child dies, as she thinks, to preserve the integrity of her will in its submission to the higher will. It is, with a difference, Isabella's farewell to Claudio in *Measure for Measure*.

The development of Griselda's response to the two further tests can be traced in similar terms. On the one hand there is the faithful report of her deep commitment to obedience to the higher will, which at times is hardly contained within the framework of the literal narrative situation:

> 'And certes, if I hadde prescience
> Youre wyl to knowe, er ye youre lust me tolde,
> I wolde it doon withouten necligence;
> But now I woot youre lust, and what ye wolde,
> Al youre plesance ferme and stable I holde;
> For wiste I that my deeth wolde do yow ese,
> Right gladly wolde I dyen, yow to plese.' (659–65)

The readiness to die if it is her lord's will is, in a literal sense, a blasphemy, though it has a temporary and rather paradoxical familiarity as a reversal of the usual courtly hyperbole, just as her desire to anticipate her lord in all his wishes resembles what Criseyde finds in Troilus (iii.465–7). The essentially important part of her response, though, as Donaldson (1958, pp. 917–20) in his eloquent account of the poem stresses, is the clear-eyed explicit recognition of the nature and significance of her acts, the conscious will which directs them. It is this that makes Griselda's patience, or 'vertuous suffraunce', so different from that dog-like passive submissiveness which is often the connotation of the word in modern usage. Her voluntary embrace of the will to which she has vowed obedience is a form of heroism: it creates a place for hope ('We glory in tribulations also; knowing that tribulation worketh patience; and patience, experience; and experience, hope', Romans 5.3; cf. Job 5.17), and may even have the power to win over that will. Her father is a deliberately pointed contrast: his original consent to Walter's wishes (319–22) is almost identical with Griselda's (359–64), but he lacks her depth and integrity, and his response to adversity, in a passage added by Chaucer, is to curse the day he was born (901–3). He has the impatience of the early Job, unillumined and unreconstructed, where his daughter has the 'humblesse', and more, of the developed Job (932–8). There is no heroism here, and his death is the death of one whose grudging submission brings only sadness and confusion of heart, and whose spirit is broken by circumstance:

> His wyves fader in his court he kepeth,
> Til that the soule out of his body crepeth. (1133–4)

At the same time, though, that he gives full expression to Petrarch's vision of exemplary patience and fortitude, Chaucer also adds a number of humanising touches that increase the poignancy of Griselda's situation and increase the strain upon the narrative of the exemplary reading. In her speech of assent to the removal of her son, she speaks with pitiable but unselfpitying frankness of her experience of motherhood:

> I have noght had no part of children tweyne
> But first siknesse, and after, wo and peyne. (650–1)

The bitter symmetry of the pain of bearing and of losing her children is Chaucer's addition. Likewise, in her long speech of submission when she is dismissed from the palace by Walter, she is seemingly overcome momentarily by the memory of the past and gives utterance to a very human reflection on things:

> 'O goode God! how gentil and how kynde
> Ye semed by youre speche and youre visage
> The day that maked was oure mariage!' (852–4)

How touchingly her reference to 'the day that maked was oure mariage' echoes Walter's use of the same words (497) when he reminded her of the same day and her promise of obedience. The quizzical, slightly sardonic awareness of the realities of her situation, the awareness of its unjustness as well as the necessity of embracing it willingly, makes her submission the more meaningful and, paradoxically, the more an expression of power. It is she who has to remind Walter of the respect he owes to himself as well as to her in not obliging her to return naked to her father's home:

> Lat me nat lyk a worm go by the weye.
> Remembre yow, myn owene lord so deere,
> I was youre wyf, though I unworthy weere. (880–2)

The reproof is proud yet submissive; the striking image of the 'worm' is recognised by Kean (1972, p. 127) to be an allusion to the *via dolorosa* of Christ; the evidence is of a will freely consenting and aware of the nature of and reasons for that consent. Her remarks to Walter at the 'wedding' feast, when he asks for her appraisal of his new 'bride', are similarly quizzical and reflexive, and, though not new, are given added force and sharpness by Chaucer (1037–43). These are the high points of Griselda's career of 'vertuous suffraunce', or, to put it more strongly, of her exemplification of the Christian theology of freewill in its actual mode of operation. At the end of the tale, the release of tension in the emotion of discovery and recognition produces a scene of pure pathos, much extended by Chaucer (1079–106), which takes us back into the simpler world of the Man of Law's Tale and the Prioress's Tale, the world of the 'sentimental experiment' (Payne, 1963, p. 164), where the emotional response tends to overwhelm the rational and intellectual faculties. It may be that Chaucer recognises this as a dramatic necessity, given the checks and restraints he has applied to emotion throughout the tale.

If Walter, throughout all this, had been treated as a mysterious and inscrutable figure, a kind of 'Duke of dark corners', manipulating Griselda's suffering as a means of offering her the opportunity to demonstrate the temper of her will, the story would stand firm as an *exemplum*, with not too many questions to be asked. What Chaucer does with Walter, though, and in so doing makes his most systematic series of departures from Petrarch, is audacious in the extreme. From the time of the first test, he embarks on a tirade of denunciation of Walter for his wickedness and cruelty, where Petrarch merely remarks neutrally on the extraordinary and inexplicable nature of his actions:

> This markys in his herte longeth so
> To tempte his wyf, hir sadnesse for to knowe,
> That he ne myghte out of his herte throwe
> This merveillous desir his wyf t'assaye;
> Nedelees, God woot, he thoghte hire for t'affraye.
>
> He hadde assayed hire ynogh bifore,
> And foond hire evere good; what neded it
> Hire for to tempte, and alwey moore and moore,
> Though som men preise it for a subtil wit?
> But as for me, I seye that yvele it sit
> To assaye a wyf whan that it is no nede,
> And putten hire in angwyssh and in drede. (451–62)

Subsequently, Petrarch remarks frequently on Walter's subterfuges, his close scrutiny of his wife's reactions, and his concealment of his true feelings, suggesting some hidden intention (513, 579, 599, 671, 708, 733, 893). Chaucer keeps all this, and further sharpens the bitterness of Walter's taunting of Griselda – his exhortation to her to bear calmly 'the strook of Fortune or of aventure' (812) when he turns her out, his promise that her dower shall be returned (807), which Griselda ruefully recognises for the cutting irony it is (845–51), and his assurance to her that he values her contribution to the preparations for his new wedding:

> Thou knowest eek of old al my plesaunce. (964)

Chaucer, however, in addition, persistently pursues Walter with accusations of tyrannical cruelty (579–81), of something close to sadism (621–3), and of compulsive exercise of will (701–5). The suggestions of motive are not at all of a dark and inscrutable and potentially benevolent purpose, but of a streak of cruelty which is, as Spearing (1972, p. 97) says, all too recognisably human, though a horrifying disfigurement of humanity. The desire to torment helpless and submissive creatures, to exercise power over the powerless, is a reality of human existence, not an aspect of the instrumentality of a divine providence, and marriage has traditionally been an institution which sanctioned and even enforced such cruel displays of power. Walter, in fact, comes to seem as wicked as Satan himself, to whom God committed the privilege of testing Job. His 'wikke usage' (785) is deep-seated in his sinful self. The story is different though: Griselda may be like Job, but she is married to Walter and has to love and respect him and ground her willing 'suffraunce' in that love and respect.

At this point a good many critics throw up their hands in despair, and admit that the story, as an *exemplum*, has fallen apart. The pressure of Chaucer's dramatic realisation of the story causes it to crack and break down. As Burrow (1982) says, speaking generally of the exemplary relation of stories and general truth:

> When the scale of the narrative is increased, complications of a different sort may arise; for those details of human motive and behaviour which show up in larger-scale narrative tend to put at risk the general truth which the story claims to exemplify. (pp. 113–14)[15]

A more ingenious version of this explanation of the Clerk's Tale, and one which has the attraction that it does not actually accuse Chaucer of artistic failure, is that which claims that Chaucer, in stressing the role of the Clerk as 'a moral critic' of the story he tells, is deliberately setting up a tension 'between the teller and the tale', which is expressive of the 'tension between divine law and the law of the flesh' (Spearing, 1972, pp. 81, 93, 98); or that Chaucer is demonstrating the inadequacy of exemplary tales to sustain any weight of imaginative realisation (Middleton, 1973–4, p. 15). This, though, to be of any more than technical interest, would have to be an intrinsically interesting kind of inadequacy, and the value of such an interpretation for the understanding of the Clerk's Tale seems limited. There has therefore been a good deal of recourse to 'dramatic' explanations, or explainings-away, of the Clerk's Tale. The failures of the tale are attributed to the Clerk, who cannot understand the nature of the relationship between the exemplary world of moral abstraction and the real world, since he is so remote from the latter (Grennen, 1971–2; David, 1976, p. 167); or they reflect the unresolved state of his thinking about authority and the individual, because of the current Oxford debate concerning realism and nominalism (Morse, 1958). The most extravagant attempts to salvage the tale, and give it a 'dramatic' interest (since it so manifestly lacks any other), are those which, following Kittredge (1911–12), see it as a *riposte* to the Wife of Bath's Tale, and part of the continuing debate about sovereignty in marriage. The evidence of the epilogue (1163–212), where the Clerk refers openly to the Wife of Bath and the difficulty of finding women like Griselda in a world peopled by her and her sect, is pressed into service to demonstrate that the tale, rather dull and sentimental in itself, is made lively by the consciousness we have of the Wife's face going redder and redder at this subtle rebuke to her heretical manifesto concerning women's sovereignty. No-one, it is true, could miss the rich humour of these two closing stanzas (1163–76), with their direct invitation to read the story in the way the Clerk has just declared to be improper, nor the irony of the envoy, in which the Clerk exhorts all women to follow the example of the Wife of Bath in beating and bullying their husbands into submission. Muscatine (1957, p. 197) calls it 'an excellent example of "concessionary" comedy. The Clerk admits the opposition purposely, so willingly and extravagantly as to make safe from vulgar questioning the finer matter that has gone before.' The whole passage is introduced, like the close of the Pardoner's Tale (VI.919), as a distinct stepping-out of the narration of the tale –

But o word, lordynges, herkneth er I go (1163)

and there is ample evidence, in Brown (1933, pp. 1041–4), Manly and Rickert (1940, vol. 2, p. 244) and Dempster (1953, pp. 1143–7), that it is also distinct, as to date of composition, from the tale itself. This would not in itself inhibit the reader from recognising some retrospective reinterpretation of the tale that it might offer, and there are of course enough references to marriage and sovereignty in the tale to make such a reinterpretation superficially plausible. The argument against accepting it is the impoverishment that is brought about in the tale if it is subdued to such a comparatively trivial 'dramatic' interpretation. The role of the epilogue and envoy seems rather, as is often the case in the *Canterbury Tales*, to draw us out of the experience of the tale and return us to the surrounding fiction of the *Canterbury Tales*, like blinking surprisedly awake in the sunlight after a harrowing dream.

The Clerk's Tale remains a painful experience and a precariously rewarding one. No tale of Chaucer's remains so poised on the knife-edge between success and failure, or will record, on different readings by the same reader, such different responses. It is certainly, in the intensity of its imaginative enagement with its material, at different levels, an example of Chaucer's innovative narrative technique at its most daring. It is also deeply serious, and at its most serious prompts the reader to enquire more deeply into the apparent collision of different modes of narration. The intensification of awareness, as well as pathos, in Griselda may be related to the dramatically realistic motivation of Walter in more significant ways than merely as demonstrations of the way Chaucer's imaginative response to the story may take him in two different direct-ions at once. The voluntariness of Griselda's actions appears all the more striking a demonstration of patience and fortitude and faith if they are performed in the fullness of knowledge of the unjustness of the circum-stances in which they are required. This knowledge is a source of power, and its influence upon Walter is not so much to convince him that his plan to test Griselda has succeeded as to persuade him to a change of heart:[16]

> And whan this Walter saugh hire pacience,
> Hir glade chiere, and no malice at al,
> And he so ofte had doon to hire offence,
> And she ay sad and constant as a wal,
> Continuynge evere hire innocence overal,
> This sturdy markys gan his herte dresse
> To rewen upon hire wyfly stedfastnesse. (1044–50)

The willing embrace of undeserved suffering as part of the determination to accord the will to a higher will in the end reforms that higher will in its own image. So, in the theological terms that constantly press for recognition in the Clerk's Tale, absolute potency, postulated as a theological necessity,[17] is subdued to and constrained by love, the Father by the Son.

THE PHYSICIAN'S TALE

The Physician's Tale is the third in this group of exemplary tales, and, like the Man of Law's Tale and the Clerk's Tale, has as its heroine a woman of marvellous patience and obedience. In this case, the patience and obedience are demanded of her, not by her husband, as in the Clerk's Tale, nor by apparently malignant fate, as in the Man of Law's Tale, but by her father, who decrees that she must die rather than submit to the lustful designs of the wicked judge Appius (221–4). Virginia begs for mercy, asks if there is any alternative, and, when told that there is none, requests a moment to lament her fate, as did Jephthah's daughter:

> And, God, it woot, no thyng was hir trespas. (242)

She then, her debt paid to her humanity, meekly accepts her death. These fifty lines (207–57) constitute the central episode of the story, and in themselves they suggest what might have first drawn Chaucer to the story, which he found in the *Roman de la Rose*, as an opportunity to develop the human pathos of superhuman virtue. In the back of our minds there is the story of Iphigenia as well as that of Jephthah's daughter, and, more potent still, the fearful acquiescence of Isaac, as he is portrayed in the mystery plays, in his father's and God's will.[18] Behind this, there is a deeper recognition of the horrifying aptness, according to certain views of a father's role, and of God's, of this *exemplum* of ruthless benevolence.

The failure of Chaucer's poem, in its attempt to treat a story so promising as a vehicle for another 'sentimental experiment', is worth trying to understand. There is a clue in the conclusion to the tale, which says nothing of Virginia's exemplary virtue, nor, more understandably, of her father's care for her chastity, but expatiates rather on the cunning vengeance that God has prepared for the wicked (277–86). It has been argued by Kean (1972) that this moral is explicable if we can assume that we have been watching a more or less explicitly allegorical 'contest between vice and virtue, between Luxuria and Castitas, in which Luxuria, although victorious for a time, is finally defeated' (p. 183). But the more immediate reason that Chaucer resorts to such commonplaces seems to be that he cannot find it in his heart to extol the virtue of Virginia, which is so much an enactment of her father's will, nor the virtue of her father, whose act is bound to seem brutal in the absence of any explicit role for him, as there is for Jephthah, Agamemnon or Abraham, as the instrument of destiny or of a divine providence. Lacking these forms of moral and spiritual endorsement, the story is thrust back upon its literal meaningfulness, and here Chaucer's failures are predictable. What he has done is to omit from the story all those elements of political and social circumstance which originally made it, in the version told by Livy, and to some extent in the versions retold by Jean de Meun, Boccaccio and Gower, intelligible. The struggle between the factions represented by Appius and Virginius, the corruption of law and state by the patriciate, in the person of Appius, the demonstration of the power of the people to overthrow a wicked tyrant when one brave man shows the way – all those things which made the story potentially significant as a political and social *exemplum* of Roman history – are either removed or misrepresented in Chaucer.

> Chaucer systematically obliterates the traditional social content of the legend of Virginius *and* fails to replace it with explicit social commentary in his own or a narrator's voice. In so doing . . . he deprives the story of convincing dramatic motivation and his characters of plausible psychological and ethical motives. (Delany, 1981, p. 51)

After this, there is no need to belabour Chaucer with the other inadequacies of the tale, such as the strangely intrusive warning to governesses and parents to train up their children strictly, setting them a good example and chastising them firmly (72–102). Even to allow the straying across one's mind of the thought that a well-brought-up daughter should follow Virginia's example is to court hilarity. If Chaucer did intend some topical allusion in this digression, as has been, desperately, suggested (see Robinson, 1957, pp. 727–8), the only interest would be the demonstration of how little he cared, when he was not imaginatively engaged, about his art.

Various attempts at salvaging the tale have been mounted. It is really rather difficult to operate the 'dramatic principle', and attribute the inadequacies of the tale to the inadequacies of the narrator, and thereby make it interesting as a satire upon him.[19] Nothing in the tale relates to any possible physician, and the passing reference to St Augustine as the source of a *sententia* about Envy –

(The doctour maketh this descripcioun) (117)

– is a clear indication of how absent he is from Chaucer's mind. The bravest and most ingenious effort to rescue Chaucer from the consequences of his lack of interest has been made by Anne Middleton (1973–4), who suggests that the unconvincingness of the story is part of a demonstration by Chaucer that stories do not always make good *exempla*:

> In the *Physician's Tale*, as in the *Canterbury Tales* generally, Chaucer encourages us to examine, define, and redefine ethical abstractions that are treated as given in his originals or regarded as unexamined moral categories by their Canterbury narrators ... The tales as Chaucer adapts them become consistently less neat, less economical, and far less palatable as ethical examples than their sources are – and they succeed with us largely to the extent that they fail their tellers. (p. 15)

There is much here that is certainly true of the Clerk's Tale, and to some extent of the other exemplary and hagiographic tales too. The difference perhaps is that there the 'problem' and its working-out does genuinely provoke interest – both a sense of uneasiness and also a conviction, communicated through the poetry, that the uneasiness is the necessary prelude to some new insight. In the Physician's Tale, however, the 'problem', though it may well be there, remains a problem that Chaucer has not really become engaged in addressing, and the reader may be forgiven if the absence of incentive makes him reluctant to work hard at understanding something that Chaucer has worked less than hard at making understandable.

THE MONK'S TALE

The hundred lines that link *Melibee* and the Monk's Tale contain some of Chaucer's freest and most vigorous dramatic writing. They are mostly spoken by the Host, who gives a vivid and comical picture of his wife Goodelief, and subjects the Monk to some good-humoured chaffing. The Monk waits patiently for all these volleys of raillery to pass, and, standing not unexpectedly upon his dignity, offers to do his best

> To telle yow a tale, or two, or three.
> And if yow list to herkne hyderward,
> I wol yow seyn the lyf of Seint Edward;
> Or ellis, first, tragedies wol I telle,

Of whiche I have an hundred in my celle.
Tragedie is to seyn a certeyn storie . . . (1968–73)

What could be more obliging? And what could be a more conclusive
put-down for the Host, with technical terms flying like missiles about his
head, and the prospect of 'tragedies' stretching out to the crack of doom?
Even then there may still be 'the lyf of Seint Edward' to come.

What follows, sure enough, is a string of 'tragedies', ranging in
historical time from Lucifer and Adam to Barnabo Visconti, duke of
Lombardy, who died in 1385, and in length from one stanza to sixteen.
Lucifer, Adam, Barnabo and Peter of Cyprus are each dismissed in one
stanza, while Samson has ten, Nero eleven, and Zenobia, for no very
good apparent reason, sixteen. The hundred tragedies do not, happily,
all materialise, since the Knight interrupts at the end of the story of
Croesus, the seventeenth unfortunate. This, at any rate, is the dramatic
fiction of 'incompleteness' established in the framing narrative: it is not
necessarily how the Monk's Tale was originally conceived. A pleasing
hypothesis would run thus: Chaucer composed a series of poetic exercises in the 'fall of princes' tradition, modelled upon the examples in the
Roman de la Rose and in Boccaccio's encyclopaedic prose works, *De
Casibus Illustrium Virorum* and *De Claris Mulieribus*, and drawing further
upon Boethius, the Bible, the encyclopaedias of Vincent of Beauvais, and
other works; he subsequently added the group of 'Modern Instances'
(Peter of Spain, Peter of Cyprus, Barnabo and Ugolino), in order to give
the theme a contemporary relevance, as was usual with writers working
in the 'fall of princes' tradition (Pearsall, 1970, pp. 250–2); and, at the
same time or subsequently, allocated the series to the Monk, to whose
profession he may have felt such miscellaneous and patchwork erudition
was appropriate. The Host had picked on one stereotype of 'the Monk',
that of the virile 'outridere', as he is represented in the General Prologue
and the Shipman's Tale; the Tale represents him according to another
stereotype, that of the eclectic monastic compiler of histories, poring
over his old books.

The underlying theme of the stories brought together in the Monk's
Tale is fully expounded in Boethius's *Consolation of Philosophy* and in the
long passage in the *Roman de la Rose* (4807–6870) in which Reason
explains to the Lover that it is entirely within the power of his own mind
to rise above and recognise the true nature of the sufferings, misfortunes
and frustrations of life. This part of the *Roman* is by Jean de Meun, who
himself did a complete translation into French of the *Consolation*.

Chaucer likewise did a translation of Boethius into English, using Jean de Meun as a 'crib', and also translated part of the *Roman*, including a portion of Reason's discourse on Fortune. He was thus thoroughly imbued with these Boethian ideas. Boethius's argument, briefly, is that 'Fortune' is in effect no more than a name that men give to the causes of circumstances that they do not understand, but which they have the power to understand if they raise their minds from worldly concerns and commitments to the contemplation of the way all things show the working out of divine providence. It is, Philosophy explains, a question of point of view:

> Nothyng is wrecchid but whan thou wenest it . . . And ayenward, alle fortune is blisful to a man by the aggreablete or by the egalyte of hym that suffreth it. (Book II, prose 4, lines 109–16 in Chaucer's translation)

The wise man therefore reckons nothing of Fortune, recognising that it is in the power of his mind and will alone to judge at their true value her visitations of worldly joy and sorrow alike. Lady Philosophy is thus able to come to her conclusion that 'alle fortune is good', in other words that there is no such thing as fortune, as it is commonly understood (Book IV, prose 7, 7–14).

The paradox of Boethius's influence upon the Middle Ages – a paradox that Jean de Meun recognised in having Reason as one of a number of discordant voices within a dramatic allegory – is that the illusions of Fortune's power that Philosophy so authoritatively dispels proved more potent and resilient as images than the rational arguments demonstrating their non-existence. Medieval literature is full of portraits of the awesome goddess Fortuna, and particularly fond of demonstrations of the remorseless and arbitrary power of her Wheel; there is much less interest, on the whole, in the philosophical arguments concerning the power of the cognitive will to dispel these images as fictions. Where an answer is sought to the problem of Fortune's apparently limitless power, it is sought in religion rather than philosophy, and the philosophical recognition of the transitoriness of the things of the world in relation to the permanence of mind is converted into the contempt of the world in comparison with the promised world hereafter. The ease with which this transition could be made is evident, though it results in a misrepresentation of Boethius.

The further paradox is that the definition of 'tragedie' which the Monk quotes from Boethius (1973–7) is actually the definition of something that is recognised to be insignificant by both Boethius and his Christian interpreters.

What other thyng bywaylen the cryinges of tragedyes but oonly the dedes of Fortune? (Book II, prose 2, 67–8).

Subsequently, Philosophy will show that such arguments against Fortune are not only futile but irrelevant, will show indeed that 'tragedye', like Fortune, is a name men give to something they do not but could understand. There is, for the wise man, nothing 'tragic' about *tragedye*.

The Christian version of Boethius must come to the same conclusion. Where rational understanding fails, faith supervenes, and asserts the providential order. The human consciousness does not confront, or constitute itself an objection to the predicament of life, but rises above circumstance, informed by a higher consciousness of the will of God. Within such a system of belief, therefore, there can be no 'tragedy' in the Greek or Shakespearian sense.

It may be that in his greatest poems, the Knight's Tale and *Troilus and Criseyde*, Chaucer enlarges Boccaccio's stories so as to bring them close to the tragic confrontation with the predicament of life. Perhaps there was in the Middle Ages an embryonic notion of tragedy, an idea of tragedy struggling to emerge from beneath the blankets of consolation offered by stoic and Christian morality. It can be seen from time to time in Boccaccio's account of the multitude of complainants who appear before him in the *De Casibus*: a generous respect for high Roman virtue in the face of death, admiring descriptions of suffering stoically born or defiantly greeted, a sense of poignancy at the undeserved abasement of grandeur and the eclipse of nobility.

It cannot be said that in the Monk's Tale Chaucer, though he adopts something of Boccaccio's personal tone of lamentation (e.g., 1991, 2000, 2079, 2090) and rhetorical manner of presentation (e.g., 2004, 2007, 2015, 2052, 2075, 2095), rises far beyond a conventional medieval view of 'tragedye'. Among those who make up the procession of the unfortunate, there are some who fall because they are wicked and proud (Lucifer, Adam, Belshazzar, Nero, Holofernes, Antiochus, Croesus), some who fall despite the fact that they are good (Hercules, Zenobia, Peter of Cyprus, Alexander, Julius Caesar) or at least not specifically said to be bad (Barnabo, Ugolino), and some who are the victims of others' machinations without Fortune being mentioned at all (Samson, Peter of

Spain). Antiochus is clearly said to have been destroyed by God, not by Fortune, because of his attacks on God's chosen (2600, 2609, 2615); Nebuchadnezzar learns by experience and lives out his life in proper fear of God (his story is thus not a 'fall', but might be regarded as a prelude to the following story of Belshazzar). The arbitrariness and fickleness of Fortune is constantly invoked, but not with much sense of the unfolding of a grand design, since all that one needs to be in this litany of the unfortunate is to be dead. There seems little point in elaborating at length on so indiscrimate a fate. What is missing is any extended or eloquent statement of the Christian theme of the grand design, namely, that man's chief cause of concern is not that he is doomed to die, but that he is doomed to live.

Eclectically derived, therefore, partly emerged from the theology of *contemptus mundi* and mortality, and only partly committed to any rational account of history, the Monk's Tale is bound to seem a thing of threads and patches. In this it is no more than characteristically medieval. It is not, as Lepley (1977–8) reminds us, incoherent, or without explicit rationale. The theme is announced at the beginning:

> For certein, whan that Fortune list to flee,
> Ther may no man the cours of hire withholde.
> Lat no man truste on blynd prosperitee;
> Be war by thise ensamples trewe and olde. (1995–8)

and it is reasserted at the end, with emphasis on trust in Fortune as a form of pride (2761–6). The story of Hercules concludes with a clear statement of the Boethian alternative of self-knowledge as the means to rise above the world's mischances (2136–9). The effect of these interventions, however, is glossarial and annotatory; they do not act to elucidate the great providential plan which lies behind the mutations of circumstance, and the sequence of stories tends to remain a mere catalogue. The most distinctive failure, and again it is the product of a characteristically medieval habit of mind, is the failure of history. The world of the Old Testament, of Greece and Rome, is faded into a tapestry of 'ensamples trewe and olde'. Even the Modern Instances seem to be deliberately extracted and distanced from a historical reality with which Chaucer must in this case have been intimately familiar, and subordinated to the purposes of dignified platitude. The story of Ugolino is the one exception, the one example of a story in the Monk's Tale in which the special circumstances of the narrative are imaginatively attended to. Chaucer

omits of course the monstrous account in Dante of the discovery of
Ugolino in the lowest circle of Hell, gnawing at the head of his ertswhile
enemy, the archbishop Roger (*Inferno*, xxxii–xxxiii), and alludes only
briefly to the context of the story in Italian history. He responds fully,
however, to the pathos of Dante's story of the incarceration of Ugolino
with his children, and expands on the dramatic detail of their fear and
bewilderment with that touchingly evocative sympathy that we have seen
so effectively displayed in the Prioress's Tale and Man of Law's Tale
(2431–8). He removes, however, any mention of the boys' names, and
the sense of reality that attaches to them, removes any hint of unbearable
reproach to the father's helplessness (*Inferno*, xxxiii, 67–9), and suffuses
the climactic scene with a more distinctive symbolic and quasi-religious
sacrificial allusiveness:[20]

> 'Oure flessh thou yaf us, take oure flessh us fro,
> And ete ynogh,' – right thus they to hym seyde,
> And after that, withinne a day or two,
> They leyde hem in his lappe adoun and deyde. (2451–4)

Chaucer averts his eyes completely from the horror of Dante's last images
of the blinded father fumbling among the corpses of his little sons.
Pathos is quite enough for Chaucer.

The attribution of a catalogue of falls of princes to the Monk is
perfectly appropriate: his monastic library would have been full of the
patchwork encyclopaedias and collections of *exempla* from which such
catalogues were compiled, and his more cloistered colleagues would have
been engaged in just such historical joinery-work. It is a remarkable
premonition of the monk Lydgate, whose longest poem, *The Fall of
Princes*, is a gigantic amplification of this same theme. Chaucer is not
making fun of the Monk: it is rather that the dramatic context he
provides for the Tale allows him to suggest the limitations of such an
approach to adversity and misfortune. The retrospective view of a tale
provided by the subsequent frame-narrative can sometimes produce a
merely quizzical effect, especially where the tale is firmly established
within the framework of understanding of its own genre, as is the case
with the Clerk's Tale. Where this centripetal tendency is weaker, as with
the Squire's Tale, the retrospect may produce a more radical kind of
re-evaluation. Here, the interruption of the Monk's Tale by the Knight
enables Chaucer to express, dramatically, some dissatisfaction with the
formlessness of the catalogue-method and also, in contrast to the

Knight's own more sophisticated handling of 'tragedye', with the conceptual naïveté of Fortune-tragedy (see Kaske, 1957). This is not to say that he wrote the tale badly in order to prove his point and to demonstrate the inadequacy of the Monk.[21] Such a literal-minded application of the 'dramatic principle' is ludicrously trivialising. And in fact, of course, the tale is not told 'badly'. There are awkwardnesses here and there – the explanations of Zenobia's restrictions on marital intercourse (2279–94) or of Nero's plans for Seneca's removal (2503–18) are not notably perspicuous – but there is variety in the rhetoric of narration, some vivid touches:

> . . . Oloferne, which Fortune ay kiste
> So likerously, and ladde hym up and doun,
> Til that his heed was of, er that he wiste. (2556–8)

and many hints, similar to those in *The Legend of Good Women*, of the swift, pregnant narrative technique of the Pardoner's Tale and the *exempla* in the Nun's Priest's Tale. There is also the tale of Ugolino. We must clearly take the Monk's Tale seriously, at the same time that we recognise how happily Chaucer was able to take advantage of the structure of the *Canterbury Tales* in implying some criticism of its form.

CHAUCER'S TALE OF MELIBEE

His tale of Sir Thopas having been so decisively cut off in its dubious career by the Host's rude interruption, Chaucer is much put out. However, when the Host relents, and gives him a second chance, he offers 'a litel thyng in prose', something that cannot possibly give offence, 'a moral tale vertuous'. The Tale of *Melibee*, which follows, is certainly the latter, and certainly in prose,[22] though no 'litel thyng'. In wordage, it is slightly bulkier than the longest of the verse tales, the Knight's Tale, and is only exceeded in length by the other prose tale, the Parson's Tale. Some wry laughter at such a 'litel thyng' is appropriate, though of course it is confined to the dramatic comedy of the frame, and does not extend to the reception of the tale. The idea that Chaucer tells a dull and boring moralistic tale as a way of revenging himself on the Host for stinting his tale of Sir Thopas is a trivial one, and promises little pleasure to the reader who has to suffer the same fate as the Host (he could of course increase his pleasure by not reading it, which would be a new kind of recommendation for one of the *Tales*). Likewise, the tale offers little room for manoeuvre for those (e.g., Whittock, 1968, p. 214; Norton-Smith, 1974, pp. 146–9; Palomo, 1974) who would redeem it by interpreting it as some kind of satire on the genre of moralistic allegory. Chaucer simply does not do enough with the tale to earn even such doubtful credit.

The comedy of the frame remains, though, and Chaucer's attempt to prove that, if anything goes wrong with his telling of the tale – if there are rather more proverbs in it, for instance, than people might expect, or if the words are not what they have heard before – it does not affect its 'sentence', is surely part of this comedy. The comparison with the Gospels, which all have the same 'sentence',

Al be ther in hir tellyng difference (948)

is rather audacious, but hardly suggests that this prologue to *Melibee* should be treated as a serious statement by Chaucer concerning his purposes in the *Canterbury Tales*. The argument put forward by Robertson (1962, pp. 367–9) that the other versions of this 'moral tale' told 'in sondry wyse/Of sondry folk' (941–2) are actually the other *Canterbury Tales*, that 'this litel tretys heere' (957) is the *Tales* as a whole and not the *Melibee*, and that the 'sentence' of all is, like the Gospels, 'al oon' (952), is strained in every detail and inappropriate in context, and Olson (1975–6) has sensibly reasserted the traditional interpretation.

The 'murye tale' that Chaucer promises is not much of a tale, and not very 'murye' (i.e., 'pleasant'), except in so far as what is edifying must be pleasing. The story is chiefly a peg on which to hang a vast quantity of moral discourse on a variety of matters, including the role of women and the value of their advice, the choosing of counsellors, the ethics of revenge, and the merits of poverty as against riches and of peace as against war. The discourse is organised to accommodate a great number of *sententiae* culled from classical, biblical and patristic authorities. Every new move in the dialogue between Melibeus and Prudence, which constitutes the bulk of the narrative, triggers off an avalance of authorities, 'sentences' and proverbs, and no further progress can be made until the new mountainside has been removed. Schematic, quasi-logical organisation is more important than the progress of the narrative (e.g., 1172, 1355). For all this, Chaucer takes little more responsibility than that of a translator, since his tale is a close paraphrase of the French *Livre de Melibee et de Dame Prudence* of Renaud de Louens, which in its turn is an abridged paraphrase of the

mid-thirteenth-century *Liber Consolationis et Consilii* of Albertanus of
Brescia.

Any complaints about the tale should therefore properly be addressed
elsewhere. The irreconcilability of the two levels of the allegory, for
instance, the moral-psychological (the soul under attack from world,
flesh and devil) and the moral-social-political, is a 'given' of the sources.
The absurdity of any continued consciousness of the former during the
development of the latter would reach its peak when Melibeus makes his
final reconciliation with his three enemies, who show a truly religious
penitence (1745–6), and choose the wisest of the three as their spokesman
(1816). The moral-psychological allegory, in fact, is evidently imposed
on the basic narrative, and the two passages in which it is implied
(967–72) and expounded (1410–26) could be removed without creating
any incoherence. The Middle Ages, however, clearly felt no distress at
the juxtaposition of the two modes of interpretation, as Owen (1972–3)
explains in replying to the objections of Strohm (1967–8).

They must also have enjoyed the remorseless good sense of this kind of
schematised anthology of moral commonplaces, and we should be wrong
to assume that Chaucer did not share that enjoyment. It is possible that
his translation of a work which promoted peace and conciliation as
against war and revenge had a special point in the 1380s, when government was divided into war and peace factions concerning the desirability
of renewing hostilities with France.[23] It may be that he chose the work
for translation with its topical relevance in mind, though he does nothing
whatever to draw out that relevance. It is perhaps more instructive to
look for the significance of the tale of *Melibee* in another quarter. Like
the translations of Boethius and of the Latin treatise or treatises that
provide the source for the Parson's Tale, and like the lost translation of
the *De Miseria Condicionis Humane* of Innocent III, the tale of *Melibee* is
a sort of quarrying work, its aim to provide the raw material for
subsequent imaginative transmutation. Translation into English prose is
a course or discipline that Chaucer proposed for himself so that he might
absorb and make available to himself a representative sampling of some
of the great encyclopaedic anthologies of moral, philosophical and
religious commonplaces of the Middle Ages. His choice of texts was
remarkably shrewd if what he wanted was, not the best that had been
thought and written, but what had been thought and written about most.
The demonstration of the value of such an enterprise, as a way of
stocking the storehouses of the mind, whether or not it was consciously
entered upon, is in the large number of echoes and reminiscences of

Melibee in others of the *Canterbury Tales*. The discourse on women clearly provides raw material for the Wife of Bath, such as the mention of women's inability to keep a secret (1061), or the three things that drive a man out of his house (1086), echoed in her Tale (III.945–82) and Prologue (III.534, 278–81). There is a specific verbal parallel for the Wife of Bath's Prologue, line 112, in *Melibee*, 1088, and some of the proverbial sayings that besprinkle the other tales (e.g., I.3530, VII.2800) may well have been first caught up in this work of translation (1003, 1047). *Melibee* is not of course the source of every parallel that can be found (and there are many more noted in Robinson, 1957): some common material is evidently derived from a common source, and there may also be some cross-fertilisation. But on the whole it seems likelier that the direction of internal borrowing is from the translated to the independently conceived work rather than vice versa. Chaucer's second tale is thus, though not itself poetry, the cause of poetry in other tales: a fat dung-heap.

THE PARSON'S TALE

The Prologue to the Parson's Tale seems to mark the drawing to an end of an original one-way scheme for the *Canterbury Tales*. The sense of things coming to an end is strong: the time of day, elaborately computed in a paragraph strikingly reminiscent of the opening lines of the Introduction to the Man of Law's Tale (Owen, 1977, pp. 25–31) and iconographically very suggestive (Wood, 1970, pp. 272–97), is 4 p.m.; the pilgrims enter 'at a thropes ende' (X.12), and the Host urges the Parson to make haste, for 'the sonne wole adoun' (70). Night draws on; there is a chill in the air. The lively exchange between Host and Parson is not without its humour, but humour is quickly dispersed as the Parson describes how he will conclude the proceedings by showing how their pilgrimage is an emblem of the pilgrimage of the life of man, from the earthly to the heavenly city, or, as it were, from London to Canterbury:

> And Jhesu, for his grace, wit me sende
> To shewe yow the wey, in this viage,
> Of thilke parfit glorious pilgrymage
> That highte Jerusalem celestial. (48–51)

The assent of the pilgrims to his proposal, and their appointment of the Host as their spokesman in giving their assent (67), is done with unprecedented and significant formality. It is like a formal handing-over of the true conduct of the pilgrimage to the Parson.

The Parson's Tale is not a tale at all, not even in the limited sense appropriate to *Melibee*, for it contains no narrative. It is a treatise on penitence and its three parts, Contrition, Confession and Satisfaction, into the second of which is incorporated a lengthy account of the Seven Deadly Sins and their remedies. The Sins take up nearly two-thirds of a treatise which in total bulk is over half as long again as the Knight's Tale or *Melibee* and thus by far the longest of all the *Tales*. The place of the Parson's Tale in the tradition of the general penitential treatise has long been recognised, and has been authoritatively restated by Patterson (1978, pp. 332–41), though it is still occasionally called a 'sermon'. This is misleading, as Wenzel (1981–2) makes clear, except in so far as one might recognise occasionally within the Tale certain homiletic features such as the use of short *exempla* or illustrative stories (e.g., 363, 670), or brief similes (e.g., 411, 698, 816, 870, 899), and some lively turns of phrase and pungent descriptive writing (e.g., 422–5). The structure and method of the Tale, however, is that of a treatise, not a sermon.

The actual source of the Tale, if it be presumed that it is drawn from a single source, is still not known. It is commonly assumed that it was drawn from the vast thirteenth-century Latin compilations of Guilielmus Peraldus (*Summa seu Tractatus de Viciis*) and Raymund of Pennaforte (*Summa Casuum Poenitentiae*), but Chaucer is unlikely to have done the elaborate scissors-and-paste work that would have been needed to make his (comparatively brief) Tale out of these comprehensive encyclopaedias. Some intermediary or independent compilation that gave him more or less what we have got in the Tale is likely to have been his source, and recent research has turned up a Latin treatise on the remedies for sin which is close enough to be itself, or at one remove, part of a compilation on which Chaucer might have drawn.[24]

The Parson's Tale is important for the history of religion and religious ideas, and for the history of the dissemination of those ideas; it is also important because it is by Chaucer. It is not, itself, 'literature', though it is of interest and importance for the understanding of literature. It gives, in comparatively clear and succinct form, an account of human behaviour and the scheme of salvation which acts as the official framework of understanding (not necessarily the means of understanding) for the writings of Chaucer and indeed for all medieval literature. It expresses a deep and orthodox piety, in the practice of which, as a man, Chaucer would not have wished to be separated from his fellow men. He does little to make it his own, as a writer,[25] nor to carry alive its truth into the heart by passion or the power of his imagination. No attempt on Chaucer's part should be detected in this to 'distance' himself from these orthodox pieties: only a recognition, perhaps temperamental in origin, that they are not the appropriate material of his art. At the same time, the poet in him is not averse to the plundering of this rich storehouse of quotations, sententious sayings, images, motifs and themes for the purposes of his imaginative writings. The Parson's Tale is thus, like the other prose translations, a quarry, from which crude ore can be extracted for transmutation into the material of art. A nice example comes at the beginning of the description of Pride:

> And yet is ther a privee spece of Pride, that waiteth first to be salewed er he wole salewe, al be he lasse worth than that oother is, peraventure; and eek he waiteth or desireth to sitte, or elles to goon above hym in the wey, or kisse pax, or been encensed, or goon to offryng biforn his neighebor ... (407)

Extracted from its section and sub-section in the moral grid of the Sins, this last illustration of Pride provides a moment of vivid individual characterisation for the Wife of Bath in the General Prologue:

> In al the parisshe wif ne was ther noon
> That to the offrynge bifore hire sholde goon. (I.449–50)

It is the specificity of detail – which of course is a necessary element in a penitential treatise designed to promote self-examination and proper confession – that is seized upon by Chaucer as a good and borrowable piece of observation. The illustrative function of the detail of behaviour as an example of Pride remains, but it is absorbed into the larger human and dramatic picture of the Wife, all bustling and indignant. Likewise, in the account of Lechery Chaucer found a little anecdote that he was to turn to good effect in the Merchant's Tale:

> And for that many man weneth that he may nat synne, for no likerousnesse that he dooth with his wyf, certes, that opinion is fals. God woot, a man may sleen hymself with his owene knyf, and make hymselve dronken of his owene tonne. (859)

The instinct that prompted Chaucer here can be traced to the surrounding context, where the mention of 'thise olde dotardes holours', who will 'kisse, though they may nat do' (857), brings January irresistibly to mind. And it is January of course who, in the lunatic oblivion of his sensuality, turns the anecdote absurdly on its head (IV.1835–41). There is no need to return to the Parson's Tale to understand the point of this passage in its context: it is interesting to do so, for the purpose of understanding Chaucer's methods, but the significant direction of the change is all *from* the Parson's Tale *to* the Merchant's Tale.

There is much else of a similar kind, full exposition of which would take us on a Chaucerian road to Xanadu: biblical quotations, sayings from the Fathers, *sententiae* of all kinds, that Chaucer first picked up here and then adapted for dramatic or narrative use elsewhere in the *Tales*. Some of the links and references and cross-connections may be accidental, and may arise simply from the fact that the Parson's Tale, as a systematic dissection of all aspects of human behaviour, is bound to cut across the interests of other tales at many points. A case has been made by Baldwin (1955) and Huppé (1964) – though repudiated by Donaldson (1970, pp. 172–3) – that the Parson's Tale makes explicit in orthodox religious language the truths that Chaucer has been representing by dramatic and indirect means in the other tales, that it is, so to speak, the court of moral arbitration to which interpretative disputes may be referred, and therefore 'the best' of the tales. In one very obvious sense, this is true, and Chaucer accepts and promotes the truth of it, as a man and as a Christian, in his Retraction. According to this truth, there is no good reason for the existence of anything other than the Parson's Tale: everything else exists on suffrance, as a form of indulgence and a covert means of communicating the doctrinal truths that the Parson's Tale inculcates by explicit precept. The lover of Chaucer's poetry can hardly be expected to acquiesce in such a proposition, and must reaffirm, with Ruggiers (1965, pp. 249–52) and Jordan (1967, pp. 227), that the Parson's Tale, though of interest to the student of literature, is not literature: it is autonomous, and *different*. The end of the treatise is an act of penitence and the denial of art.

The attempts that have been made to salvage the Parson's Tale for literature, as for instance by suggesting that it is deliberately designed, and the sources adapted, to characterise the religious opinions of a ruthless ideologue,[26] are ill-advised. It is, of course, 'the Parson's Tale', and as such, like all the other tales, it stands at a certain distance from its author. But the distance, in the light of the description of the Parson in the General Prologue, and in the light of the Parson's Prologue, is infinitesimal, and is removed altogether in the Retraction. The most that could be said is that the Parson's Tale is part of the *Canterbury Tales*, and that the truth it embodies is recognised to be one of a number of versions of 'truth', given added weight, perhaps, by the final position of the Tale and the retrospective realignment of point of view that it may contribute to.

Even this modified account of an artistic role for the Parson's Tale in the whole scheme of the *Canterbury Tales* has in the end, however, to be withdrawn. The manner of the treatise, and its demonstration of the abstract, coherent, all-inclusive and definitive nature of all that is known, is not merely something to set beside the various kinds of fictionality that have gone before, but a denial of the validity of fiction. Finally, Chaucer acquiesces completely in this, and moves at the end of the Tale not back into the uncompleted fiction of the pilgrimage but directly into the realm of action in relation to his own life. The deliberate denial of art, with the Retraction, is his own most truthful response to the call for penitence, and penitence *now*, which is the imperative logic of the closing paragraphs of the Tale. Patterson (1978) says of the Tale,

> Its very nature is terminal. It begins within the fictional construct but becomes the tale to end all tales, and its conclusion inevitably escapes from the narrative frame and now refers to the larger context of biography. (p. 380).

The Retraction, in which Chaucer begs forgiveness for and formally revokes all his 'translacions and enditynges of worldly vanitees', grows inevitably out of the Parson's Tale, and confirms the passing of artistic into historical consciousness. It is Chaucer's own act of Satisfaction. The Parson had spoken of the pilgrimage to Canterbury as a symbol of man's spiritual journey to a celestial Canterbury, but proceeded to turn that symbol into reality, the only ultimate reality. What was allegory has become plain fact.

The Retraction has caused some problems for modern commentators, who are tempted to see it as a betrayal of artistic principle.[27] Chaucer must surely, it is said, have had more respect for poetry and for himself as a poet than to assent to a sullen orthodoxy that would see no more in his six major poems that mere 'worldly vanitees', and that would wish to have remembered only the translation of Boethius and some anonymous 'bookes of legendes of seintes, and omelies, and moralitee, and devocioun'. The Retraction has been dismissed as inauthentic or as merely conventional (and in accord with a convention observed or rediscovered by writers as diverse as Boccaccio and Tolstoy), or as a mere sop to orthodoxy; signs of irony, or at least of hankering after the world, have been detected in the single line of verse embedded in the surrounding prose,

and many a song and many a leccherous lay

or in the mischievously undocumented – because non-existent – quantity of edifying works that are to be laid in the other side of the balance. These views can hardly be taken seriously. Equally, it will not do to see the Retraction as confirming a moral interpretation of the *Canterbury Tales* as a whole. The reference to 'this litel tretys' at the beginning is certainly, as Clark (1971–2) affirms, to the Parson's Tale itself and not to the *Tales* as a whole, which have receded enough from the immediate field of consciousness to be cited as a separate work in the list of poems to be revoked, those at least of 'the tales of Caunterbury' that 'sownen into synne'. The defence of the 'litel tretys' as written under correction, yet serviceable according to Paul's dictum that 'Al that is writen is writen for oure doctrine', is appropriately modest in relation to the Parson's Tale, but quite inappropriate to the *Canterbury Tales* in general, given that they are about to be revoked, at least in part. A 'literary' context for Paul's dictum is provided by the ending of the Nun's Priest's Tale, and to some extent by the prologue to *Melibee*; there is no literary context here.

The Retraction remains physically part of the *Canterbury Tales* through its connection with the Parson's Tale, which itself passes from the fictional world of the *Canterbury Tales* into the real world of Chaucer's life as a Christian. The passage, however, is a decisive one, and creates a discontinuity, so that in the sequence of reading there is no uneasy juxtaposition of the two worlds in the Retraction. There is a contrast here with the similarly unequivocal assertion of Christian belief at the end of *Troilus and Criseyde*, where the juxtaposition is more abrupt and painful. The epilogue to the *Troilus* remains an acute problem for the reader and literary commentator; the Retraction is of interest primarily to the speculative biographer, who might be left to decide whether it has to have been written at the end of Chaucer's life, or to determine the truth of Thomas Gascoigne's accusation (see Wurtele, 1980) that Chaucer's death-bed repentance came too late.

CHAPTER 7

Audience and Reception

Questions concerning the audience of the *Canterbury Tales* in Chaucer's own time, and concerning the reception of the work in the centuries since then, are important and need to be asked, not because they produce answers that will guide our own responses, or determine their permissibility, but because they make clear the relation of our reading of the poem to earlier readings of the poem as integral parts of the history of the work. No reading, except a totally trivial one, exists in isolation, and it is better that the reader should be aware of the nature of the predetermining expectations, or predispositions, to which he is subject, even if he accepts that he cannot entirely escape their influence, than that he should assume he is not subject to any.

With regard to the contemporary audience of the *Canterbury Tales*, the audience that Chaucer had in mind when he wrote or that was actually familiar with the *Tales* during his lifetime or in the years immediately after his death, there is little external evidence available. In the absence of such evidence – not a single one, for instance, of the multitude of records relating to his life (Crow and Olson, 1966) refers to his activities as a poet – there has been a surfeit of speculation based on internal evidence. Examples of rhetorical apostrophe within particular tales, for instance, have been literalistically misread as indications of the original specialised audience for which the tale was designed. The addresses to merchants in the Prologue to the Man of Law's Tale (II.122), to governesses in the Physician's Tale (VI.72), to 'lordes' in the Nun's Priest's Tale (VII.3325), and to 'worshipful chanons religious' in the Canon's Yeoman's Tale (VIII.992) have all been interpreted in this way.[1] More widespread, and perhaps more generally misleading, has been the tendency to allow speculation concerning the audience of the love-vision poems and *Troilus* to stand unexamined as applying also to the *Canterbury Tales*.

Generally speaking, the discussion there has been (see Pearsall, 1977), of Chaucer's status as 'a poet of the court', and of the supposed practice by which he would read his poems aloud to 'the court', is irrelevant to the

Canterbury Tales. The characteristic techniques of the poet writing for oral delivery are clearly present, as is pointed out in the discussion of the Knight's Tale above, but these mannerisms are readily carried over into verse intended for private reading, since the relationship of the poet and the reader can always be happily understood as a private version of the public and immediate contact of poet and listener. References to the poet speaking or the reader listening and present are never felt to be inappropriate in private reading: by contrast, references to the poet writing or the reader reading (of which there are many in the *Tales*) are out of place in the context of oral delivery and may be taken to indicate that it is not the form of communication assumed by the poet. It is easy to imagine that Chaucer's poetry was often read aloud, by himself or others, in intimate and exclusive groups, in a manner not substantially different from that of 'poetry readings' in all ages; it is natural to assume that its primary existence was in written copies, designed for private reading.

Whatever the value of these speculations, it is clear that Chaucer has answered all questions concerning the audience and mode of publication of the *Tales* by incorporating the answers in the very structure of the poem: the audience is the other pilgrims, and the tales are 'published' by being told to them. All the subterfuges into which Chaucer had traditionally entered in order to distance the author, as a reality, from the audience are now unnecessary. The author reports now, not dreams or the contents of books, but simply experience, and the audience, with the author, enter a world of his own creation which has the appearance of being totally autonomous. Chaucer's power of creating the sense of a listening group, which is so present a part of the experience of reading *Troilus*, is now given complete freedom of operation, since the 'actual' audience is the fictional audience, and the actual audience mere eavesdroppers. Chaucer has deliberately planted the audience in the work, so that their presence and their responses become part of the complex material with which the reader has to deal (Mehl, 1978).

Chaucer, in fact, makes it almost impossible to talk about the 'historical' audience of the *Canterbury Tales* on the basis of internal evidence. There can be no easy conclusion, either, about the manner in which the *Tales* were first published. It seems very reasonable to assume that Chaucer circulated copies of single tales or other portions of the work among his friends during the 1390s. Indeed, if he had any friends at all, it is unimaginable that he could have done otherwise than let them see some of his new work. Presumably Sir John Clanvowe took the opening lines of *The Book of Cupid* (*The Cuckoo and the Nightingale*) from a written copy of the Knight's Tale, or its pre-*Canterbury Tales* predecessor, and how else was 'maister Bukton' expected to make himself acquainted with the Wife of Bath?

> The Wyf of Bathe I pray yow that ye rede
> Of this matere that we have on honde. (*Envoy to Bukton*, 29–30)

It is an equally natural assumption that from time to time Chaucer would read portions of the work to a group of friends, though there was now, for the first time, a general expectation of private reading built into the work as a whole, in several allusions, both in tales and links (e.g., I.1201, 3177, VIII.78).

Whatever circulation there was, before Chaucer's death in 1400, of written copies of portions of the *Canterbury Tales*, it may be presumed to have been very limited. The Knight's Tale and the Second Nun's Tale were probably 'released' in their pre-*Canterbury Tales* form before 1387, since there would be little point in the references to the two poems in the Prologue to the *Legend of Good Women* if they were not known to the audience of the Prologue, but Chaucer's inference that Bukton knew or could get to know of the Wife of Bath is the only indication that copies of portions of the *Tales* were in circulation during the *Canterbury Tales* period. All literary references to Chaucer during his lifetime are to the translator of the *Roman de la Rose* and the imitator of French love-visions (Deschamps), to 'the noble philosophical poete in Englissh' of 'the boke of Troylus' (Thomas Usk), and to the disciple and poet of Venus, author of many love-lyrics, who is called upon to make his 'testament of love' (Gower).[2] There are no references to the *Canterbury Tales*, and no manuscript of the work, in part or whole, survives from before 1400. It seems clear that Chaucer, though he must have allowed his friends to see or hear portions of the work, kept the poem as a whole to himself, constantly revising and reallocating and reordering the tales. At his death, the work remained unfinished, in the form of a series of unconnected fragments.

The speed with which Chaucer's literary executors set to work to produce a full copy of the poem from these fragments (in the Hengwrt manuscript), the care and skill that was lavished on a more complete and fully edited copy a few years later (in the Ellesmere manuscript), are early evidence of the immediate recognition that was granted to the *Canterbury Tales* as the major work of an already famous poet.

The *Canterbury Tales* continued throughout the fifteenth century as a 'best-seller', and there are more manuscripts of the poem surviving, in whole or in part (see Appendix A), than of any other work written in English, with the exception of *The Prick of Conscience* (see note 8 to Chapter 1). The manuscripts range in quality from the most ordinary to the *de luxe*, though very few are illustrated (they are described by Margaret Rickert in Manly and Rickert, 1940, vol. 1, pp. 561–605), and there are no manuscripts of the *Tales* to compare in luxury and expensiveness with some of the manuscripts of Lydgate's *Troy-Book* and *Fall of Princes*, or even with the lavish but unfulfilled promise of Corpus Christi College, Cambridge, MS 61 of the *Troilus*. The absence of any conventional precedent for a programme of illustration was perhaps a factor here, though the more obvious explanation is that the *Canterbury Tales* was not in itself the kind of work to which ostentation of presentation was appropriate. No buyer of manuscripts who wanted his social and cultural status to be properly appreciated through his financial outlay on expensively produced manuscripts could be unaware that the familiar Englishness of the *Tales* would undercut such pretension at every point. Lydgate's poems, by contrast, seem designed, both in their choice of subject-matter and in their size, structure and style, for ostentatious presentation and prestige publication. Another reason that suggests itself for the comparative paucity of illustration in *Canterbury Tales* manuscripts is that it is a work that people wished, above all, to read, and which needed less, therefore, the alternative attractions and distractions of accompanying pictures. A last reason, that might more tentatively be proffered, is that the *Tales*, being divided by their nature into readily identifiable units, are less in need of the visual 'punctuation' (Lawton, 1983, pp. 41, 44, 51, 60) that pictures provided in long continuous texts like the *Roman de la Rose*.

Some manuscripts, including Hengwrt and Ellesmere, presumably catering for readers with an interest in learned allusion, are equipped with Latin glosses and side-notes which explain references or indicate their Latin sources. Some of these glosses may go back to Chaucer and may have a more integral function in relation to the text (Silvia, 1965; Caie, 1975–6). Some manuscripts, such as British Library Lansdowne 851 and Cambridge University Library Gg.4.27, are dignified with Latin rubrics and headings instead of the more usual English or occasional French. But these are a few among many, and the range and variety of types of manuscript of the *Canterbury Tales*, and the different kinds of owner suggested by indications of provenance (Manly and Rickert, 1940, vol. 1) would militate against any definite indentification of a special class of owners, buyers or readers. There are perhaps fewer copies in the hands of royal and aristocratic owners than one might expect, and fewer in proportion than for *Troilus*, or Lydgate's two long poems, or Gower's *Confessio Amantis*. The principal ownership is among the business and administrative classes, especially in London, and landed country families: there is no surprise in this, since these groups would constitute together the greater part of the fifteenth-century reading or book-owning public. Among those leaving copies of the *Canterbury Tales* in their wills, if this might be considered a fair cross-section of owners, there are John Brinchele, a citizen and assize-man of London (1420), Sir Thomas Cumberworth, a wealthy Lincolnshire landowner (1451), Dame Elizabeth Bruyn, of Essex (1471), John Parmente, a high-ranking Canterbury diocesan official (1479), and Margaret, Countess of Richmond, mother of Henry VII (1509).[3]

The bulk of the manuscripts were produced by the professional London scribes of whose activities we have a fascinating glimpse in an important essay by Doyle and Parkes (1978), but particular manuscripts show evidence of more specialised production and tastes. British Library Harley 7333, for instance, was made and kept at the Austin priory of Leicester: some of the tales have been subjected to a process of censorship, sometimes aimed at removing what was perceived as obscenity, but sometimes, as in the Reeve's Tale, at removing the suggestion of anti-clericalism (Manly and Rickert, 1940, vol. 1, p. 212). A particularly interesting manuscript is Bibliothèque Nationale MS fonds anglais 39, which was made for Jean d'Angoulême, brother of Charles d'Orléans, who like his brother spent most of his mature years as a prisoner in England. The manuscript contains marginalia in his own hand, and the selection and treatment of the *Tales* presumably reflect his own literary judgement (see Strohm, 1971). Jean shows no interest in the structure or framework of the *Tales*, which was usually a major preoccupation of editors and scribes, and rearranges tales to suit himself: he cuts away most of the Squire's Tale, which he calls *valde absurda*, and also cuts the Monk's Tale to a bare three tragedies, as being *valde dolorosa*. These are interesting and intelligible judgements.

In several respects, the *Canterbury Tales*, with its strongly marked elements of humour, realism and colloquial style, cuts across fifteenth-century critical preconceptions about poetry. Official praise of Chaucer, in the lavish eulogies of Hoccleve, Lydgate and his other disciples, tends to concentrate on his qualities as a poet of sententious utterance and the high rhetorical style.[4] For Lydgate, he is 'the noble Rethor that alle dide excelle' (*Troy Book*, iii.553), who first refined and enriched the English language from its primitive rudeness:

> Noble Galfride, poete of Breteyne,
> Amonge oure englisch that made first to reyne
> The gold dewe-dropis of rethorik so fyne
> Oure rude langage only t'enlwmyne. (*Troy Book*, ii.4697–700,
>   in Brewer, 1978, vol. 1, p. 47)

For Hoccleve he is the 'flour of eloquence' and 'Mirour of fructuous entendement', whose death

> Despoiled hath this land of the swetnesse
> Of rethorik; for unto Tullius
> Was never man so lyk amonges us. (*Regiment of Princes*, 1962–3,
>   2084–6, in Brewer, 1978, vol. 1, p. 63)

Every writer who speaks of Chaucer in the fifteenth century speaks of him in similar terms, which by the middle of the century have hardened into a formula. Their imitation of his work reflects the same attitude: the poems to which they turn again and again for subject-matter, thematic details, stylistic devices, phrases and words, are the poems which respond most readily to the demand for high 'sentence', of love and philosophy, and the high style, namely *The Parliament of Fowls*, the *Troilus*, *The Legend of Good Women*, and the Knight's Tale (see Pearsall, 1970, pp. 49–63). The *Canterbury Tales* in general are less highly regarded, or at least less imitated.

There is much in this that may occasion surprise. Modern critics would praise Chaucer for his humour, realism and irony, for his sense of character, for his breadth and subtlety of observation, for his complex sense of point of view in narrative and constant withdrawal from positions of authority, and for his cultivation of an idiomatic conversational style. It may seem that the fifteenth century, in selecting for special commendation Chaucer's sententiousness and rhetoric, has perversely chosen to praise him for the very things he strove to avoid. There are some historical considerations to apply here, of course: the gloss of Chaucer's style may have appeared more brilliant, his diction more select, in early days, before continual currency had worn them to the familiar and fluent idiom that we think we recognise, while the modern distaste for sententiousness of all kinds may have acted to suppress the recognition of its presence in Chaucer, or to see it as ironical. But beyond that it should be emphasised that their language of praise is to some extent conventional. Writers speak of Chaucer, when they wish to praise him, in the language appropriate to the praise of poetry, and Chaucer is praised for 'sentence' and 'rethoryk' because these are the twin foundations of medieval poetic theory. Poetry teaches moral virtue – 'Al that is written is writen for oure doctrine' (Retraction, X.1083; cf. VII.3441–2) – and it teaches by sweetening the instruction with rhetoric. These were the terms available for the praise of a great poet, and, since Chaucer demanded to be praised, these were the topics of praise. There is nothing peculiarly medieval about this: in later times, and still today, Chaucer will be annexed to prevailing critical opinion in the same way – sententiousness and rhetoric then, ambiguity and irony now – not so much because this alone is what readers observe and experience, but because this provides the current vocabulary of comment and appreciation. There is a case for saying that in the reading of great literature there is a core of common experience which remains constant, but which finds only imperfect expression in the fashionable critical language of the day.

Evidence that fifteenth-century readers saw more in Chaucer than they were able to express in the current vocabulary of conventional eulogy, and in particular that they relished those qualities of humour and dramatic realism in the *Canterbury Tales* to which later ages were to give pre-eminence, is not difficult to come by. Lydgate's Prologue to his *Siege of Thebes* (ed. Erdmann and Ekwall, 1911, 1920), for instance, is a Canterbury link in Chaucer's low comic style, and shows the monk gambolling in elephantine playfulness after his master. There is a similarly boisterous response on Lydgate's part, in the *Mumming at Hertford*, to the cruder and more violent aspects of Chaucer's portrait of the Wife of Bath, perhaps drawing more on the grotesque and comic distortion of that portrait in the Clerk's Envoy than on the Prologue itself. The *Tale of Beryn*, which appears in one manuscript (ed. Furnivall and Stone, 1887) as the first tale of the homeward journey, told by the Merchant, provides another example, and a better one, of a fifteenth-century poet who has a full appreciation of the rich dramatic comedy of the *Canterbury Tales*, especially the links. In the Prologue, which again introduces a very serious poem, the pilgrims are shown arriving in Canterbury: the Pardoner and the Miller take it upon themselves to give explanations, all wrong, of the subject-matter of the stained glass in the cathedral; the Summoner and Miller filch trinkets from the souvenir-selling stall; the Prioress and the Wife of Bath take a turn in the garden together; the Knight and the Squire go out to view the fortifications of the city. In the central episode of the Prologue narrative, the Pardoner is gulled by a cunning barmaid and her paramour, who make fun of him and his amatory protestations: there may be some recognition here of the hints of effeminacy in Chaucer's portrait.

Inevitably, though, it will be Chaucer's courtly and serious poetry that is most admired and imitated in the fifteenth century, and to the general evidence of commendation and imitation one would have to add, in the case of the *Canterbury Tales*, the evidence of excerpting (see Silvia, 1974). Not counting those manuscripts that consist of or contain single leaves or fragments of individual tales, and that represent what might have been originally complete texts of the *Tales*, there are some twenty manuscripts (see Appendix A) which include one or more selected tales as part of an anthology or other kind of collection: twelve manuscripts contain a single tale, six contain two tales, one four, and one five. The tales most commonly selected are the Clerk's Tale and the Prioress's Tale, with six instances each, closely followed by *Melibee*, with five. A number of tales appear twice, namely, those of the Second Nun, Man of Law, Knight, Wife of Bath, Monk and Parson. The dominance of the serious didactic and religious tales of course is immediately striking. It would be possible to discount some of the weight of evidence that suggests a preference for such tales by pointing to external factors such as the incentive for copying that derived from the moral benefit presumed to accrue to the copyist, and the better chances of survival of religious manuscripts, but some recognition must be given here to genuine taste, whether that taste is interpreted as ideological conformism or not.

However, a possibly stronger argument for the more generous receptivity of fifteenth-century readers to the *Tales* is provided by the large number of complete, or originally complete texts of the *Tales*, in which no attempt is made to expurgate or otherwise adapt the collection to prevailing courtly, didactic or religious preferences. Indeed, copyists show an enthusiastic response to the scheme of the *Tales* as a whole, and are constantly trying to rationalise or fill out the dramatic framework of the *Tales*, or make it more internally consistent, by adding links, by completing unfinished tales or by providing new tales for pilgrims whose tales are unfinished or missing. The *Tale of Gamelyn*, assigned to the Cook in several manuscripts, is the best example of such an addition. The programme of illustration devised for the Ellesmere manuscript, and imitated in Cambridge University Library Gg.4.27 and in the fragmentary 'Oxford' manuscript, whereby portraits of the pilgrims are placed in the margin at the beginnings of the tales assigned to them, is a clear indication of the desire to stress the 'dramatic principle' in the ordering of the *Tales*, and to keep in the mind of the reader the presence of the pilgrim in his tale (see Doyle and Parkes, 1978, pp. 190–1). In this connection, it should be remarked also that the two 'Canterbury links' described above, those that act as Prologues to the *Siege of Thebes* and the *Tale of Beryn*, offer evidence of the liveliest response to the dramatic framework of the *Canterbury Tales*. The Prologue to *Beryn* gives a fuller account of the activities of the pilgrims as a group than anything in Chaucer, while Lydgate even goes to the length of returning on occasion, during the narrative of *Thebes* itself, to the fiction of roadside narration, commenting on the journey and the places on the road that the pilgrims are passing and have passed (*Thebes*, 324, 1044–60, 4522–4). One is inclined to see these elaborations of the framework narrative as a rather naive response to the exciting suggestiveness of Chaucer's scheme, and to believe that his own comparative restraint in developing the links is a mark of his wise recognition that the illusion of roadside drama, though in itself part of a valuable framing structure, would become ultimately trivial if over-indulged.

Further evidence of the readiness to respond to the *Tales* as a whole is provided by the knowledge displayed by writers such as Lydgate, Hoccleve and Dunbar, for all the lofty terms of their eulogies, of the underworld of the *Tales*,[5] and also by the terms in which the *Tales* are explicitly described. Some problems are presented to the conventional view of poetry by the *Tales*, and the response to these problems by writers who have occasion to describe the *Tales* is to acknowledge frankly and give value to the principle of variety and diversity. Lydgate, following Chaucer's own remarks concerning dramatic propriety (I.725–42, 3171–86), relates this variety and diversity explicitly to the varied character of the pilgrims:

> The tyme in soth whan Canterbury talys
> Complet and told at many sondry stage
> Of estatis in the pilgrimage,
> Everich man lik to his degre,
> Some of desport, some of moralite,
> Some of knyghthode, love and gentillesse,
> And some also in soth of Ribaudye
> To make laughter in the companye. (*Thebes*, Prologue, 18–26)

The author of the *Tale of Beryn* makes the same point, rather more apologetically:

> When all this fresshe feleship were com to Cauntirbury,
> As ye have herd to-fore, with talys glad and merry,
> Som of sotill centence, of vertu and of lore,
> And som of othir myrthis, for hem that hold no store
> Of wisdom, ne of holynes, ne of Chivalry,
> Nethir of vertuouse matere, but holich to foly
> Leyd wit and lustis all, to suche nyce japis ... (*Beryn*, 1–7)

Caxton, in introducing his second edition of the *Canterbury Tales* in 1484, seems to be under greater pressure to claim traditional virtues for the *Tales*, perhaps because of his desire to cultivate a particular kind of status-conscious reader:

> I purpose temprynte by the grace of god the book of the tales of Cauntyrburye/in whiche I fynde many a noble hystorye/of every astate and degre/Fyrst rehercyng the condicions/and tharraye of eche of them as properly as possyble is to be sayd/And after theyr tales whyche ben of noblesse/wysedom/gentylesse/Myrthe/and also of veray holynesse and vertue/wherin he fynysshyth thys sayd booke. (Brewer, 1978, vol. 1, p. 76)

'Myrthe', it will be seen, is smuggled in almost unobserved, and at the end of the 'Prohemye' Caxton withdraws even this concession, praying, in terms reminiscent of the Retraction, that all readers of the book shall have remembrance of Chaucer's soul and take good heed of 'the good and vertuous tales'. Hawes, while speaking in the most traditional terms of Chaucer's poetry, as kindling our hearts with 'the fyry leames of morall vertue', nevertheless acknowledges the variety of the tales:

> And upon his ymagynacyon
> He made also the tales of Caunterbury,
> Some vertuous, and some glade and mery. (*Pastime of Pleasure*,
> 1321–3, 1328–30, in Brewer, 1978, vol. 1, p. 82)

Skelton speaks in the same terms

> Of the Tales of Caunterbury,
> Some sad storyes, some mery (*Philip Sparrow*, 615–16, in
> Brewer, 1978, vol. 1, p. 83)

and further, perhaps because of the lighter and more humorous context in which he is writing, he gives nearly all his specific attention to the Wife of Bath.

The popularity of the *Canterbury Tales*, as these last remarks indicate, continued unabated into the sixteenth century. It was not the first book that Caxton printed, and not the first work by Chaucer – a small pamphlet of his minor poems and the translation of Boethius preceded it (Blake, 1969, pp. 224–6) – but it was the first major poem and the first major work of English literature that he printed. He was conscious enough of its importance, too, to issue a second edition six years later, in 1484, incorporating corrections that he took from a better manuscript delivered to him by a certain 'gentylman'. He speaks in the loftiest terms of his sense of responsibility to his author to print a correct text, and expresses the greatest regret for having been obliged to use a defective manuscript for his first edition, and, though his protestations are not matched by his performance (see Blake, 1969, pp. 104–6; Pearsall, 1983, pp. 106–8), his care and attention to the work in bringing out a revised edition are quite exceptional. Further editions of the *Canterbury Tales*, all taken from Caxton's second edition, were put out by Richard Pynson in 1492, by Wynkyn de Worde in 1498, and again by Pynson, as part of a collected series of Chaucer's works, in 1526. It must be presumed that, in these first fifty years of the printing era, the *Canterbury Tales* was reaching and pleasing a wider audience than ever before.

With the publication of William Thynne's edition of Chaucer's collected works in 1532, the reputation of Chaucer entered upon a secure inheritance among readers, which lasted until well into the eighteenth century; by that time, conditions were propitious for a new kind of reappraisal of Chaucer in the light of historical scholarship, as demonstrated in Thomas Tyrwhitt's great edition of the *Canterbury Tales* in 1775. Throughout these centuries, Chaucer's collected works were regularly printed.[6] A reprint of Thynne came out in 1542, with the spurious 'Plowman's Tale' added, and another reprint a few years later, possibly in 1545, with the added tale moved to a new position before the Parson's Tale. John Stow brought out another reprint of Thynne in 1561, with additional apocryphal material, and with the inclusion of Lydgate's *Siege of Thebes* as a 'Canterbury tale'. He prints this at the end of the volume, and makes no pretence that it is Chaucer's: like the scribes of the fifteenth century, and like all Chaucer editors before Tyrwhitt, he clearly regards the *Canterbury Tales* as an open-ended and expandable collection, which it is the editor's responsibility to augment with whatever can be found that masquerades as a 'Canterbury tale', whether specifically attributed to Chaucer or not. Stow's text was reprinted by Thomas Speght in 1598, with the addition of a more elaborate introductory apparatus, a glossary and some annotations, as well as other editorial material; and again in 1602, with extensive correction of the text and a revised and expanded apparatus. Finally, in 1721, after the booksellers' reprint of Speght's second edition in 1687, comes the edition that goes under the name of John Urry (though he died in 1714), in which both the *Tale of Beryn* and the *Tale of Gamelyn*, which we have seen incorporated into manuscripts of the *Tales* in the fifteenth century, are included.

Throughout this period, the *Canterbury Tales* are always placed first in the order of Chaucer's works – as has remained the conventional practice up to the present day, despite the chronological anomaly – and the influence of this choice should not be underestimated. Since readers have a natural tendency to begin at page one, and to go on until their interest wanes not many pages afterwards, it is not difficult to believe that the position of the *Tales* at the beginning of the collected works contributed something to their special popularity. The emergence of the General Prologue in the eighteenth and nineteenth centuries as the touchstone of Chaucer's poetic genius may be not unconnected, though there are more respectable reasons.

This, though, is to look ahead, for in the sixteenth century the *Canterbury Tales* still faced difficulties. The comparatively open and generous response of Lydgate, Caxton, Hawes and Skelton to the variety and diversity of the *Tales* was no longer enough: Chaucer was on his way to being canonised as a 'classic', and the *Canterbury Tales* do not obviously have the elevation of style and subject-matter that would be expected in the writing of a poet who is to be compared with the classical poets of antiquity and the great Italians. There is no sign of discrimination against the *Tales* in the eulogy of Chaucer in the letter of Sir Brian Tuke, prefixed as a dedication to Henry VIII in Thynne's Chaucer of 1532, nor in the fulsome tributes of Leland and Bale (Brewer, 1978, vol. 1, pp. 87–96; Spurgeon, 1925, vol. 3, part iv, pp. 13–27): all conform to fifteenth-century convention in praising Chaucer for his eloquence and sententiousness, though there is now additional emphasis on his learning. There is also, at this time, a particular boost given to the reputation of the *Tales* by a mere accident of historical circumstance. The satire on the clergy in the *Canterbury Tales*, and even more in the Lollard polemic of the Plowman's Tale, which was added to the canon in 1542, was very welcome to the England of the Reformation, and Chaucer was hailed as a stalwart anti-Papist and Protestant by premonition. The 'Canterburye tales', along with 'psalters, prymers, prayers, statutes and lawes of the Realme, Cronycles', and others, were expressly exempted from an act for the abolition of forbidden books in 1542 (Brewer, 1978, vol. 1, p. 98), and in 1570 John Foxe, who already attributed to Chaucer the Lollard treatise of *Jack Upland* that Speght was to add to the canon in 1602, greeted Chaucer as 'a right Wiclevian' (ibid., p. 108). We may smile at the error, but it is salutary to recognise the more or less universal truth it demonstrates, that a great poet can only be shown to be great if his ideas and attitudes can be shown to be similar to those of his contemporary admirers.

Chaucer's reputation as a Wycliffite lasted until the late seventeenth century, when it was no longer historically relevant. It was always a subsidiary interest, and could not counteract the more serious kinds of erosion to which the literary reputation of the *Canterbury Tales* was subject. The levity of many of the tales, and the general atmosphere of familiar good humour, were not in accord with what was expected of a serious poet, and the *Tales* suffered further from the general prejudice against unedifying fictions which had always lain beneath the surface in the fifteenth century. So it was, by an unhappy chance, that 'Canterbury Tales' came to be a synonym for idle and trivial and worthless stories. The first recorded use of the opprobrious phrase seems to be in 1535 (Spurgeon, 1925, vol. 1, p. 81), and the characteristic usage is well illustrated by Turbervile, for instance, who speaks in 1575 of a recommendation for an operation on a hawk that he does not approve of as 'a thing not only frivolous to talke of and a verie olde womans fable or Cantorburie tale, but also verie perillous to be put in practise' (ibid., p. 111). In 1795, 'Canterbury tales' is still being used as a synonym for 'cock and bull stories' (ibid., p. 498). One might wonder how much the reception of the *Canterbury Tales* was influenced during these centuries by the existence of this disparaging idiom.

More generally, the *Canterbury Tales* were exposed, like the rest of Chaucer's poetry, to increasing objection because of the old and obscure language in which they were written. Skelton had recognised as early as 1507 the existence of this objection, and had defended Chaucer stoutly:

> Chaucer, that famus clerke,
> His termes were not darke
> But plesaunt, easy, and playne;
> No worde he wrote in vayne. (*Philip Sparrow*, 801–4, in Brewer, 1978,
>   vol. 1, p. 85)

But with the passage of time it was inevitable that Chaucer's language would grow more difficult to understand. His editors were in something of a dilemma: whilst they did not restrain compositors from their regular practice of introducing the occasional modernisations of spelling and trivial substitutions of a modern for an older form of word, they did not wish to engage in any wholesale programme of modernisation since they knew that for many readers the antiquity of the language was actually a source of attraction. These readers might be the very ones who would buy their books. For this reason, too, they continued to print Chaucer in Caxton's black-letter or Gothic type, even though it was completely obsolete: Urry's edition of 1721 was the first to be printed in roman. So for every Puttenham who said that Chaucer, for his antiquated language, should be put down, there was a Spenser who, for the same reason, would take him up (Spurgeon, 1925, vol. 1, pp. 117, 125).

The *Canterbury Tales*, however, were under specially severe attack, since they seemed to lack any compensating virtues of nobility or solid sense. Harington acknowledged the 'flat scurrilitie' of some of them, though he defended them on the grounds of decorum (Brewer, 1978, vol. 1, p. 130). It was unfortunate, in a way, that Gascoigne, in 1575, in the midst of the doubts that were current concerning the correctness of Chaucer's versification, should have identified the metre of the *Canterbury Tales* as 'ryding rime', a sort of easy jogging four-stress couplet suitable for 'delectable and light enterprises' (ibid., p. 110). His remarks were taken up by Puttenham in 1589 in a manner still more dismissive of the *Tales*:

> His meetre Heroicall of *Troilus and Cresseid* is very grave and stately, keeping the staffe of seven, and the verse of ten, his other verses of the Canterbury Tales be but riding ryme, nevertheless very well becomming the matter of that pleasaunt pilgrimage in which every mans part is played with much decency. (ibid., p. 127)

Puttenham's distinction between the more serious and respectable part of Chaucer's work and the light-hearted *Canterbury Tales* is one that is commonly maintained. Sidney, for instance, in his *Apology for Poetry*, selects *Troilus and Criseyde* for special commendation, passing by the rest as having 'great wants, fitte to be forgiven in so reverent antiquity' (ibid., p. 120). The more worthy of the *Canterbury Tales*, or rather those that fitted in best with current opinion on what constituted worthiness in poetry, were sometimes exempted from the general condescension: the

Knight's Tale is always highly regarded, and it is noteworthy that the Squire's Tale, to us one of the least important of the *Tales*, is treated with special respect by Spenser and Milton. The general reputation of the *Tales* as a whole, as popular literature of a rather low sort, is well represented in the imitation of the work offered in *The Cobbler of Caunterburie*, a collection of 'tales that were told in the Barge betweene Billingsgate and Gravesend: imitating herein *old father Chaucer*, who with the like Method set out his Canterbury tales' (Spurgeon, 1925, vol. 1, pp. 132–3).

Fortunately, rescue was at hand, and in the editions of 1598 and 1602 Speght and his friends mounted an important campaign to establish Chaucer as a serious and learned writer. The title-pages refer to him as 'our Antient and lerned English Poet', and the new work of the editors can be seen as an endeavour, quite strenuous for its time, to present Chaucer as a poet capable of being compared with the classical poets of antiquity and the poets of the Italian and French Renaissance. The apparatus imitates what would be provided for such poets: a series of commendations, a Life, a list of 'arguments' for each work, a glossary, annotations and index of authors cited. It is the work of university-trained men, and Speght got his old friend of Cambridge days, Francis Beaumont, to write an epistle, printed among the prefatory matter to the edition, which sets out the new view of Chaucer, and specifically of the *Canterbury Tales*. Beaumont defends Chaucer at length against the objections commonly alleged against him, namely that 'many of his wordes (as it were with overlong lying) are growne too hard and unpleasant, and next that hee is somewhat too broad in some of his speeches' (Brewer, 1978, vol. 1, p. 136). More positively, he establishes a classical pedigree for the *Canterbury Tales* by comparing them with the comedies of Plautus and Terence, asserting indeed that Chaucer is superior in the originality of his matter and the comprehensiveness of his satire.

> His drift is to touch all sortes of men, and to discover all vices of that Age, and that he doth in such sort, as he never failes to hit every marke he levels at. (ibid., p. 138)

The application to the *Tales* of the criteria of approbation appropriate to classical satire is a very important new stage in the denizenation of the *Tales* as a recognised genre.

Speght himself returns to classical comparisons in his own account of the General Prologue in 'The Argument to the Prologues':[7]

The Author in these Prologues to his Canterbury Tales, doth describe the reporters thereof for two causes: first, that the Reader seeing the qualitie of the person, may judge of his speech accordingly: wherein Chaucer hath most excellently kept that *decorum*, which Horace requireth in that behalfe. Secondly to shew, how that even in our language, that may be perfourmed for descriptions, which the Greeke and Latine Poets in their tongues have done at large. (Spurgeon, 1925, vol. 3, part iv, p. 52)

Speght declares Chaucer to be no whit inferior to these 'Greeke and Latine Poets' in his powers of satirical portraiture, and he commends him especially for the skill with which 'he comprehendeth all the people of the land, and the nature and disposition of them in those daies'. He concludes:

In the Tales is shewed the state of the Church, the Court, and Countrey, with such Arte and cunning, that although none could deny himselfe to be touched, yet none durst complaine that he was wronged.

The allusion to 'decorum' has precedent, as we have seen, if not the explicit reference to Horace (*Ars Poetica*, 99–118, 220–50), but the direct comparison with the tradition of the satirical portrait in classical poetry is new, as is the direct reference in the last sentence to the principle on which satirical poetry was defended, as morally normative rather than slanderous (Horace, *Satires*, I.iv.78–129). Speght refers here to the *Tales* generally, though evidently the General Prologue is very much in his mind, being certainly the part of the *Tales* that could most aptly be equipped with proper classical precedent. The General Prologue also receives more annotatory comment than any other poem, which may not be merely because it comes first and has much matter for annotation.

Speght did his work well. His critical comments provided an important stimulus for Dryden in his Preface to the *Fables*, while his 1602 text was the one used by Tyrwhitt as his base-text in his edition of the *Canterbury Tales* in 1775. In the seventeenth century, however, the *Canterbury Tales*, and Chaucer's poetry generally, were at their lowest ebb. The increasing obscurity of his language, the roughness of his versification as it was now represented in the degenerate texts of successive printings, meant that the efforts of Speght and Beaumont, and others, to render him acceptable to neo-classical taste were for the time being ignored. Henry Peacham, writing in 1622 of the kind of books that a gentleman should have on his shelves, is eager to recommend Chaucer as 'among the best of your English bookes in your librarie', but he has to make a definite effort to excuse the language:

> Although the stile for the antiquitie, may distast you, yet as under a bitter and rough rinde, ther lyeth a delicate kernell of conceit and sweete invention. (Brewer, 1978, vol. 1, p. 149)

The inevitable decay of his language was a constant theme of comment, and writers will often repeat Peacham's distinction of 'mouldy words' and 'solid sense' (Samuel Cobb, 1700, in Spurgeon, 1925, vol. 1, p. 271), or, as Waller puts it,

> *Chaucer* his sense can only boast,
> The glory of his numbers lost. (ibid., p. 244)

A harsher view sees the mouldering of Chaucer's verse as an irremediable loss:

> But Age has rusted what the *Poet* writ,
> Worn out his Language, and obscur'd his Wit. (Joseph Addison, 1694, ibid., p. 266)

In the midst of these conventional and patronising commonplaces, it is refreshing to come upon Dryden's Preface to his *Fables* of 1700. Dryden, in offering his modernisations of the Knight's Tale, the Nun's Priest's Tale, the Wife of Bath's Tale and the Parson's portrait (as well as *The Flower and the Leaf* and some tales from Boccaccio), is under no misapprehensions about the language and versification of his author. '*Chaucer*, I confess', he says, 'is a rough Diamond, and must first be polish'd, e'er he shines' (Brewer, 1978, vol. 1, p. 168). His metre is allowed to have 'the rude Sweetness of a *Scotch* tune in it', but the opinion recently put about that 'there were really Ten Syllables in a Verse where we find but Nine' is declared to be 'not worth confuting' (ibid., p. 165). More generally, says Dryden, in his lordly fashion:

> The Words are given up as a Post not to be defended in our Poet, because he wanted the Modern Art of Fortifying. The Thoughts remain to be consider'd ... (ibid., p. 163)

However, in his response to his reading of Chaucer, as distinct from these critical platitudes, Dryden shows a much more discerning taste, and a generous readiness to accept Chaucer into the neoclassical pantheon as a portrayer of general Nature. He draws much upon Speght and Beaumont for his comments, though he communicates them to a much wider audience and may indeed be said to have established the language of commendation and the topics of praise for the *Canterbury Tales* that are still today most widely current, if now in more sophisticated garb. Here, for instance, echoing Beaumont's comments on Chaucer's powers of visual realism,[8] is how Dryden compares Chaucer and Ovid:

> Both of them understood the Manners; under which Name I comprehend the Passions, and, in a larger Sense, the Descriptions of Persons, and their very Habits: For an Example, I see ... all the Pilgrims in the *Canterbury* Tales, their Humours, their Features, and their very Dress, as distinctly as if I had supp'd with them at the *Tabard* in *Southwark*. (ibid., pp. 162–3)

Later, after offering Chaucer the ultimate accolade of neo-classical realism ('*Chaucer* follow'd Nature every where, but was never so bold to go beyond her', p. 164), Dryden develops his critique of the *Canterbury Tales* in the most famous passage of the Preface:

> He must have been a Man of a most wonderful comprehensive Nature, because, as it has been truly observ'd of him [by Speght, as cited above], he has taken into the Compass of his *Canterbury Tales* the various Manners and Humours (as we now call them) of the whole *English* nation, in his Age. Not a single Character has escap'd him. All his pilgrims are severally distinguish'd from each other; and not only in their Inclinations, but in their very Phisiognomies and Persons ... The Matter and Manner of their Tales, and of their Telling, are so suited to their different Educations, Humours, and Callings, that each of them would be improper in any other Mouth. (ibid, p. 166)

Dryden gives some examples of the exercise of this decorum, commenting on the manner in which the ribald characters are severally distinguished in their ribaldry, and concludes:

But enough of this: There is such a Variety of Game springing up before me, that I am distracted in my Choice, and know not which to follow. 'Tis sufficient to say according to the Proverb, that here is God's Plenty. (ibid., pp. 166–7)

Dryden subsequently makes a special point of praising the Knight's Tale, for predictable reasons, but it is clear that in building this substantial neo-classical platform for Chaucer's reputation, with all the hints that he took from his predecessors concerning Chaucer's sense of decorum, his realism, his comprehensiveness, and the truth of his observation of Nature, Dryden has in the forefront of his consciousness the General Prologue and the dramatic appropriateness of the tales to the pilgrims as portrayed there.

There were other attractions for the early eighteenth-century reader of the *Canterbury Tales*. Dryden himself speaks of the 'immodesty' of some of the tales, and of his concern to steer clear of them (p. 167), but subsequent modernisations showed no such delicacy, and Chaucer's unofficial reputation as a teller of bawdy tales flourished. Pope's own 'Imitation of Chaucer' is a concession to this taste. Official commendation of Chaucer, however, constantly echoes Dryden. John Dart, in the life of Chaucer prefixed to Urry's Chaucer, speaks of him as one who 'discovered Nature in all her appearances, and stript off every disguise with which the *Gothick* Writers had cloathed her . . . he copied her close', adding that 'he was a true Master of Satyr' (Brewer, 1978, vol. 1, p. 183). Thomas Morell, who proposed an edition of the *Canterbury Tales* and brought out the General Prologue and the Knight's Tale in 1737, praised the liveliness of Chaucer's descriptions of 'his merry Crew', and concluded thus:

From whence we may observe, that Nature is still the same, however alter'd in her outward Dress, and the Man that, like *Chaucer* and *Shakespear*, can trace her in her most secret Recesses, will be sure, in every Age, to please. (ibid., p. 197)

George Ogle, introducing his own version of the Clerk's Tale, praises Chaucer's powers of characterising, 'whether in the Comic or in the Satiric way,' and says 'these turns of Satire are not unworthy of PERSIUS, JUVENAL or HORACE himself.' (ibid., p. 205). Thomas Warton, in his *History of English Poetry* (1774), speaks of his 'talents for satire, and for observation on life' (Brewer, 1978, vol. 1, p. 229).

Tyrwhitt's edition of the *Canterbury Tales* came out in the following year, and was frequently reprinted, with or without acknowledgment, over the next 120 years. Thomas Wright's edition of 1847 claimed superiority on the grounds that it was set up from a manuscript, but since the manuscript that it was set up from (Harley 7334) was not a good one, it achieved only partial success. Tyrwhitt provided a text that was exceptionally good for its time, and also valuable annotation and discussion of sources. He offers little in the way of critical commentary, but his readers hardly needed it, since the manner in which the *Tales* were to be read, and the qualities for which they were to be admired, were now well-established and widely accepted. To follow out the critical commentary on the *Tales* in the next century or so, until Skeat's edition of 1894, is to follow out a series of variations on a set theme: Chaucer is the realistic and sympathetic portrayer of general human nature, his gifts mainly comic and satiric, and the *Tales* are his masterpiece. William Godwin, whose remarks in his *Life of Geoffrey Chaucer* (1803) can be taken as representative, especially since he shows no signs of having any thoughts of his own, speaks of the *Tales* as 'the great basis of the fame of the Chaucer', their excellence residing in 'his power of humour, of delineating characters, and of giving vivacity and richness to comic incidents' (Spurgeon, 1925, vol. 2, p. 8). *Troilus*, by contrast, 'is merely a love-tale' (ibid., p. 2). The famous engravings of Thomas Stothard (1808) and William Blake (1809), representing the procession of Chaucer's pilgrims to Canterbury, make almost tangible the reality of Chaucer's descriptions, and Blake speaks of Chaucer as 'the great poetical observer of men', whose 'characters live age after age' (Brewer, 1978, vol. 1, pp. 252, 254):

> Some of the names or titles are altered by time, but the characters themselves for ever remain unaltered, and consequently they are the physiognomies or lineaments of universal human life, beyond which Nature never steps. (ibid., p. 251)

William Hazlitt, comparing Chaucer with the other three great poets, Spenser, Shakespeare and Milton, in his *Lectures on the English Poets* (1818), says that in comparison with the others 'Chaucer excels as the poet of manners, or of real life ... Chaucer most frequently describes things as they are' (Spurgeon, 1925, vol. 2, p. 105). His conviction of the *reality* of the Summoner, for instance, is so profound that he wonders what has become of him in the present day, and into what profession that character – for the characters of men never change – now lurks (Brewer, 1978, vol. 1, pp. 280–1). Leigh Hunt, though like others he recognises touches of pathos in Chaucer's works, praises him as having 'the strongest imagination of real life' and as being 'in comic painting inferior to none' (Spurgeon, 1925, vol. 2, p. 254), and he analyses Chaucer's humour in his well-known essay on *Wit and Humour*, drawing his examples almost exclusively from the General Prologue (Brewer, 1978, vol. 2, pp. 70–5).

There are some remarks in a book on *Early English Literature* (1837) by John Henry Hippisley which reveal an interesting early sense of historical perspective. Hippisley gives the first account of the history of Chaucer criticism, and comments on the way taste has shifted from 'the pathetic poems' (*Troilus* and the Knight's Tale), which were most admired in the sixteenth century, to the comic, and how 'From the days of Shakspeare, the comic powers of Chaucer have been the constant theme of admiration both with critics and poets' (Spurgeon, 1925, vol. 2, p. 215). The comic genius is located principally in the General Prologue and 'the ludicrous tales,' and Hippisley remarks on the originality of these poems and the shift towards the representation of 'the habits of middle and low life' (ibid., p. 217). In this he anticipates the securing of the chronology of Chaucer's writings, and the manner in which, with the *Tales* moored at the end of his life, his career could be seen as a progress from imitation and artificiality to originality and real life. So Lounsbury expressed it, in the first respectable full-length study of Chaucer's life and writings (1891):

> For the shadowy beings who dwell in the land of types he substituted living men and women; for the allegorical representations of feelings and beliefs, the direct outpourings of passion. (Brewer, 1978, vol. 2, p. 229)

The matter, and the profundity of the prejudice, had been put more bluntly by a writer called William Cyples in the Cornhill Magazine in 1877, who pointed out 'how very small a portion of Chaucer's work decides the special impression of him which now is historically transmitted from generation to generation'. If a tenth of his writing were put away, he would be unrecognisable.

> Instead of appearing a broad humourist, with an overpowering love of nature, painting persons and scenes with exact reality, there would then seem to be no English poet so artificial, so romantic, so lackadaisical as Chaucer. The truth is, that the literary associations for which the

mention of his name is the cue, belong to the *Canterbury Tales* only . . .
If the matchless Introduction had not been written, or had been
different, and if he had not included in the list two or three of the
stories, or not given prologues to the others, Chaucer could not have
survived in our literature. (Brewer, 1978, vol. 2, p. 190)

If one thinks of this as an unrepresentative view, or a specially narrow
view, one has only to turn to Matthew Arnold's comments on Chaucer in
his essay on 'The Study of Poetry', where he speaks of the superior
substance and style of Chaucer's poetry:

His superiority in substance is given by his large, free, simple, clear yet
kindly view of human life . . . he has gained the power to survey the
world from a central, a truly human point of view. We have only to call
to mind the Prologues of *The Canterbury Tales*. The right comment
upon it is Dryden's 'It is sufficient to say, according to the proverb,
that *here is God's plenty*'. And again: 'He is a perpetual fountain of good
sense'. It is by a large, free sound representation of things, that poetry,
this high criticism of life, has truth of substance. (Brewer, 1978, vol. 2,
p. 217)

The dominance of the General Prologue in the critical reception of
Chaucer, and of Dryden's comments mainly based on it, is well demonstrated here.

All this time, while German and American scholars such as Ten Brink,
Child, Manly and Kittredge were laying the foundations of a proper
understanding of Chaucer's language, English scholars were engaged in a
radical reappraisal of the text and canon. The work of Henry Bradshaw,
the Cambridge University Librarian, on the text and order of the
Canterbury Tales led to the foundation of the Chaucer Society in 1867,
with F. J. Furnivall as its moving spirit, and to the publication of the
Six-Text edition of the *Canterbury Tales* during the years 1868–77.
Throughout the examination of the evidence of the manuscripts for the
ordering of the sequence of the *Tales*, the criterion of judgement for the
validity of an interpretation was the assumption of a thoroughgoing and
consistent dramatic realism in Chaucer's plan for the *Tales*. The tales
themselves were moved about like so many counters, to fill a hypothetical
afternoon here, or a hypothetical interval between tea and dinner there,
on the journey. The powerful role of the General Prologue in determin-
ing the conditions for the reading of the *Tales* is again well demonstrated,

and in the many editions of single tales or pairs of tales that were now coming out for school or university use (Richard Morris's edition of Prologue, Knight's Tale and Nun's Priest's Tale in 1867 is the first), the General Prologue or the appropriate portrait from it was generally included.

The important consequence of all this scholarly endeavour, upon which the modern study of the *Tales* rests, was the publication of the great six-volume edition of Chaucer's works edited by W. W. Skeat in 1894. It makes a watershed in the history of the reading, study and criticism of Chaucer, and after its publication one has the conviction for the first time that those who are writing about Chaucer have actually read a reasonable quantity of his poetry in the original. W. P. Ker's review of the edition in 1895 (Brewer, 1978, vol. 2, p. 249) can be taken as ushering in the modern age of criticism. His emphasis on the *Troilus* ('It is difficult to speak moderately of Chaucer's "Troilus"') is a sign of the times.

It is impossible to deal at length with the developments that have taken place in the reception and interpretation of the *Canterbury Tales* since the turn of the century. The vast increase in the professional study of the poem has created a corresponding volume of scholarly publication, and the availability of the individual tales as potential subject-matter for independent essays has contributed much to the disproportionate concentration on the *Tales* in the learned journals. However, a number of main lines of interpretation can be described.[9]

The view that the nineteenth century inherited of the poet of the *Canterbury Tales* as a comic realist *par excellence* and an expert delineator of character has remained strong, though not dominant in more recent years. The work of Manly (1926) on the historical actuality of Chaucer's pilgrims, and the real-life models that Chaucer might have used, was a particular example of this continuity, almost in its way a fulfilment of the nineteenth-century dream of a dramatic realism so close to life as to be virtually part of it.[10] Kittredge (1911–12, 1913) has been the strongest influence, and his image of the *Canterbury Tales* as Chaucer's version of 'The Human Comedy' has remained a persuasive one, not least because of the way in which it associates Chaucer with the nineteenth-century novel of psychological realism, which is generally admired. Kittredge is the most convincing proponent of the 'dramatic principle' – or what was long before called the principle of decorum – by which the tales are understood as characterising their speakers, or, in more extreme terms, as existing for the sake of doing so. This view has found much favour,

and not surprisingly, when one sees the delightful fantasies that if feeds
on and may feed:

> A group of men are gathered in the smoking compartment of a Pullman
> car. The cigars burn freely, and the bars come down. The captain of
> industry lets himself be known by stories of big business; the soldier
> has tales of the trenches; the Californian sings the glories of his State in
> dazzling anecdote; the college professor strives to seem unacademic,
> but the damned spot will not out; the commercial traveller tells the
> story of his life, and the clergyman discreetly seeks his berth ...
> (Lowes, 1919, pp. 73–4)

W. W. Lawrence's full-length study (1950) is a sober reading of the *Tales*
in terms of dramatic realism; R. M. Lumiansky's consistent advocacy of
the 'dramatic principle' (1955) has done something to indicate its severe
limitations; C. A. Owen (1977) draws towards the latter in some respects,
though his criticism of individual tales is astute and sensitive. A particular temptation in the dramatic reading of the *Tales*, present in Kittredge but never fully succumbed to by that wise critic, is the tendency to
read individual tales as indications of the inadequacy of the speaker.
Some basis for such an interpretation exists in certain tales, and very
obviously so in *Thopas*, but the dangers of such an approach are evident.
Any tale that a modern reader finds unsatisfactory, because of his lack of
the historical understanding appropriate to the reading of the tale, can be
taken as a demonstration of the inadequacy of the narrator, and a means
of ensuring that Chaucer shares the reader's sense of dissatisfaction. The
system can operate on any level to refute or ironise the apparent meaning
of a text: a tale can be demonstrated to be artistically inadequate and
therefore a means of exposing the shallowness and pretence of the narrator in that respect (Man of Law's Tale, Monk's Tale, Squire's Tale); or it
can be shown to be morally inadequate or confused or pernicious, and
therefore a means of further exposing the corruptness of its teller (any of
the fabliaux); or spiritually inadequate with similar effect (Prioress's
Tale, Man of Law's Tale, Second Nun's Tale); or it can be shown to be
ideologically inadequate, thereby revealing the narrow prejudices of its
narrator, and his inability to understand that larger perspective of social
and political conduct that Chaucer shares with his modern reader
(Knight's Tale, Franklin's Tale). The last method has been particularly
fruitful in accommodating Chaucer to particular kinds of modern development in attitudes to war, wealth, government and women.

These, though, are relics of nineteenth-century attitudes, and perhaps less important in the long run than the development of the New Criticism. This approach takes as its basic assumption that literary works are structures in which meaning is embodied in local detail and texture of style and in larger kinds of formal patterning as much as in traditional conceptual content. Its development may be seen as in part prompted by the decay of a common body of moral and social values, and of a sense of the relation of literature to those values. Whatever the explanations of its origins, it has contributed much to the understanding of Chaucer, especially in the work of Muscatine (1957), whose account of the blending and conflict of bourgeois and courtly stylistic techniques has helped to demonstrate the existence in Chaucer's poetry of that kind of 'unresolved dialectic' which is the special need of late twentieth-century readers. Payne (1963) and Jordan (1967) work according to similar principles of stylistic and structural analysis, though to somewhat different effect. Donaldson (1954, 1958, 1970) is difficult to place, because of his elusive and eclectic critical approach, but he has had considerable influence. He will tend sometimes to interpret the narrator *in*, according to the old-fashioned dramatic principle, but then he will interpret him *out* again by ironising the whole act of narration in *The Canterbury Tales*, thus creating, in the same way as Muscatine but by different means, a richly ironic effect of multiple perspectives. The constant questioning of the narrator's role, the constant demand for a critical self-questioning on the part of the reader, are central to Donaldson's reading of the *Tales*, and have had much influence on writers such as Howard (1976) and David (1976) who are principally devoted to a sophisticated kind of dramatic reading.

At some polar extreme stand the 'historical' critics, such as Robertson (1962) and Huppé (1964), whose claim, not unreasonably, is that the *Tales* should be interpreted according to rules that may be deduced from medieval aesthetic theory. In effect, this has meant the application of a rigidly dogmatic reading of the poems in accordance with Augustinian doctrine of Charity and Cupidity. Like the New Criticism, this approach to medieval literature is the product of a particular crisis in modern culture, in this case the crisis of the orthodox conscience, which, finding itself outflanked on every side by what are seen as unsavoury developments in modern society, finds consolation in a dogmatic interpretation of the literature of the past. The exegesis applied to the *Tales* by the 'historical' critics has done much to uncover authentic levels of meaning, but the inflexibility of method and the implied denial of any special mode of understanding that may be appropriate to narrative or other imaginative literature has been a limitation. A more moderate form of 'historical' criticism has been that which goes to literary and scholastic theorists rather than patristic writers for guidance on interpretation: the effect, however, in the work of Allen (1981, 1982), has again been a tendency to prescribe readings on the grounds that other readings are historically unviable. One can understand the attractions of such positivism in the face of the chaos created by the uncontrolled subjectivism of dramatic reading, and of some of the more spurious kinds of New Criticism, but the result again is a loss of necessary flexibility.

A particular consequence of both 'new critical' and 'historical' reading has been the fragmentation of the *Tales* and the decline of the General Prologue. Since a higher order of meaning is sought, and one which does not depend on the cultivation of dramatic illusion, the particular order in which the *Tales* are taken is of no great moment – though exegetical criticism has been pleased to take advantage of the final position of the Parson's Tale and the influential essay of Baldwin (1955). It happens that this fragmentation has coincided with the revised scrutiny of the textual assumptions of Skeat, who provided the model for the edition of Chaucer that has been in almost universal scholarly use (Robinson's first edition of 1933 and second edition of 1957), and the gradual absorption of the repeated message of Manly and Rickert, in their 1940 edition of the *Tales*, that none of the manuscript orders of the *Tales* is Chaucer's. The fullest statement of their case has been made by Blake (e.g., 1981), who goes so far as to suggest that the *Tales*, as a whole work, are virtually inaccessible to criticism. The austerity of such a view is not likely to gain much favour, especially among critics who have the urge to write full-length studies of the *Tales*, and one can see the impetus of the desire to create real unity out of apparent disunity in the work of David (1976), and in more extravagant form in the books on the *Canterbury Tales* by Howard (1976) and by Allen and Moritz (1981).

It will be observed that the vast majority of the critics whose interpretation of the *Tales* has been so far discussed are North American. English critics have tended to be more pragmatic and eclectic in their approach to the *Tales* and have generally attached less importance to the dramatic framework of the *Tales*. They have inevitably been influenced by the techniques of reading developed by the New Criticism, though their employment of these techniques is generally more informal; they have remained impervious to 'historical' criticism, which appears to be an exclusively American phenomenon. The nearest that traditional English criticism offers to a systematic mode of interpretation is in the work inspired by F. R. Leavis, such as that of Speirs (1951), Whittock (1968) and Robinson (1972), though even here the insistence on the serious moral business of poetry as a criticism of life has to allow much to the individuality of the tales and the flexibility of response that they demand; Whittock is also one of the few English critics to give much attention to the significance of the dramatic framework. Apart from these, criticism has been dominated by the mild and humane eclecticism that derives ultimately from the tradition established by W. P. Ker and which is most fully and richly represented in C. S. Lewis (1936) – neither of whom, incidentally, had much to say about the *Canterbury Tales*. There have been individual variations on the themes of this central tradition: in Brewer (e.g., 1973) a special regard for the understanding of the *Tales* that is to be derived from a full account of the social and cultural and literary-historical context in which they stand; in Burrow (1971), Kean (1972) and Ruggiers (1965, an intruder in these English groves) a particular attention to the importance of narrative genre, as well as structure and style, in the analysis of the manner in which Chaucer brought into the *Tales* the preoccupations and dominant ideas of his age; and in Salter (1962, 1983) a readiness to recognise the creative conflict in certain of the *Tales* between traditional materials and the manner of Chaucer's imaginative engagement with those materials, and the emergence of a highly sophisticated and subtle yet interestingly flawed technique from this conflict.

Something has been said here of the general lines of critical approach that have affected the reading and interpretation of the *Tales*. Nothing has been said of the great quantity of valuable work that has been done to make possible a richer understanding of Chaucer's poem through fuller and more enlightened study of its sources and intellectual and literary background, as in the classic study of the General Prologue by Mann (1973). To do so would be to rehearse the matter of the notes to the present book. Nor has much been said of the application to the *Canterbury Tales* of the more modern kinds of theory of literary narrative. This is partly because not much yet has been done in this field, though there are some preliminary surveys in Bloomfield (1981), Ridley (1981), Minnis (1981) and Wetherbee (1981). One could confidently predict, however, that the methods of interpretation so satisfyingly provided for modern readers by this kind of theorising will certainly be visited on the *Canterbury Tales*, and that understanding will be the richer thereby.

APPENDICES

(A) MANUSCRIPTS OF THE CANTERBURY TALES

Manuscripts are listed in alphabetical order by location and, if appropriate, additionally by library and by collection. Manuscripts may be presumed to be complete, or near-complete and defective only by mechanical loss; in the case of excerpts and fragments, the contents are briefly described. Approximate dates of copying are indicated either directly or by the use of conventional symbols. Most of the information is derived from Manly and Rickert (1940, Vol. 1), Brown and Robbins (1943) and Robbins and Cutler (1964), but it has been supplemented and corrected with the help of Jeremy Griffiths, Charles Owen, and others. SC (Summary Catalogue) numbers are given in brackets for Bodleian Library manuscripts.

ENGLAND, SCOTLAND AND WALES

Aberystwyth, National Library of Wales	
Peniarth 392D (the Hengwrt manuscript)	XVin
21972D (the Merthyr fragment, formerly the property of L. C. Simons of Merthyr Maw, Bridgend)	
Three leaves of the Nun's Priest's Tale	c1400
Alnwick, Northumberland (home of the Duke of Northumberland)	
Northumberland 455	XV3/4
Cambridge, Cambridge University Library	
Dd.4.24	XV1/4
Ee.2.15 The Man of Law's Tale, in a religious collection	XVex
Gg.4.27 (Part 1)	XV2/4
Ii.3.26	XV2/4
Kk.1.3 (Part 20) One leaf of the Prioress's Tale in a composite volume	XV2/4
Mm.2.5	XVmed
Cambridge, Fitzwilliam Museum	
Fitzwilliam McClean 181	XV3/4
Cambridge, Magdalene College	
Pepys 2006 *Melibee* and the Parson's Tale form one section of a three-part miscellany	XV4/4
Cambridge, Trinity College	
Trinity College R.3.3 (James Catalogue 582)	XVmed
Trinity College R.3.15 (James Catalogue 595)	XV4/4
Trinity College R.3.19 (James Catalogue 599)	
Extracts from the Monk's Tale combined with extracts from Lydgate's *Fall of Princes* in a fascicular collection	XV4/4

Chatsworth House, Derbyshire (home of the Duke of Devonshire)
  Devonshire MS (sold at Christie's, June, 1974)   XVmed
  Devonshire fragment   Two leaves, fragments of the Man of
    Law's Tale   XV2/4
Glasgow, University of Glasgow, Hunterian Library
  Hunterian U.1.1. (197)   1476
Holkham Hall, Norfolk (home of the earl of Leicester)
  Holkham 667   XV2/4
Lichfield, Staffordshire, Lichfield Cathedral Library
  Lichfield Cathedral Library 2   XV2/4
Lincoln, Lincoln Cathedral Library
  Lincoln Cathedral Library 110   XV2/4
London, British Library
  Additional 5140   XV4/4
  Additional 10340   General Prologue description of Parson
    quoted from memory on a flyleaf in a manuscript of Chaucer's
    Boece   c1400
  Additional 25718   XV2/4
  Additional 35286   XV2/4
  Arundel 140   *Melibee* in a generally didactic miscellany   XVmed
  Egerton 2726   XV2/4
  Egerton 2863   XV2/4
  Egerton 2864   XV3/4
  Harley 1239   Knight's Tale, Man of Law's Tale, Wife of Bath's
    Tale, Clerk's and Franklin's Tales, with *Troilus*   XV3/4
  Harley 1704   Prioress's Tale in a miscellany of prose and verse   XV3/4
  Harley 1758   XVmed
  Harley 2251   Prioress's Tale in a large miscellany   XV3/4
  Harley 2382   Prioress's Tale and Second Nun's Tale in a
    religious miscellany   XV4/4
  Harley 5908   One leaf of the Clerk's Tale   XV2/4
  Harley 7333   XVmed
  Harley 7334   XV1/4
  Harley 7335   XV3/4
  Lansdowne 851   XV1/4
  Royal 17.D.xv   XV3/4
  Royal 18.C.ii   XV2/4
  Sloane 1009   *Melibee* in a collection of religious pieces   XV4/4
  Sloane 1685   XV2/4
  Sloane 1686   XV4/4
London, Royal College of Physicians
  Royal College of Physicians 13   XV3/4
London, Sion College
  Sion College Arch.L.40.2/E.23   Clerk's, Wife of Bath's, Friar's

and Summoner's Tales c1475
Longleat House, Wiltshire (home of the marquess of Bath)
  Longleat 29   Parson's Tale in a miscellany of religious verse and
    prose c1425
  Longleat 257   Knight's Tale and Clerk's Tale in a 'romance'
    collection XV3/4
Manchester, Chetham's Library
  Chetham 6709   Prioress's Tale and Second Nun's Tale, copied
    from Caxton (1484) in a collection of saints' lives 1490
Manchester, University of Manchester, John Rylands Library
  Manchester (Rylands) English 63   Two leaves of the Miller's
    Tale, forming one of the two fragments (see Philadelphia,
    Rosenbach) of the 'Oxford' manuscript XVmed
  Manchester (Rylands) English 113 1483–5
Oxford, Bodleian Library
  Barlow 20 (SC 6420) XV3/4
  Bodley 414 (SC 27880) XV3/4
  Bodley 686 (SC 2527) XV2/4
  Douce d.4 (SC 21981)   A single leaf of the General Prologue XV3/4
  Hatton Donat.1 (SC 4138) XVmed
  Laud Misc.600 (SC 1476) XV2/4
  Laud Misc.739 (SC 1234) XV4/4
  Rawlinson poet.141 (SC 14635) XVmed
  Rawlinson poet.149 (SC 14641) XV3/4
  Rawlinson poet.223 (SC 14714) XVmed
  Rawlinson C.86 (SC 11951)   Clerk's Tale and part of the
    Prioress's Tale in a fascicular collection XV4/4
  Selden Arch.B.14 (SC 3360) XV3/4
Oxford, Christ Church
  Christ Church 152 XV3/4
Oxford, Corpus Christi College
  Corpus Christi College 198 c1410–20
Oxford, New College
  New College D.314 XV3/4
Oxford, Trinity College
  Trinity College Arch.49 1461–83
Petworth, Sussex (home of Lord Leconfield)
  Petworth 7 c1425
Stonyhurst College, Lancashire
  Stonyhurst B.XXIII   *Melibee* in a collection of religious
    pieces XVmed
FRANCE
  Paris, Bibliothèque Nationale
    B.N. fonds anglais 39 1422–36

ITALY
  Naples, Royal Library
    Naples, Royal Library XIII.B.29   Clerk's Tale in a romance
      collection   1457
JAPAN
  Tokyo, private collection of Professor Toshiyuki Takamiya
    Takimiya 8 (formerly the Delamere MS)   XV3/4
SWITZERLAND
  Geneva (Coligny), Bibliotheca Bodmeriana
    Bodmer Library (formerly Phillipps 8136)   XV3/4
UNITED STATES
  Austin, Texas, University of Texas
    University of Texas Humanities Research Center MS 46
      Two fragments, each of 12 consecutive leaves, containing (a)
      the Pardoner's Tale (part), Shipman's Tale, Prioress's Tale,
      Thopas and *Melibee* (part), (b) the latter half of the Parson's
      Tale. Formerly Phillipps 6570 (later Rosenbach 159, later
      Louis H. Silver Collection MS 1)   XV3/4
    University of Texas Humanities Research Center MS 143
      (formerly the Cardigan MS)   XV3/4
  Chicago, University of Chicago Library
    Chicago 564 (formerly McCormick)   XVmed
  New York, Columbia University Library
    Plimpton Collection 253 (formerly Phillipps 9970)
      Two leaves containing fragments of the Merchant's and
      Squire's Tales   XV2/4
  New York, Pierpont Morgan Library
    Morgan M.249   XVmed
  Philadelphia, Rosenbach Collection
    Rosenbach 1084/1 (formerly 157; formerly Phillipps 8137)   XV2/4
    Rosenbach 1084/2 (formerly 158)   Eleven leaves containing
      portions of the Reeve's Tale, Man of Law's Tale, Squire's
      Tale, Canon's Yeoman's Tale, *Thopas* and Parson's Tale,
      forming one of the two fragments (see Manchester) of the
      'Oxford' manuscript   XVmed
  Princeton, New Jersey, Princeton University
    Princeton University Library
      MS 100 (formerly the Helmingham MS)   c1425 (part)
                                                                    +c1455 (part)
    San Marino, California
    Huntington Library E1.26.C.9 (the Ellesmere MS)   XVin
    Huntington Library HM 140 (formerly Phillipps 8299)
      Clerk's Tale in a collection of Chaucer and Lydgate pieces,
      mainly religious   XV3/4

Huntington Library HM 144   *Melibee* and Monk's Tale in a
mainly religious miscellany   XV4/4

The following manuscripts are sometimes listed as containing the *Canterbury Tales*, or part thereof, but are not included above:
 Oxford, Bodleian Library, Ashmole 45, Part 3 (SC 6928)
  Contains a 17th c. copy of the Cook's Tale
 Oxford, Bodleian Library, Douce 170 (SC 21744)
  A 17th c. transcript of the *Tales*

(B) PRINCIPAL EDITIONS OF THE CANTERBURY TALES

1478   Caxton, William, [*The Canterbury Tales*]
1484   Caxton, William, [*The Canterbury Tales*]
1492   Pynson, Richard, [*The Canterbury Tales*]
1498   Wynkyn de Worde, *The boke of Chaucer named Caunterbury tales*
1526   Pynson, Richard, *Here begynneth the boke of Caunterbury tales dilygently and truely corrected and newly printed*. Part 3 of an edition of the works.
1532   Thynne, William, *The Workes of Geffray Chaucer newly printed, with dyuers workes whiche were neuer in print before.*
1542   Thynne, William, *The workes of Geffray Chaucer newly printed, with dyuers workes whych were neuer in print before.*
1545   Thynne, William, *The workes of Geffray Chaucer newly printed, with dyuers workes whiche were neuer in print before.*
1561   Stow, John, *The workes of Geffrey Chaucer, newly printed with diuers addicions, whiche were neuer in print before.*
1598   Speght, Thomas, *The Workes of our Antient and Lerned English Poet, Geffrey Chavcer, newly Printed.*
1602   Speght, Thomas, *The Workes of Ovr Ancient and learned English Poet, Geffrey Chavcer, newly Printed.*
1687   Speght, Thomas, *The Works of our Ancient, Learned, & Excellent English Poet, Jeffrey Chaucer.*
1721   Urry, John, *The Works of Geoffrey Chaucer.*
1775   Tyrwhitt, Thomas, *The Canterbury Tales of Chaucer*, 4 vols. (London: T. Payne, 1775), with the addition of a 5th volume (Glossary) in 1778.
1847   Wright, Thomas, *The Canterbury Tales of Geoffrey Chaucer*, 3 vols., being Vols. 24–26 of the Percy Society's *Early English Poetry, Ballads, and Popular Poetry of the Middle Ages* (vols. 1 and 2, 1847, some copies 1848; vol. 3, 1851).
1868–77 Furnivall, Frederick J., *A Six-Text Print of Chaucer's Canterbury Tales in parallel columns*, Chaucer Society, series 1, no. 1, 14, 15, 23, 30, 31, 37, 49; series 2, no. 3. Diplomatic prints of Ellesmere, Hengwrt, Gg.4.27, Corpus 198, Lansdowne 851 and Petworth.

1894   Skeat, Walter W., *The Complete Works of Geoffrey Chaucer*, 6 vols. (Oxford: Clarendon Press).

1898   Pollard, Alfred W., *et al.*, *The Works of Geoffrey Chaucer*, The Globe Edition (London: Macmillan).

1928   Manly, John Matthews, *The Canterbury Tales, by Geoffrey Chaucer* (London: Harrap). Selected tales.

1933   Robinson, F. N., *The Poetical Works of Chaucer* (Boston: Houghton Mifflin; London: Oxford University Press).

1940   Manly, John Matthews, and Rickert, Edith M., *The Text of the Canterbury Tales, studied on the basis of all known Manuscripts*, 8 vols. (Chicago: University of Chicago Press).

1957   Robinson, F. N., *The Works of Geoffrey Chaucer* (Boston: Houghton Mifflin; London: Oxford University Press).

1958   Donaldson, E. Talbot, *Chaucer's Poetry: An Anthology for the Modern Reader* (New York: Ronald Press Company, 1958). Some tales omitted.

1963   Baugh, Albert C., *Chaucer's Major Poetry* (New York: Appleton-Century-Crofts).

1974   Pratt, Robert A., *The Tales of Canterbury, by Geoffrey Chaucer* (Boston: Houghton Mifflin).

1980   Blake, N. F., *The Canterbury Tales*, York Medieval Texts, second series (London: Edward Arnold, 1980).

1983   Ruggiers, Paul G., and Baker, Donald C., *A Variorum Edition of The Works of Geoffrey Chaucer* (Norman: University of Oklahoma Press), Vol. II *The Canterbury Tales*, Parts Three (The Miller's Tale, ed. Thomas W. Ross) and Nine (The Nun's Priest's Tale, ed. Derek Pearsall).

NOTES

CHAPTER 1 DATE AND MANUSCRIPTS

1 These passages occur, respectively, in the F version of the Prologue to the *Legend*, lines 329–34, 417–30, and in the *Canterbury Tales*, fragment II, lines 45–76, and fragment X, lines 1085–8. (All quotations from Chaucer are taken from Robinson, 1957.)

2 *Legend of Good Women*, Prologue, F version, 417–26, with the two lines in square brackets as added to the G version, 405–16, which otherwise differs only in the bowdlerising change of *holynesse* to *besynesse* (F 424, G 412). In the first of the added lines, I have changed Robinson's spelling 'of' to 'Of', since the reference is clearly to a translation with an English title imitating Latin 'De...' (namely, the *De Miseria Condicionis Humane*: see Lewis, 1978).

3 The stanza is printed in Robinson (1957) as IV.1212a–g. It appears after the revised conclusion in the best manuscripts (e.g. Hengwrt and Ellesmere) and was probably originally taken up by mistake from an imperfectly cancelled draft in the author's copy, the revised conclusion having perhaps been inserted on an added sheet. That the Host's stanza (1212a–g) is to be cancelled is clear from the re-use of its material and phrasing in the Host's words after *Melibee* (VII.1893–4) and from the direct link of new 1212 and 1213. For a full discussion of the matter, see Manly and Rickert (1940, vol. 2, p. 265).

4 This is the view vigorously put forward by Owen in a series of articles and essays, and most fully stated in Owen (1977). Owen's further argument, that it was the Wife of Bath that inspired Chaucer to expand the whole plan of the *Tales* to allow for four tales per pilgrim, and that he began to plan the tales for the homeward journey to include principally hers and those of her successors (see his plan, 1977, pp. 38–9), is highly speculative. For a full statement of the more traditional view, see Pratt (1961). For the 'Marriage-group', see Kittredge (1911–12) and the summary of subsequent discussion in Schoeck and Taylor (1960, p. 158).

5 The added lines (575–84, 609–12, 619–26, 717–20 in Robinson, 1957) appear in Ellesmere and other good manuscripts but not in Hengwrt. See Manly and Rickert (1940, vol. 2, p. 191). This is the obvious but not the only possible interpretation of the textual variation here. See further the discussion of the Wife of Bath's Prologue in Chapter 3 below.

6 E.g. Sunday 3 May in Knight's Tale, I.1463, 2188, and Friday 3 May in Nun's Priest's Tale, VII.3190, 3347. See Robinson (1957, pp. 669, 673–4) for the opinions of early speculators; for recent and more mature fantasy, see North (1969). Eisner (1976) accepts that Chaucer's dates are 'useful only for symbolic purposes' (p. 22).

7 E.g. Giffin (1956), who argues that the Second Nun's Tale was written for presentation to the monks at Norwich Cathedral priory in 1383, and the Man of Law's Tale addressed to merchants who might support the expedition to Castile (in support of Constance) in 1382–3.

8 See Appendix 5, 'Preservation of Texts', in Brown and Robbins (1943, p. 737); also Robbins and Cutler (1965), Appendix D, p. 521. The table gives a figure of 64 manuscripts for the *Canterbury Tales*, which presumably excludes most of the manuscripts containing only excerpts (see Appendix A here). *Piers Plowman* and Gower's *Confessio Amantis* come next, with just over 50 manuscripts each, if one ignores the intervention of Lydgate's *Dietary* ahead of *Piers Plowman*. Latin works, of course, often survive in far larger numbers: there are, for instance, some 672 manuscripts of the *De Miseria Condicionis Humane* (Lewis, 1978, p.3).

9 For instance: the absence of any clear statement of principle or of the assumptions

underlying the analysis of the texts (a defect partly remedied in an important article by Dempster, 1946); the excessive reliance on the techniques of genetic classification through agreement in error, where the evidence of significant error and the non-evidence of coincidental error (or 'convergent variation') are often conflated; and the tendency to treat shifts in textual affiliation in terms of individual tales rather than in terms of blocks of text lost and replaced through mechanical causes (e.g. loss of leaves or quires).

10 See Manly and Rickert (1940, vol. 2, pp. 41–2), and the chronological list of manuscripts, p. 48, which shows eleven manuscripts from before 1430. Dempster (1946) questions the absolute value placed on this group of manuscripts (p. 413), and of course there are occasional exceptions to the general truth of what Manly says. But I have found it borne out in my own work on the Nun's Priest's Tale for the Variorum Chaucer (Pearsall, 1983).

11 Most of these examples are taken from the Nun's Priest's Tale and will be found further discussed in my edition of that tale (Pearsall, 1983). A convenient source for comparison of Hengwrt (Hg) and Ellesmere (El) is Ruggiers (1979), which provides a full collation from El beside the transcription of Hg.

12 The scrupulous care for the correct grammatical use of final -e is a notable feature of Hengwrt, and of course a vital element in Chaucer's metrical technique. Here, as elsewhere, Hengwrt can be shown to be very close to what Chaucer must have written. Ellesmere's handling of final -e is good, but not so secure. These matters are dealt with in an article by Burnley (1982) which, incidentally, along with the important earlier essays of Donaldson (1948) and Samuels (1972), demonstrates further, if demonstration were needed, that the proponents of the 'non-metrical' Chaucer (one who did not sound final -e and who wrote a looser, rhythmical, predominantly four-stress line), such as Southworth (1954), are wrong. Evidence of the further authority of Hengwrt as a witness to Chaucer's orthography is given by Samuels (1983).

13 For a detailed description of Hengwrt, and an account of the information to be derived from the physical evidence of the manuscript concerning the stages of copying, see the Introduction by Doyle and Parkes to Ruggiers (1979).

14 That the scribe is one and the same is demonstrated, on the basis of orthographical evidence, by Samuels (1983). Samuels (p. 61) suggests tentative dates: c.1402–4 for Hengwrt, and 1410–12 for Ellesmere.

15 There has been some dispute about this: Manly and Rickert (1940) certainly held that there was quite extensive circulation of tales or fragments from the *Canterbury Tales* before 1400 (see Dempster, 1946, pp. 387–90), and Benson (1981, pp. 109–10) agrees, but Tatlock (1935, pp. 104–6) and Blake (1979, pp. 2–3) argue against such circulation. It seems, however, unlikely that Chaucer would have kept the whole thing to himself for so many years, and he does tell his friend Bukton to 'rede' about the Wife of Bath, as mentioned above. See Chapter 7, below.

16 On the order of the *Tales* as represented in the manuscripts and as presumed to be intended by Chaucer, see Tatlock (1935), Manly and Rickert (1940, vol. 2, pp. 475–94), Dempster (1946; 1948; 1949; 1953), Lawrence (1950), Pratt (1951), Donaldson (1970b), Blake (1981b), Benson (1981).

17 The pilgrim Chaucer's 'second chance' (VII.926–35), and the similar offer made to the Monk (VII.2805), are not presented as anything other than special 'dramatic' privileges, whereas the Cook, at the end of the late-developed fragment I, seems to assume that he will be telling a later tale (I.4358–62). In fragment IX the Cook is introduced as if for the first time, another unadjusted discrepancy.

18 See Manly and Rickert (1940, vol. 2, p. 95; vol. 3, p. 423). The discrepancy in numbering has provoked a number of other explanations, conveniently summarised in Eckhardt (1975), whose own explanation – that the discrepancy is real ('the text' is sacrosanct, of course) and was intended by Chaucer as ironic mockery of the narrator's

glib certainty – is not the least ingenious. A thorough reappraisal of all the evidence by Brosnahan (1981–2) concludes that the half-line is scribal.

19 It might be thought that the reference in the first line of Fragment X to the completion of the Manciple's Tale indicates that IX and X are really one group. But the reading 'Manciple' (written over an erasure in Hengwrt) is possibly editorial, and of course there is nothing very satisfactory about a link between fragments which allows at least six hours (see IX.16, X.5) for the telling of the Manciple's Tale.

20 See the charts of the 'Order of Tales' in Manly and Rickert (1940), in vol. 2 on unnumbered pages following p. 494.

21 In an important essay, Doyle and Parkes (1978) argue that Ellesmere, though by the same scribe, is not based directly on Hengwrt (p. 186). On the evidence of text, however, Ellesmere is certainly very closely related to Hengwrt, and on the evidence of tale order it must be derived from something approximate: see Dempster (1949, pp. 1138–9) and Blake (1979, pp. 14–18). Owen (1982) uses the marginal glosses as further evidence that Ellesmere is derived from Hengwrt.

22 For Ellesmere as a *compilatio*, see Doyle and Parkes (1978, pp. 190–1); also Parkes (1976, p. 130). Many of the Latin glosses are certainly not attributable to Chaucer (e.g. the gloss 'Petrus Comestor' in both Hg and El at Nun's Priest's Tale VII.3209, which completely misses the comic point of the line), but others, especially sequences of quotations from acknowledged Latin sources, may well derive from Chaucer's copy. On the glosses generally, see Manly and Rickert (1940, vol. 3, pp. 483–527) and, for their comments on the possible authenticity of some glosses, pp. 525–7. For a persuasive argument that some glosses are genuine 'authorial memoranda', see Silvia (1965); and likewise Caie (1975–6). For the argument that the glosses to the Clerk's Tale go back to Chaucer, see Dempster (1943–4); and for similar argument concerning the glosses to the Man of Law's Tale, see Lewis (1967).

23 This is the scheme devised by Furnivall, widely known in the form adopted, with some variations, in French (1947, pp. 197–8). It does not allow for the complications of a possible return journey, though Bradshaw had raised the issue, and it has not been neglected by later writers, such as Owen (1977).

24 It was used by Furnivall in the Six-Text edition and has therefore been extremely influential. Manly and Rickert (1940) follow it, and it is supported by Pratt (1951) in an important article. Robinson (1957) provides a dual line-numbering system for Fragment VII (B^2).

25 The sequence II–VII is in one manuscript only, Selden B.14, notorious for its unreliability. The Bradshaw shift is rejected by Baker (1962), Donaldson (1970b) and Benson (1981). They argue that Ellesmere represents not merely the best but Chaucer's order.

26 Most of the manuscripts that have picked up the Epilogue have 'Somnour' in II.1179, though a few, recognising that this is impossible, have 'Squyer', since the Squire's Tale is one of those that begins a fragment (though the language of II.1178–90, and the tone of the promised story, are spectacularly inappropriate for the Squire's Tale). Only the Selden MS has 'Shipman'.

CHAPTER 2 PLAN AND ORDER

1 These unadjusted discrepancies, and the general evidence of stratification, are discussed at length in Chapter 1 above. It follows, of course, that the present 'ending' of the *Tales*, with the pilgrims arriving, presumably, at Canterbury (X.48–51), was intended to be superseded.

2 For confirmation of the accuracy of Chaucer's numbering of the pilgrims, 'Wel nyne and twenty in a compaignye' (I.24), see note 18 to Chapter 1 above.

3 See the *Siege of Thebes* (ed. Erdmann and Ekwall, 1911, 1920), lines 322–4, 1044–60, 4522–4, and cf. 2667, 3401–5, 4420–5; *The Tale of Beryn* (ed. Furnivall and Stone, 1909). The two poems are discussed further in Chapter 7 below. Chaucer's sense of group activity, as Howard (1976, pp. 169–71) points out, is almost entirely of spiteful quarrelling and teasing, but this may be, not because he wants to present 'the darker side of group dynamics' (p. 169) and a pessimistic view of human behaviour, but because conflict is a natural and spontaneous generator of tales.

4 Salter (1969, p. 31). Cf. her remarks on the Proem to Book II of Troilus, in Salter (1966, p. 93): 'It seems to spring from a need to say something about artistic responsibility'. By contrast, and with some straining of the natural sense of the General Prologue passage, Taylor (1982b) makes it into an ironic recognition of the manner in which language may be abused if it is treated as a mere reflector of surface realities, and suggests that it affirms 'that Chaucer's view of language is that of a Christian Platonist, and that he aspires toward a linguistic realism [as against nominalism] in which intent informs deeds through the ministry of words' (p. 325).

5 Chaucer takes his cue from *Le Roman de la Rose*, where Jean de Meun apologises in similar ironic terms for words that may seem 'trop baudes ou trop foles', explaining that 'ce requeroit la matire' (ed. Lecoy, 1965–70, lines 15112, 15143). The forceful defence by Dame Raison of her use of words like *coilles* and *vit* (6915–7154) is less relevant to matters of authorial strategy (but cf. Manciple's Tale, IX.210–37).

6 As in Coghill (1949, pp. 94–105, 113–14, 177); compare the more sophisticated presentation of his argument in Coghill (1956, pp. 49–59). See also the chapter on 'auctoritee' and 'pref' in Lawlor (1968, pp. 140–63). For the recognition that 'authority' itself may be equivocal, and the claim that experience and authority ('tradition') are complementary, not antithetical ('Experience, mediated through art, generates tradition; tradition helps us to evaluate experience', p. 110), see Delany (1972). Josipovici (1971, pp. 52–74), who is chiefly concerned with the nature of the fictional illusion and its relation to 'truth', sees Chaucer's poetry as an invitation to inspect the fallibility of both experience and authority. Burlin (1977, pp. 3–22), similarly, sees an increasing questioning of the 'epistemological validity' (p. 22) of the two terms.

7 Lanham (1967) draws attention to the language of 'game' and 'play' in Chaucer (the whole of the *Tales* is a tale-telling 'game') and relates it to game-theory, also role-playing theory, and a way of perceiving human behaviour which is essentially comic: 'Once a poet has become aware of the *poseur* in all of us, indeed that we are little else, it is difficult for him to be other than a comic poet' (p. 24). On the notion of art as game in Chaucer, see also Josipovici (1971, pp. 87–99), Manning (1979), and Olson (1982, pp. 145–7).

8 I am not so much concerned here with whether Chaucer knew the *Decameron* and was influenced by it, though it is almost impossible to believe that he did not or that he did and was not. For a recent discussion of the matter, with full reference to the previous literature on the subject, see McGrady (1977–8). The translation used below is that of Aldington (1930); for the original, see Branca (1976).

9 At one point, after his tale of sodomy (Day 5, Tale 10), he is asked not to sing a rude song, rather as the 'gentils' cry out that they want to hear no 'ribaudye' from the Pardoner (VI.323–4).

10 How he came to hear is of course not explained, but a beautifully disingenuous explanation is offered in a miniature in a mid-fifteenth-century French copy (now Bodleian MS Douce 213) of the French translation of the *Decameron* by Laurens de Premierfait, where Boccaccio is shown sitting outside the gate of a walled garden, busily copying down on a scroll what he hears from inside the garden, where a young man is telling a tale to his nine companions. The miniature is reproduced in Pächt and Alexander (1966), vol. 1, Plate LV (no. 717).

11 There is useful comment on the limitations of the 'dramatic principle' in Hulbert

(1948), Malone (1951, pp. 210–35), Jordan (1967, pp. 118–30), and Allen and Moritz (1981, pp. 7–11: 'Because it [the dramatic principle] is thus so insidious, it needs especially to be put down', p. 11).

12 For the wider literary context in which the practice of 'ironisation' is to be regarded, see Booth (1974). There is a lively defence of Shakespeare from the assaults of the ironists in Levin (1979). On ideological 'appropriation', see Sinfield (1981).

13 As Burrow (1982, p. 80) points out, Chaucer, by this means, also 'blurs the distinction between the fiction of the pilgrimage and the fictions which it encloses', and creates 'one of those rich confusions that he loved to explore'.

14 'It does not matter who the tellers are or what they are like, so long as we are made aware of the fact that they are tellers' (Josipovici, 1971, p. 86). Josipovici emphasises tone and rhetoric, not the personality of the teller, as the means by which we are pulled back 'from participation in the *event* and into a contemplation of the *words*' (p. 85).

15 It is so used in Guillaume de Deguileville's *Pèlerinage de la Vie Humaine*, written in 1330, the work from which Chaucer translated his *ABC* poem in praise of the Virgin; and of course pilgrimage is a dominant image in *Piers Plowman* (see Salter and Pearsall, 1967, Introduction, pp. 41–7). See also Chaucer's poem *Truth*, lines 17–21; Wenzel (1973). There is a useful brief chapter on medieval attitudes to and practice of pilgrimage in Zacher (1976, pp. 42–59).

16 This of course is what is done, tale by tale, and without reference necessarily to any unifying frame, in the work of D. W. Robertson and his followers, as we shall have frequent occasion to remark in the treatment of individual tales. For his general comments on the pilgrimage-frame, see Robertson (1962, pp. 373–4).

17 For some valuable brief comments on 'the border where the exemplary and the imitative meet' in medieval narrative, see Silverstein (1967); also the illuminating discussion of 'Modes of meaning' in medieval poetry in Burrow (1982, pp. 82–118), especially the 'more problematic cases, where the fundamental exemplary relation between story and general truth is itself in question' (p. 112).

18 E.g. Payne (1963, pp. 147–70: the tales are experiments in 'the possibilities of the form' of various genres, p. 162); Ruggiers (1967), where the tales are divided into two broad groups of 'comedies' and 'romances' (p. 48) expressive of principally secular and principally spiritual interests respectively (p. 15); Pearsall (1970), where the tales are discussed under four genre headings – romance, fable, pious tale and saint's legend, and fabliau – corresponding more or less to the categories of subject-matter proposed by Chaucer in the introduction to the Miller's Tale quoted above: 'gentillesse . . . moralitee and hoolynesse . . . harlotrie' (I.3179–80, 3184).

19 See especially Howard (1976, e.g. pp. 192–209, 320–32). The inspiration for this approach is the few pages on 'Gothic Form' in Muscatine (1957, pp. 167–73). For development of the idea, see Jordan (1967). 'Gothic Chaucer' is the title of Brewer's essay in Brewer (1974, pp. 1–32: see p. 4). For some warnings against analogies with the visual arts (and some better examples), see Salter (1969).

20 The quotation is from the excellent brief account of the *Tales* in Harrington (1975–6, p. 190). Hanning (1975) speaks similarly, though not solely in terms of frame versus tale, of two 'polar impulses' in the *Tales*, 'one toward mimetic variety and the illusion of a self-effacing art that reproduces life "as it is", the other toward artistic ordering, on various principles, which shatters the mimetic illusion by making us aware of the artist's power to organize experience for thematic or aesthetic purposes' (p. 23).

CHAPTER 3   SOME PORTRAITS

1 Baldwin (1955), as reprinted in Schoeck and Taylor (1960, p. 20). Baldwin goes on to emphasise the coexistence of persistent secularity of tone with the implication, 'in a

rough and unrealized state', of a divine *sovrasenso* (p. 21). Hoffman (1954), in his excellent account of the duality of impulse in the General Prologue, emphasises more the 'sustained hovering effect' (p. 37). Speirs (1951, pp. 100–2) offers an interesting comparison with the opening of *The Waste Land*.

2   For discussion of the ordering of the portraits, see e.g. Swart (1954), Brooks (1962), Howard (1976, pp. 94–106, 149–57), Morgan (1978).

3   The technique can be examined in the *Ars Versificatoria* of the twelfth-century rhetorician Matthew of Vendôme, printed in Faral (1923, pp. 106–93: see pp. 121–32). See note 4 to Chapter 5 below; also the excursus on 'The "General Prologue" and the "Descriptio" Tradition' in Mann (1973, pp. 176–86).

4   E.g. Kimpel (1953), where it is argued that the narrator of the *Tales* (not just the Prologue) is not presented as a consistent 'character'; Major (1960), where the 'personality of Chaucer the pilgrim' is said to be 'little more than a shadowy extension of the poet himself, put forth and withdrawn to suit the poet's needs' (p. 160); Leicester (1980: 'the voice of the text' is the only reality, p. 219). There is an excellent essay by Stevens (1978) on a closely related subject. For some acute brief comments on the limitations of the idea of the 'fictional version of the author or narrator' as 'a self-consciously contrived projection', see. Norton-Smith (1974, pp. 103–4).

5   See Lumiansky (1956) on Benoit; Patch (1925) on treatises on vices and virtues; Curry (1926) for medical and physiognomical diagnoses of Summoner, Cook, Pardoner, Reeve and Miller; Robertson (1962, pp. 242–8, 253–6) for iconographic analysis of Miller, Prioress, Knight, Monk.

6   An exception should be made for the essay by Morgan (1977), which is clear in its insistence on the function of concrete detail as illustrating the universal validity of the conception that lies behind the portrait, and not as contributing to a sense of 'individuality'. See also the sensible remarks of Gradon (1971, pp. 314–17).

7   *Roman de la Rose*, 12775 (cf. Wife of Bath's Prologue, 1–3); 12734–9, 12894–918 (cf. Prol. 469–79); 13011 (cf. Prol. 409–17); 14047–76 (cf. Prol. 621–6); 14441–507 (cf. Prol. 453–502). There are some perceptive brief comments on Chaucer's adaptation of La Vieille in Muscatine (1957, pp. 204–6) and an excellent extended discussion in Kean (1972, pp. 149–56).

8   Aers (1980) gives a good 'feminist' account of the necessarily limited nature of the Wife's challenge to orthodox views: 'While Chaucer presents her rebellion as real, he simultaneously discloses the complexities involved in opposing dominant social and ideological forms. He dramatizes the affirmation of the established culture in her negation of it, creating an aesthetic representation of the way subordinate groups or individuals may so internalize the assumptions and practices of their oppressors that not only their daily strategies of survival but their very acts of rebellion may perpetuate the outlook against which they rebel' (p. 147). Weissman (1975) speaks similarly of 'Chaucer's profound and sympathetic insight into the effects of antifeminism on the feminine nature' (p. 107).

9   See Carruthers (1979, p. 210). For a detailed account of the Wife's business background and legal position, see Robertson (1979–80). Robertson is much concerned to prove that the Wife is a bondwoman. A rather surprising essay by Weissman (1980–1) develops the association between Bath and bath-houses, and of the latter with prostitution; she thinks of the Wife as a successful 'bathhouse madam' (p. 25).

10 Line 624 seems to be directly inspired by La Vieille's admiring account of the indiscriminate appetite of horses: 'Non pas morele contre morele / seulement, mes contre fauvele, / contre grise ou contre liarde . . .' (*Roman*, 14031–3).

11 For emphasis on the educative function of the homily, see the useful essay by Malone (1962, pp. 484–5). It might be regarded too as a rebuke to the merely superficial

courtly ethic which permitted him to take advantage of an ordinary 'mayde' in the first place, though it is doubtful whether the rebuke should be generalised into a protest by the Wife of Bath on behalf of the middle classes against class-oppression, as Colmer (1973) argues. See also the densely facetious account of the Wife's technique for putting down husbands in Silverstein (1960–1).

12 The 'pun' was first noted, it appears, by Baum (1956, p. 232). The existence of the pun, which has been generally accepted, is made doubtful by the elaboration of the expected musical reference of *burdoun* in the next line, line 674.

13 For the influence of the more general 'confessional' tradition in medieval literature, see the important essay by Patterson (1976).

14 Howard (1976, p. 372). He says elsewhere, 'It is like watching an actor perform whom we have heard backstage boasting and chuckling over his power to make people laugh and cry' (p. 349). The Pardoner Howard has created is in fact a Vice who knows he is a Vice. For a view of the Pardoner as a Vice who knows he is one and is trying to stop being one, see Condren (1973). Aers (1980, pp. 89–106) historicises the Vice as a self-reflexive commentator on the corrupt practices and values of an institution that has someone like himself as part of it.

15 This is the passage that Owen (1977) refers to so suggestively as 'the litany of "I wol"' (p. 174). For a thorough account of the corruption and hypostasis of the will that orthodox theology associated with persistence in evil, see Kellogg (1951).

16 For a particularly good account of the multiple implications of 'death' in the tale, see Bishop (1967); also Robertson (1962, pp. 333–4), Pittock (1974).

17 This is evidently the primary interpretation in the Pardoner's Tale also: see Hamilton (1939). For further discussion of the Old Man, see Owen (1951); Steadman (1964), who sees him principally as a *memento mori*; Hatcher (1974–5), who points out that he represents the horror of what the rioters seek, life without death.

18 Writing to Elizabeth Barrett on 16 November 1845: quoted in Ian Jack, *Browning's Major Poetry* (Oxford: Clarendon Press, 1973), p. 195.

19 Similarly Patterson (1976): 'The tale is, in turn, transformed by the context of its telling from an *exemplum* about avarice into a psychological allegory that reveals the Pardoner as a man in despair' (p. 162) . . . 'Like the sterile quaestor whom he [the Old Man] faithfully expresses, he is condemned to a life-in-death of Cain-like wandering, and in his fruitless penitential yearnings he has descended into a hell of despair' (p. 166). David (1976) gives a similar account of the Old Man, who, he says, 'expresses the other side of the Pardoner's nature, the terrible weariness of carrying his burden of sin' (p. 201).

20 The effectiveness of the contrast between the two tales has been frequently noticed: see note 9 to Chapter 6.

21 This passage (1428–71) received some attention from late medieval and Renaissance alchemists, who considered Chaucer to be an initiate of the mysteries of 'the secree of secrees' (1447). Some modern interpreters such as Damon (1924) believe the same. There is a valuable article by Duncan (1968) on the background of Chaucer's poem in medieval alchemical treatises and discussions of alchemy.

22 The view that the Canon's Yeoman's Prologue and Tale are spurious is that of Blake (e.g. 1981, pp. 107–9). For some discussion of the question, see Brown (1983).

23 That the *Pars Secunda* was originally written for performance before an audience of canons (whence the address to 'chanons religious', 992–1011) is suggested by Manly (1926, p. 246), who also exhumes the older theory that Chaucer wrote it because he had himself had an unfortunate experience with a swindling alchemist. There is a careful defence of the simpler and more persuasive hypothesis that the *Pars Secunda* was originally written as an independent poem, and subsequently adapted to the *Tales* with the invention of the Canon's Yeoman, in Hartung (1977–8).

CHAPTER 4   ROMANCES

1   The classic statement of this interpretation of romance (in relation to Chrétien de Troyes) is in Auerbach (1957), chapter 6: 'The Knight Sets Forth' (reprint, pp. 107–24). For some comment on the relationship between Chaucer and the general traditions of medieval romance, see Stevens (1973) and Lenaghan (1974).

2   The note in Robinson (1957, p. 669) gives examples from Clerk's Tale, IV.812, Merchant's Tale, IV.1967, *Troilus*, i.568, and suggests the influence of Dante, e.g. *Inferno*, xv.46; xxi.82; xxxii.76. It is not beyond possibility that Chaucer intends a hint that the Host has managed the lottery in order to get the result he wants, a sly foretaste of the role of Saturn in the ensuing tale.

3   See Burrow (1971, pp. 54–7, 94–5): 'this Ricardian lack of interest in fighting' (p. 95). There are some long battle-scenes, though, in the alliterative *Morte Arthure*. For further reference to this question, see the account of the General Prologue description of the Knight in Chapter 3 above, and the account of *Melibee* in Chapter 6 below.

4   *Teseida*, Book XII, stanza 84, ed. Marti (1970). Boccaccio explicitly answers the challenge of Dante, who said that no Italian poet had sung of war (*De Vulgari Eloquentia*, II.ii.9). There is a translation of the whole of the *Teseida* by McCoy (1974), and a much better translation of the parts immediately relevant to the Knight's Tale in Havely (1980).

5   *Chiose al Teseida*, VII.50 (ed. Marti, 1970, p. 713). For some account of the background to these ideas, see Robertson (1962, pp. 125–6, 370–3), Schreiber (1975), Hollander (1977b).

6   Frankis (1979) speaks of paganism in *Troilus*, and in the Knight's Tale and Franklin's Tale too (pp. 67–70), as 'a myth of mankind without God' (p. 72). Similarly Robinson (1972), in his account of the Knight's Tale: 'The setting of the poem in the distant past gave Chaucer his opportunity of taking the gods seriously without insulting the church . . . he has used the gods to describe some of the things to be met with in life – which is to say in our life – without depriving the gods of their divinity' (p. 129). Ruggiers (1965, p. 157) speaks of the resemblance between Chaucer and Boethius in their attempt to make a bridge between the meaningless pagan cosmos and the Christian universe in which Fortune is only a name. Cf. also Burlin (1977, pp. 99–100).

7   The Boethian section of Arcite's speech (1251–67) is specially indebted to the *Consolation*, Book III, prose 2, and Book IV, prose 6, and the Boethian section of Palamon's speech (1303–22) to *Consolation*, Book I, metre 5, and Book III, prose 7.

8   Critics have often noted a resemblance between Theseus's tone of voice and that of the narrator: compare, for instance, Theseus's speech here and the narrator's remarks on Arcite's moodiness in 1528–39. But the tone of voice is characteristically 'Chaucerian', and there seems little reason for associating it specifically with the Knight (as does, e.g. Fyler, 1979, pp. 139–47), except in so far as both he and Theseus, as well as Chaucer, may be presumed to be middle-aged (see Burrow, 1971, pp. 53–4, 116–17). For some discussion of the doctrine of 'the Ages of Man' and the conduct appropriate to each in the Knight's Tale, see Burrow (1971, pp. 116–18, 126–7).

9   In her eloquent and forceful account of the poem, Salter (1962) finds Theseus's speech quite incapable of resolving 'the imaginative issues' (p. 33) which have been raised by the poem, particularly 'the spectacle of human life subject to cruel and disproportionate strokes of destiny' (p. 32). She describes the 'basic illogicality' of the speech (p. 35). She extends and develops this view of the poem in Salter (1983, pp. 141–81). Compare the account of the speech in Kean (1972, pp. 41–8): 'Theseus's speech is thus, philosophically speaking, much more comprehensive and closely argued than has sometimes been allowed' (p. 48). Others see the speech as containing but not resolving the opposition of order and disorder which is present throughout the poem, e.g. Fichte (1975, p. 345).

10 Aers (1980, pp. 174–95), sees the speech as the expression of the tyrant's will to rule: 'He will use any portion of any system of ideas which seem to bolster up his own exercise of power' (p. 192). Chaucer wishes to reflect, here and throughout the poem, upon the principle of 'order' of which Theseus is so powerful a representative.

11 See Curry (1960, pp. 139–48). Kean (1972), throughout her long and important study of the Knight's Tale (pp. 1–52), stresses the significance of the new role created for Saturn by Chaucer (pp. 28–35). In the long term, he is a 'composer of strife and a bringer of order out of disorder' (p. 33). In terms of the story, however, and the reader's emotional response to it, his influence is bound to seem, as here, baneful.

12 It is Muscatine (1950) who argues most eloquently, on the basis of the poem's symmetry of organisation, richness of texture and slow narrative pace, that it is 'essentially neither a story, nor a static picture, but a poetic pageant, and that all its materials are organized and contributory to a complex design expressing the nature of the noble life' (in Wagenknecht, 1959, p. 69). For the distinction I make between 'story' and 'argument', see Shepherd's essay on 'Troilus and Criseyde' in Brewer (1966, p. 73).

13 'The whole treatment of the gods . . . shows them not merely as destinal forces, but also as aspects of the behaviour of the human beings to whom they are so closely linked' (Kean, 1972, p. 5). The hints and allusions as to the psychological significance of planetary influences need to be understood, however, as elements in the context of the story, as strands in the thread of argument, rather than as 'the meaning' of the poem, which is how they are expounded in the over-schematic account of the poem given by Brooks and Fowler (1970).

14 For a brilliant demonstration of the significances to be attached to 'locus of action' in narrative, and other elements of spatial setting (with particular reference to Dante and Langland), see Muscatine (1963).

15 Arcite argues that he did see her, as a *woman*, first; that even if he didn't, it makes no difference, since all the usual rules of conduct are swept aside by love (he makes what is usually the bitter recognition of a sad fact into a recommendation for future action, an irony that Chaucer underlines with the allusion to Boethius, Book III, metre 12: 'Who shal yeve a lovere any lawe?'); and finally turns the fable of the two dogs and the bone on its head by declaring its point to be 'Ech man for hymself'. The whole speech (1153–86) is added by Chaucer, and is expressive of 'anarchic appetitiveness' (Norton-Smith, 1974, p. 133). For further analysis of the speech, see Robertson (1962, pp. 106–8) and Brooks and Fowler (1970, p. 136).

16 This is why one might feel hesitant about the promotion of Theseus as the embodiment of the principle of order in the poem, as in Muscatine (1950, pp. 72–3), Halverson (1960, pp. 614–16), Robertson (1962, pp. 260–6), Kean (1972, pp. 21–5, 41–8). On the other hand, one would not wish to accept as an alternative the views of those who see Theseus as himself radically flawed, and guilty of acts of rashness and brutality, e.g. Webb (1947), Underwood (1959), Neuse (1962), Blake (1973), Justman (1978). By contrast, Aers (1980, pp. 174–95) recognises Theseus as the embodiment of the principle of order, but questions, and has Chaucer question, the nature of that order.

17 Cresseid, in Henryson's *Testament of Cresseid*, is trapped on what might seem a fine point of law, and ruthlessly punished; but her 'blasphemy' against meaningless 'gods' comes to be revealed as a symptom of a deeper transgression against her own best self.

18 'Juppiter' is used ambiguously in the Knight's Tale: on the one hand, as the name for the good-natured but rather ineffectual planetary influence (2442); on the other hand, and much more significantly, as the name given to the figurative representative, in the classical pantheon, of the Prime Mover (3035). It is the latter which is referred to here. The separation of Jupiter from the pattern of planetary influences is a part of Chaucer's strategy that makes it difficult to see any systematic correspondence between the

natural (Aegeus – Theseus – Palamon – Arcite – Emelye) and supernatural (Saturn – Jupiter – Venus – Mars – Diana) actors of the poem. There are of course many suggestive parallels, as Everett (1955, p. 168) points out.

19 What Chaucer leaves out here is Boccaccio's description of Emilia's sacrifice of the little white lambs, whose hearts she draws out still warm and beating (*Teseida*, VII.76).

20 There are accounts of Chaucer's debt to the native English tradition in Brewer (1966, pp. 1–38), Kean (1972, vol. 1, pp. 1–31), and Burrow (1971, pp. 12–23). It is Burrow who speaks further of the 'insufficiencies' of English in the late fourteenth century, and of the 'many improvisations and accommodations, ironies and silences', into which Ricardian poets were forced (1971, p. 12).

21 See Pearsall (1964). Similar interpretations have been offered by Neville (1951), who sees a certain gaucheness in the Squire's attempt to imitate his father; Haller (1965); McCall (1966–7). Stillwell (1948) also draws attention to humorous and realistic touches that seem out of place in a romance (especially the opening of part two), but he regards them as signs that Chaucer 'is not altogether at home in Tartary' (p. 179), and that his natural humanity and subtle humour prevented him from maintaining 'the wide-eyed *naïveté* and quaint curiosity required by his theme' (p. 188). He does not associate this with any inadequacy on the Squire's part. Kahrl (1972–3) has given a further twist to the analysis of the weaknesses of the tale, suggesting that they are intended by Chaucer to exemplify and expose the emptiness of the 'new' chivalry that the Squire represents, its concern with mere outward form. Kahrl is satisfactorily answered in a sensible essay by Goodman (1983).

22 Coghill (1949, p. 123). This view has been frequently elaborated, e.g. Pearsall (1964, pp. 90–1), Peterson (1970–1), Duncan (1970–1).

23 For a recent translation of the relevant part of the *Filocolo*, see Havely (1980, pp. 154–61). The version in the *Decameron* (Day 10, Tale 5) is essentially similar.

24 *Guigemar*, lines 19–21 (ed. Ewert, 1944). For general accounts of the Breton lay, see Hoepffner (1959) and Donovan (1969). Beston (1974) gives an account of the form as it was known in fourteenth-century England.

25 See note 6 above, and Frankis (1979). A similar interpretation of the pagan setting in the Franklin's Tale is made by Hume (1972, 1972b).

26 Wood (1970), who devotes some pages (pp. 245–71) to the disappearance of the rocks, concluding that it was a trick, clearly believes that it does matter. For him it is a demonstration of the web of deceit, illusion and self-deception in which all the characters, including the Franklin, are enmeshed. His interpretation of the astrological passage (1273–96) is questioned by Eade (1982, pp. 58–69). It is nice to find the astrological experts disagreeing.

27 As Donaldson (1958) says, in his eloquent account of the tale, 'she promises to be untrue to her own nature if Aurelius manages to rearrange creation' (p. 925). Cf. also Kearney (1969).

28 As Dempster (1937) points out, 'Valeria's glory had consisted in refusing to remarry, Rhodogune's, in killing her nurse, and Bilia's, in never remarking on the smell of her husband's breath' (p. 20). See further, Dempster (1939). Dempster's analysis of Chaucer's work on the *compleynt*, where she shows him sifting three times through the examples in Jerome's *Adversus Jovinianum*, leaves her with an impression of Chaucer as a hasty and casual worker. Morgan (1977b), however, treats the complaint as perfectly serious: 'The organisation of the *exempla* into three clearly defined groups enables him to articulate in a lucid and consecutive fashion the three central moral issues of chastity, fidelity and honour, and at the same time to leave with his audience a disturbing sense of moral conflict' (pp. 93–4). Morgan's opinion that 'mediaeval poetry is distinguished by its moral and not its psychological subtlety' (p. 97) has weight, but his exposition here is complicated, requires a theory of

Chaucerian revision, and ignores the *dramatic* effect of such a very long complaint.

29 This is the argument of Baker (1961). Ruggiers (1965), likewise, considers that the complaint gives a true impression of 'an emotionally distressed woman contemplating the choice of death or dishonor' (p. 233). His excellent account of the tale stresses 'the terrible burden of freedom' (p. 230) which she bears, 'the terrible freedom to choose' (p. 233). Robinson (1972), who similarly sees the theme of the tale as 'the terrifying openness of the bond of love' (p. 197), incorporates the rhetorical excess of the complaint into his interpretation of Dorigen as 'imprisoned in a convention that can't properly express her feelings . . . this is where the guarantees of love have led, to this insufficiency and insincerity' (pp. 192–3).

30 He comments, for instance, on Trollope's use of narratorial digression and aside, 'Such a betrayal of a sacred office seems to me, I confess, a terrible crime': 'The Art of Fiction', in *The House of Fiction: Essays on the Novel by Henry James*, ed. Leon Edel (London: Rupert Hart-Davis, 1957), pp. 23–45 (p. 26). The most famous narratorial intrusion of this kind in Chaucer is *Troilus*, ii.666–79; see also ii.29–35.

31 'Hannah Arendt has some enlightening pages on the nature of promises in her *The Human Condition* [Chicago: University of Chicago Press, 1958, pp. 243–7]. She refers to Nietzsche, who "saw in the faculty of promises . . . the very distinction which marks off human from animal life", and shows how promises give men, who would otherwise be carried along helplessly in the flux of the world, some control over the future by providing "isolated islands of certainty in an ocean of uncertainty"; she shows, also, how mutual promise has always been taken to be the foundation of civilized society'. So Fox (1968, p. 9), explaining why Gawain finds himself in a dead land, in a dead season, seeking his own death, because of a promise.

32 Much of Langland's exploration of the concept of 'patient poverty' is concerned to make the same distinction, though of course he speaks of attitudes to external circumstances rather than to other people. The Clerk's Tale is closer to Langland than the Franklin's Tale.

33 Burrow (1971) draws attention to the ways in which *Thopas* 'represents the vigorous wild stock upon which were grafted Chaucer's other more literary and sophisticated styles' (p. 21), and how many of its characteristic 'minstrel features', such as the address to the audience and the use of superlative epithets and stock phrases, are found elsewhere in Chaucer. 'The poem, where it is bad, is often bad in a strikingly Chaucerian way' (pp. 14–15). See also Kean (1972, p. 61) and note 20 above.

34 This is the view put forward by Manly (1928b), and opposed, with good reason, by Lawrence (1935). Burrow (1984), comparing *Thopas* with a genuine satire on the Flemings, concludes that it is 'essentially a literary burlesque' (p. 55).

35 For the 'accomplished incompetence' of the bob-line in *Thopas*, and the reaction of scribes, see Stanley (1972). Burrow (1971b) notes the occurrence of the bob-line stanzas in association with other features, and concludes that a true second 'fit' begins at line 833. The three 'fits' so elicited have 18, 9 and 4½ stanzas respectively, fitting to the principle of 'progressive diminution' in the poem (p. 57), the dwindling away to nothingness.

CHAPTER 5   COMIC TALES AND FABLES

1 There is a good account of this process in Rowland (1979); see also Brewer (1968). One should remember too the pioneering study of Hart (1908), written at a time when most Chaucer scholars were still delicately side-stepping the question of the fabliaux.

2 The many echoes of 'pryvetee' in the tale (3454, 3558, 3603, 3623), and the obscene pun suggested, whereby the carpenter, in seeking to penetrate 'Goddes pryvetee', loses his wife's, have often been noted, and especially in Neuss (1974).

3 For an excellent analysis of the comic effects created by sprinkling description and conversation with 'clichés borrowed from the vernacular versions of the code of courtly love', see Donaldson (1951). Lewis (1981–2) gives specific examples of the kinds of sources that Chaucer might have borrowed from, such as the poem of *Dame Sirith* and the dramatic *Interludium de Clerico et Puella*.

4 For examples of *descriptio feminae* in the rhetorical arts of poetry, see Matthew of Vendome, *Ars Versificatoria*, I.56, and Geoffrey of Vinsauf, *Poetria Nova*, 536–621, in Faral (1923), pp. 129, 214. For a full account of the convention, see Brewer (1955). The portrait is beautifully analysed by Muscatine (1957, pp. 228–30) and by Donaldson (1951, as reprinted in Donaldson, 1970, pp. 22–5). See also Hill (1973) and Kiernan (1975–6).

5 This description of the Reeve's character is much indebted to Muscatine (1957, p. 200); also to the valuable but variable article by Copland (1962, pp. 24–31). Garbáty (1973–4) makes the interesting point that Norfolk men, since they formed a large part of the immigrant population in the period, would in any case 'have been regarded with a jaundiced eye' by Londoners (p. 4).

6 Baugh (1937) suggests that the tale was originally designed for the Friar. This suggestion, along with the earlier theory of Manly (1928, pp. 596, 624) that it was written for the Monk, is refuted by Dempster (1938). Manly's theory has been more recently exhumed by Garbáty (1969–70).

7 There has been some debate about the tone of the mock-encomium. Baugh (1937, pp. 18–19) did actually argue that it was not ironical at all, and Jordan (1967) argues that the voice is that of 'the familiar Chaucerian innocent' (p. 138). Sedgewick (1948) detects a complex interweaving of 'four different voices' (p. 341). Pittock (1967) describes well how the discourse on marriage can be seen 'to throw the tale out of moral gear from the beginning' (p. 35). There is a thorough analysis of the problems of tone and voice in the mock-encomium by Benson (1979–80). He draws attention especially to the strongly marked elements of argument and exhortation, with 'strong indications of a sermon model', in the rhetoric of the passage (p. 57), and considers it in the end 'a tantalizing anomaly' (p. 59) within the tale.

8 One of the consequences of the imaginative intensity of the Merchant's Tale is the effect it has in fusing and charging with ironic implication certain repetitions of words and images through the poem. Note here the later picking-up of 'warm wex' (2117), first remarked by Dempster (1932, p. 51), and cf. 'worth a bene' (1263, 1854), 'laurer' (1466, 2037), 'twiste' (2005, 2349).

9 'The poem is thus constantly affronting our aesthetic sense, bringing our emotions into play in such a way as to confuse our moral judgment, which finds no safe place to settle' (Donaldson, 1970, pp. 34–5). Burrow (1957) speaks too of the cruelty of the close-up technique, and the unexpected engagement of the moral sense (p. 199). Schleusener (1979–80) describes the way in which the reader is implicated in the poem's meanness.

10 See the analysis by Donaldson (1970, pp. 40–1). Burnley (1976) regards the description of the marriage-service as the core of a network of related words and images which create 'a deliberate scheme of association by which the significance of marriage in Christian doctrine is juxtaposed with its reality in the case of May and Januarie' (p. 23), and which assert, for 'an audience accustomed to analogical habits of thought', 'familiar positive values ... no less forceful than the impression of negation and amorality often gained by the modern reader' (p. 25).

11 The 'unrelieved acidity' of the tale was first thoroughly explored by Tatlock (1935–6). His view of the tale is substantially that of Muscatine (1957), Donaldson (1970, pp. 30–45) and Brewer (1973, pp. 143–5), of Harrington (1971) and Brown (1978–9), in important essays of reappraisal, and of many others. Dissenting voices have been those of Bronson (1961), who considers that the tale, originally a piece of 'traditional

anti-feminist japery', only became 'impregnated ... with a mordant venom' when it was attributed to the misogynistic Merchant (p. 596); Jordan (1967), who sees 'an extremely varied and discordant mixture of many of the voices which Chaucer habitually uses', and a moral unity behind the aesthetic disunity which provides 'reassurances about the nature of things' (p. 143); and Stevens (1972–3), who, in a persuasive essay, finds principally a 'spirit of bawdry and uncontained merriment' (p. 128). All seem to have missed something in an understandable attempt to inhibit 'dramatic' reading of the tale in relation to the character of the Merchant.

12   Donaldson (1958, pp. 921–3) places some stress on the bitterness and cynicism of the tale as a revelation and implied condemnation of the Merchant and his mercantile values; so does Olson (1961). But David (1976, pp. 179–80) and Stevens (1972–3, pp. 121–5) are effectively critical of such views.

13   For some discussion of Chaucer's unexpectedly favourable portrait of the merchant, and some parallels, see Stillwell (1944), McGalliard (1975), and Scattergood (1976–7). As Copland (1966) says, 'this merchant is as honest and likeable as any man can be who has subordinated his whole life to "th'encrees of his wynnyng"' (p. 19).

14   This aspect of the tale is well analysed by Beichner (1961), though he insists on the presence and consciousness of the Friar-as-narrator throughout. If this view is persisted with, the Friar is inevitably implicated as a further victim of the 'ironies' of the tale: see Lenaghan (1972–3). The perils of such a reading are sensibly avoided in the accounts of the ironies of the tale by Birney (1959) and Richardson (1970, pp. 73–85).

15   The reflection in the poem of the kind of charges brought against friars in anti-mendicant satire of the thirteenth and fourteenth centuries is described by Williams (1953) and Fleming (1966). For the debt to Jerome, see the notes in Robinson (1957, pp. 707–8). For the use of John of Wales's *Communiloquium* in the sermon on Ire, see Pratt (1966, pp. 627–31).

16   The ironies of the tale are well analysed by Birney (1960b) and Adams (1962).

17   For some remarks on the significance of the reference to lay confraternity in the context of the tale, see Fleming (1967–8, pp. 101–5). The general purpose of Fleming's essay, it should be noted, is to add weight to the 'exegetical' interpretation of the tale, and to stress the 'moral urgency' which informs the tales of both Friar and Summoner: 'We have in these two tales an agonizing *tableau* of the profound spiritual crisis of late medieval Christendom' (p. 106).

18   The idea of 'complicity' is taken from a statement by Michael Seidel, in his book, *Satiric Inheritance: Rabelais to Sterne* (Princeton: Princeton University Press, 1979), p. 3: 'The rhetorical, forensic, and moral justification for satire and for the positioning of the satirist against his subject tends to ignore the complicity of the satirist in the degenerate record he formally records'. The difference of course is that Seidel, following a famous essay by Wyndham Lewis, 'The Greatest Satire is Nonmoral', is arguing for satire as 'a subversive deforming mode' (p. 10), where Chaucer's reluctance to take up the traditional positions of the satirist is, in its medieval context, a movement towards a subversive affirming mode.

19   There are shrewd expressions of scepticism concerning the 'dramatic' interpretation of the Nun's Priest's Tale in Harrington (1965), Muscatine (1957, p. 272) and Brewer (1973, p. 132). However, the more modest case, that the tale is appropriate to a *preacher*, is adequately made by Friedman (1972–3).

20   The view of Manly (1926b) that Chaucer is here mocking the practice of rhetoric as such is fully answered by Payne (1963; 1968).

21   The division of opinion, between those who see this passage as confirming the exemplary mode of the tale and those who see it as subverting it, is stark. For the former view, see Robertson (1962, pp. 316–17, 335–6); for the latter, Manning (1960), Burrow (1971, p. 90), Burlin (1977, p. 237).

22 This is the substance of the very influential reading of the tale in Donaldson (1958, pp. 941–2); cf. also David (1976, pp. 23–30), Howard (1976, pp. 283–6), Burlin (1977, pp. 230–4).

23 Hazelton (1963) makes this point much more emphatically (pp. 22–5) in an elaborate essay which perhaps overstrains its central thesis that the tale is 'a parodic version of the romanticized moral fable' (p. 3).

24 'The Manciple sneers at those who can be distracted from empirical reality by language, which creates a bogus reality of its own' (Harwood, 1971–2, p. 268).

CHAPTER 6   RELIGIOUS TALES

1 E.g. in the revised *Manual of Writings in Middle English* (Severs, 1967); also, generally, see the chapter on 'Homiletic Romances' in Mehl (1969, pp. 120–58). For discussion of some particular cases, see Braswell (1965) and Hume (1970). The essay on the Man of Law's Tale by Clogan (1977) is relevant to the question of generic definition.

2 For this distinction between 'literary' and other uses of language, see Burrow (1982, p. 13). It should be stressed that the lack of interest in the imaginative capacities of prose is Chaucer's, and not of course a lack of capacity in prose as such. Devotional writing in Middle English illustrates this well enough.

3 For the fullest statement of this view, see Schoeck (1956). Forceful support is given by Preston (1961). Wordsworth did a modernisation of the Prioress's Tale, commenting: 'The fierce bigotry of the Prioress forms a fine background for her tenderhearted sympathies with Mother and Child'. See *Poems*, ed. John O. Hayden (Harmondsworth: Penguin, 1977), vol. 1, p. 486.

4 E.g. Donaldson (1958, pp. 932–4), Howard (1976, p. 276: her 'frame of mind . . . is deplorable'). For a measured statement of the 'historical' view, see Ridley (1965) and Friedman (1974–5). The eloquent and sensitive account of the tale by Russell (1969) pays no regard to 'dramatic' significances.

5 For the argument that 'sone of Eve', since it echoes the words of the invocation to Mary – 'Hail! to thee we crien, exciled sones of eve' – sung every day by nuns in the anthem *Salve Regina*, is quite appropriate to a Nun, see Gardner (1947).

6 A full discussion of Chaucer's sources and the way he handled them is given by Reames (1978–9 and 1980). The argument in the second essay that Chaucer's retelling shows 'increasing theological pessimism' (p. 40) is interesting, but not a necessary conclusion from the evidence.

7 Whittock (1968, p. 254). Whittock cites the etymologising of the Prologue as a further example of language as a series of 'analogues of transcendental things' (p. 254). An elaborate account of the Prologue as the introductory exposition of the essential 'figural meaning' of the tale is given by Clogan (1972). The idea that the tale exploits the resources of language and imagery to demonstrate the difference between physical and spiritual sight is developed by Collette (1975–6).

8 The Peterborough Psalter is Corpus Christi College, Cambridge, MS 53 (the Crucifixion scene is at folio 15b). There is a reproduction of the Sherborne Missal miniature in Rickert (1954, plate 165).

9 For accounts of such and similar relationships, see Grennen (1966). Other writers have noticed other relationships: Muscatine (1957, pp. 216–17) compares the two passages on blindness, VIII.498–504 and 1412–21; Whittock (1968, p. 252) notes the contrast of 'leveful bisynesse' (VIII.5) and misplaced industry; Harrington (1975–6) contrasts the calm certainty of being in the former tale with the hectic sense of life in flux in the latter; Olson (1981–2) deals with images of purgation, here and in Dante.

10 Sullivan (1953) has a lively account of the humour of the whole speech (lines 39–96), but overdoes the 'dramatic' interpretation. David (1976, pp. 118–34) does not

abandon the dramatic interpretation, but sees the discourse principally as a comic rehearsal of Chaucer's own self-questionings about morality and the proper subject of narrative poetry.

11 Mann (1983) speaks of this 'astonishing vision of the cosmos which presents an unnatural cruelty as fundamental to its structure and operation' (p. 169). She finds the answer to the question of the 'relationship between suffering and a benevolent providence, the apparently cruel operations of omnipotent love' (p. 175), in a series of reversals of apparent power ('enthralled lords', p. 171).

12 The reversal by providence of an apparently irreversible fate is what Curry (1926, p. 187) sees as the theme of the Man of Law's Tale. Wood (1970, pp. 219–34) disagrees both with the technical interpretation of the astrology and the conclusion Curry draws. He argues that the Man of Law gets everything wrong. Kean (1972, pp. 114–22) confirms Curry's general interpretation, as does Bethurum (1979). The astrology is technically approved, at least at one level of understanding, by Eade (1982, pp. 76–82).

13 The distancing effect of traditional rhetorical modes in the tale is stressed by Bloomfield (1972), and noted also by Paull (1970–1). Delany (1974–5), by contrast, considers that the disharmony of mode is a means of directing the reader's attention to other, non-literal, emblematic levels of meaning (pp. 64–7). For the reflection upon contemporary religious values, see Weissman (1979); also Johnson (1981–2): 'Chaucer projects an intentional psychological ambivalence toward the religious ideas in his source and, by implication, his age' (p. 202).

14 This comparison is made by Bronson (1960, p. 112), in the course of his general argument that the dramatic and pathetic treatment of the story exposes its false morality. Spearing (1972, pp. 99–101) elaborates the same comparison, but sees in the 'conflict' between the dramatic and the exemplary, in both Chaucer's tale and the plays (and in biblical parables too), an articulation of the necessary 'tension between the divine law and the law of the flesh' (p. 98).

15 Burrow goes on to speak specifically of the 'equivocal' effect of the Clerk's Tale: 'We hardly know in the end what to make of the story' (1982, p. 115). The classic statement of 'the reader's dilemma', and of the unresolved clash of the 'two worlds' of religious symbolism and dramatic realism, is Salter (1962, pp. 37–65). The view of Sledd (1953–4) is essentially similar. Jordan (1967) locates the 'broken back' (p. 198) of the story, its essential 'narrative . . . and moral discontinuity' (p. 201), in the transition from Part 1 to Part 2.

16 This argument is well developed by Mann (1983): 'Walter is "bounden" to his cruel obsession: appearing to enjoy complete independence, he is in fact helplessly enslaved to his own will. Griselda, in contrast, turns "subjeccioun" into "governance" by the complete absorption of her vow to be obedient to Walter into her own will: [quot. 509–11]. And if Walter is bound by his own will, he is liberated from it by Griselda's patience' (pp. 178–9). Mann also stresses the Christ-like role of Griselda, as does . McCall (1966). His general argument is this: 'By the free and total submission of the human will, the will itself becomes sovereign . . . the final submission, a submission to "death", is the means by which death itself is conquered' (p. 261). See lines 1090–2.

17 There are useful remarks on the particular development, in Ockham, Bradwardine and other fourteenth-century writers, of the theology of God's *potentia absoluta*, in Stepsis (1975–6); but some important qualifications, and a warning against taking Walter as the allegorical representative of such a 'God', in Steinmetz (1977–8).

18 Compare the role of Griselda in relation to her husband in the Clerk's Tale (see note 14 above), and see Lancashire (1974–5).

19 It has been tried, though, as by Howard (1976), who says 'The Physician's Tale

reflects his mentality' in its 'misguided moralism' (p. 334), its shallow and hypocritical sententiousness (p. 336), and its 'callous estimate of human life' – so appropriate to an 'avaricious physician' (p. 337). Whittock (1968) finds the narrator to be 'a bigot with a strong religious and anti-sexual bias' (p. 182), but does not think this a particularly appropriate description of the Physician. For other examples of such interpretation, see Hoffman (1967–8), Hanson (1972–3) and Brown (1981), who calls the tale 'a literary projection of a mind incapable of dealing with causes' (p. 134). Ramsey (1971–2), on the other hand, argues that the tale deliberately thwarts the impulse towards easy moralising.

20   Noted by Speirs (1951, p. 184). For a description of the changes by which Chaucer converts a story illustrative of a moral system of sin and retribution into a touching account of an emotional situation, see Spencer (1934) and Boitani (1976). Donaldson (1958, p. 1102) is rather scornful of the intruded sentimentality.

21   According to Howard (1976), the tale reveals 'the Monk's obsession with power and dignity', his 'moral chaos', and his 'powerlessness' (pp. 280–1). Whittock (1968) sees Chaucer to be mocking 'the Monk's inadequacies as story-teller' (p. 220), though unexpectedly the Monk 'found himself inspired' in retelling Dante's story of Ugolino (p. 222). Criticism of the Monk is considered to be the point of the tale in most modern interpretations, e.g. Berndt (1971, p. 442: the Monk is 'an acedious person'); Burlin (1977, pp. 184–5); Olsson (1978–9: the Monk is a pedantic grammarian, inspired by mere idle *curiositas*).

22   An oddity, by which much in the opening few paragraphs falls very naturally into lines of 'iambic pentameter' (e.g. '... and leften hire for deed, and wenten awey ... rentynge his clothes, gan to wepe and crie. Prudence, his wyf, as ferforth as she dorste, bisoghte hym of his wepyng for to stynte ...' 972–4), is noted by Baum (1946). There is discussion of the prose of *Melibee* in Bornstein (1977–8). Her argument for the influence of the style of the French source (the 'officialese' of its day, characterised by the use of formulaic expressions, long interlaced sentences, polysyllabic words and synonymous 'doublets') is much more convincing than that of Schlauch (1950; 1966) for the influence of the *cursus* of Latin prose.

23   The argument for the topical relevance of *Melibee*, as Chaucer's advocacy of a policy of peace, is put forward by Lawrence (1940), Stillwell (1944b), Scattergood (1981) and Göller (1982).

24   See Wenzel (1971). This is the Latin treatise that he calls *Postquam*. The relation of two other Latin treatises, called for brevity *Quoniam* and *Primo*, both abbreviated versions of Peraldus, to Chaucer's treatment of the vices is more enigmatic: see Wenzel (1974).

25   Patterson (1978) argues, on the contrary, that the work is more coherently structured than other penitential treatises, and that this is Chaucer's doing: 'In his revisions Chaucer has elected to use just those elements from the paradigms of religious writing that will enforce a sense of theoretical cohesion' (p. 340). This ignores what seems to be a real confusion in Chaucer's handling of certain specialised aspects of his source-material; see Shaw (1982).

26   This is the view put forward in a lively, interesting and wide-ranging essay by Kaske (1975). There are similar arguments in Finlayson (1971–2, p. 112: the tale is 'the product of a distinct personality', pedantic, tedious, sarcastic, and preoccupied with sex), Allen (1973) and Aers (1980, pp. 106–16).

27   There are accounts of the critical response to the Retraction in Gordon (1961) and Sayce (1971). The latter gives an excellent account of the tradition of the 'literary confession', but, in placing the Retraction firmly within it, neglects the special effect created by the close connection between the Retraction and the preceding discourse on penitence. A similar criticism might be made of Schricker (1981), who places the Retraction in the context of the endings of Chaucer's earlier poems.

CHAPTER 7 AUDIENCE AND RECEPTION

1 See, respectively, Giffin (1956); the notes in Robinson (1957, pp. 727–8); Baum (1958, p. 221); Manly (1926, p. 246). The reference to 'men of dignitee' in Prioress's Tale, VII.456, is similarly taken by Ferris (1980–1) as an indication that the poem was written for presentation before a great court and church assembly in the chapter-house at Lincoln in 1387.

2 For these allusions, see Brewer (1978, vol. 1, pp. 39, 42, 43). For convenience, the many allusions to Chaucer cited in the following pages are taken from this publication, or, where appropriate, from its predecessor, Spurgeon (1925).

3 Spurgeon (1925, vol. 1, p. 25; vol. 3, part 4, p. 6; vol. 1, pp. 56, 60, 71). For some recent discussion of the significance of this kind of evidence, see Salter (1983, pp. 36–41).

4 See Pearsall (1966, pp. 202–3; 1970, pp. 64–7). For a much fuller discussion, with important qualifying observations ('The fifteenth and early sixteenth centuries, we may surely conclude, showed a much deeper and wider appreciation of Chaucer's art than has sometimes been allowed', p. 237), see Kean (1972, pp. 210–39).

5 Lydgate frequently gives evidence of his knowledge of the Wife of Bath, as noted above, and so do Hoccleve (*Dialogue*, 694–7) and Dunbar (*The Twa Mariit Wemen and the Wedo*). Lydgate refers to several of the tales, including the Merchant's Tale, in *The Temple of Glass* (e.g. 184–5).

6 For accounts of these editions, see Skeat (1894, vol. 1, pp. 27–46), Hammond (1908), Muscatine (1963), Brewer (1969b), Miskimin (1975, pp. 226–61), Brewer (1978, vol. 1, pp. 33–6), Pearsall (1983, pp. 110–20). See also Appendix B below. For the later period, see Alderson and Henderson (1970). For general accounts of Chaucer's reputation during this period, and up to modern times, see Spurgeon (1925, vol. 1, pp. xv–cxliv), Brewer (1966, pp. 240–70), Burrow (1969, pp. 19–23, 33–9, 113–18), Brewer (1978, vol. 1, pp. 1–29, vol. 2, pp. 1–23).

7 The plural form indicates that each portrait was thought of as the 'prologue' to that pilgrim's tale. The thinking is similar to that of the Ellesmere illustrator, and that of modern editors of single tales, who will often place the General Prologue portrait at the head of the tale.

8 'Besides, one gifte hee hath above other Authours, and that is, by the excellencie of his descriptions to possesse his Readers with a stronger imagination of seeing that done before their eyes, which they reade, than any other that ever writ in any tongue' (Brewer, 1978, vol. 1, pp. 138–9).

9 There is a useful account of twentieth-century criticism of Chaucer in Brewer (1969) and, later, in Ridley (1979).

10 The dream was present even earlier to a social historian like Joseph Strutt, who, in his book on the history of 'the Dress and Habits of the people of England', spoke thus: 'The different characters exhibited by Chaucer, in his Canterbury Tales, are drawn with a masterly hand: they are, undoubtedly, pictures of real life, and throw great light upon the manners and customs of the age in which the Poet flourished' (Spurgeon, 1925, vol. 1, p. 502).

BIBLIOGRAPHY

The following titles of journals are conventionally abbreviated:

English Literary History	*ELH*
Journal of English and Germanic Philology	*JEGP*
Publications of the Modern Language Association of America	*PMLA*

The Bibliography is the key to the author–date reference system used in the text and notes. Second and subsequent works by the same author in the same year are designated b, c, etc.

(1) EDITIONS AND TRANSLATIONS

(Editions of the *Canterbury Tales* are listed in Appendix B)

Aldington, Richard (trans.), *The Decameron of Giovanni Boccaccio* (Garden City, New York: Garden City Books, 1949; first published 1930).

Andreas Capellanus. *See* Walsh (1982).

Banks, Mary M. (ed.), *An Alphabet of Tales*, Early English Text Society, Original Series, 126–7 (1894–5). Fifteenth-century English translation of the *Alphabetum Narrationum*.

Beryn, The Tale of, ed. F. J. Furnivall and W. G. Stone, Early English Text Society, Extra Series, 105 (1909).

Boccaccio, Giovanni, *Teseida*, ed. Mario Marti, *Opere*, vol. 2 (Milano: Rizzoli Editore, 1970).

Boccaccio, Giovanni, *Teseida*, trans. McCoy (1974).

Branca, Vittore (ed.), Giovanni Boccaccio, *Tutte le Opere*, 12 vols. (Milan: I Classici Mondadori (1976). The *Decameron* is in vol. 4.

Brunner, Karl (ed.), *The Seven Sages of Rome*, Early English Text Society, Original Series, 191 (1933).

Burrow, John (ed.), *English Verse 1300–1500* (London: Longman, 1977). Includes text of and excellent notes on the Prioress's and Shipman's Tales.

Chichmaref, Vladimir (ed.), *Guillaume de Mauchaut, Poésies Lyriques*, 2 vols. (Paris, 1909; Geneva: Slatkine Reprints, 1973).

Erdmann, A. and Ekwall, E. (eds.), Lydgate, *The Siege of Thebes*, Early English Text Society, Extra Series, 108, 125 (1911, 1920).

Ewert, Alfred (ed.), *Marie de France: Lais* (Oxford: Blackwell, 1944).

Faral, Edmond, *Les Arts Poétiques du XIIe et du XIIIe siècle*, Bibliothèque de l'École des Hautes Études, fasc. 238 (1923; reprint, Paris: Champion, 1971).

Fox, Denton (ed.), *The Poems of Robert Henryson* (Oxford: Clarendon Press, 1981).

Furnivall, F. J and Stone, W. G. (eds.), *The Tale of Beryn*, Early English Text Society, Extra Series, 105 (1909).

Gibbs, A. C. (ed.), *Middle English Romances*, York Medieval Texts (London: Edward Arnold, 1966).

Gower. *See* Macaulay (1900).

Hammond, Eleanor Prescott (ed.), *English Verse between Chaucer and Surrey* (Durham, N. Carolina: Duke University Press, 1927).

Havely, N. R. (ed. and trans.), *Chaucer's Boccaccio: Sources of Troilus and the Knight's and Franklin's Tales*, Chaucer Studies 5 (Cambridge: D. S. Brewer; Totowa, New Jersey: Rowman and Littlefield, 1980).

Henryson, Robert. *See* Fox (1981).

Hoepffner, Ernest (ed.), Guillaume de Machaut, *Oeuvres*, Société des Anciens Textes Français (Paris, 1911).

Langland, William. *See* Pearsall (1978), Salter and Pearsall (1967).

Lecoy, Félix (ed.), Guillaume de Lorris et Jean de Meun, *Le Roman de la Rose*, 3 vols., Les Classiques Français du Moyen Age (Paris: Champion, 1965–70).

Lewis, Robert E. (ed.), *Lotario dei Segni (Pope Innocent III), De Miseria Condicionis Humane*, The Chaucer Library (Athens: University of Georgia Press, 1978).

Lydgate, *Siege of Thebes*, ed. Erdmann and Ekwall (1911, 1920).

Macaulay, G. C. (ed.), *The English Works of John Gower*, 2 vols. (Oxford: Clarendon Press, 1900).

Machaut, Guillaume de, *Dit dou Lyon*, ed. Hoepffner (1911).

Marti, Mario (ed.), *Giovanni Boccaccio, Opere* (Milano: Rizzoli Editore, 1970). The *Teseida* is in vol. 2.

McCoy, Bernadette Marie (trans.), *The Book of Theseus: Teseida delle Nozze d'Emilia*, by Giovanni Boccaccio (New York: Medieval Text Association, 1974).

Musa, Mark, and Bondanella, Peta E., *Giovanni Boccaccio, The Decameron: a new translation of 21 Novelle, Contemporary Reactions, Modern Criticism* (New York: W. W. Norton, 1977).

Pearsall, Derek (ed.), William Langland, *Piers Plowman: An Edition of the C-text*, York Medieval Texts, second series (London: Edward Arnold, 1978).

Piers Plowman. See Langland.

Roman de la Rose. See Lecoy.

Salter, Elizabeth, and Pearsall, Derek (eds.), *Piers Plowman: Selections from the C-text*, York Medieval Texts (London: Edward Arnold, 1967).

Sinicropi, G. (ed.), Giovanni Sercambi, *Novelle*, 2 vols. (Bari: Gius, Laterza & Figli, 1972).

Skeat, Walter William (ed.), *Chaucerian and other Pieces* (Oxford: Oxford University Press, 1897). Vol. 7 of Skeat, 1894 (Appendix B).

Walsh, P. G. (ed.), *Andreas Capellanus on Love*, with English translation (London: Duckworth, 1982).

(2) SECONDARY WORKS

(a) General.

Allen, Judson Boyce, *The Ethical Poetic of the Later Middle Ages: A Decorum of Convenient Distinction* (Toronto: University of Toronto Press, 1982).

Auerbach, Erich, *Mimesis: The Representation of Reality in Western Literature*, trans. Willard R. Trask (Princeton: Princeton University Press, 1953; reprinted Garden City, New York: Doubleday Anchor Books, 1957; first published in German, 1946).

Bakhtin, Mikhail, *Rabelais and his World*, trans. Helene Iswolsky (Cambridge, Mass.: M.I.T. Press, 1965; originally published in Russian).

Benson, Larry D. (ed.), *The Learned and the Lewed: Studies in Chaucer and Medieval Literature*, Harvard English Studies, 5 (Cambridge, Mass.: Harvard University Press, 1974).

Beston, John B., 'How much was known of the Breton Lai in Fourteenth-Century England?' in Benson (1974), pp. 319–36.

Blake, N. F., *Caxton and his World* (London: André Deutsch, 1969).

Boitani, Piero, and Torti, Anna (eds.), *Literature in Fourteenth-Century England: The J. A. W. Bennett Memorial Lectures, Perugia 1981–1982* (Tübingen: Guntar Narr Verlag; Cambridge: D. S. Brewer, 1983).

Bolton, W. F. (ed.), *The Sphere History of Literature in the English Language*, vol. 1: *The Middle Ages* (London: Sphere Books, 1970).

Booth, Wayne C., *A Rhetoric of Irony* (Chicago: University of Chicago Press, 1974).

Branca, Vittore, *Boccaccio: The Man and his Works*, translated by Richard Monges (New York: New York University Press, 1976b).

Braswell, Laurel, '"Sir Isumbras" and the Legend of Saint Eustace'. *Mediaeval Studies*, vol. 27 (1965), pp. 128–51.

Brewer, D. S., 'The Ideal of Feminine Beauty in Medieval Literature, especially "Harley Lyrics", Chaucer, and some Elizabethans', *Modern Language Review*, vol. 50 (1955), pp. 257–69.

Brewer, Derek, *Symbolic Stories: Traditional narratives of the family drama in English literature* (Cambridge: D. S. Brewer; Totowa, New Jersey: Rowman and Littlefield, 1980).

Brown, Carleton, and Robbins, Rossell Hope, *The Index of Middle English Verse* (New York: Columbia University Press, 1943).

Burrow, J. A., *Ricardian Poetry: Chaucer, Gower, Langland, and the Gawain Poet* (London: Routledge and Kegan Paul, 1971).

Burrow, J. A., *Medieval Writers and their Work: Middle English Literature and its Background* (Oxford: Oxford University Press, 1982).

Carruthers, Mary J., and Kirk, Elizabeth D. (eds.), *Acts of Interpretation: The Text in its Contexts 700–1600. Essays on Medieval and Renaissance Literature in Honor of E. Talbot Donaldson* (Norman, Oklahoma: Pilgrim Books, 1982).

Cooke, Thomas D., *The Old French and Chaucerian Fabliaux: A Study of their Comic Climax* (Columbia: University of Missouri Press, 1978).

Coss, P. R., 'Literature and Social Terminology: The Vavasour in England', in *Social Relations and Ideas: Essays in Honour of R. H. Hilton*, ed. T. H. Aston *et al.* (Cambridge: Cambridge University Press, 1983), pp. 109–50.

Curtius, E. R., *European Literature and the Latin Middle Ages*, trans. Willard R. Trask, Bollingen Series 36 (New York: Pantheon Books, 1953; originally published in German, Bern, 1948).

De Sanctis, Francesco, *Storia della Letteratura Italiana*, ed. Benedetto Croce, 2 vols. (Bari: Gius, Laterza & Figli, 1949; first published 1870–1).

Donovan, Mortimer J., *The Breton Lay: A Guide to Varieties* (Notre Dame: University of Notre Dame Press, 1969).

Fox, Denton (ed.), *Twentieth Century Interpretations of Sir Gawain and the Green Knight* (Englewood Cliffs, N.J.: Prentice-Hall, 1968).

Gradon, Pamela, *Form and Style in Early English Literature* (London: Methuen, 1971).

Hoepffner, Ernest, 'The Breton Lais', in *Arthurian Literature in the Middle Ages: A Collaborative History*, ed. Roger Sherman Loomis (Oxford: Clarendon Press, 1959), pp. 112–21.

Hollander, Robert, 'The Validity of Boccaccio's Self-Exegesis in his *Teseida*', *Medievalia et Humanistica*, vol. 8 (1977), pp. 163–83.

Hollander, Robert, *Boccaccio's Two Venuses* (New York: Columbia University Press, 1977b).

Hume, Kathryn, 'Structure and Perspective: Romance and Hagiographic Features in the Amicus and Amelius Story', *JEGP*, vol. 69 (1970), pp. 89–107.

Iser, Wolfgang, *The Implied Reader: Patterns of Communication in Prose Fiction from Bunyan to Beckett* (Baltimore and London: The Johns Hopkins University Press, 1974).

Josipovici, Gabriel, *The World and the Book: A Study of Modern Fiction* (London: Macmillan, 1971).

Langbaum, Robert, *The Poetry of Experience: The Dramatic Monologue in Modern Literary Tradition* (New York: Random House, 1957).

Lawton, Lesley, 'The Illustration of Late Medieval Secular Texts, with Special Reference to Lydgate's *Troy Book*', in Pearsall (1983), pp. 41–69.

Leach, MacEdward (ed.), *Studies in Medieval Literature in Honor of Albert Croll Baugh* (Philadelphia: University of Pennsylvania Press, 1961).

Levin, Richard, *New Readings vs. Old Plays* (Chicago: University of Chicago Press, 1979).

Lowes, John Livingston, *Convention and Revolt in Poetry* (1919; 2nd edn., London: Constable, 1930).

Luttrell, Claude, *The Creation of the First Arthurian Romance: A Quest* (London: Edward Arnold, 1974).

Mehl, Dieter, *The Middle English Romances of the Thirteenth and Fourteenth Centuries* (London: Routledge and Kegan Paul, 1969).

Meiss, Millard, *French Painting in the Time of Jean de Berry: the Boucicaut Master* (London: Phaidon, 1968).

Muscatine, Charles, 'Locus of Action in Medieval Narrative', *Romance Philology*, vol. 17 (1963), pp. 115–22.

Muscatine, Charles, 'The Social Background of the Old French Fabliaux', *Genre*, vol. 9 (1976), pp. 1–19.

Nykrog, Per, 'Courtliness and the Townspeople: The Fabliaux as a Courtly Burlesque', in *The Humor of the Fabliaux: A Collection of Critical Essays*, ed. Thomas D. Cooke and Benjamin L. Honeycutt (Columbia: University of Missouri Press, 1974), pp. 59–73.

Nykrog, Per, *Les Fabliaux: Étude d'histoire littéraire et de stylistique médiévale* (Copenhagen: Ejnar Munksgaard, 1957).

Pächt, Otto, and Alexander, J. J. G., *Illuminated Manuscripts in the Bodleian Library, Oxford* (Oxford: Clarendon Press, 1966).

Parkes, M. B., 'The Influence of the Concepts of *Ordinatio* and *Compilatio* on the Development of the Book', in *Medieval Learning and Literature: Essays presented to R. W. Hunt*, ed. J. J. G. Alexander and M. T. Gibson (Oxford: Clarendon Press, 1976), pp. 115–41.

Patch, H. R., 'Characters in Medieval Literature', *Modern Language Notes*, vol. 40 (1925), pp. 1–14.

Pearsall, Derek, 'The English Chaucerians', in Brewer (1966), pp. 201–39.

Pearsall, Derek, *John Lydgate* (London: Routledge and Kegan Paul, 1970).

Pearsall, Derek (ed.), *Manuscripts and Readers in Fifteenth-Century England: The Literary Implications of Manuscript Study* (Cambridge: D. S. Brewer; Totowa: Biblio, 1983).

Rickert, Margaret, *Painting in Britain: The Middle Ages* (Penguin Books, London: The Pelican History of Art, 1954).

Robbins, Rossell Hope, and Cutler, John L., *Supplement to the Index of Middle English Verse* (Lexington: University of Kentucky Press, 1964).

Robertson, D. W., Jr., 'The Doctrine of Charity in Mediaeval Literary Gardens: A Topical Approach through Symbolism and Allegory', *Speculum*, vol. 26 (1951), pp. 24–49.

Robertson, D. W., Jr., 'Some Medieval Literary Terminology, with Special Reference to Chrétien de Troyes', *Studies in Philology*, vol. 48 (1951b), pp. 669–92.

Salter, Elizabeth, 'Medieval Poetry and the Visual Arts', *Essays and Studies*, vol. 22 (1969), pp. 16–32.

Salter, Elizabeth, *Fourteenth-Century English Poetry: Contexts and Readings* (Oxford: Clarendon Press, 1983).

Scattergood, V. J., and Sherborne, J. W. (eds.), *English Court Culture in the Later Middle Ages* (London: Duckworth, 1983).

Schreiber, Earl G., 'Venus in the Medieval Mythographic Tradition', *JEGP*, vol. 74 (1975), pp. 519–35.

Severs, J. Burke (ed.), *A Manual of the Writings in Middle English 1050–1500*, revised, Fascicule 1: *Romances* (New Haven: The Connecticut Academy of Arts and Sciences, 1967).

Silverstein, Theodore, 'Allegory and Literary Form', *PMLA*, vol. 82 (1967), pp. 28–32.

Sinfield, Alan, 'Against Appropriation', *Essays in Criticism*, vol. 31 (1981), pp. 181–95.

Stevens, John, *Medieval Romance: Themes and Approaches* (London: Hutchinson University Library, 1973).

Stevens, Martin, 'The Performing Self in Twelfth-Century Culture', *Viator*, vol. 9 (1978), pp. 193–212

Tillyard, E. M. W., *Poetry Direct and Oblique*, rev. edn. (London: Chatto and Windus, 1945; first published 1934).

Tuve, Rosemond, *Allegorical Imagery: Some Mediaeval Books and their Posterity* (Princeton: Princeton University Press, 1966).

Vinaver, Eugene, *The Rise of Romance* (Oxford: Clarendon Press, 1971).

Wenzel, Siegfried, 'The Pilgrimage of Life as a Late Medieval Genre', *Mediaeval Studies*, vol. 35 (1973), pp. 370–88.

Zacher, Christian K., *Curiosity and Pilgrimage: The Literature of Discovery in Fourteenth-Century England* (Baltimore and London: The Johns Hopkins University Press, 1976).

(b) *General Studies of Chaucer, and studies of works by Chaucer other than the* Canterbury Tales

Aers, David, *Chaucer, Langland and the Creative Imagination* (London: Routledge and Kegan Paul, 1980).

Alderson, William, L., and Henderson, Arnold C., *Chaucer and Augustan Scholarship*, University of California Publications, English Studies, No. 35 (Berkeley and London: University of California Press, 1970).

Baum, Paull F., 'Chaucer's Metrical Prose', *JEGP*, vol. 45 (1946), pp. 38–42.

Baum, Paull F., 'Chaucer's Puns', *PMLA*, vol. 71 (1956), pp. 225–46.

Baum, Paull F., *Chaucer: A Critical Appreciation* (Durham, North Carolina: Duke University Press, 1958).

Bennett, H. S., *Chaucer and the Fifteenth Century*, Oxford History of English Literature, vol. 2, part 1 (Oxford: Clarendon Press, 1947).

Bennett, J. A. W., *Chaucer at Oxford and Cambridge* (Oxford: Clarendon Press, 1974).

Bloomfield, Morton W., 'Authenticating Realism and the Realism of Chaucer', *Thought*, vol. 39 (1964), pp. 335–58.

Bloomfield, Morton W., 'Contemporary Literary Theory and Chaucer', in Rose (1981), pp. 23–36.

Boitani, Piero, *Chaucer and Boccaccio*, Medium Ævum Monographs, new series VIII (Oxford, 1977).

Brewer, D. S. (ed.), *Chaucer and Chaucerians: Critical Studies in Middle English Literature* (London and Edinburgh: Nelson, 1966).

Brewer, D. S., 'The Relationship of Chaucer to the English and European Traditions', in Brewer (1966), pp. 1–38.

Brewer, D. S., 'Images of Chaucer 1386–1900', in Brewer (1966), pp. 240–70.

Brewer, D. S., 'The Criticism of Chaucer in the Twentieth Century', in Cawley (1969), pp. 3–28.

Brewer, D. S. (ed.), *Geoffrey Chaucer, The Works 1532*, facsimile, with supplementary material from the editions of 1542, 1561, 1598 and 1602 (London: Scolar Press, 1969b).

Brewer, D. S., *Chaucer*, 3rd edn. (London: Longman, 1973). There were earlier editions in 1953 and 1960.

Brewer, D. S., 'Honour in Chaucer', *Essays and Studies*, vol. 26 (1973b), pp. 1–19.

Brewer, Derek (ed.), *Writers and their Background: Geoffrey Chaucer* (London: G. Bell & Sons, 1974).

Brewer, Derek (ed.), *Chaucer: The Critical Heritage*, 2 vols. (London: Routledge and Kegan Paul, 1978).

Brewer, Derek, 'The Arming of the Warrior in European Literature and Chaucer', in Vasta and Thundy (1979), pp. 221–43.

Bronson, Bertrand H., *In Search of Chaucer* (Toronto: University of Toronto Press, 1969).

Burlin, Robert B., *Chaucerian Fiction* (Princeton: Princeton University Press, 1977).

Burnley, David, 'Inflexion in Chaucer's Adjectives', *Neuphilologische Mitteilungen*, vol. 83 (1982), pp. 169–77.

Burrow, J. A. (ed.), *Geoffrey Chaucer: A critical anthology* (Harmondsworth: Penguin, 1969).

Cawley, A. C. (ed.), *Chaucer's Mind and Art* (Edinburgh and London: Oliver and Boyd, 1969).

Coghill, Nevill, *The Poet Chaucer*, Home University Library of Modern Knowledge, no. 185 (London: Oxford University Press, 1949).

350 *Canterbury Tales*

Coghill, Nevill, *Geoffrey Chaucer*, Writers and their Work, no. 79 (London: Longmans, Green & Co. for the British Council, 1956).

Crow, Martin M., and Olson, Clair C., *Chaucer Life-Records* (Oxford: Clarendon Press, 1966).

Curry, Walter Clyde, *Chaucer and the Mediaeval Sciences* (Oxford: Oxford University Press, 1926; 2nd edn., revised and enlarged, New York: Barnes and Noble, 1960).

David, Alfred, *The Strumpet Muse: Art and Morals in Chaucer's Poetry* (Bloomington and London: Indiana University Press, 1976).

Delany, Sheila, *Chaucer's House of Fame: The Poetics of Skeptical Fideism* (Chicago and London: University of Chicago Press, 1972).

Dempster, Germaine, *Dramatic Irony in Chaucer*, Stanford University Publications in Language and Literature, vol. 4, no. 3 (Stanford: Stanford University Press, 1932).

Diekstra, F., 'Chaucer's Way with his Sources: Accident into Substance and Substance into Accident', *English Studies*, vol. 62 (1981), pp. 215–36.

Donaldson, E. Talbot, 'Chaucer's Final -e', *PMLA*, vol. 63 (1948), pp. 1101–24.

Donaldson (1958). *See* Appendix B.

Donaldson, E. Talbot, *Speaking of Chaucer* (London: The Athlone Press, 1970).

Donaldson, E. Talbot, 'Medieval Poetry and Medieval Sin', in Donaldson (1970), pp. 164–74.

Eade, J. C., ' "We ben to lewed or to slowe": Chaucer's Astronomy and Audience Participation', *Studies in the Age of Chaucer*, vol. 4 (1982), pp. 53–85.

Economou, George D. (ed.), *Geoffrey Chaucer: A collection of original articles* (New York: McGraw Hill, 1975).

Eisner, Sigmund, 'Chaucer's Use of Nicholas of Lynn's Calendar', *Essays and Studies*, vol. 29 (1976), pp. 1–22.

Elbow, Peter, *Oppositions in Chaucer* (Middletown, Connecticut: Wesleyan University Press, 1973).

Everett, Dorothy, 'Some Reflections on Chaucer's "Art Poetical" ', in her *Essays on Middle English Literature*, ed. Patricia Kean (Oxford: Clarendon Press, 1955), pp. 149–74.

Frankis, John, 'Paganism and Pagan Love in *Troilus and Criseyde*', in Salu (1979), pp. 57–72.

French, Robert D., *A Chaucer Handbook* (New York: Appleton-Century-Crofts, 1st edn., 1927; 2nd edn., 1947).

Fyler, John M., *Chaucer and Ovid* (New Haven and London: Yale University Press, 1979).

Giffin, Mary, *Studies on Chaucer and his Audience* (Hull, Quebec: Editions L'Eclair, 1956).

Göller, K.-H., 'War and Peace in the Works of Chaucer and his Contemporaries', *Veröffentlichungen der Universität Innsbruck*, vol. 137 (1982), pp. 213–22.

Hammond, Eleanor Prescott, *Chaucer: A Bibliographical Manual* (New York: Macmillan, 1908).

Hanning, Robert W., 'The Theme of Art and Life in Chaucer's Poetry', in Economou (1975), pp. 15–36.

Hazelton, Richard, 'Chaucer and Cato', *Speculum*, vol. 35 (1960), pp. 357–80.

Jordan, Robert M., *Chaucer and the Shape of Creation: The Aesthetic Possibilities of Inorganic Structure* (Cambridge, Mass.: Harvard University Press, 1967).

Kean, P. M., *Chaucer and the Making of English Poetry*, 2 vols. (London: Routledge and Kegan Paul, 1972), Vol. I: *Love Vision and Debate*, Vol. II: *The Art of Narrative*. All references are to Vol. II, unless otherwise specified.

Kittredge, George Lyman, *Chaucer and his Poetry* (Cambridge, Mass.: Harvard University Press, 1951).

Knight, Stephen, *rymyng craftily: Meaning in Chaucer's Poetry* (Sydney: Angus and Robertson, 1973).

Kolve, V. A., 'Chaucer and the Visual Arts', in Brewer (1974), pp. 290–320.

Lanham, R. A., 'Game, Play, and High Seriousness in Chaucer's Poetry', *English Studies*, vol. 48 (1967), pp. 1–24.

Lawlor, John, *Chaucer* (London: Hutchinson University Library, 1968).

Lenaghan, R. T., 'The Clerk of Venus: Chaucer and Medieval Romance', in Benson (1974), pp. 31–43.

Loomis, Laura Hibbard, 'Chaucer and the Breton Lays of the Auchinleck Manuscript', *Studies in Philology*, vol. 38 (1941), pp. 14–33.

Malone, Kemp, *Chapters on Chaucer* (Baltimore: The Johns Hopkins Press, 1951).

Manly, John Matthews, *Some New Light on Chaucer* (London: Bell, 1926).

Manly, John Matthews, 'Chaucer and the Rhetoricians', *Proceedings of the British Academy*, vol. 12 (1926b), pp. 95–113.

Manning, Stephen, 'Rhetoric, Game, Morality, and Geoffrey Chaucer', *Studies in the Age of Chaucer*, vol. 1 (1979), pp. 105–18.

McCall, John P., 'Chaucer's May 3', *Modern Language Notes*, vol. 76 (1961), pp. 201–5.

McGrady, Donald, 'Chaucer and the *Decameron* Reconsidered', *Chaucer Review*, vol. 12 (1977–8), pp. 1–26.

Mehl, Dieter, 'Chaucer's Audience', *Leeds Studies in English*, new series, vol. 10 (1978), pp. 58–73.

Minnis, Alastair J., 'Chaucer and Comparative Literary Theory', in Rose (1981), pp. 53–69.

Miskimin, Alice S., *The Renaissance Chaucer* (New Haven and London: Yale University Press, 1975).

Mitchell, Jerome, and Provost, William (eds.), *Chaucer the Love Poet* (Athens: University of Georgia Press, 1973).

Muscatine, Charles, *Chaucer and the French Tradition: A Study in Style and Meaning* (Berkeley, Los Angeles and London: University of California Press, 1957).

Muscatine, Charles, *The Book of Geoffrey Chaucer: An account of the publication of Geoffrey Chaucer's Works from the Fifteenth Century to Modern Times* (San Francisco: Book Club of California limited edition, 1963).

North, J. D., 'Kalenderes Enlumyned ben they', *Review of English Studies*, new series, vol. 20 (1969), pp. 129–54, 257–83, 418–44.

Norton-Smith, John, *Geoffrey Chaucer* (London: Routledge and Kegan Paul, 1974).

Payne, Robert O., *The Key of Remembrance: A Study of Chaucer's Poetics* (New Haven: Yale University Press, 1963).

Payne, Robert O., 'Chaucer and the Art of Rhetoric', in Rowland (1968), pp. 38–57.

Pearsall, Derek, 'The *Troilus* Frontispiece and Chaucer's Audience', *Yearbook of English Studies*, vol. 7 (1977), pp. 68–74.

Pratt, Robert A., 'Conjectures regarding Chaucer's Manuscript of the *Teseida*', *Studies in Philology*, vol. 42 (1945), pp. 745–63.

Pratt, Robert A., 'Chaucer's Use of the *Teseida*', *PMLA*, vol. 62 (1947), pp. 598–621.

Ridley, Florence, 'The State of Chaucer Studies: A Brief Survey', *Studies in the Age of Chaucer*, vol. 1 (1979), pp. 3–16.

Ridley, Florence, 'A Response to "Contemporary Literary Theory and Chaucer"', in Rose (1981), pp. 37–51.

Robbins, Rossell Hope (ed.), *Chaucer at Albany* (New York: Burt Franklin, 1975).

Robertson, D. W., Jr., *A Preface to Chaucer: Studies in Medieval Perspectives* (Princeton: Princeton University Press, 1962).

Robinson (1933, 1957). *See* Appendix B.

Robinson, Ian, *Chaucer and the English Tradition* (Cambridge: Cambridge University Press, 1972).

Rose, Donald M. (ed.), *New Perspectives in Chaucer Criticism* (Norman, Oklahoma: Pilgrim Books, 1981).

Rowland, Beryl (ed.), *Companion to Chaucer Studies* (Toronto, New York and London: Oxford University Press, 1968).

Rowland, Beryl (ed.), *Chaucer and Middle English Studies in Honour of Rossell Hope Robbins* (London: Allen and Unwin, 1974).

Salter, Elizabeth, '"Troilus and Criseyde": A Reconsideration', in *Patterns of Love and Courtesy: Essays in Memory of C. S. Lewis*, ed. John Lawlor (London: Edward Arnold, 1966), pp. 86–106.

Salu, Mary (ed.), *Essays on Troilus and Criseyde*, Chaucer Studies 3 (Cambridge: D. S. Brewer; Totowa, New Jersey: Rowman and Littlefield, 1979).

Samuels, M. L. 'Chaucerian Final -e', *Notes and Queries*, vol. 217 (1972), pp. 445–8.

Samuels, M. L., 'Chaucer's Spelling', in *Middle English Studies presented to Norman Davis in Honour of his Seventieth Birthday*, ed. Douglas Gray and E. G. Stanley (Oxford: Clarendon Press, 1983), pp. 17–37.

Schlauch, Margaret, 'Chaucer's Prose Rhythms', *PMLA*, vol. 65 (1950), pp. 568–89.

Schlauch, Margaret, 'The Art of Chaucer's Prose', in Brewer (1966), pp. 140–63.

Schricker, Gale C., 'On the Relation of Fact and Fiction in Chaucer's Poetic Endings', *Philological Quarterly*, vol. 60 (1981), pp. 13–27.

Shepherd, G. T., '*Troilus and Criseyde*', in Brewer (1966), pp. 65–87.

Skeat (1894). *See* Appendix B.

Southworth, J. G., *Verses of Cadence* (Oxford: Basil Blackwell, 1954).

Spearing, A. C., 'Chaucerian Authority and Inheritance', in Boitani and Torti (1983), pp. 185–202.

Speirs, John, *Chaucer the Maker* (London: Faber and Faber, 1951).

Spurgeon, Caroline F. E., *Five Hundred Years of Chaucer Criticism and Allusion*, 3 vols. (Cambridge: Cambridge University Press, 1925). Originally published in 5 Parts and an Index by the Chaucer Society, 1908–17. Volume II contains

Parts ii and iii, Volume III Parts iv and v and the Index, all separately paginated.

Strohm, Paul, 'Jean of Angoulême: a fifteenth-century reader of Chaucer', *Neuphilologische Mitteilungen*, vol. 72 (1971), pp. 69–76.

Tatlock, J. S. P., 'The domestic "our"', in 'The Source of the Legend, and other Chauceriana', *Studies in Philology*, vol. 18 (1921), pp. 419–28 (see pp. 425–8).

Taylor, Paul Beekman, '*Peynted Confessiouns*: Boccaccio and Chaucer', *Comparative Literature*, vol. 34 (1982), pp. 116–29.

Taylor, P. B., 'Chaucer's *Cosyn to the Dede*', *Speculum*, vol. 57 (1982b), pp. 315–27.

Tuve, Rosemond, 'Spring in Chaucer and before him', *Modern Language Notes*, vol. 52 (1937), pp. 9–16.

Vasta, Edward, and Thundy, Zacharias P. (eds.), *Chaucerian Problems and Perspectives: Essays presented to Paul E. Beichner* (Notre Dame: University of Notre Dame Press, 1979).

Wagenknecht, Edward (ed.), *Chaucer: Modern Essays in Criticism* (New York: Oxford University Press, A Galaxy Book, 1959).

Weissman, Hope Phyllis, 'Antifeminism and Chaucer's Characterization of Women', in Economou (1975), pp. 93–110.

Wetherbee, Winthrop, 'Convention and Authority: A Comment on Some Recent Critical Approaches to Chaucer', in Rose (1981), pp. 71–81.

Wimsatt, James I., 'Chaucer and the Canticle of Canticles', in Mitchell and Provost (1973), pp. 66–90.

Wood, Chauncey, *Chaucer and the Country of the Stars: Poetic Uses of Astrological Imagery* (Princeton: Princeton University Press, 1970).

(c) Studies of The Canterbury Tales, *or of individual tales or groups of tales*

Adams, John F., 'The Structure of Irony in *The Summoner's Tale*', *Essays in Criticism*, vol. 12 (1962), pp. 126–32.

Aiken, Pauline, 'Vincent of Beauvais and Dame Pertelote's Knowledge of Medicine' *Speculum*, vol. 10 (1935), pp. 281–7.

Allen, Judson Boyce, 'The old way and the Parson's way: an ironic reading of the Parson's Tale', *Journal of Medieval and Renaissance Studies*, vol. 3 (1973), pp. 255–71.

Allen, Judson Boyce, and Moritz, Theresa Anne, *A Distinction of Stories: The Medieval Unity of Chaucer's Fair Chain of Narratives for Canterbury* (Columbus: Ohio State University Press, 1981).

Allen, Judson Boyce, 'The Ironic Fruyt: Chauntecleer as Figura', *Studies in Philosophy*, vol. 66 (1969), pp. 23–35.

Baker, D. C., 'A Crux in Chaucer's *Franklin's Tale*: Dorigen's Complaint', *JEGP*, vol. 60 (1961), pp. 56–64.

Baker, Donald C., 'The Bradshaw Order of the "Canterbury Tales": A Dissent', *Neuphilologische Mitteilungen*, vol. 63 (1962), pp. 245–61.

Baldwin, Ralph, 'The Unity of *The Canterbury Tales*', *Anglistica*, vol. 5 (Copenhagen: Rosenkilde and Bagger, 1955). Reprinted in abridged form in Schoeck and Taylor (1960), pp. 14–51. Citations are from this reprint.

Baugh, Albert C., 'The Original Teller of the Merchant's Tale', *Modern Philology*, vol. 35 (1937–8), pp. 15–26.

Beichner, Paul E., 'Absolon's Hair', *Mediaeval Studies*, vol. 12 (1950), pp. 222–33. Reprinted as 'Characterization in the *Miller's Tale*' in Schoeck and Taylor (1960), pp. 117–29.

Beichner, Paul E., 'Chaucer's Hende Nicholas', *Mediaeval Studies*, vol. 14 (1952), pp. 151–3.

Beichner, Paul, '*Non Alleluia Ructare*', *Mediaeval Studies*, vol. 18 (1956), pp. 135–44.

Beichner, Paul E., 'Daun Piers, Monk and Business Administrator', *Speculum*, vol. 34 (1959), pp. 611–19.

Beichner, Paul E., 'Baiting the Summoner', *Modern Language Quarterly*, vol. 22 (1961), pp. 367–76.

Beichner, Paul E., 'Confrontation, Contempt of Court, and Chaucer's Cecilia', *Chaucer Review*, vol. 8 (1973–4), pp. 198–204.

Benjamin, E. B., 'The Concept of Order in the *Franklin's Tale*', *Philological Quarterly*, vol. 38 (1959), pp. 119–24.

Benson, Donald R., 'The Marriage "Encomium" in the *Merchant's Tale*: A Chaucerian Crux', *Chaucer Review*, vol. 14 (1979–80), pp. 48–60.

Benson, Larry D., 'The order of *The Canterbury Tales*', *Studies in the Age of Chaucer*, vol. 3 (1981), pp. 77–120.

Benson, Larry D., and Andersson, Theodore M., *The Literary Context of Chaucer's Fabliaux: Texts and Translations* (Indianapolis and New York: Bobbs-Merrill, 1971).

Berndt, David E., 'Monastic *Acedia* and Chaucer's Characterization of Daun Piers', *Studies in Philology*, vol. 68 (1971), pp. 435–50.

Birney, Earle, '"After his Ymage": The Central Ironies of the "Friar's Tale"', *Mediaeval Studies*, vol. 21 (1959), pp. 17–35.

Birney, Earle, 'The Inhibited and the Uninhibited: Ironic Structure in the "Miller's Tale"', *Neophilologus*, vol. 44 (1960), pp. 333–8.

Birney, Earle, 'Structural Irony within the Summoner's Tale', *Anglia*, vol. 78 (1960b), pp. 204–18.

Birney, Earle, 'Chaucer's "Gentil" Manciple and his "Gentil" Tale', *Neuphilologische Mitteilungen*, vol. 61 (1960c), pp. 257–67.

Bishop, Ian, 'The Narrative Art of *The Pardoner's Tale*', *Medium Ævum*, vol. 36 (1967), pp. 15–24.

Bishop, Ian, '*The Nun's Priest's Tale* and the Liberal Arts', *Review of English Studies*, new series, vol. 30 (1979), pp. 257–67.

Blake, Kathleen A., 'Order and the Noble Life in Chaucer's *Knight's Tale*?', *Modern Language Quarterly*, vol. 34 (1973), pp. 3–19.

Blake, N. F., 'The Relationship between the Hengwrt and Ellesmere Manuscripts of the *Canterbury Tales*,' *Essays and Studies*, vol. 32 (1979), pp. 1–18.

Blake (1980). *See* Appendix B.

Blake, N. F., 'On Editing the *Canterbury Tales*', in *Medieval Studies for J. A. W. Bennett*, ed. P. L. Heyworth (Oxford: Clarendon Press, 1981), pp. 101–19.

Blake, N. F., 'Critics, Criticism and the order of *The Canterbury Tales*', *Archiv*, vol. 218 (1981b), pp. 47–58.

Bleeth, Kenneth A., 'The Image of Paradise in the *Merchant's Tale*', in Benson (1974), pp. 45–60.

Block, Edward A., 'Originality, Controlling Purpose, and Craftsmanship in Chaucer's *Man of Law's Tale*', *PMLA*, vol. 68 (1953), pp. 572–616.

Bloomfield, Morton W., 'The Man of Law's Tale: A Tragedy of Victimization and a Christian Comedy', *PMLA*, vol. 87 (1972), pp. 384–90.

Boitani, Piero, 'The *Monk's Tale*: Dante and Boccaccio', *Medium Ævum*, vol. 45 (1976), pp. 50–69.

Bolton, W. F., 'The "Miller's Tale": An Interpretation', *Mediaeval Studies*, vol. 24 (1962), pp. 83–94.

Bornstein, Diane, 'Chaucer's *Tale of Melibee* as an Example of the *Style Clergial*', *Chaucer Review*, vol. 12 (1977–8), pp. 236–54.

Brewer, D. S., 'The Fabliaux', in Rowland (1968), pp. 247–67.

Broes, Arthur T., 'Chaucer's Disgruntled Cleric', *PMLA*, vol. 78 (1963), pp. 156–62.

Bronson, Bertrand H., 'Afterthoughts on the Merchant's Tale', *Studies in Philology*, vol. 58 (1961), pp. 583–96.

Brooks, Douglas, and Fowler, Alastair, 'The Meaning of Chaucer's *Knight's Tale*', *Medium Ævum*, vol. 39 (1970), pp. 123–46.

Brooks, Harold F., *Chaucer's Pilgrims: The Artistic Order of the Portraits in the Prologue* (London: Methuen, 1962).

Brosnahan, Leger, 'Does the Nun's Priest's Epilogue Contain a Link?', *Studies in Philology*, vol. 58 (1961), pp. 468–82.

Brosnahan, Leger, 'The Authenticity of "And preestes thre"', *Chaucer Review*, vol. 16 (1981–2), pp. 293–310.

Brown, Carleton, 'The Evolution of the Canterbury "Marriage Group"', *PMLA*, vol. 48 (1933), pp. 1041–59.

Brown, Carleton, 'The Man of Law's Headlink and the Prologue of the Canterbury Tales', *Studies in Philology*, vol. 34 (1937), pp. 8–35.

Brown, Carleton, 'The Prioress's Tale', in Bryan and Dempster (1941), pp. 447–85.

Brown, Emerson, 'Chaucer, the Merchant, and their Tale: Getting beyond old Controversies', *Chaucer Review*, vol. 13 (1978–9), pp. 141–56, 247–62.

Brown, Emerson, 'What is Chaucer doing with the Physician and his Tale?', *Philological Quarterly*, vol. 60 (1981), pp. 129–49.

Brown, Peter, 'Is the "Canon's Yeoman's Tale" Apocryphal?', *English Studies*, vol. 64 (1983), pp. 481–90.

Bryan, W. F., and Dempster, Germaine (eds.), *Sources and Analogues of Chaucer's Canterbury Tales* (Chicago: University of Chicago Press, 1941).

Burnley, J. D., 'The Morality of *The Merchant's Tale*', *Yearbook of English Studies*, vol. 6 (1976), pp. 16–25.

Burrow, J., 'Irony in the Merchant's Tale', *Anglia*, vol. 75 (1957), pp. 199–208.

Burrow, J. A., '"Sir Thopas": An Agony in Three Fits', *Review of English Studies*, new series, vol. 22 (1971b), pp. 54–8.

Burrow, J. A., 'Chaucer's *Sir Thopas* and *La Prise de Neuvile*', *Yearbook of English Studies*, vol. 14 (1984), pp. 44–55.

Burton, T. L., 'The Wife of Bath's Fourth and Fifth Husbands and her Ideal Sixth: The Growth of a Marital Philosophy', *Chaucer Review*, vol. 13 (1978–9), pp. 34–50.

Caie, Graham D., 'The Significance of the Early Chaucer Manuscript Glosses (with Special Reference to the *Wife of Bath's Prologue*)', *Chaucer Review*, vol. 10 (1975–6), pp. 350–60.

Calderwood, J. L., 'Parody in *The Pardoner's Tale*', *English Studies*, vol. 45 (1964), pp. 302–9.

Camden, Carroll, 'The Physiognomy of Thopas', *Review of English Studies*, vol. 11 (1935), pp. 326–30.

Carruthers, Mary, 'The Wife of Bath and the Painting of Lions', *PMLA*, vol. 94 (1979), pp. 209–22.

Chamberlain, David S., 'The Nun's Priest's Tale and Boethius's *De Musica*', *Modern Philology*, vol. 68 (1970–1), pp. 188–91.

Chapman, R. L., '*The Shipman's Tale* was meant for the Shipman', *Modern Language Notes*, vol. 71 (1956), pp. 4–5.

Clark, John W., '"This Litel Tretys" Again', *Chaucer Review*, vol. 6 (1971–2), pp. 152–6.

Clogan, Paul M., 'The Figural Style and Meaning of *The Second Nun's Prologue and Tale*', *Medievalia et Humanistica*, new series, vol. 3 (1972), pp. 213–40.

Clogan, Paul M., 'The Narrative Style of The Man of Law's Tale', *Medievalia et Humanistica*, new series, vol. 8 (1977), pp. 217–33.

Collette, Carolyn P., 'A Closer Look at Seinte Cecile's Special Vision', *Chaucer Review*, vol. 10 (1975–6), pp. 337–49.

Collette, Carolyn P., 'Sense and Sensibility in the *Prioress's Tale*', *Chaucer Review*, vol. 15 (1980–1), pp. 138–50.

Colmer, Dorothy, 'Character and Class in *The Wife of Bath's Tale*', *JEGP*, vol. 72 (1973), pp. 329–39.

Condren, Edward I., 'The Pardoner's Bid for Existence', *Viator*, vol. 4 (1973), pp. 177–205.

Conley, John, '"The Peculiar Name Thopas"', *Studies in Philology*, vol. 73 (1978), pp. 42–61.

Cook, James W., '"That she was out of alle charitee": Point-Counterpoint in the *Wife of Bath's Prologue and Tale*', *Chaucer Review*, vol. 13 (1978–9), pp. 51–65.

Cooper, Geoffrey, '"Sely John" in the "Legende" of the *Miller's Tale*', *JEGP*, vol. 79 (1980), pp. 1–12.

Copland, Murray, '*The Reeve's Tale*: Harlotrie or Sermonyng?', *Medium Ævum*, vol. 31 (1962), pp. 14–32.

Copland, Murray, '*The Shipman's Tale*: Chaucer and Boccaccio', *Medium Ævum*, vol. 35 (1966), pp. 11–28.

Copland, R. A., 'A Line from Chaucer's Prologue to the Canterbury Tales', *Notes and Queries*, vol. 215 (1970), pp. 45–6.

Craik, T. W., *The Comic Tales of Chaucer* (London: Methuen, 1964).

Cunningham, J. V., 'The Literary Form of the Prologue to the *Canterbury Tales*', *Modern Philology*, vol. 49 (1951–2), pp. 172–81.

Dahlberg, Charles, 'Chaucer's Cock and Fox', *JEGP*, vol. 53 (1954), pp. 277–90.

Dalbey, Marcia A., 'Pluto and Proserpine in Chaucer's "Merchant's Tale"', *Neuphilologische Mitteilungen*, vol. 75 (1974), pp. 408–15.

Damon, S. Foster, 'Chaucer and Alchemy', *PMLA*, vol. 39 (1924), pp. 782–8.

David, Alfred, 'An ABC to the Style of the Prioress', in Carruthers and Kirk (1982), pp. 147–57.

Delany, Sheila, 'Clerks and Quiting in the *Reeve's Tale*', *Mediaeval Studies*, vol. 29 (1967), pp. 351–6.

Delany, Sheila, 'Womanliness in the *Man of Law's Tale*', *Chaucer Review*, vol. 9 (1974–5), pp. 63–72.

Delany, Sheila, 'Politics and the Paralysis of Poetic Imagination in *The Physician's Tale*', *Studies in the Age of Chaucer*, vol. 3 (1981), pp. 47–60.

Delasanta, Rodney, 'And of great reverence: Chaucer's Man of Law', *Chaucer Review*, vol. 5 (1970–1), pp. 288–310.

Dempster, Germaine, 'Chaucer at Work on the Complaint in *The Franklin's Tale*', *Modern Language Notes*, vol. 52 (1937), pp. 16–23.

Dempster, Germaine, 'The Original Teller of the *Merchant's Tale*', *Modern Philology*, vol. 36 (1938–9), pp. 1–8.

Dempster, Germaine, 'A Further Note on Dorigen's *Exempla*', *Modern Language Notes*, vol. 54 (1939), pp. 137–8.

Dempster, Germaine, 'Chaucer's Manuscript of Petrarch's Version of the Griselda Story', *Modern Philology*, vol. 41 (1943–4), pp. 6–16.

Dempster, Germaine, 'Manly's Conception of the Early History of the *Canterbury Tales*', *PMLA*, vol. 61 (1946), pp. 379–415.

Dempster, Germaine, 'A Chapter of the Manuscript History of the *Canterbury Tales*: The Ancestor of Group *d*, the Origin of its Texts, Tale-order, and spurious Links', *PMLA*, vol. 63 (1948), pp. 456–84.

Dempster, Germaine, 'The Fifteenth-Century Editors of the *Canterbury Tales* and the Problem of Tale Order', *PMLA*, vol. 64 (1949), pp. 1123–42.

Dempster, Germaine, 'A Period in the Development of the *Canterbury Tales* Marriage Group and of Blocks B^2 and C', *PMLA*, vol. 68 (1953), pp. 1142–59.

Diekstra, F. N. M., 'Chaucer's Digressive Mode and the Moral of *The Manciple's Tale*', *Neophilologus*, vol. 67 (1983), pp. 131–48.

Donaldson, E. Talbot, 'Chaucer the Pilgrim', *PMLA*, vol. 69 (1954), pp. 928–36. Reprinted in Schoeck and Taylor (1960), pp. 1–13. Citations are from this reprint.

Donaldson, E. Talbot, 'Idiom of Popular Poetry in the Miller's Tale', in *English Institute Essays 1950*, ed. A. S. Downer (New York: Columbia University Press, 1951), pp. 116–40. Reprinted in Donaldson (1970), pp. 13–29. Citations are from this reprint.

Donaldson, E. Talbot, 'The Effects of the Merchant's Tale', in Donaldson (1970), pp. 30–45.

Donaldson, E. Talbot, 'The Ordering of the *Canterbury Tales*', in *Medieval Literature and Folklore Studies: Essays in Honor of Francis Lee Utley*, ed. Jerome Mitchell and Bruce A. Rosenberg (New Brunswick, N.J.: Rutgers University Press, 1970b), pp. 192–204.

Donovan, Mortimer J., 'The *Moralite* of the Nun's Priest's Sermon', *JEGP*, vol. 52 (1953), pp. 498–508.

Doyle, A. I., and Parkes, M. B., 'The production of copies of the *Canterbury Tales* and the *Confessio Amantis* in the early fifteenth century', *Medieval Scribes, Manuscripts and Libraries: Essays presented to N. R. Ker*, ed. M. B. Parkes and Andrew G. Watson (London: Scolar Press, 1978), pp. 163–210.

Duffey, Bernard I., 'The Intention and Art of *The Man of Law's Tale*', *ELH*, vol. 14 (1947), pp. 181–93.

Duncan, Charles F., '"Straw for youre Gentillesse": The Gentle Franklin's Interruption of the Squire', *Chaucer Review*, vol. 5 (1970–1), pp. 161–4.

Duncan, Edgar H., 'The Literature of Alchemy and Chaucer's Canon's Yeoman's Tale: Framework, Theme, and Characters', *Speculum*, vol. 43 (1968), pp. 633–56.

Eckhardt, Caroline D., 'The Number of Chaucer's Pilgrims: A Review and Reappraisal', *Yearbook of English Studies*, vol. 5 (1975), pp. 1–18.

Engelhardt, George J., 'The Ecclesiastical Pilgrims of the *Canterbury Tales*: A Study in Ethology', *Mediaeval Studies*, vol. 37 (1975), pp. 287–315.

Fairchild, H. N., 'Active Arcite, Contemplative Palamon', *JEGP*, vol. 26 (1927), pp. 285–93.

Ferris, Sumner, 'Chaucer at Lincoln (1387): The *Prioress's Tale* as a Political Poem', *Chaucer Review*, vol. 15 (1980–1), pp. 295–321.

Fichte, Joerg O., 'Man's Free Will and the Poet's Choice: The Creation of Artistic Order in Chaucer's *Knight's Tale*', *Anglia*, vol. 93 (1975), pp. 335–60.

Finlayson, John, 'The Satiric Mode and the *Parson's Tale*', *Chaucer Review*, vol. 6 (1971–2), pp. 94–116.

Fleming, John V., 'The Antifraternalism of the *Summoner's Tale*', *JEGP*, vol. 65 (1966), pp. 688–700.

Fleming, John V., 'The Summoner's Prologue: An Iconographic Adjustment', *Chaucer Review*, vol. 2 (1967–8), pp. 95–107.

French, W. H., 'The Lovers in the *Knight's Tale*', *JEGP*, vol. 48 (1949), pp. 320–8.

Friedman, Albert B., 'The Prioress's Tale and Chaucer's Anti-Semitism', *Chaucer Review*, vol. 9 (1974–5), pp. 118–29.

Friedman, John Block, 'The *Nun's Priest's Tale*: The Preacher and the Mermaid's Song', *Chaucer Review*, vol. 7 (1972–3), pp. 250–66.

Frost, William, 'An Interpretation of Chaucer's Knight's Tale', *Review of English Studies*, vol. 25 (1949), pp. 290–304.

Fulk, R. D., 'Reinterpreting the *Manciple's Tale*', *JEGP*, vol. 78 (1979), pp. 485–93.

Furnivall, Frederick, J., *A Temporary Preface to the Six-Text Edition of Chaucer's Canterbury Tales*, Part 1, Chaucer Society, second series, no. 3 (1868).

Garbáty, Thomas J., 'The Monk and the *Merchant's Tale*: An Aspect of Chaucer's Building Process in the *Canterbury Tales*', *Modern Philology*, vol. 67 (1969–70), pp. 18–24.

Garbáty, Thomas J., 'Satire and Regionalism: The Reeve and his Tale', *Chaucer Review*, vol. 8 (1973–4), pp. 1–8.

Gardner, William B., 'Chaucer's "Unworthy Sone of Eve"', *Studies in English*, University of Texas, no. 26 (1947), pp. 77–83.

Gaylord, Alan T., 'The Promises in *The Franklin's Tale*', *ELH*, vol. 31 (1964), pp. 331–65.

Gaylord, Alan T., 'Sentence and Solaas in Fragment VII of the *Canterbury Tales*: Harry Bailly as Horseback Editor', *PMLA*, vol. 82 (1967), pp. 226–35.

Gellrich, Jesse M., 'The Parody of Medieval Music in the *Miller's Tale*', *JEGP*, vol. 73 (1974), pp. 176–88.

Gibbons, Robert F., 'Does the Nun's Priest's Epilogue contain a Link?', *Studies in Philology*, vol. 51 (1954), pp. 21–33.

Goodman, Jennifer R., 'Chaucer's *Squire's Tale* and the Rise of Chivalry', *Studies in the Age of Chaucer*, vol. 5 (1983), pp. 127–36.

Gordon, J. D., 'Chaucer's Retraction: A Review of Opinion', in Leach (1961), pp. 81–97.

Grennen, Joseph E., 'The Canon's Yeoman's Alchemical "Mass"', *Studies in Philology*, vol. 62 (1965), pp. 546–60.

Grennen, Joseph E., 'St. Cecelia's "Chemical Wedding": The Unity of the *Canterbury Tales*, Fragment VIII', *JEGP*, vol. 65 (1966), pp. 466–81.

Grennen, Joseph E., 'Science and Sensibility in Chaucer's Clerk', *Chaucer Review*, vol. 6 (1971–2), pp. 81–93.

Hahn, Thomas, and Kaeuper, Richard W., 'Text and Context: Chaucer's *Friar's Tale*', *Studies in the Age of Chaucer*, vol. 5 (1983), pp. 67–101.

Haller, Robert S., 'Chaucer's *Squire's Tale* and the Uses of Rhetoric', *Modern Philology*, vol. 62 (1965), pp. 285–95.

Halverson, J., 'Aspects of Order in the Knight's Tale', *Studies in Philology*, vol. 57 (1960), 606–21.

Hamilton, Marie Padgett, 'Death and Old Age in *The Pardoner's Tale*', *Studies in Philology*, vol. 36 (1939), pp. 571–6.

Hanson, Thomas B., 'Chaucer's Physician as Storyteller and Moralizer', *Chaucer Review*, vol. 7 (1972–3), pp. 132–9.

Harder, Kelsie B., 'Chaucer's Use of the Mystery Plays in the *Miller's Tale*', *Modern Language Quarterly*, vol. 17 (1956), pp. 193–8.

Harrington, David V., 'The Undramatic Character of Chaucer's Nun's Priest', *Discourse*, vol. 8 (1965), pp. 80–9.

Harrington, Norman T., 'Chaucer's Merchant's Tale: Another Swing of the Pendulum', *PMLA*, vol. 86 (1971), pp. 25–31.

Harrington, Norman T., 'Experience, Art, and the Framing of the *Canterbury Tales*', *Chaucer Review*, vol. 10 (1975–6), pp. 187–200.

Hart, Walter Morris, 'The Reeve's Tale: A Comparative Study of Chaucer's Narrative Art', *PMLA*, vol. 23 (1908), pp. 1–44.

Hartung, Albert E., '"Pars Secunda" and the Development of the *Canon's Yeoman's Tale*', *Chaucer Review*, vol. 12 (1977–8), pp. 111–28.

Harwood, Britton J., 'Language and the Real: Chaucer's Manciple', *Chaucer Review*, vol. 6 (1971–2), pp. 268–79.

Harwood, Britton J., 'The Wife of Bath and the Dream of Innocence', *Modern Language Quarterly*, vol. 33 (1972), pp. 257–73.

Hatcher, Elizabeth R., 'Life without Death: The Old Man in Chaucer's *Pardoner's Tale*', *Chaucer Review*, vol. 9 (1974–5), pp. 246–52.

Havely, N. R. (ed.), *Geoffrey Chaucer: The Friar's, Summoner's and Pardoner's Tales from The Canterbury Tales* (London: University of London Press, 1975).

Hawkins, Sherman, 'Chaucer's Prioress and the Sacrifice of Praise', *JEGP*, vol. 63 (1964), pp. 599–624.

Hazelton, Richard, 'The *Manciple's Tale*: Parody and Critique', *JEGP*, vol. 62 (1963), pp. 1–31.

Hemingway, Samuel B., 'Chaucer's Monk and the Nun's Priest', *Modern Language Notes*, vol. 31 (1916), pp. 479–83.

Herz, Judith Scherer, '*The Canon's Yeoman's Prologue* and *Tale*', *Modern Philology*, vol. 58 (1960–1), pp. 231–7.

Hieatt, Constance B., 'The moral of the "Nun's Priest's Tale"', *Studia Neophilologica*, vol. 42 (1970), pp. 3–8.

Hill, Betty, 'Chaucer: *The Miller's* and *Reeve's Tales*', *Neuphilologische Mitteilungen*, vol. 74 (1973), pp. 665–75.

Hirsh, John C., 'Reopening the *Prioress's Tale*', *Chaucer Review*, vol. 10 (1975–6), pp. 30–45.

Hirsh, John C., 'The Politics of Spirituality: The Second Nun and the Manciple', *Chaucer Review*, vol. 12 (1977–8), pp. 129–46.

Hoffman, Arthur W., 'Chaucer's Prologue to Pilgrimage: The Two Voices', *ELH*, vol. 21 (1954), pp. 1–16. Reprinted in Wagenknecht (1959), pp. 30–45. Citations are from this reprint.

Hoffman, Richard, 'Jephthah's Daughter and Chaucer's Virginia', *Chaucer Review*, vol. 2 (1967–8), pp. 20–31.

Holbrook, David, 'The Nonne Preestes Tale', in *The Age of Chaucer* (Vol. 1 of the Pelican Guide to English Literature), ed. Boris Ford (London: Penguin Books, 1954), pp. 118–28.

Howard, Donald R., *The Idea of the Canterbury Tales* (Berkeley, Los Angeles and London: University of California Press, 1976).

Hulbert, J. R., 'The *Canterbury Tales* and their Narrators', *Studies in Philology*, vol. 45 (1948), pp. 565–77.

Hume, Kathryn, 'Why Chaucer Calls the *Franklin's Tale* a Breton Lai', *Philological Quarterly*, vol. 51 (1972), pp. 365–79.

Hume, Kathryn, 'The Pagan Setting of the *Franklin's Tale* and the Sources of Dorigen's Cosmology', *Studia Neophilologica*, vol. 44 (1972b), pp. 289–94.

Huppé, Bernard F., *A Reading of the Canterbury Tales* (Albany: State University of New York Press, 1964).

Johnson, William C., 'The *Man of Law's Tale*: Aesthetics and Christianity in Chaucer', *Chaucer Review*, vol. 16 (1981–2), pp. 201–21.

Jones, Claude, 'The "Second Nun's Tale", A Mediaeval Sermon', *Modern Language Review*, vol. 32 (1937), p. 283.

Jones, Terry, *Chaucer's Knight: The portrait of a medieval mercenary* (London: Weidenfeld and Nicolson, 1980).

Justman, Stewart, '"Auctoritee" and the *Knight's Tale*', *Modern Language Quarterly*, vol. 39 (1978), pp. 3–14.

Kahrl, Stanley J., 'Chaucer's *Squire's Tale* and the Decline of Chivalry', *Chaucer Review*, vol. 7 (1972–3), pp. 194–209.

Kaske, Carol V., 'Getting around the Parson's Tale: An Alternative to Allegory and Irony', in Robbins (1975), pp. 147–77.

Kaske, R. E., 'The Knight's Interruption of the "Monk's Tale"', *ELH*, vol. 24 (1957), pp. 249–68.

Kaske, R. E., 'An Aube in the *Reeve's Tale*', *ELH*, vol. 26 (1959), pp. 295–310.

Kaske, R. E., 'January's "Aube"', *Modern Language Notes*, vol. 75 (1960), pp. 1–4.

Kaske, R. E., 'The *Canticum Canticorum* in the *Miller's Tale*', *Studies in Philology*, vol. 59 (1962), pp. 479–500.

Kearney, A. M., 'Truth and Illusion in *The Franklin's Tale*', *Essays in Criticism*, vol. 19 (1969), pp. 245–53.

Keen, Maurice, 'Chaucer's Knight, the English Aristocracy and the Crusade', in Scattergood and Sherborne (1983), pp. 45–61.

Keiser, George R., 'In Defense of the Bradshaw Shift', *Chaucer Review*, vol. 12 (1977–8), pp. 191–201.

Kellogg, Alfred L., 'An Augustinian Interpretation of Chaucer's Pardoner', *Speculum*, vol. 26 (1951), pp. 465–81.

Kellogg, Alfred L., and Haselmayer, Louis A., 'Chaucer's Satire of the Pardoner', *PMLA*, vol. 66 (1951), pp. 251–77.

Kiernan, Kevin S., 'The Art of the Descending Catalogue, and a Fresh Look at Alisoun', *Chaucer Review*, vol. 10 (1975–6), pp. 1–16.

Kimpel, Ben, 'The Narrator of the *Canterbury Tales*', *ELH*, vol. 20 (1953), pp. 77–96.

Kittredge, George Lyman, 'Chaucer's Pardoner', *The Atlantic Monthly*, vol. 72 (1893), pp. 829–33. Reprinted in Wagenknecht (1959), pp. 117–25. Citations are from this reprint.

Kittredge, George Lyman, 'Chaucer's Discussion of Marriage', *Modern Philology*, vol. 9 (1911–12), pp. 435–67.

Kolve, V. A., 'Chaucer's *Second Nun's Tale* and the Iconography of Saint Cecilia', in Rose (1981), pp. 137–74.

Lancashire, Anne, 'Chaucer and the Sacrifice of Isaac', *Chaucer Review*, vol. 9 (1974–5), pp. 320–6.

Lawrence, W. W., 'Satire in Sir Thopas', *PMLA*, vol. 50 (1935), pp. 81–91.

Lawrence, William Witherle, 'The Tale of Melibeus', in *Essays and Studies in Honor of Carleton Brown* (New York: New York University Press, 1940), pp. 100–10.

Lawrence, William Witherle, *Chaucer and the Canterbury Tales* (New York: Columbia University Press, 1950).

Leicester, H. Marshall, 'The Art of Impersonation: A General Prologue to the *Canterbury Tales*', *PMLA*, vol. 95 (1980), pp. 213–24.

Leicester, H. Marshall, '"Synne Horrible": The Pardoner's Exegesis of his Tale, and Chaucer's', in Carruthers and Kirk (1982), pp. 25–50.

Lenaghan, R. T., 'The Irony of the *Friar's Tale*', *Chaucer Review*, vol. 7 (1972–3), pp. 281–94.

Lepley, Douglas L., 'The Monk's Boethian Tale', *Chaucer Review*, vol. 12 (1977–8), pp. 162–70.

Lester, G. A., 'Chaucer's Knight and the Medieval Tournament', *Neophilologus*, vol. 66 (1982), pp. 460–8.

Levitan, Alan, 'The Parody of Pentecost in Chaucer's *Summoner's Tale*', *University of Toronto Quarterly*, vol. 40 (1970–1), pp. 236–46.

Levy, Bernard S., and Adams, George R., 'Chauntecleer's Paradise Lost and Regained', *Mediaeval Studies*, vol. 29 (1967), pp. 178–92.

Lewis, Robert E., 'Glosses to the *Man of Law's Tale* from Pope Innocent III's *De Miseria Humane Conditionis*', *Studies in Philology*, vol. 64 (1967), pp. 1–16.

Lewis, Robert E., 'The English Fabliau Tradition and Chaucer's "Miller's Tale"', *Modern Philology*, vol. 79 (1981–2), pp. 241–55.

Leyerle, John, 'Thematic Interlace in "The Canterbury Tales"', *Essays and Studies*, vol. 29 (1976), pp. 107–21.

Linn, Irving, 'The Arming of Sir Thopas', *Modern Language Notes*, vol. 51 (1936), pp. 300–11.

Loomis, Dorothy Bethurum, 'Constance and the Stars', in Vasta and Thundy (1979), pp. 207–20.

Lumiansky, R. M., *Of Sondry Folk: The Dramatic Principle in the Canterbury Tales* (Austin: University of Texas Press, 1955).

Lumiansky, R. M., 'Benoit's Portraits and Chaucer's General Prologue', *JEGP*, vol. 55 (1956), pp. 431–8.

Major, John M., 'The Personality of Chaucer the Pilgrim', *PMLA*, vol. 75 (1960), pp. 160–2.

Malone, Kemp, 'The Wife of Bath's Tale', *Modern Language Review*, vol. 57 (1962), pp. 428–91.

Manly, John Matthews (ed.), *Chaucer's Canterbury Tales* (New York: Harrap, 1928).

Manly, John Matthews, '*Sir Thopas*: A Satire', *Essays and Studies*, vol. 13 (1928b), pp. 52–73.

Manly and Rickert (1940). See Appendix B.

Mann, Jill, *Chaucer and Medieval Estates Satire: The Literature of Social Classes and the General Prologue to the Canterbury Tales* (Cambridge: Cambridge University Press, 1973).

Mann, Jill, 'The *Speculum Stultorum* and the *Nun's Priest's Tale*', *Chaucer Review*, vol. 9 (1974–5), pp. 262–82.

Mann, Jill, 'Chaucerian Themes and Style in the *Franklin's Tale*', in *The New Pelican Guide to English Literature*, ed. Boris Ford, Vol. I: *Medieval Literature*, Part 1: *Chaucer and the Alliterative Tradition* (Harmondsworth: Penguin Books, 1982), pp. 133–53.

Mann, Jill, 'Parents and Children in the "Canterbury Tales"', in Boitani and Torti (1983), pp. 165–83.

Manning, Stephen, 'The Nun's Priest's Morality and the Medieval Attitude towards Fables', *JEGP*, vol. 59 (1960), pp. 403–16.

Manning, Stephen, 'Chaucer's Constance, Pale and Passive', in Vasta and Thundy (1979), pp. 13–23.

Matthews, William, 'The Wife of Bath and All her Sect', *Viator*, vol. 5 (1974), pp. 413–43.

McAlpine, Monica E., 'The Pardoner's Homosexuality and How it Matters', *PMLA*, vol. 95 (1980), pp. 8–22.

McCall, John P., 'The *Clerk's Tale* and the Theme of Obedience', *Modern Language Quarterly*, vol. 27 (1966), pp. 260–9.

McCall, John P., 'The Squire in Wonderland', *Chaucer Review*, vol. 1 (1966–7), pp. 103–9.

McClintock, Michael W., 'Games and the Players of Games: Old French *Fabliaux* and the *Shipman's Tale*', *Chaucer Review*, vol. 5 (1970–1), pp. 112–36.

McGalliard, John C., 'Chaucerian Comedy: *The Merchant's Tale*, Jonson, and Molière', *Philological Quarterly*, vol. 25 (1946), pp. 342–70.

McGalliard, John C., 'Characterization in Chaucer's *Shipman's Tale*', *Philological Quarterly*, vol. 54 (1975), pp. 1–18.

Merrill, Thomas F., 'Wrath and Rhetoric in "The Summoner's Tale"', *Texas Studies in Language and Literature*, vol. 4 (1962–3), pp. 341–50.

Middleton, Anne, 'The *Physician's Tale* and Love's Martyrs: "Ensamples mo than ten" as a Method in the *Canterbury Tales*', *Chaucer Review*, vol. 8 (1973–4), pp. 9–32.

Miller, Milton, 'The Heir in the *Merchant's Tale*', *Philological Quarterly*, vol. 29 (1950), pp. 437–40.

Miller, Robert P., 'Chaucer's Pardoner, The Scriptural Eunuch, and The Pardoner's Tale', *Speculum*, vol. 30 (1955), pp. 180–99. Reprinted in Schoeck and Taylor (1960), pp. 221–44. Citations are from this reprint.

Moore, Arthur K., '*Sir Thopas* as Criticism of Fourteenth-Century Minstrelsy', *JEGP*, vol. 53 (1954), pp. 532–45.

Morgan, Gerald, 'The Self-Revealing Tendencies of Chaucer's Pardoner', *Modern Language Review*, vol. 71 (1976), pp. 241–55.

Morgan, Gerald, 'The Universality of the Portraits in the *General Prologue* to the *Canterbury Tales*', *English Studies*, vol. 58 (1977), pp. 481–93.

Morgan, Gerald, 'A Defence of Dorigen's Complaint', *Medium Ævum*, vol. 46 (1977b), pp. 77–97.

Morgan, Gerald, 'The Design of the *General Prologue* to the *Canterbury Tales*', *English Studies*, vol. 59 (1978), pp. 481–98.

Morgan, Gerald, 'Rhetorical Perspective in the *General Prologue* to the *Canterbury Tales*', *English Studies*, vol. 62 (1981), pp. 411–22.

Morse, J. Mitchell, 'The Philosophy of the Clerk of Oxenford', *Modern Language Quarterly*, vol. 19 (1958), pp. 3–20.

Muscatine, Charles, 'Form, Texture, and Meaning in Chaucer's *Knight's Tale*', *PMLA*, vol. 65 (1950), pp. 911–29.

Muscatine, Charles, '*The Canterbury Tales*: style of the man and style of the work', in Brewer (1966), pp. 88–113.

Neuse, Richard, 'The Knight: the First Mover in Chaucer's Human Comedy', *University of Toronto Quarterly*, vol. 31 (1962), pp. 299–315.

Neuss, Paula, '*Double-Entendre* in *The Miller's Tale*', *Essays in Criticism*, vol. 24 (1974), pp. 325–40.

Neville, Marie, 'The Function of the *Squire's Tale* in the Canterbury Scheme', *JEGP*, vol. 50 (1951), pp. 167–79.

Nevo, Ruth, 'Chaucer: Motive and Mask in the "General Prologue"', *Modern Language Review*, vol. 58 (1963), pp. 1–9.

Nicholson, Peter, 'The "Shipman's Tale" and the Fabliaux', *ELH*, vol. 45 (1978), pp. 583–96.

Olson, Glending, 'The *Reeve's Tale* as a Fabliau', *Modern Language Quarterly*, vol. 35 (1974), pp. 219–30.

Olson, Glending, 'A Reading of the *Thopas-Melibee* link', *Chaucer Review*, vol. 10 (1975–6), pp. 147–53.

Olson, Glending, 'Chaucer, Dante, and the Structure of Fragment VIII (G) of the *Canterbury Tales*', *Chaucer Review*, vol. 16 (1981–2), pp. 222–36.

Olson, Paul A., 'Chaucer's Merchant and January's "Hevene in Erthe Heere"', *ELH*, vol. 28 (1961), pp. 203–13.

Olson, Paul A., 'The *Reeve's Tale*: Chaucer's *Measure for Measure*', *Studies in Philology*, vol. 59 (1962), pp. 1–17.

Olson, Paul A., 'Poetic Justice in the *Miller's Tale*', *Modern Language Quarterly*, vol. 24 (1963), pp. 227–36.

Olsson, Kurt, 'Grammar, Manhood, and Tears: The Curiosity of Chaucer's Monk', *Modern Philology*, vol. 76 (1978-9), pp. 1–17.

Owen, Charles A., Jr., 'The Crucial Passages in Five of *The Canterbury Tales*: A Study in Irony and Symbol', *JEGP*, vol. 52 (1953), pp. 294–311. Reprinted in Wagenknecht (1959), pp. 251–70. Citations are from this reprint.

Owen, Charles A., Jr., 'Chaucer's *Canterbury Tales*: Aesthetic Design in Stories of the First Day', *English Studies*, vol. 35 (1954), pp. 49–56.

Owen, Charles A., Jr., 'The *Tale of Melibee*', *Chaucer Review*, vol. 7 (1972–3), pp. 267–80.

Owen, Charles A., Jr., *Pilgrimage and Storytelling: The Dialectic of 'Ernest' and 'Game'* (Norman: University of Oklahoma Press, 1977).

Owen, Charles A., Jr., 'The Alternative Reading of *The Canterbury Tales*: Chaucer's Text and the Early Manuscripts', *PMLA*, vol. 97 (1982), pp. 237–50.

Owen, W. J. B., 'The Old Man in *The Pardoner's Tale*', *Review of English Studies*, new series, vol. 2 (1951), pp. 49–55.

Palomo, Dolores, 'What Chaucer Really Did to *Le Livre de Mellibee*', *Philological Quarterly*, vol. 53 (1974), pp. 304–20.

Parker, David, 'Can We Trust the Wife of Bath?', *Chaucer Review*, vol. 4 (1969–70), pp. 90–8.

Patterson, Lee W., 'Chaucerian Confession: Penitential Literature and the Pardoner', *Medievalia et Humanistica*, new series, vol. 7 (1976), pp. 153–73.

Patterson, Lee W., 'The "Parson's Tale" and the Quitting of the "Canterbury Tales"', *Traditio*, vol. 34 (1978), pp. 331–80.

Paull, Michael R., 'The Influence of the Saint's Legend Genre in the *Man of Law's Tale*', *Chaucer Review*, vol. 5 (1970–1), pp. 179–94.

Payne, F. Anne, 'Foreknowledge and Free Will: Three Theories in the *Nun's Priest's Tale*', *Chaucer Review*, vol. 10 (1975–6), pp. 201–19.

Pearcy, Roy J., 'Chaucer's Franklin and the Literary Vavasour', *Chaucer Review*, vol. 8 (1973–4), pp. 33–59.

Pearsall, D. A., 'The Squire as Story-teller', *University of Toronto Quarterly*, vol. 34 (1964), pp. 82–92.

Pearsall, Derek, 'The Canterbury Tales', in Bolton (1970), pp. 163–94.

Pearsall, Derek (ed.), *Chaucer: The Nun's Priest's Tale*, Part Nine of Volume II (*The Canterbury Tales*) of *A Variorum Edition of the Works of Geoffrey Chaucer*, ed. Paul G. Ruggiers and Donald C. Baker (Norman: University of Oklahoma Press, 1983).

Peterson, Joyce E., 'The Finished Fragment: A Reassessment of the *Squire's Tale*', *Chaucer Review*, vol. 5 (1970–1), pp. 62–74.

Peterson, Joyce E., 'With Feigned Flattery: The Pardoner as Vice', *Chaucer Review*, vol. 10 (1975–6), pp. 326–36.

Pittock, Malcolm, 'The Merchant's Tale', *Essays in Criticism*, vol. 17 (1967), pp. 26–40.

Pittock, Malcolm, '*The Pardoner's Tale* and the Quest for Death', *Essays in Criticism*, vol. 24 (1974), pp. 107–23.

Pratt, Robert A., 'The Knight's Tale', in Bryan and Dempster (1941), pp. 82–105.

Pratt, Robert A., 'Chaucer Borrowing from himself', *Modern Language Quarterly*, vol. 7 (1946), pp. 259–64.

Pratt, Robert A., 'The Order of the *Canterbury Tales*', *PMLA*, vol. 66 (1951), pp. 1141–67.

Pratt, Robert A., 'The Development of the Wife of Bath', in Leach (1961), pp. 45–79.

Pratt, Robert A., 'Jankyn's Book of Wikked Wyves: Medieval Antimatrimonial Propaganda in the Universities', *Annuale Mediaevale*, vol. 3 (1962), pp. 5–27.

Pratt, Robert A., 'Chaucer and the Hand that Fed him', *Speculum*, vol. 41 (1966), pp. 619–42.

Pratt, Robert A., 'Three Old French Sources of the Nonnes Preestes Tale', *Speculum*, vol. 47 (1972), pp. 422–44, 646–68.

Pratt (1974). See Appendix B.

Pratt, Robert A., 'Chaucer's Title: 'The tales of Caunterbury''', *Philological Quarterly*, vol. 54 (1975), pp. 19–25.

Pratt, Robert A., 'Some Latin Sources of the Nonnes Preest on Dreams', *Speculum*, vol. 52 (1977), pp. 538–70.

Pratt, Robert A., and Young, Karl, 'The Literary Framework of the Canterbury Tales', in Bryan and Dempster (1941), pp. 1–81.

Preston, Raymond, 'Chaucer, his Prioress, the Jews, and Professor Robinson', *Notes and Queries*, vol. 206 (1961), pp. 7–8.

Ramsey, Lee C., '"The Sentence of it Sooth is": Chaucer's *Physician's Tale*', *Chaucer Review*, vol. 6 (1971–2), pp. 185–97.

Reames, Sherry L., 'The Sources of Chaucer's "Second Nun's Tale"', *Modern Philology*, vol. 76 (1978–9), pp. 111–35.

Reames, Sherry L., 'The Cecilia Legend as Chaucer inherited it and retold it: The Disappearance of an Augustinian Ideal', *Speculum*, vol. 55 (1980), pp. 38–57.

Richardson, Janette, *Blameth Nat Me: A Study of Imagery in Chaucer's Fabliaux* (The Hague and Paris: Mouton, 1970).

Ridley, Florence H., *The Prioress and her Critics*, University of California Publications, English Studies 30 (Berkeley and Los Angeles: University of California Press, 1965).

Robertson, D. W., Jr., 'Why the Devil wears green', *Modern Language Notes*, vol. 69 (1954), pp. 470–2.

Robertson, D. W., Jr., 'Chaucer's Franklin and his Tale', *Costerus: Essays in English and American Language and Literature*, new series, vol. 1, ed. James L. W. West III (Amsterdam: Rodopi, 1974), pp. 1–26.

Robertson, D. W., Jr., '"And for my land thus hastow mordred me?": Land Tenure, the Cloth Industry, and the Wife of Bath', *Chaucer Review*, vol. 14 (1979–80), pp. 403–20.

Robertson, Stuart, 'Elements of Realism in the Knight's Tale', *JEGP*, vol. 14 (1915), pp. 226–55.

Rowland, Beryl, 'Animal Imagery and the Pardoner's Abnormality', *Neophilologus*, vol. 48 (1964), pp. 56–60.

Rowland, Beryl, 'The Play of the *Miller's Tale*: A Game within a Game', *Chaucer Review*, vol. 5 (1970–1), pp. 140–6.

Rowland, Beryl, 'Chaucer's Dame Alys: Critics in Blunderland?' *Neuphilologische Mitteilungen*, vol. 73 (1972), pp. 381–95.

Rowland, Beryl, 'On the Timely Death of the Wife of Bath's Fourth Husband', *Archiv*, vol. 209 (1972–3), pp. 273–82.

Rowland, Beryl, 'What Chaucer did to the Fabliau', *Studia Neophilologica*, vol. 51 (1979), pp. 205–13.

Rowland, Beryl, 'Chaucer's Idea of the Pardoner', *Chaucer Review*, vol. 14 (1979–80), pp. 140–54.

Ruggiers, Paul G., *The Art of the Canterbury Tales* (Madison, Milwaukee and London: University of Wisconsin Press, 1967).

Ruggiers, Paul G. (ed.), *Geoffrey Chaucer, The Canterbury Tales: A Facsimile and Transcription of the Hengwrt Manuscript, with Variants from the Ellesmere Manuscript*, with Introductions by Donald C. Baker, and by A. I. Doyle and M. B. Parkes (Norman: University of Oklahoma Press; Folkestone: Wm. Dawson & Sons, 1979). In citation from this facsimile, punctuation is added, and spelling adapted, according to the conventions observed in Robinson (1957).

Russell, G. H., 'Chaucer: The Prioress's Tale', in *Medieval Literature and Civilization: Studies in Memory of G. N. Garmonsway*, ed. D. A. Pearsall and R. A. Waldron (University of London: the Athlone Press, 1969), pp. 211–27.

Ryan, Lawrence V., 'The Canon's Yeoman's Desperate Confession', *Chaucer Review*, vol. 8 (1973–4), pp. 297–310.

Salter, Elizabeth, *Chaucer: The Knight's Tale and the Clerk's Tale*, Studies in English Literature, no. 5 (London: Edward Arnold, 1962).

Samuels, M. L., 'The Scribe of the Hengwrt and Ellesmere Manuscripts of *The Canterbury Tales*', *Studies in the Age of Chaucer*, vol. 5 (1983), pp. 49–65.

Sands, Donald B., 'The Non-Comic, Non-Tragic Wife: Chaucer's Dame Alys as Sociopath', *Chaucer Review*, vol. 12 (1977–8), pp. 171–82.

Sayce, Olive, 'Chaucer's "Retractions": The Conclusion of the "Canterbury Tales" and its place in Literary Tradition', *Medium Ævum*, vol. 40 (1971), pp. 230–48.

Scattergood, V. J., 'The Manciple's Manner of Speaking', *Essays in Criticism*, vol. 24 (1974), pp. 124–46.

Scattergood, V. J., 'The Originality of the *Shipman's Tale*', *Chaucer Review*, vol. 11 (1976–7), pp. 210–31.

Scattergood, V. J., 'Chaucer and the French War: *Sir Thopas* and *Melibee*', in *Court and Poet* (ARCA 5), ed. Glyn S. Burgess (Liverpool: Francis Cairns, 1981), pp. 287–96.

Scheps, Walter, 'Chaucer's Anti-Fable: *Reductio ad Absurdum* in the *Nun's Priest's Tale*', *Leeds Studies in English*, new series, vol. 4 (1970), pp. 1–10.

Scheps, Walter, 'Chaucer's Man of Law and the Tale of Constance', *PMLA*, vol. 89 (1974), pp. 285–95.

Scheps, Walter, '"Up roos oure Hoost, and was oure aller cok": Harry Bailly's Tale-telling Competition', *Chaucer Review*, vol. 10 (1975–6), pp. 113–28.

Schlauch, Margaret, *Chaucer's Constance and the Accused Queens* (New York: New York University Press, 1927).

Schlauch, Margaret, 'The Marital Dilemma in the *Wife of Bath's Tale*', *PMLA*, vol. 61 (1946), pp. 416–30.

Schleusener, Jay, 'The Conduct of the *Merchant's Tale*', *Chaucer Review*, vol. 14 (1979–80), pp. 237–50.

Schoeck, Richard J., 'Chaucer's Prioress: Mercy and Tender Heart', in *The Bridge: A Yearbook of Judaeo-Christian Studies*, vol. 2 (1956), pp. 239–55. Reprinted in Schoeck and Taylor (1960), pp. 245–58.

Schoeck, Richard J., and Taylor, Jerome (eds.), *Chaucer Criticism*, 2 vols. (Notre Dame: University of Notre Dame Press, 1960–1), Vol. 1: *The Canterbury Tales* (1960). All citations are from this volume.

Sedgewick, G. G., 'The Progress of Chaucer's Pardoner, 1880–1940', *Modern Language Quarterly*, vol. 1 (1940), pp. 431–58. Reprinted in Wagenknecht (1959), pp. 126–58. Citations are from this reprint.

Sedgewick, G. G., 'The Structure of the *Merchant's Tale*', *University of Toronto Quarterly*, vol. 17 (1948), pp. 337–45.

Severs, J. Burke, *The Literary Relationships of Chaucer's Clerkes Tale*, Yale Studies in English 96 (New Haven: Yale University Press, 1942).

Severs, J. Burke, 'Is the *Manciple's Tale* a Success?', *JEGP*, vol. 51 (1952), pp. 1–16.

Severs, J. Burke, 'Author's Revision in Block C of *The Canterbury Tales*', *Speculum*, vol. 29 (1954), pp. 512–30.

Shallers, A. Paul, 'The "Nun's Priest's Tale": An Ironic Exemplum', *ELH*, vol. 42 (1975), pp. 319–37.

Shaw, Judith, 'Corporeal and Spiritual Homicide, the Sin of Wrath, and the "Parson's Tale"', *Traditio*, vol. 38 (1982), pp. 281–300.

Shumaker, Wayne, 'Alisoun in Wander-Land: A Study in Chaucer's Mind and Literary Method', *ELH*, vol. 18 (1951), pp. 77–89.

Silverman, Albert H., 'Sex and Money in Chaucer's *Shipman's Tale*', *Philological Quarterly*, vol. 32 (1953), pp. 329–36.

Silverstein, Theodore, 'The Wife of Bath and the Rhetoric of Enchantment: or, How to make a Hero see in the Dark', *Modern Philology*, vol. 58 (1960–1), pp. 153–73

Silvia, Daniel S., 'Glosses to the *Canterbury Tales* from St. Jerome's *Epistola Adversus Jovinianum*', *Studies in Philology*, vol. 62 (1965), pp. 28–39.

Silvia, Daniel S., 'Some Fifteenth-Century Manuscripts of the *Canterbury Tales*', in Rowland (1974), pp. 153–63.

Sledd, James, 'Dorigen's Complaint', *Modern Philology*, vol. 45 (1947–8), pp. 36–45.

Sledd, James, 'The *Clerk's Tale*: The Monsters and the Critics', *Modern Philology*, vol. 51 (1953–4), pp. 73–82.

Spearing, A. C., 'Chaucer's Clerk's Tale as a Medieval Poem', in his *Criticism and Medieval Poetry*, 2nd edn. (London: Edward Arnold, 1972; 1st edn. 1964), pp. 76–106.

Specht, Henrik, *Chaucer's Franklin in the Canterbury Tales: The Social and Literary Background of a Chaucerian Character*, Publications of the Department of English, University of Copenhagen, vol. 10 (Copenhagen: Akademisc Forlag, 1981).

Spector, R. D., 'Chaucer's "The Manciple's Tale"', *Notes and Queries*, vol. 202 (1957), p. 26.

Spencer, Theodore, 'The Story of Ugolino in Dante and Chaucer', *Speculum*, vol. 9 (1934), pp. 295–301.

Stanley, E. G., 'The Use of Bob-Lines in *Sir Thopas*', *Neuphilologische Mitteilungen*, vol. 73 (1972), pp. 417–26.

Statler, Margaret H., 'The Analogues of Chaucer's *Prioress's Tale*: The Relation of Group C to Group A', *PMLA*, vol. 65 (1950), pp. 896–910.

Steadman, John M., '"Hir gretteste ooth": The Prioress, St. Eligius, and St. Godebertha', *Neophilologus*, vol. 43 (1959), pp. 49–57.

Steadman, John M., 'Old Age and *Contemptus Mundi* in *The Pardoner's Tale*', *Medium Ævum*, vol. 33 (1964), pp. 121–30.

Steinmetz, David C., 'Late Medieval Nominalism and the *Clerk's Tale*', *Chaucer Review*, vol. 12 (1977–8), pp. 38–54.

Stepsis, Robert, '*Potentia Absoluta* and the *Clerk's Tale*', *Chaucer Review*, vol. 10 (1975–6), pp. 129–46.

Stevens, Martin, '"And Venus Laugheth": An Interpretation of the *Merchant's Tale*', *Chaucer Review*, vol. 7 (1972–3), pp. 118–31.

Stillwell, Gardiner, 'Chaucer's "Sad" Merchant', *Review of English Studies*, vol. 20 (1944), pp. 1–18.

Stillwell, Gardiner, 'The Political Meaning of Chaucer's *Tale of Melibee*', *Speculum*, vol. 19 (1944b), pp. 433–44.

Stillwell, Gardiner, 'Chaucer in Tartary', *Review of English Studies*, vol. 24 (1948), pp. 177–88.

Stokoe, William C., 'Structure and Intention in the First Fragment of *The Canterbury Tales*', *University of Toronto Quarterly*, vol. 21 (1951–2), pp. 120–7.

Strohm, Paul, 'The Allegory of the *Tale of Melibee*', *Chaucer Review*, vol. 2 (1967–8), pp. 32–42.

Stugrin, Michael, 'Ricardian Poetics and Late Medieval Cultural Pluriformity: the Significance of Pathos in the *Canterbury Tales*', *Chaucer Review*, vol. 15 (1980–1), pp. 155–67.

Sullivan, William L., 'Chaucer's Man of Law as a Literary Critic', *Modern Language Notes*, vol. 68 (1953), pp. 1–8.

Swart, J., 'The Construction of Chaucer's *General Prologue*', *Neophilologus*, vol. 38 (1954), pp. 127–36.

Szittya, Penn R., 'The Friar as False Apostle: Antifraternal Exegesis and the *Summoner's Tale*', *Studies in Philology*, vol. 71 (1974), pp. 19–46.

Tatlock, J. S. P., *The Harleian Manuscript 7334 and Revision of the Canterbury Tales*, Chaucer Society, second series, no. 41 (1909).

Tatlock, J. S. P., 'The Canterbury Tales in 1400', *PMLA*, vol. 50 (1935), pp. 100–39.

Tatlock, J. S. P., 'Chaucer's *Merchant's Tale*', *Modern Philology*, vol. 33 (1935–6), pp. 367–81.

Thro, A. Booker, 'Chaucer's Creative Comedy: A Study of the *Miller's Tale* and the *Shipman's Tale*', *Chaucer Review*, vol. 5 (1970–1), pp. 97–111.

Thundy, Zacharias P., 'Matheolus, Chaucer, and the Wife of Bath', in Vasta and Thundy (1979), pp. 24–58.

Tolkien, J. R. R., 'Chaucer as Philologist: *The Reeve's Tale*', *Transactions of the Philological Society* (1934), pp. 1–70.

Tyrwhitt (1775). See Appendix B.

Underwood, Dale, 'The First of the Canterbury Tales', *ELH*, vol. 26 (1959), pp. 455–69.

Webb, H. J., 'A Reinterpretation of Chaucer's Theseus', *Review of English Studies*, vol. 23 (1947), pp. 289–96.

Weissman, Hope Phyllis, 'Late Gothic Pathos in *The Man of Law's Tale*', *Journal of Medieval and Renaissance Studies*, vol. 9 (1979), pp. 133–53.

Weissman, Hope Phyllis, 'Why Chaucer's Wife is from Bath', *Chaucer Review*, vol. 15 (1980–1), pp. 11–36.

Wenzel, Siegfried, 'The Source for the "Remedia" of the Parson's Tale', *Traditio*, vol. 27 (1971), pp. 433–53.

Wenzel, Siegfried, 'The Source of Chaucer's Seven Deadly Sins', *Traditio*, vol. 30 (1974), pp. 351–78.

Wenzel, Siegfried, 'Notes on the *Parson's Tale*', *Chaucer Review*, vol. 16 (1981–2), pp. 237–56.

Whitesell, J. Edwin, 'Chaucer's Lisping Friar', *Modern Language Notes*, vol. 71 (1956), pp. 160–1.

Whiting, B. J., 'The Wife of Bath's Prologue and Tale', in Bryan and Dempster (1941).

Whittock, Trevor, *A Reading of the Canterbury Tales* (Cambridge: Cambridge University Press, 1968).

Williams, Arnold, 'Chaucer and the Friars', *Speculum*, vol. 28 (1953), pp. 499–513.

Woolf, Rosemary, 'Chaucer as Satirist in the *General Prologue* to the *Canterbury Tales*', *Critical Quarterly*, vol. 1 (1959), pp. 150–7.

Wright (1847). See Appendix B.

Wurtele, Douglas, '*Proprietas* in Chaucer's *Man of Law's Tale*', *Neophilologus*, vol. 60 (1976), pp. 577–93.

Wurtele, Douglas, 'The Penitence of Geoffrey Chaucer', *Viator*, vol. 11 (1980), pp. 335–59.

Yunck, John A., 'Religious Elements in Chaucer's *Man of Law's Tale*', *ELH*, vol. 27 (1960), pp. 249–61.

INDEX